Business, Civil Society and the 'New' Politics of Corporate Tax Justice

ELGAR POLITICS AND BUSINESS

Series Editors: Aynsley Kellow, *School of Social Sciences, University of Tasmania, Australia*, Tony Porter, *Department of Politics, McMaster University, Canada* and Karsten Ronit, *University of Copenhagen, Denmark*

Business is intrinsically woven into our societies, affecting in crucial ways how wealth is produced and distributed, the way our societies are governed and how power is exercised. Recognising this fact, the Elgar Politics and Business series is an innovative new arena for original research across the breadth of this dynamic and important area of study. Covering a broad range of topics, the series examines issues such as: the politics of business taxation, business as an 'active force' in politics, the political power of corporations, business and regulation, and the politics of global value chains. Drawing key inspiration from political science, the series is interdisciplinary in nature, and will attract submissions from across the social sciences and law. Both international and comparative in its approach, this exciting series encompasses theoretical and empirical work from both well-established researchers and emerging scholars.

Business, Civil Society and the 'New' Politics of Corporate Tax Justice

Paying a Fair Share?

Edited by

Richard Eccleston

Director, Institute for the Study of Social Change, University of Tasmania, Australia

Ainsley Elbra

Department of Government and International Relations, Faculty of Arts and Social Sciences, University of Sydney, Australia

ELGAR POLITICS AND BUSINESS

Edward Elgar PUBLISHING

Cheltenham, UK • Northampton, MA, USA

Published by
Edward Elgar Publishing Limited
The Lypiatts
15 Lansdown Road
Cheltenham
Glos GL50 2JA
UK

Edward Elgar Publishing, Inc.
William Pratt House
9 Dewey Court
Northampton
Massachusetts 01060
USA

A catalogue record for this book
is available from the British Library

Library of Congress Control Number: 2018945852

This book is available electronically in the Elgaronline
Social and Political Science subject collection
DOI 10.4337/9781788114974

MIX
Paper from responsible sources
FSC® C013056

ISBN 978 1 78811 496 7 (cased)
ISBN 978 1 78811 497 4 (eBook)

Typeset by Servis Filmsetting Ltd, Stockport, Cheshire
Printed and bound in Great Britain by TJ International Ltd, Padstow

Contents

PART III

Contributors

Allison Christians, H. Heward Stikeman Chair in the Law of Taxation, Faculty of Law, McGill University, Canada.

Richard Eccleston, Director, Institute for the Study of Social Change and Professor of Political Science, University of Tasmania, Australia.

Ainsley Elbra, Lecturer in Government and International Relations, Faculty of Arts and Social Sciences, University of Sydney, Australia.

Fred Gale, Associate Professor in Politics and International Relations, College of Arts, Law and Education, University of Tasmania, Australia.

Lachlan Johnson, PhD candidate, Institute for the Study of Social Change, University of Tasmania, Australia.

Aynsley Kellow, Professor of Politics and Policy, College of Arts, Law and Education, University of Tasmania, Australia.

Lyne Latulippe, Associate Professor, School of Management, University of Sherbrooke, Canada.

John Mikler, Associate Professor, Department of Government and International Relations, University of Sydney, Australia.

Hannah Murphy-Gregory, Lecturer in Politics and International Relations, College of Arts, Law and Education, University of Tasmania, Australia.

Tony Porter, Professor, Department of Political Science, McMaster University, Canada.

Karsten Ronit, Associate Professor, Department of Political Science, University of Copenhagen, Denmark.

Leonard Seabrooke, Professor, Department of Business and Politics, Copenhagen Business School, Denmark.

Laura Smith, PhD candidate, Sustainability Research Institute, University of Leeds, UK.

James Van Alstine, Associate Professor of Environmental Policy, Sustainability Research Institute, University of Leeds, UK.

Duncan Wigan, Associate Professor, Department of Business and Politics, Copenhagen Business School, Denmark.

Richard Woodward, Senior Lecturer in Emerging Markets, School of Strategy and Leadership, Coventry University, UK.

Acknowledgements

This book provides a political economy analysis of the global campaign against corporate tax avoidance which has emerged since the financial crisis of 2007–08. The issues examined in the study are significant because vast revenue is at stake and because we believe that questions of corporate tax avoidance represent a critical test of whether multinational corporations can be subjected to democratic accountability in the early twenty-first century.

Given that corporate taxation is a complex and technical arena, this study draws on the expertise and insights of 16 scholars from a range of disciplinary perspectives and all corners of the globe.

A research project which draws on a group of international experts not only requires a good deal of cooperation by and commitment from contributors but also demands significant financial and administrative resources. To this extent we would like to acknowledge the financial assistance of the Australian Research Council through a Discovery Project grant (DP130104088), as well as the support of the Institute for the Study of Social Change at the University of Tasmania and the Department of Government and International Relations at the University of Sydney.

We would like to thank the Institute for Marine and Antarctic Studies for providing an idyllic harbour-side setting for an initial planning meeting in Hobart where contributors presented preliminary papers and refined themes for the final volume.

Beyond the above-mentioned contributions of our colleagues we are deeply indebted to Lachlan Johnson, Julia Verdouw and Helen Smith for their tireless and thorough research assistance and substantive contributions to this volume.

Ainsley Elbra would like to thank her colleagues in the School of Social and Political Sciences at the University of Sydney for their support throughout this project. Thanks also to Tim for his dedication to the project, including accompanying me and ten-week-old baby Sam to the aforementioned idyllic harbour-side meeting. Without this support, the constant juggle of researching, writing and travel alongside our growing family would be impossible.

Richard Eccleston would like to thank the fantastic staff at the Institute for the Study of Social Change at the University of Tasmania, as well as Claire, Sam, Nick and Ben for their patience. Massive thanks also to our extended family, who provide so much support, which enables us to balance raising three little boys and two academic careers.

We would like to acknowledge the support and patience of Alex Pettifer and his team at Edward Elgar Publishing, as well as the dozens of colleagues and practitioners the world over who contributed in big ways and small to this study.

Richard Eccleston and Ainsley Elbra
March 2018

Abbreviations

ACAMS	Association of Certified Anti-Money Laundering Specialists
AML	anti-money laundering
ATO	Australian Taxation Office
BEPS	base erosion and profit shifting
BIAC	Business and Industry Advisory Committee
CbC	country-by-country
CbCR	country-by-country reporting
CPI	Corruption Perceptions Index
CRD	Capital Requirements Directive
CRS	Common Reporting Standard
CSO	civil society organisation
CSR	corporate social responsibility
CTJ	Citizens for Tax Justice
CTPA	Centre for Tax Policy and Administration
DPT	diverted profits tax
DRC	Democratic Republic of the Congo
DTA	double tax agreement
EC	European Commission
ECJ	European Court of Justice
EITI	Extractive Industries Transparency Initiative
EU	European Union
Eurodad	European Network on Debt and Development
EY	Ernst & Young
FASB	Financial Accounting Standards Board
FATCA	Foreign Account Tax Compliance Act
FATF	Financial Action Task Force
FC	Financial Crisis
FDI	foreign direct investment
FI	Fairtrade International
FoE-UK	Friends of the Earth UK
FSC	Forest Stewardship Council
FSI	Financial Secrecy Index
FTEPR	Fair Trade, Employment and Poverty Reduction
FTM	Fair Tax Mark

GAA	Global Accounting Alliance
GAAP	Generally Accepted Accounting Principles
GATJ	Global Alliance for Tax Justice
GDP	gross domestic product
GHEITI	Ghanaian Extractive Industries Transparency Initiative
GSO	global standards organisation
GVC	global value chain
GWC	global wealth chain
HDI	Human Development Index
HMRC	Her Majesty's Revenue and Customs
HTC	Harmful Tax Competition
IASB	International Accounting Standards Board
IBFD	International Bureau of Fiscal Documentation
IBFed	International Banking Federation
ICAEW	Institute of Chartered Accountants in England and Wales
ICC	International Chamber of Commerce
ICIJ	International Consortium of Investigative Journalists
ICMM	International Council on Mining and Metals
ICRICT	Independent Commission for the Reform of International Corporate Taxation
IFAC	International Federation of Accountants
IFOAM	International Federation of Organic Agriculture Movements
IFRS	International Financial Reporting Standards
IIED	International Institute for Environment and Development
IIF	Institute of International Finance
IIROC	Investment Industry Regulatory Organization of Canada
IMF	International Monetary Fund
INGO	international non-government organisation
IRS	United States Internal Revenue Service
ISEAL	International Social and Environmental Accreditation and Labelling Alliance
ISO	International Organization for Standardization
ITTO	International Tropical Timber Organization
LNG	liquefied natural gas
M&A	mergers and acquisitions
MAAL	Australia's Multinational Anti-Avoidance Law
MMSD	Mining, Minerals and Sustainable Development
MNC	multinational corporation
MNE	multinational enterprise
MSC	Marine Stewardship Council
MSG	multi-stakeholder group
NEITI	Nigerian Extractive Industries Transparency Initiative

NGO	non-government organisation
NRGI	Natural Resource Governance Institute
ODA	Overseas Development Administration
OECD	Organisation for Economic Co-operation and Development
OEEC	Organisation for European Economic Co-operation
PAC	UK Public Accounts Committee
PEFC	Programme for the Endorsement of Forest Certification
PSI	US Permanent Subcommittee on Investigations
PTR	preferential tax regime
PwC	PricewaterhouseCoopers
PWYP	Publish What You Pay
RSB	Roundtable on Sustainable Biomaterials
RSPO	Roundtable on Sustainable Palm Oil
RTRS	Roundtable on Responsible Soy
SEC	United States Securities and Exchange Commission
SGE	significant global entity
TFEU	Treaty on the Functioning of the European Union
TI	Transparency International
TIEA	tax information exchange agreement
TJN	Tax Justice Network
TNI	Transnationality Index
TRI	United States Toxic Release Inventory
UNCED	United Nations Conference on Environment and Development
UNCTAD	United Nations Conference on Trade and Development
UNECA	United Nations Economic Commission for Africa
UT + FA	unitary taxation plus formula apportionment
WB	World Bank
WTO	World Trade Organization
ZEITI	Zambian Extractive Industries Transparency Initiative

Introduction: business, civil society and the 'new' politics of corporate tax justice: paying a fair share?

Ainsley Elbra and Richard Eccleston

Blatant corporate tax avoidance has attracted the ire of politicians, citizens and consumers the world over in recent years. Since the financial crisis of 2008, international taxation has become a mainstream political issue championed by social justice campaigners and the progressive press the world over. Globally, governments and intergovernmental organisations have announced a range of reforms designed to ensure that MNCs pay their 'fair share' of tax, while some of the world's most powerful and profitable firms have been subjected to multibillion-dollar fines.

But has anything changed? Perhaps.

In 2012 Google chairman Eric Schmidt was defiantly unapologetic that his firm had avoided an estimated \$2 billion tax liability, explaining that Google was 'naturally capitalistic' (Kavoussi 2012). Yet, by early 2016, after much ridicule and condemnation, Google agreed to pay £120 million sterling in back taxes in the UK. This modest act of contrition has subsequently been dwarfed by the European Commission's €13 billion state aid case against fellow tech giant Apple handed down in September 2016. The legal ambiguity, politicisation and vast sums involved in these international tax cases clearly warrant closer examination.

Indeed, the Google and Apple cases highlight many of the questions central to this study. Has Google's tax strategy been influenced by regulatory reforms or is the company responding to activist campaigns and the threat of reputational damage? Is the tax to be paid a 'fair' amount or a token gesture? Will other lower-profile companies feel obliged to follow Google's lead? Will large-scale international tax litigation against MNC firms be upheld? Will increasing legal and financial risks influence corporate tax behaviour? Can tax justice campaigns orchestrated by NGOs have a significant and sustainable impact on tax compliance? More generally, what do these developments say about the potential for new forms of tax governance in the twenty-first century? Are they an alternative to formal regulation or are such developments complementary? This volume sets out to examine these questions, and in doing so represents the first systematic study into the effectiveness and impact of emerging forms of tax activism and its impact on corporate governance and taxation.

This study is undertaken in the context of the post-crisis global economy, where governments continue to face budgetary challenges arising from high and often unsustainable levels of public debt exacerbated by weak economic and revenue growth. Many governments have been forced to respond to the challenge of fiscal consolidation and budget repair by implementing so-called 'austerity' measures aimed at reducing government expenditure, particularly in the area of social spending. One response to these mounting budget challenges is that governments and intergovernmental organisations, such as the EU and the OECD, are also seeking ways by which they can increase tax revenues without compromising economic growth or creating a domestic political backlash. The growing need to increase tax revenue in relatively pain-free ways has created strong incentives for national governments to develop new strategies to limit multinational tax avoidance.

Yet the campaign against MNC tax avoidance has not been led from within government. Indeed, the last decade has seen a new politics of global tax justice emerge as the hitherto technical domain of international tax has received unprecedented public attention (this volume, Chapter 3). This agenda has been championed by 'tax justice' activists and the media and has resonated with voters, many of whom are negatively affected by the aforementioned austerity measures and see multinational tax avoidance as a root cause of economic inequality and as a failure of democratic governance. Growing political demands to address corporate tax avoidance have triggered a conventional regulatory response through intergovernmental organisations such as the OECD. The most recent of these efforts, the OECD's base erosion and profit shifting (BEPS) initiative, represents significant progress in reform to the global tax regime (this volume, Chapter 2). However, the initiative faces several challenges, not least of which is the need to maintain international cooperation in the context of the divergent interests of participating states. Tax justice NGOs have welcomed these initiatives and their promise of greater tax transparency but argue that more ambitious and far-reaching reforms will be necessary to counter aggressive international tax planning and avoidance (Eccleston and Smith 2016; Picciotto 2016). As will be argued in subsequent chapters, many analysts argue that addressing MNC tax avoidance demands fundamental change to the century-old legal basis of the international tax regime and deeply held norms regarding fiscal sovereignty and competition (Rixen 2008; Dietsch 2015; van Apeldoorn 2016). It is this ambitious paradigm shift which tax justice NGOs are seeking.

This Introduction sketches the emergence of tax justice NGOs, the advocacy strategies they are employing and the reforms and innovative governance regimes they are promoting. In particular, it outlines the significant political challenges associated with corporate tax reform and the incremental policy change which has been achieved to date. It concludes by presenting the theoretical and empirical aims of this volume and an overview of the study.

THE CHALLENGE OF MULTINATIONAL TAX AVOIDANCE

The financial crisis that first disrupted global markets in 2008 has had significant political and fiscal consequences. Across the OECD the crisis and its aftermath have had a profound impact on public finances, with public debt across the OECD increasing from an average of 73 per cent of GDP in 2007 to 111 per cent in 2014 (OECD 2014a). Tepid economic growth has made the task of budget repair more difficult, with many governments implementing controversial 'austerity' measures in an attempt to rein in deficits and reassure creditors. While most governments have been reluctant to increase domestic taxes for fear of compromising economic recovery or triggering a political backlash, there has been a much greater willingness to implement anti-avoidance and anti-evasion measures designed to ensure that wealthy individuals and MNCs pay more tax. In addition to bolstering revenue, proposals to crack down on aggressive international tax planning resonate with growing political demands to improve equity and fairness in the global economy.

This political context has created an environment in which emerging tax justice NGOs have been able to cultivate the media and successfully draw the wider public's attention to the issue of corporate tax avoidance through direct 'name and shame' campaigns and associated exposés (Christians 2013; Seabrooke and Wigan 2015). In addition, a series of high-profile tax avoidance scandals have contributed to growing calls for business to pay its 'fair share'. Together, these factors have led to corporate tax avoidance emerging as a key issue for policymakers and voters, many of whom see more effective multinational taxation as a solution to budgetary challenges (this volume, Chapter 3).

This study provides a detailed analysis of this 'new' political economy of international taxation in which tax justice NGOs and the media are influencing the international tax agenda, policy responses and corporate strategy. The volume not only assesses the prospects for global tax justice and the extent to which fiscally challenged governments are going to be able to extract revenues from large corporations, but also provides a critical assessment of the changing nature of power and authority in the global economy and the prospects of new modes of economic governance.

The political salience of the campaign against corporate tax avoidance is unsurprising given the growing awareness of the immense scale of the problem. As will be explained in greater detail below, the revenue forgone, or the 'tax gap' associated with legal tax planning, is notoriously difficult to estimate. The US Congressional Research Service notes that, while estimates vary greatly, it is likely that the revenue losses from tax evasion by US-based firms alone are approximately $100 billion per year (Gravelle 2015). UNCTAD (2015, p. 201) reports that multinational tax avoidance undertaken through profit shifting costs developing countries between $70 billion and $120 billion per annum. The OECD has estimated that revenue losses from base erosion and profit shifting alone are US$100 billion to US$240 billion per annum (OECD 2015).

The growing awareness of the magnitude of multinational tax avoidance has led to increased attention and scrutiny on MNCs suspected of engaging in these practices. Over the last decade this increased scrutiny has taken many forms, including media campaigns. Since the mid-2000s the UK's *Guardian* newspaper has been running a high-profile campaign against tax havens and multinational tax avoidance, including opinion pieces from individuals associated with tax justice NGOs, such as Tax Justice Network (TJN). In the US the *New York Times* has led the campaign, and in Australia the Fairfax press and the national broadcaster, the ABC, have also sought to highlight the issues of corporate tax avoidance (Aston and Wilkins 2014). Similarly, other more specific developments, such as the International Consortium of Investigative Journalists' success in obtaining and publishing the 'Luxembourg Leaks' and 'Panama Papers', have demonstrated the scale of international tax avoidance, ensuring the issue remains on the public agenda (Christians 2015).

Governments have responded to these calls by establishing various hearings and inquiries into the complex tax avoidance mechanisms used by MNCs. In 2013 the US Senate held an inquiry into 'Offshore Profit Shifting and the U.S. Tax Code'. In 2016, the UK Treasury Committee launched a hearing into 'UK Tax Policy and the Tax Base'. These efforts have been replicated in smaller jurisdictions, such as Australia, where a Senate inquiry into corporate tax avoidance was held in 2015 (Australian Senate 2015). The European Commission has also prioritised addressing tax evasion and avoidance in order to combat the negative impact of tax competition between member states, culminating in the €13 billion state aid ruling against Apple handed down in September 2016. Yet despite growing concern about corporate tax avoidance, the issue of whether tax competition ought to be regulated is deeply contested and represents a significant barrier in reaching multilateral consensus on reforming the international corporate tax regime.

These inquiries all sought to quantify the magnitude of tax avoidance and the cost to the respective national economies. In the process, representatives of multinational firms were asked to explain and justify the complex tax arrangements they employ. However, in many cases the firms engaged in the most egregious tax avoidance schemes made little attempt to deny or downplay the effects of these tax regimes. Instead, they argued that their arrangements complied with the rules of the international taxation system and simply took advantage of the existing regulations and associated loopholes that govern global taxation in order to enhance profits. Indeed, Apple CEO Tim Cook acknowledged that he 'hates the current tax system' and that Apple wants to make a 'constructive contribution to how it could be made simpler and more straightforward' (Weckler 2016). These are noble sentiments, but how might the global tax regime be made 'fairer'? If such reform is unattainable, do large corporations have ethical obligations to pay taxes beyond what is legally required? If so, what constitutes a 'fair' tax burden and how can this be determined in an objective and legitimate way? At a more pragmatic, political level, can NGOs and citizens use their resources to influence the international tax reform agenda and associated corporate behaviour?

THE DEMOCRATIC GOVERNANCE OF CONTEMPORARY CAPITALISM

The ability of business to develop complex corporate tax strategies to circumvent domestic tax regulation is but one example of modern corporations exploiting their scale and associated political power to further their commercial interests. Business is able to exploit inconsistencies and loopholes in the liberal yet state-based economic system of the early twenty-first century to avoid paying taxes in order to maximise profit. The power of MNCs in particular to avoid paying taxes has a number of dimensions. Marxist and radical liberal scholars such as Lindblom (1977) have long argued that modern capitalism privileged the norm of profitability, which in turn legitimised business power and the central role of private firms as the drivers of economic growth. In the liberalised, post-Bretton Woods international economic order, firms can make credible threats to withhold or transfer investment to jurisdictions with lower taxes and more favourable regulation. Indeed, revisionist scholars such as Bell (2012) have argued that norms regarding economic competition have become so entrenched that governments and policymakers promote capital-friendly policy irrespective of any overt threat of capital flight. As will be argued in subsequent chapters, the risk of destructive regulatory competition is particularly acute in the 'offshore world' of international taxation given that MNCs can easily transfer portfolio investment and profits to low-tax jurisdictions through the use of corporate structures and financing arrangements without relocating production.

One tangible consequence of the offshore world has been the proliferation of tax havens in the final quarter of the twentieth century. Palan (2002) rightly argues that the emergence of tax havens is the result of the combined forces of strengthened state sovereignty and financial liberalisation. He suggests that the rise of the offshore world can be attributed to a coinciding of states' enhanced ability to establish the 'legal facility for juridical relocation', and financial liberalisation (Palan 2002, p. 153). As a result, tax havens have been able to commercialise state sovereignty through the establishment of 'virtual' state systems that feed off the legal infrastructure of 'real' state systems (Palan 2002, p. 172). The increased presence of tax havens, both small and large, has therefore encouraged regime shopping or a race to the bottom as firms search for the most 'attractive' regulatory settings, while states seek to compete on the same basis.

It can be argued that the ability of firms to exploit these developments and create competition between states highlights the undemocratic nature of modern capitalism, because while states are formally sovereign they are increasingly unable to tax capital at a rate citizens desire (Dietsch 2015, chapter 1). As a result, the capacity of national governments to raise revenue is constrained, which in turn affects fiscal sustainability and spending on social services. Furthermore, individual taxpayers are then required to shoulder a greater share of the tax burden to make up for the loss of tax revenue from large firms. Lastly, businesses that do not or cannot develop complex tax arrangements and instead abide by the spirit of domestic tax laws are placed at a disadvantage when competing with those multinational firms that do take advantage of the weaknesses inherent in the global tax system. These factors highlight growing inequality in the global tax system, which unfairly affects individuals through increasing the tax burden on income and consumption while also disadvantaging small to medium firms that do not engage in tax avoidance (Clausing 2016; Henry 2016).

By examining the challenges of multinational tax avoidance, it can be shown that state-based governance is struggling to respond to the challenges of global capitalism. All but the most powerful states lack the power to act unilaterally in order to prevent tax minimisation, and efforts to challenge firms in domestic settings, such as through government inquiries, have yielded little to date in the way of reform. Yet, as outlined in the following chapters, the slow pace of multilateral reform does not offer immediate solutions to these challenges either. As a result, it appears that, despite efforts at the national and global levels, traditional forms of public governance alone are unlikely to address the challenge of tax avoidance. On a more optimistic note, there is evidence that non-state actors such as civil society groups and firms themselves have the potential to act as catalysts of reform of the global corporate tax system. Ultimately, we argue that hybrid regimes with elements of public and private authority offer the best prospects of influencing corporate behaviour in the international tax arena.

THE POLITICAL ECONOMY CHALLENGES OF ADDRESSING MULTINATIONAL TAX AVOIDANCE

The deregulation of the global financial system from the 1970s onwards provided firms with greater opportunities to shift capital, labour and operations to jurisdictions that offered more appealing investment conditions. The potential for firms to exploit this freedom has been the subject of much of the globalisation literature, and in the field of corporate taxation there is considerable evidence of firms exploiting liberalisation to minimise taxation obligations (Genschel and Schwarz 2011; Rixen 2011; Dietsch and Rixen 2016). This financial arbitrage goes to the very core of the challenge of global corporate taxation and has thus been the focus of both multilateral and unilateral reform efforts.

The OECD's first efforts at highlighting the issue of tax competition, evasion and avoidance resulted in its 1998 report *Harmful Tax Competition: An Emerging Global Issue*, which represented the first attempt by the intergovernmental organisation to define, identify and regulate tax havens. Despite these broader ambitions, subsequent reforms focused on improving tax transparency to stop tax havens being used for unlawful tax evasion, while the more contentious issues of international tax avoidance and competition were largely ignored (Eccleston 2013, chapter 2). By 2000, with the election of a Republican administration in the US, the international tax reform agenda had stalled, having become a victim of 'politics without conviction' (Palan et al. 2010). Despite a hiatus throughout the early 2000s, the financial crisis of 2008 precipitated renewed attempts to reform the global corporate tax system led by the G20, whose leaders were increasingly advocating reinvigorated efforts to reform the global tax system (Eccleston 2013).

By 2012, the OECD had shifted attention from its previous focus on bilateral information exchange agreements to address non-disclosure and offshore tax evasion, to more ambitious multilateral negotiations, in what Palan and Wigan (2014, p. 334) refer to as the emergence of 'a genuine consensus for the need for intensive multilateral efforts to tackle tax abuse'. The aim of this reform initiative (OECD 2014b, p. 34) was to promote multilateral agreements as a way to enable jurisdictions to develop an 'instrument designed to provide an innovative approach to international tax matters'. The adoption and promotion of automatic exchange of information by the OECD and other actors represent real progress. However, these reforms are only a single battle in a wider war, and do little to address the larger and more complex problems of international tax avoidance and competition which are the focus of this study.

Fundamental reform of the international tax regime may have been too politically contentious to warrant serious consideration in the early 2000s, but in the aftermath of the financial crisis the political economy of international taxation has changed, and more ambitious and fundamental reform is on the political agenda. The most significant of these developments is the OECD's BEPS initiative, which, as the name suggests, has the broader ambition of limiting the lawful tax avoidance and planning widely practised by MNCs. The BEPS initiative is discussed in greater detail in Chapter 2, where it is argued that its effectiveness requires unprecedented levels of international cooperation. BEPS enjoys significant and unprecedented political support both in the public arena and among the G20 leaders. However, its success hinges on member states' continued cooperation and an unwavering commitment to implementation and compliance amid growing resistance from some governments and large corporations.

While multilateral approaches to combating tax avoidance remain central to the OECD's efforts, they have not been embraced unequivocally by national governments. In the face of the slow pace of international political progress at the multilateral level, two of the world's largest economies, the United States and the European Union, have implemented unilateral regulations in order to combat tax avoidance. Although participation by the US and EU at the level of multilateral reform gives the impression of a reinvigorated effort at reining in tax evasion and avoidance, as Palan and Wigan (2014) argue, many of their reform efforts have been decidedly unilateral. This shift is embodied in the United States' Foreign Account Tax Compliance Act (FATCA) and related initiatives known as 'son of FATCA' agreements, which leverage the large markets of the US and EU to demand information exchange from smaller states. FATCA has ushered in a new 'not in my backyard' attitude to tax avoidance, with similar unilateral regulations introduced in other jurisdictions. These unilateral regulations also have significant extraterritorial reach, 'by deploying financial firms as tax intermediaries under the threat of withdrawal of market access' (Palan and Wigan 2014, p. 339). Evidence suggests that, while internationalisation may improve the ability of powerful states to increase taxation revenues, FATCA's unilateral nature, and its inherent rejection of multilateral efforts such as those made by the OECD, 'undermines the accountability and legitimacy of the regime' (Eccleston and Gray 2014).

These unilateral approaches, undertaken by powerful states, have reaffirmed arguments about the unfairness of the global tax regimes. Taken together, this perceived unfairness and the slow-moving nature of global tax reform have frustrated those pushing for more fundamental change, particularly tax justice NGOs.

The Rise of Tax Justice NGOs

Several vocal tax justice NGOs have played a central role in highlighting the issue of MNC tax avoidance. These organisations are particularly concerned with the fairness and equity implications of multinational tax avoidance, arguing that actions by firms to reduce their tax burdens come at the expense of individual citizens, whose social welfare is impacted and who are expected to make up for this reduction in government revenues through increased personal taxation. Much of this advocacy work has taken the form of demanding large firms pay a 'fair share' of taxation. However, while tax justice NGOs have played a significant role promoting global tax reform and highlighting the deficiencies with the current regime, their rise has been relatively recent, especially in comparison to environmental and social justice NGOs.

The first wave of tax justice advocacy groups emerged in the late 1970s when financial deregulation in the world's industrialised economies had led to rapid growth in the offshore finance industry. The first of these was arguably the US-based Citizens for Tax Justice, which was formed in 1979 with the goal of empowering US citizens to fight the country's powerful corporate tax lobby (Citizens for Tax Justice 2015). INGO Oxfam, whose focus more broadly includes campaigning for development and eliminating poverty, also began work on the impact of tax havens on development in the late 1970s (Seabrooke and Wigan 2013). At that time, however, the organisation deemed the issue of tax avoidance too complex to navigate, and it took until 2000 for the issue to reappear on Oxfam's agenda through the publication of the landmark report *Tax Havens: Releasing the Hidden Billions for Poverty Eradication* (Oxfam 2000). These early attempts at raising awareness of tax avoidance and communicating the implications for various groups indicate the complexity of governing multinational tax avoidance. Oxfam's efforts were aimed at the international or global level, while Citizens for Tax Justice were very much focused on domestic US policy – yet neither group was able to capture the attention of policymakers or the public. The abandonment of the issue by Oxfam, despite its obviously detrimental impacts, suggests a complex policy field through which NGOs and other actors struggle to effect change. It is only over the past 15 years, and especially since the financial crisis, that tax justice campaigners have re-emerged as vocal actors in the global tax avoidance debate.

Following the re-emergence of tax justice NGOs in the 2000s, three main players dominate the policy arena. These are TJN, Christian Aid and Oxfam. Each of these NGOs operates internationally. However, not all are equally resourced or structured, and they do not all have an exclusive monopoly on tax justice. For example, as will be explained in Chapter 4, TJN is wholly devoted to addressing issues of tax avoidance, tax competition and tax havens, whereas taxation forms just one area in which Oxfam and Christian Aid campaign. Of the latter, Oxfam is a much larger organisation (total 2013–2014 income £974.1 million) when compared to Christian Aid (total 2013–2014 income £103.6 million) or TJN (total 2013 income £734 559). There are significant differences in strategy that result from these organisations' structures. For example, TJN is a small expert network that leverages its connections to larger social justice NGOs. As examined in Chapter 4, the structure of TJN allows it to engage in 'identity switching', that is, moving between professional network domains to push for change in the realm of international corporate taxation. The members at the centre of TJN have expertise in the technical realms of accounting, law and economics. Yet, as Seabrooke and Wigan (2015; this volume, Chapter 4) argue, they have successfully switched identities and leveraged different network domains in order to build alliances and coalitions to reach a wider audience than would otherwise be possible with a limited technical discourse.

TJN was launched in 2003 as a network of activists, academics, lawyers and others working to draw attention to harmful tax practices. TJN's operating model works by highlighting instances of tax avoidance, drawing media attention to these issues and then allowing other organisations or activists to take over the issue (TJN 2015a). This 'agenda-setting' operating model varies greatly from that of Oxfam or Christian Aid, whose work is more focused on delivering analysis and lobbying governments to deliver solutions to the challenges of MNC tax avoidance. TJN has influenced many elements of the international tax reform agenda, including campaigning for automatic information exchange to address international tax evasion, as well as more fundamental reforms designed to address corporate tax evasion, including promoting country-by-country reporting and developing the Global Alliance for Tax Justice and the Fair

Tax Mark, both of which now exist separately from the TJN in line with the operating model outlined above (TJN 2015a). Above all else, the TJN has prosecuted an effective media engagement strategy to ensure that tax justice remains on the political agenda in many advanced democracies. Oxfam International's goals are much broader and include poverty reduction and development, with the group's tax justice programme falling into the latter category. The organisation's landmark 2000 report was one of the initial drivers of the tax justice movement, and Oxfam remains centrally involved in tax justice advocacy globally. Similarly, Christian Aid is a UK-based organisation focused on development and eliminating poverty and injustice. Its tax justice programme seeks to address the unfairness of MNC tax avoidance through the promotion of three key aims: country-by-country reporting, automatic information exchange and public registers of beneficial ownership.

In addition to these three key civil society actors other groups such as ActionAid (a Johannesburg-based INGO), Attac and UK Uncut (a grassroots protest movement focused on the UK government's austerity measures) have emerged. Additionally, coalitions such as the Global Alliance for Tax Justice (which includes ActionAid, Christian Aid and Oxfam) bring these INGOs and NGOs together to lobby for effective tax policy and to lead campaigns against tax havens or particular corporations.

While somewhat belated, the emergence of tax justice NGOs highlights civil society's potential power in this policy arena. As noted above, these groups have been successful in agenda setting or bringing the issue of multinational tax avoidance to the attention of publics and policymakers. They have done so through efforts to highlight the inconsistent and unfair nature of corporate tax avoidance in the face of mounting budget challenges and declining public spending in many economies.

The Emergence of New Forms of Tax Governance

The rise of tax justice NGOs and broader public debate about MNC tax avoidance have had a number of implications. Part of the agenda has been to promote more robust international agreements and to ensure that national governments implement their commitments. However, the growing profile and politicisation of the tax justice debate has also had a direct impact on firms themselves. As this study will highlight, business has begun to develop and participate in new systems of governance in the field of corporate taxation. These include voluntary initiatives reflecting the actions of individual firms as well as multi-stakeholder initiatives involving the NGOs highlighted above. Private governance has long existed in areas such as environmental management, occupational health and safety and human rights, where various combinations of business and civil society organisations have taken the lead in self-regulating operations to protect reputations, reassure customers and investors and avert more formal regulation. Yet firms have thus far been reluctant to participate in governance regimes pertaining to corporate taxation, and where these have emerged progress has been slow. The two key private governance regimes in this policy field include voluntary commitments to enhanced transparency in financial reporting and the development of a privately led standard, known as the Fair Tax Mark (this volume, Chapter 10). While the emergence of these governance regimes suggests 'buy-in' on the part of corporations, as Chapter 5 of this volume highlights, voluntary adoption of these initiatives has been low. While many firms have enhanced the transparency of their financial reporting, this has often been due to existing or imminent government legislation requiring this level of detail.

Private standards have also served to highlight the form and viability of more fundamental reform agendas such as a unitary taxation regime (described in more detail in this volume, Chapter 2). The core principle behind unitary taxation is country-by-country reporting, under which firms provide separate country-level revenue, profit and taxation data in all jurisdictions in which they operate. This regime requires firms to go beyond the two currently used global accounting standards, the Generally Accepted Accounting Principles (GAAP) and the International Financial Reporting Standards (IFRS), which allow multinational firms to report revenue, profit and tax paid at the regional or global level (TJN 2015b). This allows firms to conceal complex tax structures by omitting details of revenue and profits earned compared with tax paid in specific jurisdictions. Tax justice NGOs and many independent experts have campaigned for the introduction of mandatory country-by-country reporting, arguing that forcing firms to report at this level would allow a more complete picture of multinational tax arrangements and is a pre-condition of ensuring that firms pay tax in jurisdictions in which they undertake real economic activity – the so-called 'membership principle' (Dietsch 2015, p. 80; this volume, Chapter 2). This campaign has had some early success, most notably in the extractives sector, where enhanced transparency in financial reporting has been seen as a potential solution not only to multinational tax avoidance but also to corruption and human rights violations in developing states (this volume, Chapter 9). In 2013, an update to the EU Transparency and Accounting Directive saw country-by-country reporting mandated for firms in the oil, gas, mining and forestry sectors where payments to governments exceeded €100 000 (European Union 2013). This follows attempts by the US government to implement similar standards. The US Dodd–Frank Wall Street Reform and Consumer Protection Act (Dodd–Frank Act) was implemented in 2010 following the global financial crisis and included a provision that all SEC reporting firms involved in the oil, mining and gas industries report detailed financial results at the country level. However, this particular clause of the Dodd–Frank Act was suspended soon after enactment following successful litigation by the American Petroleum Institute (Mehra 2013), and other key provisions of the Dodd–Frank Act were repealed by the Trump administration's Financial Choice Act of June 2017. In both the US and the EU, proposals to enhance reporting requirements have been confined to the extractive sectors, and in the case of the US even on this limited scale efforts have been unsuccessful. We argue that these developments suggest firms are reluctant to embrace new norms around taxation transparency, and that campaigns to enhance transparency in reporting have had limited success to date.

In addition to promoting private standards such as those described above, civil society groups can have other impacts on the international tax regime. For example, they can play an important agenda-setting role as private standards may, over time, be adopted by intergovernmental organisations and implemented in treaties or domestic law. Secondly, as outlined in Chapters 4 and 6, tax justice campaigns may influence the corporate strategies and compliance behaviours of firms and their advisers, thus having a material effect on the international tax regime.

The emergence of tax justice NGOs and associated voluntary governance regimes highlights how multinational tax avoidance is a complex policy arena with competing actors including states, intergovernmental organisations, civil society and firms. Non-state actors are increasingly lobbying governments to act on the challenges of tax avoidance, and NGOs in particular have been successful at garnering popular support for measures such as increased transparency in financial reporting and a more effective international corporate tax regime. However, it has taken considerable time for these NGOs to emerge, and the governance regimes they have developed and promoted remain embryonic. The slow-moving nature of multilateral reform and the hesitance of states to erode their competitive advantage in the pursuit of greater corporate tax revenue have opened space for multi-stakeholder governance initiatives. It is these initiatives, and the civil society actors that promote them, that are the focus of this volume.

THEORETICAL AND EMPIRICAL AIMS

Why examine the role of new forms of governance in the international tax arena? The answer lies in the fact that despite several false starts the civil society campaign against multinational tax avoidance is gaining momentum. The issue of tax avoidance is becoming more salient, yet the barriers to effective governmental and intergovernmental responses highlight the persistent challenges of contemporary global governance. Thus this volume, and its analysis of the role of civil society organisations in combating corporate tax avoidance, is timely while making several theoretical and empirical claims.

Firstly, the collection contributes to debates in the globalisation literature over the drivers and effectiveness of private governance as a solution to otherwise 'ungovernable' problems. In this light, the study provides insights into the supply of and demand for new forms of governance in cases where states have been unwilling, or unable, to implement effective governance regimes. In addition it provides a critical assessment of the changing nature of power and authority in the global economy and examines the prospects of hybrid regulatory regimes more generally. In this vein, the study also addresses questions on the legitimacy and effectiveness of privately led governance and the manner in which this is assessed by governments and other non-state actors such as consumers, firms and NGOs. Lastly, the volume provides a unique contribution to the literature on activism and social movements by providing insights into the manner in which actors with technical expertise leverage connections with wider social movements.

At an empirical level, the book provides one of the first in-depth studies into the scope and potential of new forms of governance emerging in response to the challenges of corporate taxation. A central aim is to evaluate the power and influence of NGOs, and assess civil society's potential to promote international tax reform. The study offers several responses to these questions. Chapter 7 focuses on corporate responses to the push for greater transparency and highlights the continued resistance of firms to calls for greater disclosure, as evidenced by a lack of concern about corporate reputation from some of the largest and most well-known MNCs. The book also interrogates the legal basis for many of these initiatives, and by extension the legitimacy that may or may not be afforded to recent efforts at global tax reform. In particular, contributions by Christians (Chapter 10) and Gale and Murphy-Gregory (Chapter 11) evaluate the legal basis of standards promoted by activists such as TJN and the Fair Tax Mark, as well as the transparency and accountability credentials of the initiatives themselves. The study concludes with a preliminary evaluation of the prospects for global tax justice and the extent to which fiscally challenged governments are going to be able to extract revenues from large corporations.

The study employs several key concepts and terms which require elaboration owing to their contested nature. Firstly, the concept of voluntary governance is a central focus of this study. Contained within this is the notion of private governance, that is, regulation implemented by firms with significant private authority which is regarded as legitimate by other actors. It should be noted that this form of governance goes beyond self-regulation. Instead, private governance requires a level of perceived legitimacy that is reflected in the behaviour of other actors, who abide by these rules not out of self-interest but out of 'recognition of the legitimacy of the governance system' (Falkner 2003, p. 73). We argue that private governance is becoming more important in the international tax arena but often in combination with various forms of public authority, resulting in new forms of 'hybrid' governance regimes (Crouch 2004).

In terms of the analytical focus of the study we use the term 'tax avoidance' in preference to the narrower concept of 'tax evasion', which denotes illegal activity. As noted above, this study is specifically concerned with the more contested concept of MNC tax avoidance, that is, the use of complex tax structures that operate within existing legal frameworks but minimise or eliminate a firm's tax obligations. On a related note, the terms 'tax secrecy jurisdiction' and 'tax haven' are used interchangeably throughout this collection. While there is no one agreed definition of a tax haven or secrecy jurisdiction, this volume follows the OECD definition of tax havens as having 'the following key characteristics; no or only nominal taxes; lack of effective exchange of information; lack of transparency in the operation of the legislative, legal or administrative provisions' (OECD 2016). Finally, many will agree that the use of complex transnational regimes and financial structures to minimise tax liabilities constitutes tax avoidance, but this is a subjective measure, and the line between deliberate tax evasion and claiming legitimate business deductions is inherently blurred and contested. While acknowledging these ambiguities in Chapter 2, we provide an overview of key contributions from the contemporary literature on the ethics of taxation to provide some defensible guidelines as to the features of a 'fair' international tax regime and its implications for reform (Dietsch 2015).

OVERVIEW

The volume begins with a detailed assessment of the political challenges associated with taxing MNCs. Part I begins with a contextual outline of the origins and the problem of international tax avoidance associated with the rise of MNCs. Detailed consideration is given to the distinction between tax avoidance and tax evasion – a point which highlights the contested nature of fairness in the international corporate taxation system. In Chapter 1 Richard Woodward provides a historical overview of early tax campaigns and anti-avoidance measures, followed, in Chapter 2, by Richard Eccleston's analysis of the more recent shift to focusing on the tax avoidance strategies of firms and finally the introduction of BEPS. Chapter 2 concludes by presenting the philosophical and technical case for the unitary taxation of corporate income, which is increasingly the focus of the global tax justice campaign. Part I concludes with Ainsley Elbra's contribution (Chapter 3), outlining emerging forms of tax activism and private governance, including the emergence of tax justice NGOs, media and community engagement, firm-specific campaigns, standard setting and benchmarking, and investor activism.

Part II of this volume examines the strategies of various actors in the arena of private tax governance. As outlined earlier in this Introduction, the governance of corporate taxation involves multiple actors operating at various levels; Part II describes the strategies of these participants. Leonard Seabrooke and Duncan Wigan's contribution (Chapter 4) examines the strategies of tax activists, in particular TJN. This chapter highlights the key campaigns and strategies of these actors, and their links to other NGOs, tax professionals and the media. Aynsley Kellow's contribution (Chapter 5) analyses the legitimacy challenges of civil society organisations in the international tax arena and the associated limits of private governance. He highlights the centrality of norms including 'fairness' in any private governance regime and the manner in which they render the legitimacy of actors such as NGOs critical. Kellow provides an overview of the literature on NGOs and examples of legitimacy deficits, and concludes by examining the scholarship on the legitimacy of transnational activists. Following from this, Lyne Latulippe's chapter on the critical role of tax professionals (Chapter 6) examines the strategies and governing roles of professional tax advisers. She highlights the crucial role of these key intermediaries in the provision of advice as well as the implementation of complex taxation strategies. The chapter goes on to examine the interlinkages between tax professionals and NGOs and the manner in which the former respond to 'fairness' campaigns waged by the latter. Part II concludes with the contribution from John Mikler and Ainsley Elbra (Chapter 7) on corporate responses to tax justice campaigns, in particular through firms' participation in parliamentary inquiries into corporate taxation. This chapter argues there is a continued preoccupation with shareholder value maximisation over corporate reputation, and that a liberal ideological belief in free markets dominates corporate conceptions of their legitimacy in debates about paying their fair share of tax.

Part III of the book focuses on the theoretical underpinnings of private and hybrid governance and the application of these regimes in other domains of global governance. Opening Part III, Tony Porter and Karsten Ronit (Chapter 8) examine the scope and forms of private governance, including providing an overview of the theories of private governance and compliance as well as the institutional and political pre-conditions for effective private governance. The chapter concludes by examining the extent to which these pre-conditions exist in the corporate tax arena. Following this, James Van Alstine and Laura Smith (Chapter 9) examine the most established quasi-private taxation regime, the Extractive Industries Transparency Initiative (EITI). This chapter provides an overview of the EITI, including the unusual quasi-private nature of this standard, whereby the regime was developed by firms and INGOs but is implemented by national governments. Van Alstine and Smith also examine the manner in which the EITI encourages enhanced transparency on the part of firms and the future challenges for the initiative. Allison Christians's chapter (Chapter 10) discusses the legal considerations pertinent to voluntary efforts such as the Fair Tax Mark, as well as the impact of high-profile litigation such as the European Commission's 2016 state aid case against Apple. In this chapter, Christians highlights the fact that many forms of private governance do not possess a solid legal dimension. She outlines the enforcement challenges associated with these cases and asks what is the likelihood of disputes and who will adjudicate such conflicts. Next, Fred Gale and Hannah Murphy-Gregory's contribution (Chapter 11) explores lessons from the Forest Stewardship Council (FSC) and Fairtrade campaigns. Gale and Murphy-Gregory suggest that the international tax arena is something of a laggard in terms of private governance, a theme which is central to the wider study. Their contribution examines legitimacy in global private governance, how this has been achieved in the FSC and Fairtrade cases, and what lessons can be learned in the area of taxation private governance. In the final chapter, Lachlan Johnson (Chapter 12) discusses the emerging potential private governance role of whistleblowers, data leakers and investigative journalists. Drawing on survey data and accounting research, Johnson's chapter considers the impacts of reputational damage, issue salience and public awareness raised by massive data leaks – such as the Panama Papers and Paradise Papers – on the cost–benefit calculus of MNC tax planning.

The Conclusion brings the volume to a close with Richard Eccleston and Ainsley Elbra's preliminary assessment of the effectiveness of voluntary governance in the international tax arena. Eccleston and Elbra summarise the preliminary evidence presented in the study pertaining to the collective impact of the emerging governance regimes, including the central question of whether these initiatives have led to altered behaviour on the part of firms or whether they have precipitated other regulatory responses. The Conclusion ends by considering the prospects of alternative mechanisms for enhancing the global corporate taxation regime, including investor and financier activism, as well as the broader theme of the significance of private global economic governance in the early twenty-first century.

REFERENCES

Apeldoorn, L. van (2016), 'International Taxation and the Erosion of Sovereignty', in P. Dietsch and T. Rixen (eds), *Global Tax Governance: What Is Wrong with It and How to Fix It*, Colchester: ECPR Press, pp. 215–230.

Aston, H. and G. Wilkins (2014), 'ASX 200 Company Tax Avoidance Bleeds Commonwealth Coffers of Billions a Year, Report Finds', *Sydney Morning Herald*, available at http://www.smh.com.au/business/the-economy/asx-200-company-tax-avoidance-bleeds-commonwealth-coffers-of-billions-a-year-report-finds-20140927-10n3n3 (accessed 9 November 2016).

Australian Senate (2015), 'Corporate Tax Avoidance', Australian Senate Economics References Committee.

Bell, S. (2012), 'The Power of Ideas: The Ideational Shaping of the Structural Power of Business', *International Studies Quarterly* **56** (4), 661–673, doi:10.1111/j.1468-2478.2012.00743.x.

Christians, A. (2013), 'How Starbucks Lost Its Social License – And Paid £20 Million to Get It Back', *Tax Notes International* **71** (7), available at SSRN: https://ssrn.com/abstract=2308921 (accessed 6 November 2016).

Christians, A. (2015), 'Friends with Tax Benefits: Apple's Cautionary Tale', *Tax Notes International* **78** (11), available at SSRN: https://ssrn.com/abstract=2674335 (accessed 12 November 2016).

Citizens for Tax Justice (2015), 'Background and History', available at http://ctj.org/about/background.php (accessed 11 November 2016).

Clausing, K. (2016), 'The Nature and Practice of Tax Competition', in P. Dietsch and T. Rixen (eds), *Global Tax Governance: What Is Wrong with It and How to Fix It*, Colchester: ECPR Press, pp. 27–54.

Crouch, C. (2004), 'Hybrid Governance and Networked Firms', in C. Crouch, P. Le Galès, C. Trigilia and H. Voelzkow, The Changing Governance of Local Economies, Oxford: Oxford University Press, pp. 119–128.

Dietsch, P. (2015), *Catching Capital: The Ethics of Tax Competition*, New York: Oxford University Press.

Dietsch, Peter and Thomas Rixen (eds) (2016), *Global Tax Governance: What Is Wrong with It and How to Fix It*, Colchester: ECPR Press.

Eccleston, R. (2013), *The Dynamics of Global Economic Governance: The Financial Crisis, the OECD and the Politics of International Tax Competition*, Cheltenham, UK and Northampton, MA, USA: Edward Elgar Publishing.

Eccleston, R. and F. Gray (2014), 'Foreign Accounts Tax Compliance Act and American Leadership in the Campaign against International Tax Evasion: Revolution or False Dawn?', *Global Policy* **5** (3), 321–333, doi:10.1111/1758-5899.12122.

Eccleston, R. and H. Smith (2016), 'The G20, BEPS and the Future of International Tax Governance', in P. Dietsch and T. Rixen (eds), *Global Tax Governance: What Is Wrong with It and How to Fix It*, Colchester: ECPR Press, pp. 175–198.

European Union (2013), Directive 2013/34/EU of the European Parliament and of the Council on the annual financial statements, consolidated financial statements and related reports of certain types of undertakings, amending Directive 2006/43/EC of the European Parliament and of the Council and repealing Council Directives 78/660/EEC and 83/349/EEC, available at http://eur-lex.europa.eu/LexUriServ/LexUriServ.do?uri=OJ:L:2013:182:0019:0076:EN:PDF (accessed 11 November 2016).

Falkner, R. (2003), 'Private Environmental Governance and International Relations: Exploring the Links', *Global Environmental Politics* **3** (2), 72–87, doi: 10.1162/152638003322068227.

Genschel, P. and P. Schwarz (2011), 'Tax Competition: A Literature Review', *Socio-economic Review* **9** (2), 339–370.

Gravelle, J.G. (2015), *Tax Havens: International Tax Avoidance and Evasion*, Vol. R40623, Washington, DC: Congressional Research Service.

Henry, J. (2016), 'Let's Tax Anonymous Wealth!', in T. Pogge and K. Mehta (eds), *Global Tax Fairness*, Oxford: Oxford University Press, pp. 31–95.

Kavoussi, B. (2012), 'Google Chairman Eric Schmidt Defends Tax Dodge: "It's Called Capitalism"', *Huffington Post*, available at http://www.huffingtonpost.com.au/entry/google-tax-dodge_n_2292077.html?section=australia (accessed 1 November 2016).

Lindblom, C.E. (1977), *Politics and Markets: The World's Political Economic Systems*, New York: Basic Books.

Mehra, A. (2013), 'Oil Companies Are on a Slippery Slope with Their First Amendment Claim against Disclosure Rules', *Forbes.com*, available at http://www.forbes.com/sites/csr/2013/02/28/5802/ (accessed 4 November 2016).

OECD (1998), *Harmful Tax Competition: An Emerging Global Issue*, Paris: OECD Publishing.

OECD (2014a), 'Government Debt', *Economics: Key Tables from OECD*, No. 21, available at http://dx.doi.org/10.1787/gov-debt-table-2014-1-en (accessed 21 December 2017).

OECD (2014b), *OECD/G20 Base Erosion and Profit Shifting Project: Developing a Multilateral Instrument to Modify Bilateral Tax Treaties*, Paris: OECD Publishing.

OECD (2015), 'Reforms to the International Tax System for Curbing Avoidance by Multinational Enterprises', available at http://www.oecd.org/tax/g20-finance-ministers-endorse-reforms-to-the-international-tax-system-for-curbing-avoidance-by-multinational-enterprises.htm (accessed 1 November 2016).

OECD (2016), 'Glossary of Tax Terms', available at http://www.oecd.org/ctp/glossaryoftaxterms.htm#T (accessed 10 November 2016).

Oxfam (2000), *Tax Havens: Releasing the Hidden Billions for Poverty Eradication*, available at http://www.taxjustice.net/cms/upload/pdf/oxfam_paper_-_final_version__06_00.pdf (accessed 1 November 2016).

Palan, R. (2002), 'Tax Havens and the Commercialization of State Sovereignty', *International Organization* **56** (1), 151–176, doi:10.1162/002081802753485160.

Palan, R. and D. Wigan (2014), 'Herding Cats and Taming Tax Havens: The US Strategy of "Not in My Backyard"', *Global Policy* **5** (3), 334–343, doi:10.1111/1758-5899.12135.

Palan, R., R. Murphy and C. Chavagneux (2010), *Tax Havens: How Globalization Really Works*, Ithaca, NY: Cornell University Press.
Picciotto, S. (2016), 'Towards Unitary Taxation: Combined Reporting and Formulary Apportionment', in T. Pogge and K. Mehta (eds), *Global Tax Fairness*, Oxford: Oxford University Press, pp. 221–237.
Rixen, T. (2008), *The Political Economy of International Tax Governance: Transformations of the State*, New York: Palgrave Macmillan.
Rixen, T. (2011), 'Tax Competition and Inequality: The Case for Global Tax Governance', *Global Governance* **17**, 447–467.
Seabrooke, L. and D. Wigan (2013), *Emergent Entrepreneurs in Transnational Advocacy Networks: Professional Mobilization in the Fight for Global Tax Justice*, Working Paper No. 41, GR:EEN, Global Reordering: Evolution through European Networks, FP7, available at http://pipesproject.eu/assets/GREEN41.pdf (accessed 1 November 2017).
Seabrooke, L. and D. Wigan (2015), 'How Activists Use Benchmarks: Reformist and Revolutionary Benchmarks for Global Economic Justice', *Review of International Studies* **41** (5), 887–904.
TJN (Tax Justice Network) (2015a), 'About Us – Our Goals', available at http://www.taxjustice.net/about/who-we-are/goals/ (accessed 9 November 2016).
TJN (Tax Justice Network) (2015b), 'Country by Country Reporting', available at http://www.taxjustice.net/topics/corporate-tax/country-by-country/ (accessed 9 November 2016).
UNCTAD (2015), *World Investment Report 2015: Reforming International Investment Governance*, Geneva: United Nations.
Weckler, A. (2016), 'Apple and Ireland against the World', *Sunday Independent*, available at https://www.independent.ie/business/irish/apple-and-ireland-against-the-world-35018709.html (accessed 12 November 2016).

PART I

1. The evolution of the international corporate tax regime, 1920–2008

Richard Woodward

1.1 INTRODUCTION

The central focus of this book is to understand and explain the evolution of the international corporate tax regime since 2008 and the role of civil society activism and increased politicisation in this process. This chapter outlines the failings of the international corporate tax regime at the outbreak of the Financial Crisis (FC) and identifies the factors that, criticism notwithstanding, have made it resistant to change since its origins in the 1920s. Many corporate tax norms and principles devised almost a century ago still pepper contemporary tax treaties, including the allocation of taxation rights between source and residence countries, conventions governing relief from double taxation, and concepts such as permanent establishment (Jogarajan 2011). This inertia also persists in rules and decision-making procedures grounded in bilateral, rather than multilateral, agreements.

Every conundrum of global governance presents unique challenges. Nevertheless, all issues of global governance are afflicted by a common set of complications applicable to global governance challenges (Keohane 2001; Slaughter 2004; Rodrik 2011). Many arise from the mismatch between the territorially bounded authority of the primary governing units, nation states, and the global scale of the puzzle being addressed. Reluctant to forfeit their sovereignty to supranational organisations, states instead tackle these issues through international institutions and agreements. These arrangements represent, and have helped to stimulate, some impressive episodes of international cooperation; however, as products of state sovereignty, their effectiveness is constrained. A central conclusion of this book is that, despite the potential dividends of international cooperation in corporate taxation, the potential for conflict between states over the allocation of profits is an enduring threat to international tax cooperation.

Tensions between states are a hallmark of the international corporate tax regime. During the last 50 years, the surge in the number and impact of multinational corporations (MNCs) has come to symbolise economic globalisation (Mikler 2013). Although their power is sometimes exaggerated, the geographical reach and financial dexterity of MNCs has unquestionably curtailed the capacity of individual sovereign states to regulate and tax them. This predicament is exacerbated by the fact that corporate taxation remains a national prerogative and, despite numerous initiatives designed to enhance international cooperation such as bilateral treaties and international standards, the system remains vulnerable to international competition and exploitation by MNCs (Eccleston and Smith 2016; see this volume, Chapter 2).

The governance of corporate taxation is sometimes simply portrayed as a problem of collective action. From this perspective (see Thomas 2000) states have an incentive to negotiate rules to restrict fiscal practices inimical to their interest in optimising tax revenue, and to devise strong mechanisms to discourage defection. In fact, the state's interest in raising revenue is tempered by other considerations such as exploiting the tax system to boost its economic competitiveness. Lower corporate tax rates and the lenient treatment of foreign investments are indispensable tools for states eager to attract and retain mobile capital. Similarly, governments keen to stimulate expansion of domestic firms or bolster the competitiveness of 'home' MNCs are unlikely to curtail opportunities for them to profit offshore. In fact, the decentralised system of bilateral tax treaties on which the international tax regime has been built contains subtle provisions which protect the interests of powerful states and the MNCs they promote (Büttner and Thiemann 2017). The outcome is a self-defeating race to the bottom, with governments offering incentives that harm not only domestic tax revenues but those of other states.

More aggressive attempts to curb excessive or 'harmful' (OECD 1998) tax competition have clashed with tenets of state sovereignty. Taxation is 'the pre-eminent prerogative of the sovereign state' (Sharman 2012, p. 18) and is the cornerstone of the social contract on which contemporary democracy is based. Losing control over taxation has profound implications for state sovereignty, for example by undermining its ability to respond to domestic demands for welfare, security and economic competitiveness, or to protect international interests (Ring 2009). Unsurprisingly, states, even within the European Union, have ardently defended the right to design and administer domestic tax law, despite agreeing to some international norms circumscribing the reach of their tax systems (Rixen 2008). The combination of divergent and inconsistent national tax systems and competing state preferences has meant that the reform of international corporate tax laws has been incremental at best and all too often characterised by lowest-common-denominator agreements. The result is that, rather than a comprehensive multilateral agreement overseen by a World Tax Organisation, the international corporate tax regime is a matrix of bilateral treaties 'loosely coordinated' (Eccleston 2013, p. 69) by standards and model treaties agreed at the Organisation for Economic Co-operation and Development (OECD).

Accounts of the role of states and interstate relationships provide important, if incomplete, insights into the international corporate tax regime. Fully comprehending the regime's trajectory and its intransigence requires a complementary account of the role of private actors. Far from being mere subjects of the international corporate tax regime, private actors have been intrinsic to its development from the beginning. Together with national tax officials, international civil servants and academic specialists, envoys from the private sphere, including business and industry associations, MNCs, tax planning professionals and latterly civil society organisations (NGOs), have been integral parts of the community of experts whose judgements have guided the international corporate tax regime (see this volume, Chapters 6 and 7). In recent decades, private players from multinational accounting firms to global technology giants have assumed prominent positions of growing influence in the formulation and implementation of international tax rules. Before 2008 private actors were generally viewed as defenders of the status quo. The tax policy community was dominated by tax experts and professionals allied to transnational business interests that, as the key beneficiaries of a regime now recognised for its 'inadequate principles, outdated concepts and unsatisfactory policies' (Graetz 2001), worked against proposals for paradigmatic change. Since 2008, new private actors have gained entry to this closed policy community, most notably civil society organisations campaigning for tax justice. The implications of their entry into the international corporate tax regime are discussed in subsequent chapters.

This constellation of state and private interests is the primary reason why only cosmetic changes to the international corporate tax regime have been made over the last 100 years. In contrast, during the same period, the nature of corporate activity has been revolutionised. The explosion of cross-border commerce has rendered many of the regime's rules, norms and principles increasingly anachronistic. This was epitomised by the rise of MNCs and their apparent ability to exploit these rules to avoid taxes with impunity (Elbra and Mikler 2017). The next section describes the origins of the international corporate tax regime in the interwar period, while the remainder of the chapter highlights growing concerns about the capacity of the regime to effectively tax cross-border commerce.

1.2 1920–1945: THE ORIGINS OF THE INTERNATIONAL CORPORATE TAX REGIME

Intensified globalisation in the period prior to the First World War inspired the development of mechanisms to address the complications arising from cross-border commerce. By 1914, and enacted through the rudimentary forerunners of current mechanisms of global governance, states, private and professional associations and powerful individuals had developed harmonized rules and standards for trade, transport, communications, intellectual property and units of measure (Murphy 1994; Davies and Woodward 2014). At this time, the proceeds from tariffs rather than direct taxes on individuals or corporations constituted the lion's share of public revenues. From the middle of the nineteenth century, states began to develop international treaties elaborating principles for the taxation of income and profits deriving from cross-border activity (Jogarajan 2011). The objective was to galvanise international commerce by preventing double taxation, or 'the imposition of comparable taxes in two (or more) States on the same taxpayer in respect of the same subject matter and for identical periods' (OECD 2014b, p. 1).

These issues became politically charged after the First World War when the newly installed League of Nations presumed that economic liberalism would promote prospects for peace. Removing economic barriers to trade and investment would ameliorate conflict by spreading wealth and promoting interdependence, thereby making war anathema to the economic interests of leading states (Angell 1911). Against this background, the League of Nations International Financial Conference of 1920 petitioned for action to forestall double taxation, which it branded a 'serious impediment to international relations and world production, and therefore a threat to global peace' (quoted in Brooks 2013, p. 125). The following year the League of Nations Financial Committee appointed four academic economists to study the problem. Their pioneering report (League of Nations 1923) had a seminal impact on the intellectual debate and the rules that came to underpin international taxation.

The report's authors were immediately confronted with the quandary of how to establish principles that confer states with the right to tax profits gleaned from international business and investment without undermining the sovereignty of other states to raise revenue as they saw fit. To do this, they put forward three propositions. First, the right to tax should be divided between source and residence countries. Source countries, or the territory where capital was invested and a company, or its subsidiary, was permanently undertaking real economic activity, were allocated the primary taxing rights over the active income of businesses. Residence countries, or the territory inhabited by the person or company with the right to receive the returns on the investment, were allocated the primary taxing rights over 'passive' or investment income such as dividends and royalties. Second, although MNCs operate as single economic units, in a decision which would later facilitate corporate tax avoidance it was recommended that each subsidiary should be treated as a separate legal entity whose tax liability would be assessed by national fiscal authorities as a stand-alone company. Third, it was recommended that these broad conventions should underpin states' negotiations on more detailed bilateral treaties.

This report and subsequent work by a Committee of Technical Experts on Double Taxation and Tax Evasion were exercises in expediency. Their quest for politically acceptable remedies forced them to compromise on solutions identified in their academic research (see, for example, Seligman 1921; Stamp 1921; Jogarajan 2013). The Committee's malleability kept participants engaged with a package to tackle the headache of double taxation. However, members were also mindful (as the Committee's nomenclature implicitly implies) that their proposals could facilitate widespread tax avoidance. Splitting taxing rights between source and residence countries, for example, accommodates the competing preferences of both capital importing and capital exporting jurisdictions. Where source countries claim jurisdiction over activities undertaken within their borders, a tension arises with residence countries (primarily the US and the UK) that want to tax their residents' global income. In this case, as is discussed in more detail in Chapter 2, MNCs could defer residence taxation by not repatriating income made overseas.

Correspondingly the Committee of Technical Experts had lengthy discussions about whether double taxation treaties should be negotiated on a bilateral or multilateral basis. The Committee generally accepted that the superior approach was a universal multilateral pact that would manage the inconsistencies between national tax systems. Nevertheless, the Committee eventually proposed a bilateral approach, recognising that divergences amongst national fiscal systems made negotiating a collective convention 'practically impossible . . . unless it were worded in such general terms as to be of no practical value' (League of Nations 1927, p. 8). Their report sketched a prototype model convention encompassing principles applicable as a template for bilateral treaty negotiations between states. To safeguard state sovereignty, the prototype allowed contracting parties to tailor double tax agreements (DTAs) to the peculiarities of their domestic tax arrangements. The drawback of customisation was the proliferation of bilateral treaties, whose collective inconsistencies were a godsend for MNCs determined to outwit tax authorities.

Tax avoidance problems stemming from the unevenness of the treaty network were aggravated by the decision to treat each company in a corporate group as an independent entity (League of Nations 1933; Picciotto 1992). Theoretically the prices recorded for transactions between firms affiliated in the same group, so-called transfer prices, should conform to hypothetical transactions entered into at 'arm's length' (i.e. they should equate to real prices which would be charged to an unrelated company in a free market). In reality, as discussed in greater detail in Chapter 2, this system was susceptible to manipulation by corporate groups, which could reduce their overall tax liability by fixing artificial prices to funnel costs (which are tax deductible) to higher-tax jurisdictions and shift profits to low-tax environments. Throughout the 1920s and 1930s alternative proposals for unitary taxation were regularly discussed. A unitary taxation system treats corporate groups as a single entity and distributes profits amongst states according to an agreed formula related to the group's sales, assets and payroll in different jurisdictions. These proposals were confounded by a lack of international consensus on a definition of the tax base or on principles to guide its allocation (Avi-Yonah 1995). Significantly, as this book will highlight, establishing an international system of formula apportionment has become a central element of the reform agenda advocated by the tax justice movement since the Financial Crisis.

Although states were the primary shapers of the formative years of the international corporate tax regime, private actors also played a role. These private actors, with the International Chamber of Commerce (ICC) at the forefront, consisted entirely of business representatives. The ICC was consulted regularly by the Committee of Technical Experts and was granted observer status in 1929 on a new League Fiscal Committee, which masterminded a series of models for bilateral tax treaties until its conclusion in 1946. This constituency was predisposed to limit double taxation and liberalise international finance and so militated against moves to inhibit tax avoidance and evasion.

Only 60 DTAs were concluded between 1920 and 1939 (Picciotto 1992, p. 25), a modest tally that understates the progress made by the League. The League's efforts in this field established institutional and intellectual foundations upon which the post-war architects would erect a more formal international corporate tax regime. Regrettably, even before then the process of reaching consensus had shaped a regime already out of step with commercial realities by leaving a legacy of loopholes that expedited tax abuses by MNCs, flaws that would worsen after 1945 with a rapid and sustained expansion in multinational corporate activity.

1.3 1946–1996: INSTITUTIONALISATION, GLOBALISATION AND EMASCULATION

If the foundations for an international corporate tax regime were laid during the interwar period, the edifice was constructed in the second half of the twentieth century. During this time the regime became more intricate and institutionalised. The count of bilateral double tax treaties, based on refined versions of earlier model tax conventions, grew almost twentyfold to 1727 by the end of 1996 (UNCTAD 2017). Many stipulations in these agreements, however, were rendered obsolete by MNCs and their armada of tax planners. These actors, most notably the Big Four professional services firms, have increasingly wielded influence over the regime's expert policy community (this volume, Chapter 6).

After 1945, a new UN Tax Committee perpetuated the League Fiscal Committee operations but was swiftly paralysed by disagreements between capital exporting and capital importing states. Foreshadowing their later clout, international business representatives lobbied successfully to narrow dialogue to a circle of industrialised nations. In 1954, the ICC passed a resolution to sponsor a multilateral agreement on double taxation between Organisation for European Economic Cooperation (OEEC) countries. The founding of the OEEC Fiscal Committee followed two years later, and was superseded by the Organisation for Economic Co-operation and Development in 1961. Significantly the US was a full and dominant member of the OECD (unlike the OEEC), effectively ensuring that the international tax framework was consistent with American interests. The uniquely globalised nature of American MNCs left US Treasury revenues vulnerable to tax avoidance, a source of irritation for President Kennedy, who condemned the 'unjustifiable use of tax havens by growing numbers of businesses to slash their tax liabilities at home and abroad' (quoted in Houlder 2013). This hastened the arrival in 1963 of the OECD Model Tax Convention as a basis for negotiating bilateral treaties. Even within the smaller and more homogeneous setting of the OECD, reaching an agreement between states proved challenging. In practice, the Convention was simply a codification of the principles developed in the interwar years and therefore perpetuated their shortcomings.

The deficiencies of the international corporate tax regime were amplified by the changing nature and importance of MNCs. Immediately after the Second World War there were just a few hundred MNCs, whose profits came principally from foreign trade and portfolio investment. Most foreign direct investment (FDI) was from MNCs in primary industries with small numbers of affiliates looking to extract resources from specific locations. This capital was normally raised locally or financed out of retained earnings. These companies at least approximated the regime image of the MNC, with a clearly defined residence country and loosely coordinating the operations of autonomous overseas affiliates. By the 1970s things looked very different. Not only had the quantity of MNCs expanded rapidly, exceeding 9000 by 1973 (Hood and Young 1979), but the structure of companies, especially those that had emerged in the manufacturing and services sectors, increasingly bore little resemblance to that of their predecessors. Instead, modern MNCs were taking the form of single, globally integrated companies with centralised decision-making structures exerting tight control over a labyrinth of subsidiaries. These MNCs financed their FDI through borrowing on global capital markets, meaning their owners as well as their customers were geographically dispersed. The production process, value and profitability of these firms were becoming more reliant on intangible assets, most notably intellectual property rights like patents, trademarks and copyrights.

The principles on which the international corporate tax regime was constructed generated a myriad of tax avoidance opportunities for the rapidly evolving and globally integrated MNCs. The insistence on treating subsidiaries as separate companies, for example, encouraged MNCs to unbundle their assets into vast networks of offshore entities. Many of these were artificial affiliates undertaking contrived transactions to disconnect the incidence of taxation from the place where the genuine economic activity occurred (Gravelle 2009; OECD 2013). In particular, MNCs were able to manipulate corporate residence tax through the use of intangible assets, by shifting profits to low-tax jurisdictions (housing their intellectual property in tax haven subsidiaries) and then charging exorbitant fees for its use to subsidiaries in high-tax jurisdictions. MNCs also continued to capitalise on gaps and discrepancies in the network of bilateral tax treaties. For instance, it was commonplace for identical financial instruments used in cross-border activities to be differentially treated by the tax systems of the respective countries. These 'hybrid mismatches' meant that instruments regarded as debt and which generate deductible payments in one jurisdiction were regarded as non-taxable equity in jurisdictions where the proceeds were received.

MNCs' tax avoidance strategies were aided and abetted by two interconnected developments: the intensification of tax competition and the flourishing of the transnational tax planning industry. From the late 1950s, the tax havens, or jurisdictions that specialise in financial transactions for non-resident investors whom they attract by offering indulgent fiscal, regulatory and legal frameworks, grew in abundance. Small states, many of which seized on financial services as a strategy for developing and diversifying their economies, may be the most notorious tax havens, but similar enticements were intrinsic to the economic strategies of virtually all OECD countries (Woodward 2018). This is captured in the nomenclature of the now notorious 'double Irish with a Dutch sandwich', a tax avoidance technique involving two Irish companies and a Dutch one (Clyne 1977). Likewise, many OECD countries cemented their competitive position by tacitly endorsing the use of tax havens by their 'home' MNCs. Deepening their tax competitiveness enhanced tax planning opportunities for MNCs. Precipitated by the systematic selling of complex tax avoidance schemes by advanced business services firms, aggressive tax planning became a staple component of corporate strategy from the 1970s. In other words, tax was regarded as just another cost to be minimised.

Perhaps reflecting the institutionalised nature of the OECD, appetite for thoroughgoing reform to the international corporate tax regime was low. Growing reservations about the regime did result in a series of OECD working groups on double taxation, tax avoidance and transfer pricing abuses, which achieved piecemeal alterations to the Model Convention and rules on transfer pricing, including guidelines for their application (Ylonen 2017). That these groups confined their activities to incremental reform reflected a conservative bias of the OECD coupled with its reliance on consensus decision making (Carroll and Kellow 2011). This inclination is magnified in tax policy arenas, where tax reforms that may limit competition with other countries often run counter to the political interests of powerful countries which make the largest contributions to the OECD's budget.

Probabilities for regime reform were further diminished by the wholesale incorporation of the transnational tax planning industry into the underlying policy community (see this volume, Chapter 6). Narratives of corporate tax avoidance typically portray a game of cat and mouse in which the nimble tax-avoiding rodents habitually outsmart the clumsy feline tax inspector. The revolving door between the tax planning industry and bureaucracy meant swathes of the corporate tax code were being written in cahoots with the very firms that would market schemes to clients designed to circumvent these self-same laws (Brooks 2013; Sikka 2015). In other words, far from being the passive victim of provisions to shrink tax liabilities the state has, through its connivance with the tax planning industry, been their primary architect. Put another way, the cats were sabotaging their own mousetraps (Woodward 2017). These domestic trends reinforced the privileged position of private business interests at the international level. From its inception, the OECD, mainly through the Business and Industry Advisory Committee (BIAC), systematically included private sector interests in its tax deliberations. This had a rationalising effect on the regime, by undermining efforts to suppress tax avoidance. For instance, in the late 1980s, tax advisers and bankers orchestrated an energetic and successful campaign against the joint OECD–Council of Europe Convention on Mutual Administrative Assistance in Tax Matters (Picciotto 1992).

By the 1990s, the international corporate tax regime was widely regarded as anachronistic (Eccleston 2013, chapter 3). The assumptions and principles underpinning the regime correlated less and less with the reality of multinational business enterprises whose effective corporate tax rates were a fraction of the headline rate. Moreover, the system encouraged unfettered tax competition, which seemed to have locked states into a race to the fiscal bottom. This led to a dawning appreciation amongst OECD (1987) countries of the vast revenues being lost as a consequence of the estimated $5.1 trillion assets stashed offshore (Diamond and Diamond 1997), and provided the backdrop for a fresh foray into the promotion of international tax transparency.

1.4 1996–2008: PHONEY WAR AND STRATEGIC RETREAT

Commencing in 1996 at the behest of the G7, the OECD's Harmful Tax Competition (HTC) initiative marked the most serious attempt yet to overhaul the international corporate tax regime. In many respects, HTC was a pre-emptive strike by states alarmed about the impact of untrammelled tax competition in an era of mobile capital. The impetus came from a fortuitous confluence of ideational and material circumstances. The tax policy community was in thrall to liberal economic theories, portending a gloomy outlook for capital taxation (OECD 1991; Tanzi 1995). The theories forewarned that economic openness would result in capital being lost to more tax-lenient jurisdictions. This would unleash a race to the bottom amongst states seeking to attract and retain investment, the material impact of which, to borrow the phrase used in the G7 (1996) Communiqué, would be the 'erosion of national tax bases'. The OECD's (1998) preliminary report was greeted with considerable fanfare and forecasts of the 'end of offshore' (Hampton and Levi 1999; Picciotto 1999). Yet just three years later the initiative had stalled, with key states refusing to countenance an international agreement that would impinge upon their freedom to determine their tax system (see Webb 2004; Eden and Kudrle 2005; Sharman 2006).

Broadly speaking the report dubbed tax practices or tax competition 'harmful' if their consequence was to 'poach' the tax base of other countries by driving the tax rate on income from mobile activities significantly below that of other countries (OECD 1998, p. 30). Two categories of harmful tax practices were identified: tax havens and preferential tax regimes. Tax havens were defined as jurisdictions which combined low or no rates of tax with a lack of transparency or a refusal to exchange information with overseas tax authorities, or did not mandate investors to maintain substantial economic activities. In the late 1990s the agenda for identifying and sanctioning so-called tax havens was controversial. Even more arduous, however, was the related goal of identifying what the OECD called 'preferential tax regimes' (PTRs), which met transparency standards but sought to attract international investment by offering generous tax inducements. PTRs directly threatened the interests of MNCs and national governments' capacity to compete for their investment (OECD 1998). The OECD report threatened unspecified countermeasures against jurisdictions that refused to pledge to purge harmful tax practices.

Calls to reduce international tax competition through harmonisation have always raised a host of theoretical and normative concerns, and HTC was no exception. A major risk in trying to implement multilateral measures against PTRs was the lack of broad-based support for tax harmonisation across the OECD's membership. For example, France had long been apprehensive about countries such as Ireland that precipitated a destructive culture of tax avoidance competition; Ireland at the time offered a 10 per cent corporate tax rate for foreign firms that relocated (later replaced with a general 12.5 per cent corporate rate). On the other hand, the US and British governments had long opposed the agenda, arguing that it threatened the sovereign right of national governments to set budget priorities according to domestic political imperatives (Weschler 2001; Sharman 2006, p. 61).

Given this lack of consensus, the OECD HTC initiative started to unravel. Switzerland and Luxembourg had signalled their concerns by abstaining from the 1998 report, meaning that they were not bound by its contents. This led to accusations of double standards from the 41 jurisdictions identified by the OECD as tax havens. None of these territories were OECD members, yet were expected to make commitments to a project from which some OECD countries were exempted. The transnational tax planning industry and a caucus of pro-market pressure groups rallied to their aid (Easson 2004; Webb 2004), delegitimising the initiative by showing it to be inconsistent with deeply embedded norms about the value of tax competition, not least those propagated and upheld by the OECD. At this stage, civil society actors showed ephemeral interest in corporate tax justice (see Oxfam 2000) but were not prominent players and had little capacity to counter the financial wherewithal and expert prowess of the tax planning industry. The withdrawal in May 2001 of US support (US Department of the Treasury 2001) for the scheme signalled its effective end, with the OECD forced to renounce provisions such as those obliging countries to enact rules that only firms with substantial business operations could claim residency. Henceforth the HTC 'would pose little threat to the aggressive, legal, international tax planning strategies pursued by so many of the world's MNCs' (Eccleston 2013, p. 67).

By removing the potency of the HTC, the idea of tackling corporate tax avoidance lost much of its influence. After 2001, OECD reports generally endorsed broad-based tax competition and practices allowing corporations to separate the legal and physical locations of their investments (OECD 2001). Vestiges of the project were resurrected in 2009, focusing on a less gruelling agenda of promoting tax transparency and information exchange designed to make it harder for high-wealth individuals to illegally evade tax by investing in offshore tax havens. In the interim, surveys exposed the magnitude and cost of MNC tax avoidance (see Sullivan 2004, 2008; US GAO 2008; Avi-Yonah et al. 2009; Gravelle 2009; Zucman 2015), but the political will to tackle it had evaporated. However, as the next two chapters explain, the Financial Crisis strikingly altered the political calculus, and in 2012 the issue would resurface.

1.5 POST-2008: THE REVENGE OF HISTORY?

Since the Financial Crisis of 2008 there has been unprecedented interest in, and political momentum behind, reform to the international corporate tax regime (see for example Eccleston 2013; Graetz 2016; Pogge and Mehta 2016). As we have noted, austerity gave oxygen to issues of corporate tax avoidance. At a juncture when many citizens were suffering hardships inflicted by tax rises linked to austerity, the stream of stories documenting egregious cases of corporate tax avoidance has aroused considerable public anger. For states needing to placate public opinion and close yawning budget deficits, a clampdown on corporate tax avoidance is both fiscally and electorally alluring. The mobilisation of private actors campaigning under the broad banner of tax justice has also contributed to revived interest (this volume, Chapter 3). In addition to the consolidation of specialist organisations such as the Tax Justice Network (TJN), corporate tax avoidance began to intrude on the mainstream agendas of broader NGOs, including Oxfam, Christian Aid and Transparency International. Trading on their professional reputations, these bodies were able to contest ideas, and infiltrate institutions, previously exclusive to a narrow cadre of tax professionals (this volume, Chapter 4). This symbolised the emergence of a more open and expert policy community able to address complex issues of international corporate taxation and hence the possibility of meaningful revisions to the underlying regime.

Superficially, this appears to be confirmed by developments in the sphere of corporate tax governance since 2008, culminating with the endorsement of the OECD's (2015) final report on base erosion and profit shifting (BEPS) by the leaders of the Group of 20 (G20 2015). As will be discussed in greater detail in the following chapter, if the BEPS recommendations bear fruit they will represent the most dramatic amendments to the international tax rules since the 1920s. Closer inspection reveals however that the BEPS report, along with comparable developments elsewhere, does not denote a radical break with the past. Commentaries on the modifications to the international corporate tax regime assert that the proposals are much more modest than the 'change of paradigm' (quoted in *Economist* 2015) claimed by the likes of Pascal Saint-Amans, the director of the OECD's Centre for Tax Policy and Administration (CTPA). The grandfathering of supposedly obsolete concepts such as source and residence into the revamped regime, or dysfunctional regulations such as 'arm's length' laws, lends credence to Avi-Yonah and Xu's observation that 'the legal reform of international tax look[s] more like the patch-up of existing rules and principles' (2016, p. 208; see also Devereux and Vella 2014).

Echoing the past, the reasons for this are located in pathologies hereditary to global governance in general, and the international corporate tax regime in particular. Consistent with the narratives of its predecessor, the preservation of state sovereignty is of paramount consideration to the regime. Learning from its HTC experience, the OECD has sought to broker consensus with, rather than to coerce, disaffected states. The imperative of incorporating the preferences of over 100 disparate states, especially given the ambitious timescale, has again hampered fundamental change (see OECD 2014a; BIAC 2015). Moreover, despite paying lip-service to the OECD process, virtually all states continue to employ their sovereign right over fiscal matters to engage in aggressive tax competition to woo mobile corporate investment. The peer review process supporting the implementation of the BEPS minimum standards may place some restraints on tax competition. Unfortunately, the concessions made to finalise the BEPS accord have made the rules 'even more complex and in many cases contradictory' (BEPS Monitoring Group 2015), generating opportunities for tax planning experts to generate yet more tax avoidance loopholes.

BEPS has also encountered opposition from private actors in the transnational tax planning industry. The guarded public support for BEPS amongst the business community contrasts with fears expressed behind the scenes that the initiative could lead, amongst other things, to double taxation, spiralling compliance costs and the publication of commercially sensitive data. As one insider put it, the 'game plan' of many corporations remains 'to be positive but hope as little as possible happens' (Gapper 2014). Business interests also represented a strong voice in the BEPS policy process. For instance, 87 per cent of the submissions to the OECD's public consultations on the BEPS country-by-country (CbC) reporting requirements were from business stakeholders (Oxfam 2014; see also Christensen 2015). The revolving door between the Big Four accountancy firms and the upper echelons of the OECD's tax bureaucracy still turns (see Picciotto 2015). In July 2016, the OECD appointed Ernst & Young's Jefferson VanderWolk to replace Andrew Hickman, himself recruited from KPMG in 2014, as head of the CTPA's Tax Treaty, Transfer Pricing and Financial Transactions Division. Regardless of their ascent, bodies lobbying for the transnational tax planning industry and their clients vastly outnumber and outgun those agitating for action to tame tax abuses by modernising the international corporate tax regime (Woodward 2018). Predictably, these advocates have not overthrown the prevailing regime, but their interventions have nonetheless made some important contributions and achieved some significant victories. The inclusion of CbC reporting, albeit without public disclosure, in the BEPS action plan is a case in point. Conceived by Richard Murphy and John Christensen of the TJN, its elevation is the consequence of a coalition of NGOs championing its case in both domestic and international forums. NGOs have also been the watchdogs of the process, exposing examples of impropriety (see Christians 2013) and using tools such as the TJN's Financial Secrecy Index to shame corporations and states into action.

Irrespective of these successes, the aptitude of NGOs to drastically alter the international corporate tax regime, at least in the short term, should not be exaggerated. The BEPS episode serves as a reminder of the pervasiveness of the obstacles to reform identified elsewhere in this chapter and wider volume. Indeed history suggests that prophecies of thoroughgoing change should be treated cautiously.

REFERENCES

Angell, N. (1911), *The Great Illusion: A Study of the Relation of Military Power in Nations to Their Economic and Social Advantage*, New York: G.P. Putnam & Sons.

Avi-Yonah, R.S. (1995), 'The Rise and Fall of Arm's Length: A Study in the Evolution of US International Taxation', *Virginia Tax Review* **15** (1), 89–115.

Avi-Yonah, R.S. and H. Xu (2016), 'Evaluating BEPS: A Reconsideration of the Benefits Principle and Proposal for UN Oversight', *Harvard Business Law Review* **6** (2), 186–238.

Avi-Yonah, R.S., K.A. Clausing and M.C. Durst (2009), 'Allocating Business

Profits for Tax Purposes: A Proposal to Adopt a Formulatory Profit Split', *Florida Tax Review* **9** (5), 498–553.
BEPS Monitoring Group (2015), 'Overall Evaluation of the G20/OECD Base Erosion and Profit Shifting (BEPS) Project', available at https://bepsmonitoring-group.files.wordpress.com/2015/10/general-evaluation.pdf (accessed 10 October 2017).
BIAC (2015), *BEPS Position Paper*, December 2015, available at http://biac.org/wp-content/uploads/2016/01/2015-12-BIAC-BEPS-Position-Paper1.pdf (accessed 9 October 2017).
Brooks, R. (2013), *The Great Tax Robbery: How Britain Became a Tax Haven for Fat Cats and Big Business*, Oxford: OneWorld.
Büttner, T. and M. Thiemann (2017), 'Breaking Regime Stability? The Politicisation of Expertise in the OECD/G20 Process on BEPS and the Potential Transformation of International Taxation', *Accounting, Economics and Law* **7** (1), 1–17, doi:10.1515/ael-2016-0069.
Carroll, P. and A. Kellow (2011), *The OECD: A Study of Organisational Adaptation*, Cheltenham, UK and Northampton, MA, USA: Edward Elgar Publishing.
Christensen, R.C. (2015), 'Professional Competition in Global Tax Reform: The Case of BEPS Action 13', Unpublished Master's thesis, Copenhagen Business School.
Christians, A. (2013), 'How Starbucks Lost Its Social License – And Paid £20 Million to Get It Back', *Tax Notes International* **71** (7), 637–640.
Clyne, P. (1977), *New Horizons in Tax Avoidance*, Sydney: Rydge Publications.
Davies, M. and R. Woodward (2014), *International Organizations: A Companion*, Cheltenham, UK and Northampton, MA, USA: Edward Elgar Publishing.
Devereux, M.P. and J. Vella (2014), 'Are We Heading towards a Corporate Tax System Fit for the 21st Century?', *Fiscal Studies* **35** (4), 449–475.
Diamond, W.H. and D.B. Diamond (1997), *Tax Havens of the World*, New York: Matthew Bender.
Easson, A. (2004), 'Harmful Tax Competition: An Evaluation of the OECD Initiative', *Tax Notes International* **34** (10), 1037–1077.
Eccleston, R. (2013), *The Dynamics of Global Economic Governance: The Financial Crisis, the OECD and the Politics of International Tax Competition*, Cheltenham, UK and Northampton, MA, USA: Edward Elgar Publishing.
Eccleston, R. and H. Smith (2016), 'The G20, BEPS and the Future of International Tax Governance', in P. Dietsch and T. Rixen (eds), *Global Tax Governance: What Is Wrong with It and How to Fix It*, Colchester: ECPR Press, pp. 175–197.
Economist (2015), 'New Rules, Same Old Paradigm', published electronically 10 October, available at https://www.economist.com/news/business/21672207-plan-curb-multinationals-tax-avoidance-opportunity-missed-new-rules-same-old (accessed 4 October 2017).
Eden, L. and R. Kudrle (2005), 'Tax Havens: Renegade States in the International Tax Regime', *Law and Policy* **27** (1), 100–127.
Elbra, A. and J. Mikler (2017), 'Paying a "Fair Share": Multinational Corporations' Perspectives on Taxation', *Global Policy* **8** (2), 181–190.
G7 (1996), 'Economic Communiqué: Making a Success of Globalization for the Benefit of All', available at http://www.g8.utoronto.ca/summit/1996lyon/communique.html (accessed 8 October 2017).
G20 (2015), 'G20 Leaders' Communiqué', available at http://www.g20.utoronto.ca/2015/151116-communique.html (accessed 22 October 2017).

Gapper, J. (2014), 'Defensive Play in the World Cup of Corporate Taxation', published electronically 27 June, available at https://www.ft.com/content/44fe6862-10ed-3b75-ba9e-d729700a5c1c?mhq5j=e2 (accessed 12 October 2017).
Graetz, M.J. (2001), 'The David R. Tillinghast Lecture: Taxing International Income: Inadequate Principles, Outdated Concepts, and Unsatisfactory Policies', *Tax Law Review* **54** (3), 261–336.
Graetz, M.J. (2016), 'Bringing International Tax Policy into the 21st Century', *Tax Notes International* **83** (6), 315–318.
Gravelle, J.G. (2009), 'Tax Havens: International Tax Avoidance and Evasion', *National Tax Journal* **42** (4), 727–753.
Hampton, M.P. and M. Levi (1999), 'Fast Spinning into Oblivion? Recent Developments in Money-Laundering Policies in Offshore Financial Centres', *Third World Quarterly* **20** (3), 645–656.
Hood, N. and S. Young (1979), *The Economics of Multinational Enterprise*, London: Longman.
Houlder, V. (2013), 'Taxation: Unsafe Offshore', *Financial Times*, published electronically 13 January, available at https://www.ft.com/content/0dc00990-5be0-11e2-bef7-00144feab49a (accessed 10 October 2017).
Jogarajan, S. (2011), 'Prelude to the International Tax Treaty Network: 1815–1914 Early Tax Treaties and the Conditions for Action', *Oxford Journal of Legal Studies* **31** (4), 679–707.
Jogarajan, S. (2013), 'Stamp, Seligman and the Drafting of the 1923 Experts' Report on Double Taxation', *World Tax Journal* **5** (3), 368–392.
Keohane, R.O. (2001), 'Governance in a Partially Globalized World', *American Political Science Review* **95** (1), 1–13.
League of Nations (1923), *Report on Double Taxation to the Financial Committee*, Geneva: League of Nations.
League of Nations (1927), *Double Taxation and Tax Evasion: Report Presented by the Committee of Technical Experts on Double Taxation and Tax Evasion*, available at http://biblio-archive.unog.ch/Dateien/CouncilMSD/C-216-M-85-1927-II_EN.pdf (accessed 1 October 2017).
League of Nations (1933), *Taxation of Foreign and National Enterprises*, Volume IV: *Methods of Allocating Taxable Income*, Geneva: League of Nations.
Mikler, J. (2013), *The Handbook of Global Companies*, Oxford: Wiley.
Murphy, C.N. (1994), *International Organization and Industrial Change: Global Governance since 1850*, Cambridge: Polity Press.
OECD (1987), *International Tax Avoidance and Evasion: Four Related Studies*, Paris: OECD Publishing.
OECD (1991), *Taxing Profits in a Global Economy: Domestic and International Issues*, Paris: OECD Publishing.
OECD (1998), *Harmful Tax Competition: An Emerging Global Issue*, Paris: OECD Publishing.
OECD (2001), *The OECD's Project on Harmful Tax Practices: The 2001 Progress Report*, Paris: OECD Publishing, available at https://www.oecd.org/ctp/harmful/2664450.pdf (accessed 14 October 2017).
OECD (2013), *Addressing Base Erosion and Profit Shifting*, Paris: OECD Publishing.
OECD (2014a), *Tax Transparency 2014 Report on Progress*, available at http://www.oecd.org/tax/transparency/GFannualreport2014.pdf (accessed 5 October 2017).

OECD (2014b), *Model Tax Convention on Income and on Capital*, available at http://www.keepeek.com/Digital-Asset-Management/oecd/taxation/model-tax-convention-on-income-and-on-capital-2015-full-version_9789264239081-en#.WP41W0UrLIU (accessed 4 October 2017).

OECD (2015), *BEPS 2015 Final Reports*, available at http://www.oecd.org/tax/beps-2015-final-reports.htm (accessed 4 October 2017).

Oxfam (2000), *Tax Havens: Releasing the Hidden Billions for Poverty Eradication*, available at http://policy-practice.oxfam.org.uk/publications/tax-havens-releasing-the-hidden-billions-for-poverty-eradication-114611 (accessed 1 October 2017).

Oxfam (2014), *Business among Friends: Why Corporate Tax Dodgers Are Not Yet Losing Sleep over Global Tax Reform*, available at https://www.oxfam.org/sites/www.oxfam.org/files/bp185-business-among-friends-corporate-tax-reform-120514-en_0.pdf (accessed 7 October 2017).

Picciotto, S. (1992), *International Business Taxation: A Study in the Internationalization of Business Regulation*, Cambridge: Cambridge University Press.

Picciotto, S. (1999), 'Offshore: The State as Legal Fiction', in J.P. Abbott and M.P. Hampton (eds), *Offshore Finance Centres and Tax Havens*, Basingstoke: Palgrave Macmillan, pp. 43–79.

Picciotto, S. (2015), 'Indeterminacy, Complexity, Technocracy and the Taxation of Transnational Corporations', *Social and Legal Studies* **24** (2), 165–184.

Pogge, T. and K. Mehta (eds) (2016), *Global Tax Fairness*, Oxford: Oxford University Press.

Ring, D. (2009), 'What's at Stake in the Sovereignty Debate? International Tax and the Nation-State', *Virginia Journal of International Law* **49** (1), 154–223.

Rixen, T. (2008), *The Political Economy of International Tax Governance*, Basingstoke: Palgrave Macmillan.

Rodrik, D. (2011), *The Globalization Paradox: Democracy and the Future of the World Economy*, New York: W.W. Norton.

Seligman, E.R. (1921), *Essays in Taxation*, 3rd edition, London: Macmillan.

Sharman, J.C. (2006), *Havens in a Storm: The Struggle for Global Tax Regulation*, Ithaca, NY: Cornell University Press.

Sharman, J.C. (2012), 'Seeing like the OECD on Tax', *New Political Economy* **17** (1), 17–33.

Sikka, P. (2015), 'No Accounting for Tax Avoidance', *Political Quarterly* **86** (3), 427–433.

Slaughter, A.-M. (2004), *A New World Order*, Princeton, NJ: Princeton University Press.

Stamp, J. (1921), *The Fundamental Principles of Taxation*, London: Macmillan.

Sullivan, M. (2004), 'Shifting Profits Offshore Costs US Treasury $10 Billion or More', *Tax Notes* **104** (14), 1477–1481.

Sullivan, M. (2008), 'US Multinationals Shifting Profits out of the United States', *Tax Notes* **118** (11), 1078–1082.

Tanzi, V. (1995), *Taxation: An Emerging Global Issue*, Washington, DC: Brookings Institution.

Thomas, K.P. (2000), *Competing for Capital: Europe and North America in a Global Era*, Washington, DC: Georgetown University Press.

UNCTAD (2017), 'Quantitative Data on Bilateral Investment Treaties and Double Taxation Treaties', available at http://unctad.org/en/Pages/DIAE/International

%20Investment%20Agreements%20(IIA)/Quantitative-data-on-bilateral-investment-treaties-and-double-taxation-treaties.aspx (accessed 15 October 2017).
US Department of the Treasury (2001), 'Treasury Secretary O'Neill Statement on OECD Tax Havens', available at https://www.treasury.gov/press-center/press-releases/Pages/po366.aspx (accessed 1 October 2017).
US GAO (Government Accountability Office) (2008), *US Multinational Corporations: Effective Tax Rates Are Correlated with Where Income Is Reported*, Washington, DC: US GAO.
Webb, M.C. (2004), 'Defining the Boundaries of Legitimate State Practice: Norms, Transnational Actors and the OECD's Project on Harmful Tax Competition', *Review of International Political Economy* **11** (4), 787–827.
Weschler, W. (2001), 'Follow the Money', *Foreign Affairs* **90** (4), 40–57.
Woodward, R. (2017), 'UK Governance: From Overloading to Freeloading', *Political Quarterly* **89** (1), 56–64.
Woodward, R. (2018), 'Tax Havens in an Austere World: The Clash of New Ideas and Existing Interests', in S. McBride and B. Evans (eds), *The Austerity State*, Toronto: University of Toronto Press, pp. 243–263.
Ylonen, M. (2017), 'Back from Oblivion? The Rise and Fall of the Early Initiatives against Corporate Tax Avoidance from the 1960s to the 1980s', *Transnational Corporations* **23** (3), 33–57.
Zucman, G. (2015), *The Hidden Wealth of Nations: The Scourge of Tax Havens*, Chicago, IL: University of Chicago Press.

2. BEPS and the new politics of corporate tax justice

Richard Eccleston

2.1 INTRODUCTION

International taxation is the sleeping giant of the global economy. Whereas the focus of economic diplomacy and associated scholarship in the late twentieth century was on trade and financial liberalisation, now the most significant issues in international political economy are concerned with the consequences of 'globalisation' – including the growing concentration and power of multinational corporations (MNCs). The rise of MNCs, combined with growing political concern about tepid economic growth, increasing inequality and public debt, has triggered an unprecedented political campaign highlighting the tax practices of MNCs and demanding effective action from national governments, international organisations and firms themselves (this volume, Chapter 3). This 'new' politics of corporate tax justice, combined with the aforementioned political and economic factors, has transformed international taxation from what Culpepper (2011) would describe as a 'quiet' political domain, dominated by a small network of tax experts, firms and their advisers, into a 'hot' issue which commands international headlines and political attention. This burgeoning political interest in corporate tax justice will be analysed in more detail in the following chapters, but first it's necessary to examine the circumstances that gave rise to pervasive corporate tax avoidance and discuss the range of measures that must be implemented to address it.

The analysis presented in this chapter draws from Richard Woodward's (this volume, Chapter 1) key insight that the campaign to address corporate tax avoidance is related to, but conceptually distinct from, reforms designed to address international tax evasion through increased transparency and information exchange. The following section argues that the new politics of corporate tax justice is more challenging than previous reform initiatives because tax avoidance as a concept is more ambiguous and contested. Moreover, the MNCs and their advisers, who develop and implement aggressive tax avoidance strategies, are among the most powerful political actors in the global economy. Perhaps less appreciated is that international corporate tax reform has the potential to create conflict among advanced industrial economies given the potential for disagreements over the allocation, and subsequent taxation, of MNC profits.

The problem of international tax avoidance may be complex, but its consequences are clear. Research by the OECD and IMF estimates that corporate tax avoidance denies national governments between US$250 billion and US$600 billion per year (IMF 2015; OECD 2015a). What is less obvious, however, is the precise objectives of an international tax reform agenda and how they might be achieved. Even under the weight of public scrutiny Apple CEO Tim Cook steadfastly maintained that paying €334 million on total European profits of €87 billion over the decade between 2004 and 2014 was appropriate, while insisting that the onus is on governments to rewrite the rules to deliver fairer outcomes (Weckler 2016). But what is fair? As will be argued in the following pages, the effective rate of tax paid by a corporation is largely determined by the way profits and losses (or costs) are allocated across the jurisdictions in which that company operates. While delving into the technical details of how this is achieved in practice goes beyond the scope of this book, section 2.4 summarises the broad principles which should serve as the basis of a 'fair' international tax order – principles which have clear implications for the international tax reform agenda. Finally, the chapter assesses the main corporate tax reform initiatives that have been launched since 2012 by the OECD and the EU, as well as some significant unilateral national reforms. While progress has been made, it seems that more ambitious redesign of the international tax system may be required to ensure that large corporations pay their fair share of tax in a sustainable way. This agenda, of ensuring that corporate firms' profits are taxed fairly in the countries where their real economic activity occurs, is at the core of the civil society campaigns for global tax justice.

2.2 THE PROBLEMATIC POLITICS OF CORPORATE TAX JUSTICE

The problem of international taxation is high on the agenda in many domestic political debates and at many key international forums (this volume, Chapter 3), and yet formidable barriers to reform remain.

The Contested Nature of Tax Avoidance

At this point it is worth examining three of the most significant hurdles to meaningful policy change.

First, tax avoidance by its nature is a legal activity and, some would argue, an appropriate and desirable element of a competitive capitalist system. Milton Friedman (1970), for example, in his influential article on the social obligations of firms, argues that governments alone should impose taxes and that corporate executives have no right to spend stockholders' money paying additional taxes or pursuing other social objectives. While Friedman's contention that firms are obliged to minimise taxation is widely disputed, our point is that tax avoidance is arguably more contested than more tangible and emotive norms of international behaviour. Moreover, there are no formal legal standards upon which companies or individuals can make a reliable *ex ante* distinction between legal avoidance and illegal evasion (Lee et al. 2015, p. 21); such a distinction can only be made after the fact by a court or tax authority, arguably giving firms an incentive to push the envelope in search of innovative strategies to minimise their liabilities. Indeed, the testimony of a former senior PricewaterhouseCoopers employee before a UK Public Accounts Committee hearing revealed that company policy allowed the sale of tax avoidance schemes whose chances of surviving a legal challenge were judged to be as low as 25 per cent, where the other three of the 'Big Four' accounting firms set this benchmark at 50 per cent (Sikka 2015, p. 429). This strategy – insisting upon a scheme's lawfulness despite knowing the chances of it being found otherwise could be as high as 75 per cent, and that the only way for authorities to test its legality would be mounting a costly taxpayer-funded legal challenge – illustrates the complex and contested nature of the task of separating legal tax avoidance from illegal evasion.

Second, the MNCs that employ aggressive tax avoidance strategies are among the most powerful actors in the global economy – actors that have arguably become even more concentrated and powerful in recent times (this volume, Chapter 7).

Finally, the international politics of corporate tax reform is becoming increasingly volatile amid growing concerns that major states and regions will compete over the right to tax the global earnings of MNCs. In the absence of cooperation, this could result in a destructive (from a revenue perspective) race to the bottom, as discussed in Chapter 1. Given that the recent history of international tax cooperation suggests that effective multilateral or regional cooperation is dependent on great power cooperation (Eccleston 2013), recent developments (including the UK Brexit vote and Donald Trump's election as president of the United States in 2016) don't bode well for multilateral reform in the near term.

The Legitimacy of Corporate Tax Avoidance

Late-twentieth-century scholars rightly appreciated the multiplicity of ways in which norms, or widely accepted beliefs about appropriate international behaviour, could shape the preferences of actors in the global economy. By extension, they argue, these norms would also come to be reflected in formal international agreements and domestic laws over time (Finnemore and Sikkink 1998). While most accept the contention that ideas and beliefs shape political and commercial behaviour, it is equally apparent that some norms have great universal traction. For example, Keck and Sikkink (1998) suggest that norms concerning universal human rights such as torture, child exploitation and slavery have deep and widespread resonance, while other activities which have clear and tangible impacts such as pollution and environmental degradation are also likely to influence the hearts and minds of citizens and governments. Inevitably, norms that are more abstract and open to interpretation will be more contested. For example, 'fair trade' may be a laudable international policy goal, but the nature of 'fairness' and how best to achieve it are widely debated among proponents of stricter labour standards and those who promote liberalisation (Booth and Whetstone 2007). By these standards, tax avoidance is a classic case of a contested norm. Not only is it intangible and difficult to define, but by its very definition corporate tax avoidance is both legal and consistent with fundamental tenets of liberal capitalist systems concerning the desirability of market competition and the accumulation of private profit.

Given the normative ambiguity surrounding corporate tax avoidance it is unsurprising that many corporate executives are unrepentant in the face of claims that they engage in aggressive tax planning to maximise shareholder returns. For example, Google's vice-president of sales and operations in Central and Northern Europe, Matt Brittin, argued before the UK Parliamentary Public Accounts Committee that Google's choice of Ireland for its European headquarters, as well as Bermuda and the Netherlands for holding companies, was motivated by the low corporation tax rates on offer (House of Commons Committee of Public Accounts 2012, p. 40). Brittin explained that this decision, and the practice of re-routeing UK advertising sales through the Irish subsidiary, represented a desire, even an obligation, to secure the highest possible returns for Google shareholders.

Tax avoidance may be contested, but each revelation that a large and profitable company pays little or no tax in the jurisdictions in which it operates nonetheless elicits a loud and growing chorus of public dismay. For example, the 2012 revelation that Starbucks had paid only £8.6 million in UK corporate income tax over 14 years triggered an instant public backlash, with online boycott campaigns, public protestors, and even prime minister David Cameron castigating the firm's practices (Elliot and Stewart 2013). Such blatant cases of aggressive avoidance have understandably triggered strong public backlashes and firm political responses, but the problem of establishing a clear demarcation between 'fair and reasonable' tax planning and unacceptable avoidance remains. While there is an emerging consensus that in a fair and sustainable international tax regime MNCs should be taxed 'where economic activities occur and value is created' (G20 2013, p. 12), as is argued in greater detail below, there is less agreement on how this might be achieved in practice.

Corporate Power and International Taxation

The fact that large MNCs are among the most powerful actors in the global economy has also had a profound impact on the politics of corporate tax reform. Indeed, large firms can use, and have used, various strategies to influence corporate tax policy at the domestic and international level. With hundreds of billions of dollars of tax revenue at stake, and corporations spending up to US$20 billion on tax advice each year, committing hundreds of millions to advocacy and overt lobbying activities is a relatively inexpensive way to manage taxation risk. While hard data are difficult to obtain, cases of concerted corporate lobbying in relation to international tax issues abound. Recent data from US Senate filings detail consistent lobbying from a wide range of corporate actors, including drug companies like Pfizer and Merck & Co., tech companies like Microsoft, and food and beverage giants including PepsiCo, Dupont Co. and Starbucks. Many of these firms have specifically targeted the House Ways and Means Committee on issues of so-called 'stateless income' in the wake of increased government action in the BEPS arena (*Financial Times* 2013; Kleinbard 2013, p. 1516; Temple-West 2014). In addition, it has widely been reported that the OECD's initial proposal to publicly disclose country-by-country (CbC) reporting data (discussed in greater detail below) was stymied by concerted corporate lobbying (Cobham et al. 2017, p. 101). Also, recent public inquiries have revealed what many argue are overly close relations between the 'Big Four' accounting firms and national tax authorities (Hodge 2016, pp. 51–53).

Beyond overt lobbying to defend tax provisions which enable MNCs to maximise profit, large firms can exert significant structural power, which has both financial and ideational dimensions. Structural power may be subtle, in that it does not necessarily involve overt lobbying but nonetheless represents a significant barrier to corporate tax reform. For example, jurisdictions that have used tax concessions to attract corporate investment are inevitably reluctant to implement reforms which may threaten such arrangements. This was evident in the Irish government's decision to appeal the European Commission's 'state aid' ruling against Apple in September 2016, even though if implemented it would require that Apple pay more taxes in Ireland and other EU countries. Dublin's decision to appeal the decision and forgo additional revenue which may flow from it can be explained by the fact that the state aid ruling potentially threatened Apple's investment and 6000 employees in Ireland, along with the Irish government's right to attract further investment with tax concessions (Cook 2016).

In addition to national governments' structural dependence on corporate investment, as noted above, the entrenched discourse of corporate capitalism and the associated norms concerning the desirability of corporate investment and economic growth also represent a barrier to reform (Blyth 2013). While such claims are increasingly being contested, generous tax subsidies, which proponents claim promote corporate investment and growth, continue to be popular with governments.

Great Power Conflict and Its Implications for International Tax Cooperation

Effective international tax governance is dependent on high levels of international cooperation. As Rixen (2016, p. 326) has argued, international taxation is a form of 'asymmetric prisoner's dilemma', because individual countries have a strong incentive to opt out of an international agreement to share the tax base of an MNC, and thereby attract a disproportionate share of revenue or investment for themselves. Unfortunately, the high levels of international cooperation and coordination which were achieved in the aftermath of the 2007–08 financial crisis appear to be waning, with the election of Donald Trump in the United States and the UK Brexit vote in 2016 perhaps the most significant examples of growing mercantilist sentiments. While the G20 affirmed its commitment to the implementation of the OECD's BEPS programme as of the March 2017 finance ministers' meeting (G20 2017), this certainly doesn't mean that the Trump administration supports the initiative. The Trump administration's 2017 corporate tax plan, which includes cutting the statutory corporate rate to 21 per cent and providing significant tax concessions to repatriate the estimated US$1.6 trillion held offshore, may not directly undermine the international tax reform agenda but, at the very least, is likely to increase competitive pressures in the international tax regime (Oxfam America 2017; Pullar-Strecker 2017).

In addition to growing transatlantic tensions over international taxation, the other requirement of a just tax system is to ensure that low-income countries, which by their nature are more dependent on capital taxation, get a fair share of the corporate tax base (Picciotto 2017). Reflecting this imperative, tax justice is now widely recognised as a precondition for sustainable international development and a means to fund the United Nations' Sustainable Development Goals (Cobham et al. 2016; Pogge and Mehta 2016). However, governments in the developed north have historically promoted residency-based tax regimes. As a result, MNCs that invest in developing countries are taxed in the jurisdiction where they are headquartered once profits have been repatriated, and have traditionally resisted tax agreements which seek to promote greater alignment between tax and the substance of economic activity. The details of international tax agreements are extremely complex, but, given their effect is to allocate taxing rights and revenue between countries, conflicting interests and political compromises are inevitable in international tax agreements (this volume, Chapter 1). However, while distributional conflicts may represent a barrier to international tax cooperation this does not mean that it is a zero-sum game. Indeed, if a reformed international tax system could capture a portion of the estimated half a trillion dollars lost to MNC tax avoidance each year then it would become possible to devise fairer and more sustainable corporate tax regimes which could benefit governments and citizens in countries north and south (IMF 2015).

Notwithstanding the potential benefits of greater international cooperation in relation to international tax matters, the political outlook remains uncertain and volatile, putting the international tax reform agenda at risk. In this increasingly hostile political environment, civil society activism and private governance regimes are likely to become even more important in the campaign for tax justice, because when governments can't or won't act then civil society must fill the breach.

2.3 THE ANATOMY OF CORPORATE TAX AVOIDANCE

The growth of corporations and international trade in the late nineteenth and early twentieth centuries gave rise to the modern corporate income tax, with parallel developments in corporations law, creating the potential for international tax evasion and avoidance (this volume, Chapter 1). An important development contributing to the growth of corporate tax avoidance was a series of legal cases granting corporations the status of legal 'persons', and from this point on the governance of international taxation became intertwined with the effectiveness of corporate governance standards. An issue at the heart of the nexus between corporate governance and taxation is that, once corporations are regarded as separate legal entities, companies and their shareholders can be subject to taxation. Changing legal understandings of the modern corporation raised serious challenges for international business. A company's headquarters, its shareholders and the markets in which it generates profits may be in different jurisdictions, thus creating the potential for *double taxation* (where profits are taxed in multiple jurisdictions) and also the more insidious phenomenon of *double non-taxation* (where profits are moved between jurisdictions to avoid taxation).

In an international regime built on the principle of preserving sovereignty, as is the case with taxation, the fundamental governance problem concerns which state has the right to tax profits or income derived from international business (Graetz and O'Hear 1997). Indeed, many commentators correctly point out that the very notion of 'international taxation' as a concept is misleading, when the real issue is the interaction of domestic tax systems with international business transactions (Arnold and McIntyre 2016, pp. 2–3). In technical terms the challenge is to develop fair and efficient ways of allocating the international tax base between sovereign states. In practice, international transactions are taxed according to either the *source* or the *residency* principle. Under the residency principle, individuals and firms based within a jurisdiction are taxed as residents by their home government on their worldwide income irrespective of where it was earned. Under the alternative source principle, firms and individuals are taxed on their income in the jurisdiction in which it was earned. Each approach offers a sound theoretical basis upon which to establish an international tax regime, but in reality there is a real prospect of distributional conflicts between states over control of the international tax base.

Take the hypothetical (though common) example of a developing economy whose growing export sector is reliant on foreign direct investment. Such a country would benefit greatly from a source-based regime, as it could tax profits from onshore production. In contrast, a developing economy would suffer under a residence-based system, because profits would be repatriated to investing countries before being taxed. These tensions have given rise to a complex web of treaties or double tax agreements (DTAs) which attempt to 'disentangle national jurisdiction to tax by allocating the international tax base to the residence and source countries involved' (Rixen 2008, p. 63). This uncertainty regarding the allocation of the tax base, combined with most states' desire to maximise revenue, increases the risk of double taxation. This occurs when two or more overlapping jurisdictions each attempt to tax an international transaction (Picciotto 2011, pp. 216–226). While there is a risk of double taxation, the real challenge, which is the focus of this study, is the growing capacity of

MNCs to exploit their political power and the complexity of the international tax regime to minimise or eliminate their corporate tax obligations.

Corporate tax avoidance strategies, which are the focus of this book, are both complex and constantly evolving as firms and their advisers attempt to stay one step ahead of the tax authorities. However, as Sol Picciotto (1992, p. 85) argues in his seminal study of international tax regulation, most corporate avoidance strategies 'revolve around either the transfer of revenue to a lower taxed firm or of expenses (including debt on loans) to one who is more highly taxed'. Prior to assessing some of the most common corporate tax avoidance strategies and their increasing prevalence and cost to governments, it is first necessary to outline the factors which have shaped the broad regulatory context in which international taxation occurs. The critical relationship here is how the rise of the modern corporation and developments in international banking and finance have created what Ronen Palan (2003) describes as an 'offshore world', with profound implications for international taxation.

The Anatomy of Corporate Tax Avoidance

The nature and proliferation of corporate entities, and the associated growth of global production systems and value chains, has had a profound impact on international tax governance (this volume, Chapter 4). The potential tax advantages of establishing a corporate subsidiary in a low-tax offshore jurisdiction are greatly enhanced by the tax treatment of consolidated companies (Murphy and Sikka 2017). For the purposes of financial reporting, most corporations report one set of consolidated accounts, which gives the impression that they are single multinational entities (Palan et al. 2010, p. 84). Yet for taxation purposes many MNCs actually comprise a complex web of subsidiary and holding companies domiciled across several countries. In January 2009, the United States Government Accountability Office found that this type of structure was used by a majority of major American firms, with 83 of the nation's largest firms operating one or more subsidiaries in tax haven jurisdictions (US GAO 2008, p. 4). More recently, research has shown that the 50 largest US companies by market capitalisation held more than one trillion US dollars in tax havens from 2008 to 2014 (Oxfam America 2016, pp. 1–2). In Australia, 57 per cent of ASX 200 companies disclose operating subsidiaries in tax haven jurisdictions (Tax Justice Network Australia and United Voice 2014, p. 3).

Such structures offer a number of tax advantages, including the ability to 'book' profitable transactions offshore (subject to transfer pricing regulations), and to retain and reinvest profits in low-tax jurisdictions, thereby deferring the need to repatriate profits to parent companies. Perhaps the best evidence of the extent to which corporate structures are used to manage risk and minimise taxation has been the enormous growth of listed entities in tax havens in recent years. A 2008 US State Department Report (cited in Palan et al. 2010, p. 57) found that the British Virgin Islands (population 22 000) hosts over 800 000 corporations, while Panama is home to over 300 000 such entities. Yet these companies are largely constructed to minimise tax obligations rather than to undertake real economic activity. While there is ongoing debate about what constitutes corporate tax avoidance, what is clear is that since the financial crisis there has been both a growing awareness of the problem and a growing determination to address it (this volume, Chapter 3). Before turning our attention to an assessment of the international tax reform agenda – and to whether it is possible to establish a 'fair' corporate tax regime – it is first necessary to outline some of the key elements of corporate tax avoidance strategies and discuss some of the increasingly sophisticated estimates of the revenue cost of such practices: the so-called corporate tax 'gap'.

2.4 THREE AVOIDANCE STRATEGIES

1. Transfer Pricing

It has long been recognised that trade between related corporate entities creates opportunities to transfer profits from high-tax to low-tax jurisdictions. Indeed, the increased corporate concentration and associated growth in intra-firm trade, now approaching almost 50 per cent of all international trade (World Bank 2017), combined with the proliferation of corporate subsidiaries in low-tax jurisdictions, means that the potential for mispricing has never been greater. The established approach to combating transfer pricing abuse is known as the 'arm's length principle', first developed in the 1933 Carroll Report commissioned by the League of Nations Fiscal Committee (Carroll 1933, chapter 1). Under this approach, the prices paid in intra-firm transactions should be the same as would be paid by an independent party operating at arm's length from the firm. This approach may be sound in principle, but in practice it can be nearly impossible for tax authorities to calculate an arm's length price for the kinds of unique and intangible goods that are so often the objects of intra-group transactions, such as patents or algorithms (see the transfer pricing case study below).

Given that transfer pricing abuse is estimated to cost national revenue authorities hundreds of billions per annum, national tax authorities have been actively collaborating to limit transfer pricing uncertainty and abuse.

TRANSFER PRICING CASE STUDY: GLAXOSMITHKLINE AND THE CANADIAN REVENUE AGENCY

A recent case in which pharmaceutical giant GlaxoSmithKline fell foul of the Canadian Revenue Agency is illustrative of the difficult and ambiguous task of interpreting the arm's length principle in transfer pricing arrangements. The case, settled in 2015, involved intra-group trading of ranitidine, an antihistamine drug used in the production of the GSK staple Zantac. A Canadian subsidiary of the UK parent company, Glaxo Group plc, had been purchasing ranitidine from another Glaxo Group subsidiary headquartered in Switzerland for around C$1600 per kilo despite generic manufacturers acquiring it on the open market for less than one-sixth of that price. GSK's lawyers argued that the price disparity represented the value of the intellectual property for the final product, Zantac, which was held by the Swiss subsidiary. A Canadian trial judge ruled, however, that the cost of the licensing agreement for Zantac was a separate matter and that Glaxo's calculation of the arm's length price was not reasonable in the circumstances. GSK settled the matter with the Canadian Revenue Agency out of court for an undisclosed amount (Melnitzer 2015).

Yet, despite these initiatives, critics argue that incremental reforms such as those proposed under the OECD BEPS initiative (see below) are unlikely to meet the challenges posed by the digital economy of the twenty-first century (Spencer and McNair 2012). Instead, it is argued that MNCs should report profits as single entities using what is referred to as a 'unitary approach', with profits allocated among jurisdictions based on where the substance of economic activity occurs. The case for the transition to a unitary system of MNC taxation with profits allocated based on formula apportionment is presented in section 2.5.

2. Thin Capitalisation

A second strategy for transferring profits from high-tax to low-tax jurisdictions is through the manipulation of intra-group loans, as the interest on such loans can usually be claimed as a deduction against taxable income. The deductibility of interest has a number of implications for corporate finance and taxation. One perennial issue is that there are tax incentives for companies to borrow funds rather than raise capital by issuing equity, resulting in higher levels of corporate borrowing than would otherwise be the case. Thin capitalisation, or the excessive use of debt, can be used to facilitate corporate tax avoidance when an operation in a high-tax jurisdiction borrows funds from a related entity in a lower-tax one, often at above market interest rates. This internal transaction means that the interest payments can be used to offset profits in the higher-tax country, while the firm can realise significant profits on the loan issued in the low-tax jurisdiction and effectively lower the overall tax burden of the MNC. In practice, thin capitalisation regimes are more complex than this illustrative example. Furthermore, basic thin capitalisation provisions have existed in most jurisdictions since the 1980s, limiting the debt deductions corporations can claim. However, many analysts claim that intra-group loans continue to be used by many MNCs to minimise tax obligations.

The OECD's BEPS project has found that the manipulation of debt remains a serious global problem (OECD 2015a). While most countries already impose limits on the amount of offshore debt companies can hold, more sophisticated thin capitalisation provisions which consider the cost of debt and its impact on taxable income should be implemented (Sadiq 2016). In 2012, one of the most vocal and active lobbyists against reform to thin capitalisation rules was Chevron, whose submission to the *Business Tax Working Group Discussion Paper* argued that the existing framework was adequate, and that any change would 'erode the confidence required to facilitate the development of large, highly capital intensive and long term LNG projects' (Chevron Australia 2012, pp. 4–5). Chevron also lobbied against the introduction of any cap on interest deductibility, changes to the

THIN CAPITALISATION CASE STUDY: CHEVRON AUSTRALIA

Many MNCs use debt to finance expansion, research and development, or new large-scale projects, which is a perfectly legitimate practice. Chevron, however, has recently been the subject of court action by the Australian Tax Office over alleged abuse of this system. In 2003, a US subsidiary of Chevron Australia raised $2.45 billion to fund the Gorgon and Wheatstone gas projects in Australia. While the subsidiary raised the capital at an interest rate of 2 per cent, it then lent the money to Chevron Australia at almost 12 per cent, nearly six times the interest payed by its subsidiary. The interest paid on this debt was then tax deductible in Australia, as well as turning a considerable profit for the subsidiary (Chevron Finance Corporation). Debt strategies like this one have contributed to Chevron Australia having a debt-to-equity ratio (72.6 per cent) almost ten times higher than that of the Chevron Group worldwide. The ATO challenged Chevron Australia's debt strategies as a tax avoidance ploy and won in Federal Court. A judge ruled that Chevron Finance Corporation's profits from the debt raised were taxable in Australia, resulting in a tax bill (plus fines) of around A$300 million (Chenoweth 2015; ITF and Tax Justice Network Australia 2015, pp. 7–8). As of 2016, Chevron Australia owed more than A$42 billion to its Delaware shell company, paying only A$175 per year in annual filing fees to the state of Delaware and otherwise racking up enormous interest charges to be declared as a deduction on future profits from its Gorgon and Wheatstone expansion projects (Long 2016).

diminishing value rate, changes to capital asset depreciation rates, changes to tax concessions for exploration activity or R&D, and changes to the statutory cap on the determined effective life of depreciating assets.

3. Deferral

The third pillar of this trilogy of corporate tax avoidance strategies is deferral, whereby firms postpone or manipulate the timing of key international transactions or transfers to minimise tax liabilities. Reflecting the residence approach to corporate taxation, most countries make claims on the worldwide income of MNCs when profits or dividends are repatriated from offshore businesses or subsidiaries. However, MNCs have wide discretion as to when this occurs, enabling them to postpone the repatriation of profits to maximise tax advantages. In some cases, profits are held offshore almost indefinitely and reinvested in the business using intra-group loan arrangements tax-free. Debates about the impact of deferral are most acute in the United States, where until recently the federal corporate tax rate has been as high as 35 per cent. This creates a significant incentive for US-based MNCs to retain profits offshore. As of 2017 an estimated US$2.6 trillion was being held offshore, leading to calls for the US government to establish a 'tax holiday' in the form of a temporary concessional rate of taxation applied to offshored profits returned to the US.

While such strategies do create an incentive to repatriate offshore holdings, there is little evidence that the 2004 tax amnesty implemented by George W. Bush's administration made any significant contribution to longer-term employment or economic growth (Peterson 2011). Under the terms of the 2004 amnesty, repatriated profits were taxed at a discounted rate of 5.25 per cent, resulting in $362 billion returning to the United States. However, subsequent analysis revealed that the 15 firms which were the largest beneficiaries of the tax holiday cut US employment by 20000 between 2005 and 2007, leading a US Congressional Inquiry to conclude that there were few long-term economic benefits from the initiative. Furthermore, the Homeland Investment Act, which established the amnesty, stipulated that repatriated funds were to be used to spur investment in R&D and infrastructure in the United States. While the administration promoted this investment-generating aspect of the plan very strongly, in reality as much as 92 per cent of the money that returned to the US was simply paid out to shareholders in the form of buy-backs or increased dividends (Dharmapala et al. 2011, p. 782). While, at the time of writing, the Trump administration is actively considering implementing measures designed to encourage the repatriation of US profits held

> **DEFERRAL CASE STUDY: APPLE'S OFFSHORED REVENUE**
>
> Foreign-sourced income is not exempt from taxation in the US, but current tax laws stipulate that it cannot be taxed until a cash dividend is received from the source country. US MNCs have taken advantage of this ability to defer tax payments on foreign income by holding an estimated $2 trillion offshore (Rubin 2016), where these funds can be used to finance international operations and held out of reach for domestic tax authorities until they are repatriated. It is thus unsurprising that Apple, whose offshore holdings are roughly equal to the GDP of Venezuela at over US$250 billion, has vigorously lobbied the United States Congress to cut the repatriation rate from 35 per cent to a single-digit figure (Cook 2013). Moreover, Apple's overseas reserves have more than doubled in the past five years, as it awaited a tax amnesty or permanent tax cut such as granted in the Trump Administration's 2017 reforms (Titcomb 2017).

offshore, there is a strong consensus that such a strategy is no substitute for systematic tax reform.

The corporate tax avoidance strategies described above are simplified and highly stylised, but they provide some general insights into how MNCs can minimise their global tax obligations. The reality is infinitely more complex, with a 2015 OECD report providing 300 different examples of aggressive tax avoidance strategies (OECD 2015b). It is becoming increasingly clear that the cost of these arrangements – the so-called 'corporate tax gap' of additional revenue which governments could expect to receive if MNC tax avoidance was addressed is significant.

Estimating the Corporate Tax Gap: A Known Unknown

Estimating the revenue lost to governments as a result of base erosion and profit shifting is notoriously difficult, but the various efforts that have been made show it to be a significant and growing problem. Kimberly Clausing (2015) has suggested, on the basis of US Bureau of Economic Analysis survey data from 1983 to 2012, that the corporate income tax gap in 2012 likely stood at between US$77 billion and US$111 billion in the US alone. This gap represents 30 per cent of corporate income tax revenue collected per year. Moreover, Clausing estimates that the size of the tax gap increased by more than 250 per cent from 2004 to 2012. Her findings are consistent with other studies showing that the economic pressures of the financial crisis vastly increased the likelihood of corporate tax planners employing more aggressive tax planning strategies (Richardson et al. 2015). Studies of the global tax gap are arguably less accurate and more variable, with a prominent study published by the IMF estimating the corporate tax gap at

US$600 billion or about 0.6 per cent of GDP in advanced economies and reaching as high as 2 per cent of GDP in developing countries (Crivelli et al. 2015). At the more conservative end of the spectrum, Clausing (2015) estimates total revenue lost to BEPS at as much as US$280 billion.

2.5 THE REFORM AGENDA: WHAT IS A FAIR SHARE?

Tax avoidance is a notoriously contested and nebulous concept. As we have noted, avoidance by its very nature is legal, and the widely held view in corporate circles (at least until recently) is that it is appropriate and necessary to use reasonable means to minimise tax liabilities. Yet we are increasingly aware that many large and highly profitable firms have pushed aggressive tax planning to the extreme, and have rightly attracted public condemnation as a result. While claims that Apple Inc. paid 0.005 per cent tax on its European profits or that Starbucks paid £8.6 million in UK corporate income tax on £3 billion in sales were widely condemned as representing unreasonable rates, the question remains as to what would constitute a reasonable rate? Does the fact that Starbucks voluntarily opted to forgo $20 million in legal deductions mean that it has paid its fair share?

A simple but unsatisfactory solution would be for firms to pay a minimum tax rate of 10 per cent, or perhaps 15 per cent, on all profits booked within a given jurisdiction. This may seem fair and reasonable at the outset, but such a proposal is immediately beset by a fundamental problem: the central feature of any tax avoidance strategy is to manipulate intra-firm transactions so that profits are recorded in low- or no-tax jurisdictions irrespective of where economic activity occurred or wealth was created. The problem is not the statutory rate of taxation to which profits are subjected (although this matters for tax competition), but rather how profits are defined and allocated between the different jurisdictions in which MNCs operate.

Therefore, the central goal of international tax reform must be to create a fair and transparent means of allocating profits (or the tax base) among competing jurisdictions. The high-level goal is to ensure that MNEs are taxed 'where economic activities occur and value is created' (G20 2013, p. 12), rather than allowing profits to be diverted to tax havens where little real economic activity takes place. While there is a growing consensus that the right to tax corporate profits should be linked to the economic substance of business activities, there is an active debate over whether that can be achieved by incremental reform of the existing regime or whether a more fundamental root-and-branch overhaul is required.

As we have noted, the issue of corporate taxation is both technically complex and normatively contested, and there is much disagreement over whether a treaty-based regime similar to the OECD model convention described in Chapter 1 has the potential to curb the excesses of corporate tax avoidance. There is a large and growing literature describing the evolution of the international tax regime, outlining the limitations of the OECD model and proposing alternative solutions (Picciotto 1992; Rixen 2008; Picciotto 2017). However, most of this technical discussion fails to directly address the ethical issue of what constitutes a 'fair' corporate tax regime that respects the sovereign rights of states to design and manage their national tax systems while reflecting the very real limits of international cooperation and coordination in the tax arena.

One important contribution to the ethical debate about tax fairness and justice which informs this project is philosopher Peter Dietsch's 2015 study *Catching Capital: The Ethics of Tax Competition*. Dietsch's normative survey of the contemporary international tax landscape arguably provides the first comprehensive ethical framework for defining the principles that ought to underpin a 'fair' MNC tax regime. Dietsch's ethical case for tax fairness is not based around any given level or rate of taxation, but rather emphasises the importance of reinstating domestic political control over corporate taxation to ensure that 'capitalism is once again subject to democratic decision making' (Dietsch 2015, p. 21). The emphasis is on restoring fiscal sovereignty but, like most global governance scholars, Dietsch argues that this can only be achieved through international coordination designed to empower states.

Conceptually, Dietsch identifies two distinct types of tax competition:

1. *Poaching* describes the scenario when a tax base moves to another jurisdiction but the owner of capital stays put. Clearly most forms of MNC tax avoidance analysed in this study represent forms of poaching, in which elaborate tax and financial structures enable MNCs to move their tax base between jurisdictions with meagre (if any) consequences for their real business activities.
2. *Luring* is where preferential tax regimes are used to attract both owner and capital, thus attempting to attract FDI through tax concessions.

Significantly Dietsch argues that both types of competition are problematic from an ethical perspective, because the corporate tax base is eroded, forcing wealthy states to resort to regressive taxes, while low-income countries miss out altogether.

In terms of regulatory responses, Dietsch argues that the international tax regime should uphold two key principles:

1. *Membership principle:* Businesses should pay tax in the jurisdiction from whose public goods they ultimately benefit, which in turn requires country-specific reporting and high levels of transparency, alongside a prohibition on poaching.
2. *Fiscal policy constraint:* Luring is unethical if it (i) is motivated by strategic intent and (ii) compromises the fiscal capacity of other states.

Dietsch's analysis also highlights the limits of Westphalian sovereignty in the twenty-first-century world of economic integration. As with other areas of international law, the application of theoretical claims about sovereignty to the international tax arena must recognise that rights have associated obligations, and with any regime that protects and promotes state sovereignty come associated responsibilities (Dietsch 2015, pp. 186–187). For example, principles of transitional justice dictate that the interests of small and poor states must be better promoted and protected in the international tax regime. The central conclusion is that all states should be able to tax capital if they so choose – a choice clearly unavailable to many states in the current international tax system.

In practical terms, Dietsch's membership principle accords with the G20's ambition (outlined above) of aligning tax obligations with the jurisdiction in which economic value is created. In order to achieve this objective, Dietsch (2015, pp. 106–110) makes the case that, without greatly enhanced transparency, meaningful reform of the international tax regime will be elusive. On the central issue of whether fundamental reform is required, he argues that the established system of allocating corporate profits using 'separate-entity accounting and arm's length standard (ALS) transfer pricing' has been ineffective owing to the 'indeterminacy' of the standard, not to mention the challenges of enforcement. Theoretically, a system of unitary taxation in which MNCs prepared one global statement of worldwide profits for all related entities which would then be allocated among countries based on economic activity for the purposes of corporate taxation – the so-called 'unitary taxation plus formula apportionment' (UT + FA) approach – would support the membership principle. However, Dietsch is also quick to point out that there are significant political barriers to implementation, especially in relation to building an international consensus around the specific formulae to be used for allocating a unitary tax base. Considering these barriers to reform, it is argued that incremental policy changes, such as the introduction of public reporting of taxes paid on a CbC basis, would represent tangible progress towards a regime that upholds the membership principle.

In this book, we argue that reforms promoting transparency in relation to the taxation and financial affairs of MNCs and empowering national governments to tax companies based on the profits generated within their jurisdiction can provide the foundations for a fair tax system. It is then up to national governments and democratic decision-making processes to decide what level of corporate taxation should be imposed. Only time will tell whether establishing a 'fair' international tax regime is possible. If this important goal can indeed be attained, however, will it be achieved by reforming the current system, or by introducing a UT + FA framework or perhaps even another model entirely? Such questions notwithstanding, our concern is primarily with the politics of these processes, and whether citizens and civil society actors can drive international tax policy change and end the privileged position currently enjoyed by MNCs in the global economy. Having sketched the broad contours of the international tax reform agenda, this chapter concludes by assessing progress to date, including an appraisal of the OECD's high-profile Base Erosion and Profit Shifting (BEPS) initiative.

2.6 PROGRESS TO DATE? BEPs AND OTHER REFORM INITIATIVES

The OECD's *Action Plan on Base Erosion and Profit Shifting* (OECD 2013a) was launched in 2013 and quickly endorsed by the G20. The initiative was conceived amid mounting evidence of the failure of international tax standards to reflect contemporary international business practices, especially regarding intangible assets in the new digital economy (OECD 2013b). Because, as described in Chapter 1, the international taxation system was largely developed before MNCs rose to prominence, the OECD argues that both the regime and national treasuries have been weakened by exploitable gaps in the interactions between the tax rules of domestic jurisdictions and multi-jurisdictional treaties. This has been further exacerbated by the rise of e-commerce (OECD 2013a). The BEPS plan aims to rectify these problems through a series of 15 different actions, which were launched in 2015.

The BEPS agenda aims to address MNC tax avoidance by examining the strategies used by large corporations to exploit 'diverging legal provisions, secrecy, opacity and inadequate information exchange agreements' (Palan and Wigan 2014, p. 335). The goal of BEPS is to develop a multilateral instrument able to quickly and flexibly amend bilateral tax treaties and combat profit-shifting activity by requiring companies to pay tax in the jurisdictions in which the economic activity actually occurs, so that 'domestic and international instruments . . . will better align rights to tax with economic activity' (OECD 2013a, p. 11). In this sense, the BEPS project is an incremental strategy designed to reform the existing international tax regime rather than create an entirely new framework. While BEPS has been criticised for trying to reform what some argue is a fundamentally flawed framework (Sheppard 2014; Avi-Yonah and Xu 2016), other commentators have argued that, given the political risk associated with more radical reforms, the OECD has little choice other than to pursue incremental change (Büttner and Thiemann 2017).

The BEPS Action Plan devised by the OECD was fully endorsed by G20 finance ministers and central bank governors at their Moscow meeting in July 2013 and by the G20 heads of state at their St Petersburg meeting in September 2013 (OECD 2013b). Such efforts form part of a broader commitment to addressing tax avoidance through ongoing work on transparency and information sharing between jurisdictions (G20 2013, p. 13). Support for the initiative was reaffirmed at the May 2014 G20 Tax Symposium in Tokyo (G20 2014), and the OECD recommendations were again 'welcomed' at the G20 summit in Brisbane (Khadem 2014).

Yet there are some signs that, beneath the diplomatic rhetoric, the BEPS agenda is deeply politicised and contested. For instance, the OECD secretary-general's February 2014 report acknowledged that there were 'divergences' between participating states, and that more effort would be needed to achieve compromise between competing state and political interests (OECD 2014, p. 4). Fundamentally, there are conflicting economic interests and political messages within several of the critical G20 member states, undermining the ostensible unity of the G20's approach to the BEPS agenda. For example, detailed analysis of which countries stand to gain from ending MNC base erosion and profit shifting found that most G20 members would gain to varying degrees, while a handful of significant financial centres benefit from profit shifting, including the Netherlands, Ireland, Switzerland, Luxembourg and Singapore (Cobham et al. 2017).

Of the 15 interconnected BEPS Action Plans, Action 13 (which deals with corporate tax transparency) has been particularly prominent, and engages most directly with the agenda of making a transition to a system of CbC reporting as described above. The Action 13 agenda was initially concerned with giving national tax authorities sufficient information to conduct more rigorous assessments of transfer pricing practices, which included a requirement for large MNCs to disclose financial data to national tax authorities on a CbC basis. While these data are to be used for verification and compliance reporting, the provision has widely been regarded as a significant step towards a unitary tax regime (Herzfeld 2015).

While there is broad political support for both Action 13 and the BEPS program in general[1] (as of 2017 the framework had been agreed to by more than 60 countries and is likely to enhance corporate transparency and tax strategy) (Christensen 2017, p. 17), the devil is in the detail.

The BEPS program might advance the cause of CbC reporting and the broader objective of creating a more transparent and 'fair' corporate tax regime but, as Christensen (2017) argues, its long-term effectiveness will depend upon resolving numerous technical debates concerning whether tax data is made public, which firms are exempt from providing it, and how much data is provided. Already there has been a good deal of lobbying from corporate interests and OECD member states alike to ensure that CbC data are made available only to tax authorities rather than being published for more general consumption. Moreover, some argue that the persistent centrality of the benefits principle to the BEPS architecture may undermine its effectiveness. The benefits principle was designed to allocate taxing powers to the jurisdiction upon whose provision of public goods a firm draws most heavily. Avi-Yonah and Xu contend, however, that taxing active (business) income at source and passive (investment) income at residence will lead to an over-reliance on the expectation of an unrealistic environment of high-level international cooperation (Avi-Yonah and Xu 2016, pp. 188–189). Instead, they believe that the continued application of the benefits principle will create competition and sclerosis rather than cooperation, responsiveness and dynamism in the international tax regime.

EU Initiatives

International taxation is a complex issue arena in which a range of actors and institutions compete for influence (Eccleston 2013). While it has long been dominated by the OECD (see this volume, Chapter 9 and Christians 2016), the reform agenda is now influenced by the complementary reform initiatives of other intergovernmental organisations and national governments. In the field of corporate taxation, the European Union has been especially active and influential. EU attempts to establish a regionally coordinated approach to corporate taxation date back to the 1990s with the EU Code of Conduct on Business Taxation and moves to create a Common Consolidated Corporate Tax Base (Eccleston 2013, p. 102). While progress has been difficult owing to the divergent interests of member states, significant strides have been made since 2012. In June 2013, the EU Commission set up its Tax Planning Practices Task Force to investigate whether a number of high-profile deals granting favourable tax treatment to multinationals in places like Ireland, Luxembourg, the Netherlands and Belgium violated EU state aid provisions as outlined in Article 107(1) of the Treaty on the Functioning of the European Union (TFEU). According to the treaty and relevant case law, a measure that violates state aid principles will comprise four distinct elements:

1. There must be an advantage to the subject/beneficiary of the measure.
2. This advantage must be 'selective' or, in other words, not available to all other comparable businesses.
3. It is funded either by the member state or through state resources.
4. It affects trade between member states or distorts, or threatens to distort, competition within the internal market (Thomson and Hardwick 2017, p. 30).

One of the most prominent examples of state aid rules in action in the tax avoidance arena has been the European Commission's ruling on Ireland's grant of tax benefits to tech giant Apple. Apple's deal with the Irish tax authorities, struck in 1991, allowed it to pay a corporation tax rate capped at 1 per cent (the standard rate in Ireland is already relatively low at 12.5 per cent). Even with this deal, Apple managed to pay just 0.005 per cent in Ireland in 2014 (Farrell and McDonald 2016). This is because it was able to book almost all of its European sales at its 'head office' in Ireland rather than in the country of sale. European Commission competition commissioner Margrethe Vestager summarised the Commission's findings: 'The Commission's investigation concluded that Ireland granted illegal tax benefits to Apple, which enabled it to pay substantially less tax than other businesses over many years' (Vestager, quoted in Farrell and McDonald 2016). Following this finding, Apple was fined a staggering €13 billion plus interest, which is more than 40 times higher than the next highest penalty in a comparable case. By late 2016 Apple and the Irish government had appealed against the ruling.

While the use of state aid provisions in cases such as Apple's has been a much-heralded development in the fight against tax avoidance in the European Union (see Thomson and Hardwick 2017), it only addresses one aspect of the problem. This is because most tax avoidance activity relies upon the exploitation of national differences in tax policy. State aid action, though, can only combat preferential tax arrangements negotiated by a firm with one particular tax authority where the member state in question has broken its own rules to advantage one company over others (Kroes 2016). Perhaps more significant however, and contributing to moves towards a form of unitary taxation, has been the European Commission's push to require firms based or operating in the EU to adopt a form of CbC reporting. At this stage, the EU's CbC reporting system applies only to multinational companies in the extractives and forestry sectors (this volume, Chapter 9), requiring them to report on the taxes, royalties and bonuses they have paid, specifying the jurisdiction in which they have paid them. At the time of writing, the EU is considering a proposed directive to expand public CbC reporting requirements to all companies active in the single market with combined global revenues exceeding €750 000 000 per year (European Commission 2017).

Unilateral Initiatives

For a range of reasons, including domestic political pressure and anticipating new international standards, some countries are now also implementing unilateral MNC provisions. Australia is one such example, and has been more aggressive than most in targeting MNC avoidance. Australia's recent updates to its anti-avoidance provisions comprise five significant measures. First, on 1 January 2016, Australia's Multinational Anti-Avoidance Law (MAAL) came into force. The MAAL amends Australia's general anti-avoidance provisions as laid out in the Income Tax Assessment Act 1936, updating the rules to combat artificial or contrived transfer pricing arrangements whose main purpose is to avoid booking corporate profits in Australia. Second, the ATO has updated and clarified its definitions of a 'significant global entity' (SGE), introducing a set of standardised measures for determining whether a firm should be classified as an SGE (part of a corporate group generating global revenues in excess of $1 billion) for tax purposes. Third, in the 2016–17 Federal Budget, the Australian government announced a diverted profits tax (DPT). Australia's DPT applies a punitive corporate income tax rate of 40 per cent on profits from economic activity in Australia that have been found to have been diverted offshore using contrived transfer pricing practices. Fourth, Australia has doubled the penalties for firms implicated in tax avoidance or profit-shifting schemes found to be unlawful. Finally, Australia has adopted the CbC reporting standards set forth in the OECD/G20 BEPS project Action 13. Furthermore, beginning in the financial year 2013–14, Australia has published an annual register of privately owned companies with income over $200 million, detailing their income, taxable income and tax payable.

Australia is just one case where national governments are implementing policies and programmes to reduce the corporate tax gap. For example, a host of European countries led by Germany are introducing more aggressive corporate tax avoidance measures, and even Luxembourg introduced a host of new anti-avoidance measures in early 2017 in an attempt to comply with emerging BEPS standards and EU state aid provisions (EY 2017).

2.7 CONCLUSION AND IMPLICATIONS FOR REFORM

This chapter has described the nature and significance of corporate tax avoidance, highlighting the complexity of the policy debate as well as the deeply institutionalised barriers to reform. Yet this volume argues that the corporate tax arena is undergoing unprecedented change. First and foremost, the issue of corporate tax avoidance has become a prominent, mainstream political concern, which in turn has prompted a range of responses from new initiatives from established intergovernmental organisations such as the OECD to a raft of unilateral policies from national governments. However, of greater significance is the fact that these traditional policy responses have been prompted, influenced and complemented by new advocacy campaigns and strategies developed and prosecuted by civil society organisations. A central focus of this study is to describe and analyse this new civil society activism in the corporate tax arena and the extent to which it influences the corporate tax reform agenda and whether established actors such as the OECD and key national governments engage with this agenda and whether MNCs comply with it. The following chapters highlight the complex ways in which civil society and business interact with governments and intergovernmental organisations to shape contemporary global economic governance. Whether civil society groups can exert sufficient influence to ensure that MNCs pay their fair share of taxation remains to be seen. What is clear is that the battle is shaping up as a critical test of whether MNCs can be subjected to an adequate level of democratic accountability.

NOTE

1. It should be noted that, at the time of writing, the extent to which the Trump administration might attempt to undermine the regime remains unclear.

REFERENCES

Arnold, B.J. and M.J. McIntyre (2016), *International Tax Primer*, 3rd edition, The Hague: Kluwer Law International.

Avi-Yonah, R.S. and H. Xu (2016), 'Evaluating BEPS: A Reconsideration of the Benefits Principle and Proposal for UN Oversight', *Harvard Business Law Review* **6** (2), 185–238.

Blyth, M. (2013), *Austerity: The History of a Dangerous Idea*, Oxford: Oxford University Press.

Booth, P. and L. Whetstone (2007), 'Half a Cheer for Fair Trade', *Economic Affairs*, **27** (2), 29–36.
Büttner, T. and M. Thiemann (2017), 'Breaking Regime Stability? The Politicisation of Expertise in the OECD/G20 Process on BEPS and the Potential Transformation of International Taxation', *Accounting, Economics and Law* **7** (1), 1–17, doi:10.1515/ael-2016-0069.
Carroll, M.B. (1933), *Taxation of Foreign and National Enterprises*, Geneva: Economic and Financial Section, League of Nations.
Chenoweth, N. (2015), 'Chevron Paid Only $248 Tax on $1.7b Profit, Senate Tax Inquiry Told', *Australian Financial Review*, published electronically 9 November, available at http://www.afr.com/business/energy/gas/chevron-gorgon-company-paid-only-248-tax-on-17-bn-profit-senate-tax-inquiry-told-20151108-gktu7s (accessed 29 September 2017).
Chevron Australia (2012), *Submission: Business Tax Working Group Discussion Paper*, available at https://static.treasury.gov.au/uploads/sites/1/2017/06/Chevron_submission.pdf (accessed 6 October 2017).
Christensen, R.C. (2017), 'Professional Competition in Global Tax Reform: Transparency in Global Wealth Chains', available at https://osf.io/preprints/socarxiv/gu63m (accessed 1 October 2017).
Christians, A. (2016), 'BEPS and the New International Tax Order', *Brigham Young University Law Review* **2016** (6), 1603–1647.
Clausing, K.A. (2015), 'Beyond Territorial and Worldwide Systems of International Taxation', available at http://dx.doi.org/10.2139/ssrn.2567952 (accessed 5 October 2017).
Cobham, A., S.J. Klees and J. Christensen (2016), *Global Taxation: Financing Education and the Other Sustainable Development Goals*, Report to the International Commission on Financing Global Education Opportunity, available at http://www.taxjustice.net/wp-content/uploads/2016/11/Global-Taxation-Financing-Education.pdf (accessed 19 October 2017).
Cobham, A., P. Jansky and S. Loretz (2017), 'Key Findings from Global Analyses of Multinational Profit Misalignment', in S. Picciotto (ed.), *Taxing Multinational Enterprises as Unitary Firms*, Brighton: Institute of Development Studies, pp. 100–118.
Cook, T. (2013), 'Testimony of Apple Inc. before the Permanent Subcommittee on Investigations', available at http://www.hsgac.senate.gov/download/?id=E0A00AAA-F4A1-4FA0-B5B2-563B86A7588A (accessed 13 October 2017).
Cook, T. (2016), 'A Message to the Apple Community in Europe', available at https://www.apple.com/uk/customer-letter/ (accessed 24 October 2017).
Crivelli, E., R. De Mooij and M. Keen (2015), *Base Erosion, Profit Shifting and Developing Countries*, IMF Working Paper No. 15/118, available at http://www.imf.org/external/pubs/ft/wp/2015/wp15118.pdf (accessed 15 October 2017).
Culpepper, P.D. (2011), *Quiet Politics and Business Power: Corporate Control in Europe and Japan*, New York: Cambridge University Press.
Dharmapala, D., C.F. Foley and K.J. Forbes (2011), 'Watch What I Do, Not What I Say: The Unintended Consequences of the Homeland Investment Act', *Journal of Finance* **66** (3), 753–787.
Dietsch, P. (2015), *Catching Capital: The Ethics of Tax Competition*, Oxford: Oxford University Press.

Eccleston, R. (2013), *The Dynamics of Global Economic Governance*, Cheltenham, UK and Northampton, MA, USA: Edward Elgar Publishing.
Elliot, L. and H. Stewart (2013), 'David Cameron Makes Swipe at Starbucks as He Promises Focus on Tax', *Guardian Australia*, published electronically 25 January, available at https://www.theguardian.com/politics/2013/jan/24/david-cameron-starbucks-focus-tax (accessed 23 October 2017).
European Commission (2017), 'Public Country-by-Country Reporting', available at https://ec.europa.eu/info/business-economy-euro/company-reporting-and-auditing/company-reporting/public-country-country-reporting_en (accessed 12 October 2017).
EY (Ernst & Young) (2017), 'Luxembourg Transfer Pricing Legislation at a Glance', available at http://www.ey.com/lu/en/services/tax/tax-alert_20170515_tax-alert-luxembourg-transfer-pricing-legislation-at-a-glance (accessed 6 October 2017).
Farrell, S. and H. McDonald (2016), 'Apple Ordered to Pay €13bn after EU Rules Ireland Broke State Aid Laws', *Guardian UK*, published electronically 31 August, available at https://www.theguardian.com/business/2016/aug/30/apple-pay-back-taxes-eu-ruling-ireland-state-aid (accessed 1 October 2017).
Financial Times (2013), 'Starbucks Seeks Fresh US Tax Breaks', available at https://www.ft.com/content/bec4b036-ac37-11e2-a063-00144feabdc0 (accessed 6 October 2017).
Finnemore, M. and K. Sikkink (1998), 'International Norm Dynamics and Political Change', *International Organization* **52** (4), 887–917.
Friedman, M. (1970), 'The Social Responsibility of Business Is to Increase Its Profits', *New York Times Magazine*, 30 September, available at https://www.colorado.edu/studentgroups/libertarians/issues/friedman-soc-resp-business.html (accessed 23 October 2017).
G20 (2013), 'G20 Leaders' Declaration: September 6, 2013, St Petersburg', available at http://www.g20.utoronto.ca/2013/2013-0906-declaration.html (accessed 10 October 2017).
G20 (2014), 'Policy Note: The G20 and the World', available at http://www.g20.utoronto.ca/2014/policy_note_g20_world.pdf (accessed 4 October 2017).
G20 (2017), 'Communiqué: G20 Finance Ministers and Central Bank Governors March 18, 2017, Baden Baden', available at http://www.g20.utoronto.ca/2017/170318-finance-en.html (accessed 3 October 2017).
Graetz, M. and M.M. O'Hear (1997), 'The "Original Intent" of U.S. International Taxation', *Duke Law Journal* **51**, 1021–1110.
Herzfeld, M. (2015), 'The Power of a Name: Stateless Income and Its Failings', *Tax Notes International* **77**, 1019.
Hodge, M. (2016), *Called to Account: How Corporate Bad Behaviour and Government Waste Combine to Cost Us Millions*, London: Little, Brown.
House of Commons Committee of Public Accounts (2012), *HM Revenue & Customs: Annual Report and Accounts 2011–2012 – Nineteenth Report of Session 2012–2013*, available at https://publications.parliament.uk/pa/cm201213/cmselect/cmpubacc/716/716.pdf (accessed 12 October 2017).
IMF (International Monetary Fund) (2015), *Base Erosion, Profit Shifting and Developing Countries*, Working Paper No. WP/15/118, available at http://www.imf.org/external/pubs/ft/wp/2015/wp15118.pdf (accessed 9 October 2017).
ITF (International Transport Workers' Federation) and Tax Justice Network Australia (2015), *Chevron's Tax Schemes: Piping Profits out of Australia?*, available at https://d3n8a8pro7vhmx.cloudfront.net/muanational/pages/3430/

attachments/original/1445403483/ITF_Chevron_Tax_Avoidance_Report.pdf?1445403483 (accessed 5 October 2017).
Keck, M.E. and K. Sikkink (1998), *Activists beyond Borders: Advocacy Networks in International Politics*, Ithaca, NY: Cornell University Press.
Khadem, N. (2014), 'G20 Nations to Share Tax Information on Multinationals to Beat the Cheats', *Sydney Morning Herald*, published electronically 16 November, available at https://www.smh.com.au/business/g20-nations-to-share-tax-information-on-multinationals-to-beat-the-cheats-20141116-11nszo.html (accessed 15 October 2017).
Kleinbard, E.D. (2013), 'Through a Latte, Darkly: Starbucks's Stateless Income Planning', *Tax Notes*, 24 June, 1515–1535; USC CLEO Research Paper No. C13-9; USC Law Legal Studies Paper No. 13–10.
Kroes, N. (2016), 'Why EU State Aid Is Not the Right Tool to Fight Tax Avoidance', *Guardian*, 1 September, available at https://www.theguardian.com/technology/2016/sep/01/eu-state-aid-tax-avoidance-apple (accessed 7 October 2017).
Lee, B.B., A. Dobiyanski and S. Minton (2015), 'Theories and Empirical Proxies for Corporate Tax Avoidance', *Journal of Applied Business and Economics* **17** (3), 21–34.
Long, S. (2016), 'Chevron Adds $7b to 'In-House' Loan, Critics Say Move Designed to Shift Income Offshore', *Australian Broadcasting Corporation*, published electronically 6 September, available at http://www.abc.net.au/news/2016-06-09/chevrons-$7b-loan-aims-to-shift-income-offshore,-critics-say/7498002 (accessed 7 October 2017).
Melnitzer, J. (2015), 'GlaxoSmithKline Transfer Pricing Case Settled', *Financial Post*, 12 January, available at http://business.financialpost.com/legal-post/glaxo-smithkline-transfer-pricing-case-settled (accessed 20 October 2017).
Murphy, R. and P. Sikka (2017), 'Unitary Taxation: The Tax Base and the Role of Accounting', in S. Picciotto (ed.), *Taxing Multinational Enterprises as Unitary Firms*, Brighton: Institute of Development Studies, pp. 75–88.
OECD (2013a), *Action Plan on Base Erosion and Profit Shifting*, Paris: OECD Publishing.
OECD (2013b), 'OECD Secretary-General Report to the G20 Leaders: St. Petersburg, Russia, 5–6 September 2013', available at http://www.oecd.org/tax/SG-report-G20-Leaders-StPetersburg.pdf (accessed 12 October 2017).
OECD (2014), *Secretary-General's Report to Ministers 2014*, Paris: OECD Publishing, available at https://www.oecd.org/about/secretary-general/SG-Annual-Report-to-Ministers-2014.pdf (accessed 1 October 2017).
OECD (2015a), *Measuring and Monitoring BEPS: Action 11 – Final Report*, OECD/G20 Base Erosion and Profit Shifting Project, available at http://dx.doi.org/10.1787/9789264241343-en (accessed 19 October 2017).
OECD (2015b), *Neutralising the Effects of Hybrid Mismatch Arrangements: Action 2 – Final Report*, Paris: OECD Publishing, available at http://www.oecd.org/tax/neutralising-the-effects-of-hybrid-mismatch-arrangements-action-2-2015-final-report-9789264241138-en.htm (accessed 16 October 2017).
Oxfam America (2016), *Broken at the Top: How America's Dysfunctional Tax System Costs Billions in Corporate Tax Dodging*, available at https://www.oxfamamerica.org/static/media/files/Broken_at_the_Top_4.14.2016.pdf (accessed 6 October 2017).
Oxfam America (2017), 'Top 50 US Companies Stash $1.6 Trillion Offshore:

Current "Reform" Proposals Likely to Make Tax Dodging Even Worse', available at https://www.oxfamamerica.org/press/top-50-us-companies-stash-16-trillion-offshore/ (accessed 18 October 2017).

Palan, R. (2003), *The Offshore World: Sovereign Markets, Virtual Place, and Nomad Millionaires*, Ithaca, NY: Cornell University Press.

Palan, R. and D. Wigan (2014), 'Herding Cats and Taming Tax Havens: The US Strategy of "Not in My Backyard"', *Global Policy* **5** (3), 334–343, doi:10.1111/1758-5899.12135.

Palan, R., R. Murphy and C. Chavagneux (2010), *Tax Havens: How Globalisation Really Works*, Ithaca, NY: Cornell University Press.

Peterson, K. (2011), 'Report: Repatriation Tax Holiday a "Failed" Policy', *Wall Street Journal*, published electronically 10 October, available at https://www.wsj.com/articles/SB10001424052970203633104576623771022129888 (accessed 17 October 2017).

Picciotto, S. (1992), *International Business Taxation: A Study in the Internationalisation of Business Regulation*, Cambridge: Cambridge University Press.

Picciotto, S. (2011), *Regulating Global Corporate Capitalism*, Cambridge: Cambridge University Press.

Picciotto, S. (2017), *Taxing Multinational Enterprises as Unitary Firms*, Brighton: Institute of Development Studies.

Pogge, T. and K. Mehta (eds) (2016), *Global Tax Fairness*, Oxford: Oxford University Press.

Pullar-Strecker, T. (2017), 'Trump's Tax Plans Part of the Race to the Bottom by Big Countries – Expert', *Stuff – New Zealand Business Day*, available at http://www.stuff.co.nz/business/industries/92055271/Big-countries-not-playing-the-global-game-on-tax (accessed 5 October 2017).

Richardson, G., R. Lanis and G. Taylor (2015), 'Financial Distress, Outside Directors and Corporate Tax Aggressiveness Spanning the Global Financial Crisis: An Empirical Analysis', *Journal of Banking and Finance* **52**, 112–129, available at http://dx.doi.org/10.1016/j.jbankfin.2014.11.013 (accessed 14 October 2017).

Rixen, T. (2008), *The Political Economy of International Tax Governance*, Basingstoke: Palgrave Macmillan.

Rixen, T. (2016), 'Institutional Reform of Global Tax Governance', in T. Rixen and P. Dietsch (eds), *Global Tax Governance: What Is Wrong with It and How to Fix It*, Colchester: ECPR Press, pp. 325–349.

Rubin, R. (2016), 'EU Decision Upsets Treasury, Congress', *Wall Street Journal*, published electronically 31 August, available at http://online.wsj.com/public/resources/documents/print/WSJ_-A001-20160831.pdf (accessed 6 October 2017).

Sadiq, K. (2016), 'Thin Capitalisation: The Multinational Tax Avoidance Strategy the Budget Forgot', *The Conversation*, available at https://theconversation.com/thin-capitalisation-the-multinational-tax-avoidance-strategy-the-budget-forgot-58041 (accessed 6 October 2017).

Sheppard, L.A. (2014), 'Twilight of the International Consensus: How Multinationals Squandered Their Tax Privileges', *Washington University Journal of Law and Policy* **44**, 61–78.

Sikka, P. (2015), 'No Accounting for Tax Avoidance', *Political Quarterly* **86** (3), 427–433.

Spencer, D. and D. McNair (2012), 'Transfer Pricing: Will the OECD Adjust to Reality?', Tax Justice Network, available at https://www.taxjustice.net/cms/upload/pdf/Spencer_120524_OECD_.pdf (accessed 10 October 2017).
Tax Justice Network Australia and United Voice (2014), *Who Pays for Our Common Wealth? Tax Practices of the ASX 200*, available at http://www.unitedvoice.org.au/news/who-pays-our-common-wealth (accessed 16 October 2017).
Temple-West, P. (2014), 'U.S. Corporate Lobbying up on OECD Anti-Tax Dodging Push', available at http://www.reuters.com/article/us-usa-tax-beps/u-s-corporate-lobbying-up-on-oecd-anti-tax-dodging-push-idUSKBN0EA1ZZ20140530 (accessed 6 October 2017).
Thomson, A. and E. Hardwick (2017), 'The European Commission's Application of the State Aid Rules to Tax: Where Are We Now?', *Journal of Taxation of Investments* **34** (3), 29–50.
Titcomb, J. (2017), 'Apple's Cash Reserves Swell to $250bn', *Telegraph UK*, published electronically 1 May, available at http://www.telegraph.co.uk/technology/2017/05/01/apples-cash-reserves-swell-250bn/ (accessed 6 October 2017).
United States GAO (Government Accountability Office) (2008), 'Report to Congressional Requesters: International Taxation: Large U.S. Corporations and Federal Contractors with Subsidiaries in Jurisdictions Listed as Tax Havens or Financial Privacy Jurisdictions', available at http://www.gao.gov/assets/290/284522.pdf (accessed 9 October 2017).
Weckler, A. (2016), 'Apple and Ireland against the World', *Sunday Independent*, published electronically 4 September, available at https://www.independent.ie/business/irish/apple-and-ireland-against-the-world-35018709.html (accessed 10 October 2017).
World Bank (2017), 'Arm's Length Trade: A Source of Post-Crisis Trade Weakness', available at http://pubdocs.worldbank.org/en/222281493655511173/Global-Economic-Prospects-June-2017-Topical-Issue-Arms-length-trade.pdf (accessed 21 October 2017).

3. Activism and the 'new' politics of tax justice

Ainsley Elbra

3.1 INTRODUCTION

This chapter explores the roles of various actors in elevating the issue of corporate tax avoidance in the minds of publics and governments. It sketches the role of transnational activist networks, tax justice NGOs and governments in developing a nascent campaign against corporate tax avoidance. This campaign increased the salience of the issue and led to an 'opening' of the policy debate around the issue of tax in the aftermath of the Financial Crisis (FC) of 2008–09. In order to understand the challenges faced by the earliest tax justice campaigners, this chapter highlights the historically closed and technical nature of discourse around global corporate taxation. It is argued that, prior to the FC, the few significant non-governmental voices in the field of global tax regulation were those of tax practitioners and business. Corporations were able to successfully lobby against reform to the international tax system, as this arena was one of low salience, or what Culpepper (2010) would define as 'quiet politics', where issues are dominated by policy experts and vested interests and insulated from broader political considerations. These practitioners had developed close relationships with professional service firms and tax havens that benefited from tax avoidance practices, and were therefore most likely to resist reform to the global corporate tax system (this volume, Chapter 6). Despite widespread acknowledgement that firms and individuals were participating in taxation arbitrage in order to minimise tax paid, the closed nature of the debate meant that there was little chance of reform to the system. However, the FC and the resulting budgetary challenges faced by governments opened the discourse around corporate tax to a much wider range of actors. This allowed those that had been working in the policy arena since the 1970s to leverage more recent transnational activist campaigns in order to move this issue into the public spotlight.

In this chapter, the tax justice campaign is discussed in the context of the literature on transnational activist networks and the manner in which both traditional and social media have been utilised to leverage the power of tax justice NGOs. In documenting the emergence of this campaign the chapter provides analysis of the media coverage of this issue in the period since the early 1980s. It is argued that, despite the concerted earlier efforts of groups as diverse as Oxfam, the Tax Justice Network and the OECD, the ultimate driver of the campaign's relevance was the FC, which highlighted the policy problem, namely the challenge to global governance, including the distribution of the tax burden. This provided the context in which tax justice campaigners could provide policy proposals, or solutions which resonated with a newly engaged audience of governments and the public.

The chapter draws on Chapter 1 by highlighting the closed nature of the international tax arena. Here it is shown that the OECD, tasked with reforming the global corporate tax system, historically had access to a narrow range of advice which tended to resist reform of the global corporate tax system. Furthermore, it can be argued that the OECD remains a product of its powerful member states, and thus had limited scope to deviate from the status quo (Carroll and Kellow 2011). Secondly, the chapter examines the earliest attempts at a campaign against corporate tax avoidance. It sketches efforts by NGOs, INGOs and the OECD at identifying tax havens as well as attempting to increase awareness of the extent of the issue. This chapter concludes that this campaign, while it was an important precursor of later campaigns, proved too difficult for these actors. Next, the chapter discusses the significant changes that occurred post-FC, when a range of non-technical actors were able to gain traction in a campaign where technical tax issues were framed in broader political terms, specifically the inequalities emanating from corporate tax avoidance. The chapter outlines the roles of transnational activist groups and specific tax justice activists in developing a public campaign against tax avoidance. These efforts spurred several government inquiries into corporate behaviour, which are also detailed. The chapter ends with analysis of media reporting since the beginnings of the campaign. It demonstrates that the campaign against corporate tax avoidance has gained significant traction in the era since the FC, and that it is strongly linked with concepts of austerity. Tying all of these findings together, it is argued that a new politics of corporate taxation has emerged, giving rise to the potential for new forms of governance in this arena, including voluntary and private governance, possibilities explored elsewhere in this volume.

3.2 HISTORICAL TAX GOVERNANCE

The history of policy-making in the field of corporate taxation prior to 2009 is characterised by closed debate. As outlined in the preceding chapters, historically multinational corporate taxation was dominated by a technical discourse, controlled by actors such as tax practitioners and economists (Rixen 2008). The closed nature of this field of governance privileged the voices of tax practitioners, specifically transnational accounting and law firms, who have a long history of involvement in corporate tax avoidance (this volume, Chapter 6). As Webb (2004, p. 794) notes, the tax practitioners that provide advice to MNCs 'have been intimately involved in the development of offshore financial centres and tax havens', and the links between the government authorities of offshore financial centres and tax practitioners are so close that it is often difficult to distinguish between the two. Furthermore, until recently, tax practitioners and corporate interests were effectively the only actors contributing to debates about reform of the global tax system – meaning that the only non-state actors with access to decision-makers were strong advocates against reform of the international corporate tax system. By leveraging their technical expertise, these groups could control the flow of information to inter-governmental organisations, such as the OECD, that were tasked with reforming the global tax regime. The OECD was also under pressure from large member states (particularly the US) to resist calls for reform (Sharman 2006; Eccleston 2013). Until the formation of the Tax Justice Network (TJN) in 2001, there was a virtual absence of any non-governmental actors that were advocates *for* greater regulation and transparency in the global corporate tax system (Webb 2004).

The scholarly community has also been slow to highlight and respond to the challenges of effective corporate taxation. Until the 2000s, academic researchers paid little attention to the challenges of multinational tax avoidance. This is surprising given the centrality of taxation to the functioning of the state, and even more so given the changes caused by economic globalisation (Rixen 2008). The publication of early works by Picciotto (1992), Tanzi (1995) and Palan (1998) on offshore tax activities marked the beginnings of this scholarship, but it wasn't until the contributions of Webb (2004), Sharman (2006) and Rixen (2008) that scholars began to address the political and economic implications of tax avoidance and cooperation (or lack thereof) between states in this field.

The delayed response of multilateral organisations, governments and the scholarly community to identifying and responding to the challenges of corporate taxation contributed to the closed nature of this policy arena. Discussions of global corporate tax reform were largely limited to tax practitioners who continued to work closely with tax haven states to push for a continuation of the status quo. Yet, as the next section explores, while access to decision-makers was limited to tax practitioners who were overwhelmingly against reform, the beginnings of a public campaign against tax avoidance were taking place.

3.3 THE CAMPAIGN'S BEGINNINGS

The modern-day campaign against MNC tax avoidance has its roots in earlier concerns about the tax affairs of high-net-worth individuals, and the manner in which these individuals were able to circumvent domestic tax laws. The challenge of effectively taxing high-net-worth individuals in high-tax jurisdictions was first acknowledged in the 1970s and 1980s, at which time the process of deregulating the global financial system was at its height. Unprecedented financial deregulation and growing capital mobility enabled wealthy individuals to avoid taxes in high-tax regimes such as the United States and the United Kingdom. It was in response to these concerns that tax advocacy networks emerged, embarking on early attempts at 'naming and shaming' tax havens.

The first of these tax advocacy networks, the US-based Citizens for Tax Justice, was established in 1979. The organisation focuses on the impact of tax legislation on the US economy and seeks to empower citizens to fight the US corporate tax lobby on issues such as closing corporate taxation loopholes (see Citizens for Tax Justice 2017). The group's formation came just a few years before the release of the 1981 Gordon Report and 1984 US Treasury Report, which together highlighted the extent of the offshore finance zone in Caribbean states as well as the manner in which US citizens were taking advantage of this burgeoning sector (Eden and Kudrle 2005). Simultaneously, in the late 1970s, international non-governmental organisation Oxfam launched a programme aimed at understanding the link between tax havens and underdevelopment (Seabrooke and Wigan 2013). However, the issue was deemed too complex, and the programme was quickly abandoned (Seabrooke and Wigan 2013). The formation of Citizens for Tax Justice and the decision by Oxfam to focus on the issue suggest consternation around the ability of individuals and corporations to minimise their taxation obligations, yet the fact that neither group was able to elevate the issue in the minds of the public or governments also highlights the challenges of global tax reform. Despite the work of tax justice advocacy networks that highlighted the increasing ability of multinational firms to avoid and evade taxation obligations, the issue remained on the fringes of political debate until the late 1990s (Seabrooke and Wigan 2013).

The focus of governments was also on individual-level tax evasion, rather than tax avoidance undertaken by multinational firms. One of the first government attempts to formally highlight and investigate tax avoidance took place through the 1999 US Senate Hearing on Private Banking and Money Laundering, which focused on high-net-worth individuals and the proceeds of crime. A second inquiry in 2006, focused on 'Tax Haven Abuses: The Enablers, the Tools and Secrecy', broadened the focus beyond those individuals suspected of tax avoidance to the wider tax profession. The report's introduction noted 'a sophisticated offshore industry, composed of a cadre of international professionals including tax attorneys, accountants, bankers, brokers, corporate service providers and trust administrators, [that] aggressively promotes offshore jurisdictions to U.S. citizens as a means to avoid taxes' (US Senate Committee on Homeland Security and Governmental Affairs 2006, p. 1). While the 2006 report had a broader scope (when compared to the 1999 inquiry), the target of this hearing remained limited to 'U.S. citizens' rather than multinational companies.

These inquiries coincided with the HTC report (this volume, Chapter 1), which signalled the G7 and OECD's public commitment to addressing the challenge of tax avoidance. The HTC report was written in response to the G7's recognition that globalisation had created 'new challenges in the field of tax policy' and the realisation that unilateral attempts at combating tax avoidance (as ensconced in domestic tax codes) were failing (Tanzi 1995; Dietsch and Rixen 2016, p. 6). The G7 acknowledged that 'tax schemes aimed at attracting financial and other geographically mobile activities can create harmful tax competition between states, carrying risks of distorting trade and investment and could lead to the erosion of national tax bases' (G7 Finance Ministers 1996). The report sought to 'name and shame' harmful tax jurisdictions, which were defined as those that 'imposed no or only nominal tax' on corporations operating in their jurisdiction (OECD 1998). As was noted in Chapter 1, the HTC report marked the first attempt by the OECD at defining and producing a list of 'harmful tax jurisdictions' and was the organisation's 'first shot in the campaign against tax havens' (Sharman 2006, p. 45).

By the late 1990s, the campaign against corporate tax avoidance was gaining some momentum. The earliest tax justice activists emerged in this period, with groups such as Attac formed in 1998 with a focus on promoting a Tobin tax, or a levy on all spot currency conversions (Rixen 2008). Over time Attac has focused more broadly on anti-globalisation activities that include greater regulation of the global financial system, including the eradication of tax havens. Meanwhile, INGOs like Oxfam reinvigorated their efforts at addressing the issue. Oxfam and War on Want were early advocates of addressing multinational tax avoidance, with both organisations campaigning for greater transparency and regulation in the global tax regime in the early 1990s (Rixen 2008). In 2000, in response to the HTC report, Oxfam re-engaged with the issue and released a report titled *Tax Havens: Releasing the Hidden Billions for Poverty Eradication*. The report highlighted that the challenge of strengthening the global corporate taxation regime had remained unanswered, and that this was particularly harmful to developing states (Oxfam 2000). At the time, there was considerable hope that these campaigns would result in tangible progress in strengthening the global corporate tax regime. As early as 2004, the former OECD and now EY and UN tax adviser Dr Jeffrey Owens noted that the emergence of NGOs intent on exposing tax avoidance may be a sign of future success, saying that 'tax is where the environment was ten years ago' (Owens, quoted in Houlder 2004).

By the early 2000s G7 finance ministers had publicly committed to addressing the issue of tax avoidance, and in doing so they had recognised that corporate tax avoidance posed a serious challenge to national governments' budgets. Additionally, the release of the OECD HTC report was accompanied by a reinvigorated civil society campaign. Yet, as we have noted, efforts by the OECD to counter tax evasion failed to meet the goals of combating tax havens and reducing international tax avoidance and evasion. The work of the OECD was undermined by the Bush administration in the US, which, in a change of approach from that of the previous Clinton government, withdrew from the OECD initiative, arguing that the US 'does not support efforts to dictate to any country what its own tax rates or tax system should be, and will not participate in any initiative to harmonize world tax systems' (O'Neill 2001). Despite what appeared to be a promising start, combating tax avoidance was still deemed too challenging for governments and the OECD, and as a result civil society was unable to gain significant traction in its efforts to highlight the inequities in the global corporate tax regime. The withdrawal of the US from the OECD process, and the subsequent failure of the OECD to advance the issue, is a stark reminder that multinational agreements depend on the support of great powers, which is becoming more difficult to secure (Carroll and Kellow 2011). In the context of a Trump presidency and the US's apparent reluctance to commit to multilateral initiatives this challenge remains highly pertinent.

3.4 THE CONTEMPORARY CAMPAIGN AGAINST MULTINATIONAL TAX AVOIDANCE

All of this changed with the onset of the FC. Suddenly, the issue of corporate tax avoidance and the resulting forgone government revenues were central to public debates about globalisation, governance and the fairness of the global capitalist system. The remainder of this chapter outlines the emergence of a new politics of corporate tax, which built on the nascent campaign against tax avoidance led by tax justice NGOs, INGOs and the media.

The FC of 2008–09, the effects of which are still being felt by governments worldwide, was the true impetus for change in the global corporate tax regime. As governments faced large and unsustainable levels of public debt, the salience of multinational tax avoidance was suddenly heightened. Governments urgently sought ways to achieve fiscal repair and were supported in these endeavours by the OECD. As argued by Eccleston et al. (2015), the rise of tax as a focal point of global governance was not inevitable. Instead, world leaders were required to respond urgently to the FC at the same time that the OECD was promoting its international tax transparency agenda. The G20 leaders' forum endorsement of the OECD's agenda represented a window of opportunity which has reshaped debates around the global corporate tax system.

In countries such as the UK, the budget repair strategy focused on cutting public expenditure and increasing personal taxes. The impacts of these changes were felt unevenly, with citizens seemingly bearing the increased cost of governing in a post-FC environment. Adding to the ire this caused affected citizens was the realisation that multinational corporations were continuing to avoid tax obligations in these same states. Civil society groups were able to leverage this dissatisfaction to elevate the public campaign against multinational corporate tax avoidance. The campaign, waged by transnational activist networks utilising innovative communication methods, resulted in a shift in public perception and awareness of the failings of the global corporate tax regime that has led to a new politics of corporate tax. This campaign reinvigorated existing activists critical of globalisation and corporate behaviour and gave birth to new movements critical of global capitalism. It also gave governments a reason to look seriously at reforming the global tax system. Notwithstanding the power of MNCs, governments were also motivated to seek reform owing to the political logic of capturing taxation revenue on offshore earnings, as there are assumed to be fewer political costs in doing so.

The Rise of Transnational Advocacy Networks

The FC gave rise to popular movements critical of capitalism, neoliberalism and MNCs, foremost amongst which were UK Uncut and Occupy Wall Street (Occupy). UK Uncut began in 2010 as a protest against tax minimisation by high-net-worth individuals and companies in the EU but quickly spread to other jurisdictions including the US, Australia and Canada (Christians 2013). In 2011, the Occupy movement was formed. Inspired by the Arab Spring and motivated by the social injustice of post-FC austerity measures, the movement called for peaceful protest against wealth inequality, joblessness and exclusion from the democratic process. The first Occupy movement was formed in lower Manhattan in September 2011 and, like UK Uncut, spread quickly around the world (Gaby and Caren 2012). Occupy mobilised primarily against corporate elites (Steger et al. 2013). In particular, the group vocally opposed the capture of public policy by these elites, contrasting their 'corporate welfare' with the severe austerity faced by the remainder of the population (Steger et al. 2013).

Transnational activist movements, such as UK Uncut and Occupy, harnessed growing public resentment against the system that allowed MNCs to escape taxation while shifting a greater burden on to ordinary citizens. Both groups utilised framing or 'meaning-making' activities to project their issues to a global audience. Frames are 'schemata of interpretation' that allow people to 'locate, perceive, identify, and label occurrences within their life space and the world at large' (Goffman 1974, p. 21). In particular, the rallying call of the Occupy movement, 'We are the 99%', was a deliberate effort to invoke the language of battle ('us versus them') and, in doing so, expand 'us' beyond traditional groups such as workers, labour or even the middle class (Fitzgerald 2015). The framing efforts of Occupy sought to draw attention to the structural inequalities of liberalised financial markets with an additional appeal to the *unfair* nature of the unequal distribution of wealth in society. The framing efforts of transnational activist movements such as Occupy and UK Uncut were designed to mobilise new participants, raise awareness and sympathy from the public and influence public discourse (Fitzgerald 2015). Both groups effectively used framing techniques to successfully appeal to local audiences as well as INGOs, both of which were presented with a picture of tax avoidance as an issue of 'fairness' and a critique of the global capitalist system. The use of framing allowed Occupy and Uncut to connect local issues to broader contexts of injustice, whereby various participants have been united to form a 'multiple, tolerant identity' that is opposed to the injustice of MNC tax avoidance (Tarrow 2005). Furthermore, the rise of these groups opened debate about the legitimacy of the global capitalist system as well as debates about 'whose voice is entitled to be heard on what issues' (Clark 2003, p. 92).

Both Occupy and UK Uncut harnessed the power of social media to elevate the issue of corporate tax avoidance to mainstream discussion. These movements engaged in online facilitation of offline activism, a specific type of online activism where the internet is used to provide 'information on, logistical support for and/or recruitment for offline protest events such as offline marches, rallies, convergence centres etc.' (Earl et al. 2010, p. 429). This type of online activism still relies, however, on face-to-face interactions between activists, which remain central to the success of social movements such as Occupy. Occupy relied heavily on mass protest at physical sites around the globe. For this group, mobilisation relied heavily on personal ties and traditional activist tools. However, the reach of these methods was enhanced greatly by the group's online presence. Occupy is also a strong example of activism that uses an online presence to create scale-related effects, whereby 'internet usage is thought to simply accentuate or accelerate well-known processes driving activism and protest' (Earl et al. 2010, p. 427). While social movements can move quickly and inexpensively reach a wider audience, the theoretical processes underpinning activism remain unchanged. For example, the use of mass email is a similar tactic to the decades-old technique of petitions and postcards used to inform and recruit participants (Karpf 2010). In the case of Occupy, it can be argued that the movement successfully harnessed internet activism in order to attract participants who had no previous experience with political protests. In addition to growing the movement, it elevated economic inequality to the centre of public attention, particularly in the United States, and in the process highlighted the beneficiaries of this inequality (Goodwin and Jasper 2014).

While it can be argued that UK Uncut and Occupy were both central to raising the profile of corporate tax avoidance, the effectiveness of these transnational social movements in achieving change remains under question, particularly when compared with issue-focused tax justice NGOs such as TJN and Oxfam. Both groups sought to strike a balance 'between the global framing of transnational movement campaigns and the local needs of those whose claims they want to represent' (Tarrow 2005, p. 76). It is arguable that Occupy has dealt more effectively with these challenges. In doing so the group has put forward few policy proposals but seems content with a shifting configuration of supporters spread around the globe wanting, for the most part, recognition of their cause (Tarrow 2011). In fact, for Occupy, this was a major point of difference. Despite the wide range of grievances held by participants in the movement (such as anger at inequality, conventional politics, student debt, joblessness and environmental concerns), Occupy was able to provide a common enemy, that is, 'Wall Street' and the '1% with all the political and economic power' (Goodwin and Jasper 2014). Transnational activist groups successfully framed the issue of corporate tax avoidance as one tangible element of generalised inequality. Through the use of social media they were able to promote their cause to a wider global audience, in turn enhancing the campaign against corporate tax avoidance.

3.5 THE ROLE OF TAX JUSTICE ACTIVISTS

In addition to the emergence of broad transnational activist movements critical of capitalism, the FC reinvigorated the efforts of specific tax justice NGOs such as the TJN. While TJN had undertaken a long-running campaign against multinational tax avoidance since 2003 (this volume, Chapter 4), the combined effect of the FC, greater media exposure and the emergence of the transnational activist movements outlined above enhanced their platform and increased the group's contribution to the growing campaign against multinational tax avoidance. The raised profile of TJN demonstrates the increasing openness of debates around global tax governance, whereby tax justice advocates and INGOs such as Oxfam are seen as legitimate actors in the field of corporate tax.

TJN

The TJN is the most specialised, prominent and vocal of the tax justice NGOs. Unlike Oxfam or other INGOs with an interest in tax justice, the TJN is solely focused on the issue of addressing tax avoidance and evasion. As discussed in greater detail in Chapter 4, TJN was founded by a small network of technical experts from the fields of law, accounting and economics. This group of individuals had been involved separately and together in the earliest work on uncovering tax havens since the 1990s and officially launched TJN in 2003. TJN is the most specialised of the tax advocacy networks, with goals to 'create understanding and debate, and to promote reform, especially in poorer countries' in the area of global corporate taxation (Tax Justice Network 2015). The group has been at the forefront of the public campaign against tax avoidance, leveraging individual members' international networks to elevate the issue in the minds of the public and governments. TJN has access to the upper echelons of government and insiders, and therefore its tactics differ greatly from those of grassroots organisations such as Oxfam and Occupy. TJN has exploited the connections of its directors and advisers to elevate the issue of corporate tax avoidance to mainstream political discussions. The group publishes several blogs and works closely with other NGOs such as Attac and media organisations such as the *Guardian* to promote its work in the field of tax avoidance. It is through this advocacy work that the group contributes to the campaign against corporate tax avoidance.

Chapter 4 of this volume provides more detailed analysis of TJN's strategies and impact, including some of its limits and vulnerabilities. TJN has highlighted specific cases of abuse and proposed specific reforms and remedies, but the success of the group in elevating the issue to the public sphere has only been possible in the broader context of concern about inequality and contemporary business practice. Yet undoubtedly the TJN has emerged as a central actor in the campaign against tax avoidance, and the connections and influence held by the groups' members differentiate it from other groups such as Oxfam, and particularly transnational activist groups such as Occupy. Aside from the group's advocacy work, the TJN has contributed to the development of key reforms such as country-by-country reporting and private governance initiatives such as the Fair Tax Mark (see this volume, Chapter 10), as well as connecting and coordinating the efforts of other larger and better-resourced actors.

Oxfam International

As outlined above, Oxfam was the first of these groups to engage directly with the issue of tax justice. The group attempted to draw attention to the issue in the 1970s. However, the issue was deemed 'too political' and was abandoned until the turn of the century (Seabrooke and Wigan 2013). In 1999 work began on Oxfam's report *Tax Havens: Releasing the Hidden Billions for Poverty Eradication*, which included input from several individuals who would go on to form TJN (Oxfam 2000). In releasing this report, Oxfam was the only NGO to respond to the OECD's Harmful Tax Competition report, which was released in 1998 (Sharman 2006). The Oxfam report called for reforms such as: a multilateral approach to developing a common definition of the tax base and the way in which this was to be taxed; a global authority tasked with ensuring national tax systems did not have detrimental effects on the global tax system; an international convention to facilitate the repatriation of tax funds appropriated from developing country treasuries; international standards on payment of tax; and greater information sharing (Oxfam 2000). Since the publication of this report, Oxfam has continued its advocacy work on the developmental effects of tax avoidance and its contribution to global inequality.

Oxfam has focused not only on the impact of tax avoidance on developing states in terms of lost revenues, but also on the manner in which developing state tax havens may be encouraged to find politically acceptable ways to overhaul their tax systems. In the group's response to the OECD's call to identify tax havens, Oxfam argued that small developing states were unfairly targeted (in preference to tax havens such as the City of London and New York) and called for 'strategies to help small, poor and vulnerable economies to diversify from a reliance on harmful tax practices' (Oxfam 2000).

Oxfam remains committed to campaigning against corporate tax avoidance, with a particular focus on the implications for inequality and development in the world's poorest countries, and on the gender pay gap – an issue Oxfam argues is exacerbated by corporate tax avoidance (Oxfam 2016b). The organisation continues to publish reports highlighting rising global inequality and the way tax avoidance contributes to this problem. In 2016, Oxfam hosted a symposium on tax avoidance in conjunction with Oxford University titled 'Fair Tax: What Does It Look Like and How Do We Get It?' (Oxfam 2016a). Oxfam's executive director, Winnie Byanyima, notes that the organisation retains a strong focus on tax justice. She is currently lobbying for a global tax body focused on closing the tax compliance gap, especially in developing countries. Byanyima notes that 'we have international organizations for health, trade and football, even for coffee, but not tax. Why not?' (Byanyima, quoted in Reguly 2015).

Christian Aid

Christian Aid is a UK-based organisation focused on development, and eliminating poverty and injustice. The group first began campaigning against corporate tax avoidance in 2008, although as early as 2005 the NGO had published a report titled *The Shirts Off Their Backs: How Tax Policies Fleece the Poor* (Christian Aid 2005), which highlighted revenue losses to developing state governments as a result of individual and corporate tax avoidance. In the period since, Christian Aid has worked to highlight the impacts of multinational tax avoidance on developing states, particularly those in sub-Saharan Africa. Furthermore, Christian Aid has focused its attention on firms operating in the mining sector in developing countries.

In 2008 Christian Aid began campaigning for the implementation of country-by-country reporting, and this issue remains a central facet of the group's lobbying efforts. Christian Aid's tax justice programme seeks to address the unfairness of MNC tax avoidance by promoting country-by-country reporting, automatic information exchange and public registers of beneficial ownership.

The group has more recently turned its campaign focus to the local government level, lobbying for all UK councils to demand more detailed accounts from suppliers and in turn choosing not to do business with firms that avoid 'paying a fair share'. By asking local governments to demand more accountability and transparency from the businesses they deal with, Christian Aid is going beyond the current requirements, which compel councils to ask about illegal activity. Instead, the campaign asks councils to leverage the large amounts of money spent by local authorities (£45 billion per annum) to pressure suppliers to pay a greater share of tax (Cooper 2016). This campaign is being run in conjunction with the FTM, discussed in Chapter 10 of this volume, with which it shares similar normative challenges, such as questions over who is able to decide what constitutes a 'fair' share of taxation.

3.6 GOVERNMENT INQUIRIES INTO MULTINATIONAL TAX AVOIDANCE

The increased salience of multinational tax avoidance in the minds of the public enabled and encouraged (and perhaps forced) national governments to publicly respond to this issue through a series of parliamentary and congressional inquiries. These high-profile inquiries have attracted significant media attention as company representatives face questions about the legal and moral aspects of their business behaviour from various parliamentarians. Although many of these committees exist principally to highlight issues and make recommendations to governments, rather than legislate directly, their existence highlights the significance of the issue in the minds of governments and publics alike.

In the United States these inquiries have taken place through the United States Senate Committee on Homeland Security and Governmental Affairs. In May 2013, the Committee's Permanent Subcommittee on Investigations held a two-part public inquiry into offshore profit shifting and the US tax code. The first of these inquiries focused on the actions of Microsoft and Hewlett-Packard and the second on Apple Inc, which was pre-warned of the Committee's determination to 'spotlight Apple's extensive tax-avoidance'. These hearings are the latest in a series of US public inquiries into tax avoidance starting in 1999. However, it is notable that the 2013 inquiry was the first to specifically target multinational tax avoidance as opposed to individual tax evasion and/or the tax practitioners that facilitate such regimes.

In 2015 the Australian Senate held an inquiry into tax avoidance and aggressive tax minimisation by MNCs operating in Australia. This inquiry is examined in detail in Chapter 7 in this volume, where it is argued that the evidence given by representatives of Google and Apple stressed the lawfulness of their respective firms' behaviour. Not only did these representatives suggest they knew little about the finer details of their firms' tax structures, but they suggested that any tax avoidance strategies were simply a result of the structure of the international tax system in which they were operating in a way that meets the demands of shareholders. Throughout this inquiry the blame for failures to effectively tax multinational corporations operating in Australia was laid squarely at the feet of governments and inter-governmental organisations.

In January 2016 the UK Treasury Committee launched an Inquiry into UK Tax Policy and the Tax Base. This followed a 2011 report, *Principles of Tax Policy* (House of Commons Treasury Committee 2011). The latest inquiry focused on determining whether the current UK tax policy and administration are fit for purpose in the era of globalisation. The inquiry's terms of reference point directly to the ability of multinational firms to evade corporate tax obligations, suggesting this will be a significant focus of the investigation.

In May 2016, the International Consortium of Investigative Journalists (ICIJ) released a cache of documents commonly known as the Panama Papers. The leak consisted of 11 million files provided by a whistleblower, detailing the secret tax arrangements of individuals and companies that utilised the services of Panama-based professional services firm Mossack Fonseca (this volume, Chapter 12). Following this release of information, the European Parliament announced the establishment of a 'Committee of Inquiry to investigate alleged contraventions and maladministration in the application of Union law in relation to money laundering, tax avoidance and tax evasion' (European Parliament Committees 2016). This committee, known as the PANA Committee, held hearings over a 12-month period from its formation in July 2016, after which a report was released. The Committee's findings were adopted by the European Commission and the Council of Europe (European Parliament 2018).

These formal inquiries have been accompanied by public commitments from government and other politicians to remake the global corporate tax system in a way that eliminates opportunities for corporate tax avoidance. Former UK Labour prime minister Gordon Brown has called on the EU to pressure the US into imposing sanctions on tax havens in order to ensure there were no 'treasure islands for the money launderers' (Elliott 2016). In the US, a shift from Bush-era rhetoric occurred during the Obama administration when US Treasury secretary Timothy Geithner noted that the administration 'fully support[s] the legislation . . . on offshore tax centres' and will work towards a 'broader effort to address international tax evasion and close the tax gap' (Mathiason 2009). However, in February 2017, President Trump repealed anti-corruption measures included in the Dodd–Frank legislation, effectively releasing mining, oil and gas firms from the additional transparency obligations they had been actively resisting since the inception of Dodd–Frank in 2010 to improve the governance and transparency of the finance sector (Traywick 2017).

The inquiries outlined above point to growing consternation around the behaviour of large multinational corporations. Governments that have long competed on the basis of favourable tax regimes have been placed under increasing pressure to be seen to reduce opportunities for corporate tax avoidance. Unfortunately, as outlined in Chapters 7 and 10 of this volume, these inquiries have yielded little in the way of either information or significant policy change. Corporate executives called before committees have been painfully unaware of the details of their companies' corporate tax regimes, yet the information they have provided has confirmed the characteristics of inequality and unfairness that dominate the debates around tax justice. This alone has added significant momentum to the campaign for global corporate tax reform.

3.7 EVIDENCE OF AN EMERGING CAMPAIGN

The previous sections of this chapter have highlighted the emergence of a nascent campaign against corporate tax avoidance. In doing so, they have demonstrated that the debates in this field have shifted from a closed technical discourse to a more participatory conversation about fairness and inequality. The various actors as well as the techniques used to open the debate around the global corporate tax system have been outlined. This section of the chapter highlights the impact of these strategies on public discourse and the wider political agenda by analysing media reporting on the topic of tax avoidance. In doing so it highlights how the issue of corporate tax avoidance gained prominence. In this case, a crisis (the FC) 'concentrate[d] public opinion on a previously ignored topic and rendered it politically salient', in turn a pre-condition for political action and substantive change (Culpepper 2010, p. 7).

Since 2000, the *Guardian* (UK) has run a campaign against corporate tax avoidance that has benefited from the work of several key tax activist groups, including TJN. Less conspicuously, the *New York Times* has also devoted columns of print to highlighting the issue in the US context. Figure 3.1 demonstrates the closed nature of this debate prior to the early 2000s. In the years before 2000 there were fewer than 100 mentions of 'tax havens' or 'tax avoidance' per year across both the *Guardian* (UK) and the *New York Times*. These mentions also include articles focused on individual high-net-worth tax avoidance schemes. This is indicative of the lack of attention corporate tax avoidance received in this period, and is even more telling as this period captures the release of the OECD's HTC report. The relative silence around the issue of corporate tax avoidance aligns with the central argument presented in this chapter that the field was

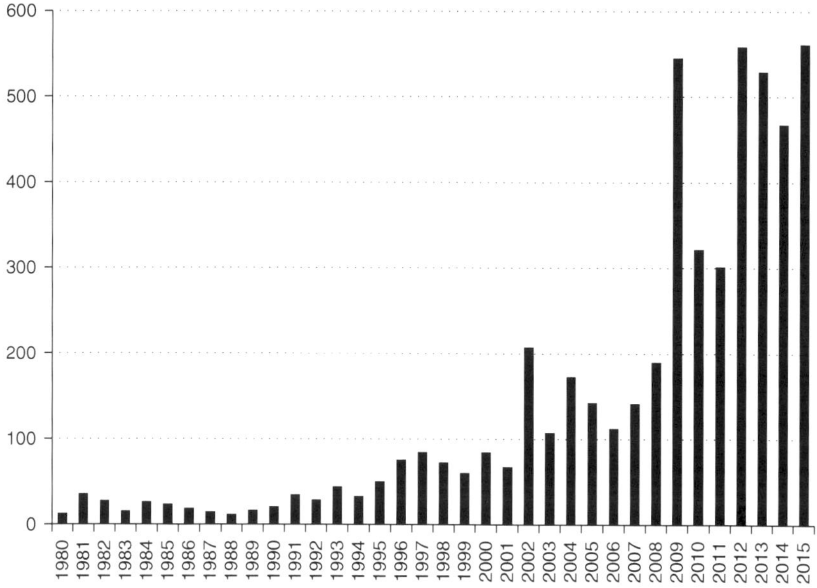

Source: Factiva.

Figure 3.1 Mentions of 'tax avoidance' or 'tax haven' in the Guardian (UK) and New York Times, 1980–2015

dominated by technical actors, such as economists and tax practitioners, with little space for more vocal actors such as tax activist groups.

After the early 2000s there is evidence that the campaign gained momentum. Figure 3.1 illustrates the manner in which media attention on this issue grew post-2001, which matched the civil society campaign outlined in this chapter. The number of mentions of 'tax avoidance' or 'tax haven' increases dramatically from 2009 onwards. While there was some discussion of tax havens and tax avoidance prior to the FC these remained in the order of 200 mentions across both news outlets per year. In 2009, this figure spikes to 590 mentions before settling at a much higher instance in the ensuing years. Of the total mentions across the period, 83 per cent appeared in the *Guardian*, and 71 per cent were focused on the UK, suggesting the campaign has been particularly effective in this country, where activists have been able to draw on the specific UK experience of austerity in framing their campaign.

There is also considerable overlap between media reports mentioning tax havens or tax avoidance, and austerity, with 71 per cent of media reports that mentioned 'tax haven' or 'tax avoidance' also including the term 'austerity'. This again suggests that the salience of the campaign has been highest in the UK, where austerity measures have been most heavily felt. Additionally, the overlap between the search terms and austerity suggests that the framing of this issue by activist groups as a question of *fairness* has been highly effective. Much of the reporting on the issue harnesses the frames of inequality and unfairness to appeal to these newspapers' readerships. These are the same themes that transnational activist groups used so successfully in their campaign against the inequalities inherent in the global capitalist system, and in particular the impacts of multinational tax avoidance.

In addition to the long-running campaigns by the *Guardian* and *New York Times*, the ICIJ's Panama Papers (discussed earlier in this chapter and in Chapter 12) provided a vast cache of documents, which were analysed by a team of investigative reporters from around the world, who then filed stories with their own media outlets detailing individuals and firms that utilised law firm Mossack Fonseca's services.

The content analysis explored in this section corroborates arguments made in this chapter. That is, prior to 2000 the debate around reform of the global corporate tax system was limited to technical actors. This remained the case despite the work of international NGOs such as Oxfam and the release of the OECD's HTC report, aimed at identifying tax havens and mandating reform in their bilateral tax treaties. However, post-FC there has been considerable growth in the public campaign against corporate tax avoidance, mirrored in the content analysis of two leading progressive newspapers.

3.8 CONCLUSION

The ongoing effects of the FC have led to widespread debate about the fairness of the global capitalist system. This debate has been keenly felt in the area of global corporate taxation, where a 'new' politics of corporate taxation has emerged. This chapter sketched the emergence of the campaign against corporate tax avoidance and the key actors involved in these debates. Firstly, it was argued that the global corporate tax system was an arena previously restricted to technical experts, who were for the most part complicit in designing and maintaining the complex structures that enabled firms and individuals to reduce their taxable income. In particular, the OECD sourced its information from actors such as economists and tax practitioners, both of which are groups with a vested interest in maintaining the status quo.

This chapter then outlined the early attempts at challenging this system and draw attention to the inequalities associated with tax avoidance, at the individual high-net-worth level as well as by corporations. Despite serious attempts to identify the costs and implications of tax avoidance and convey these to the public, the work of Oxfam and the like failed to gain traction until the onset of the FC.

After this point the campaign gained serious momentum owing to a shift in perceptions of corporate behaviour and general dissatisfaction with the global capitalist system. These frustrations were played out through the Uncut and Occupy movements, which claim to represent the 99 per cent, that is, those who have not benefited significantly from the promises of globalisation. This chapter illuminated the way in which transnational activists, and tax activists more specifically, have utilised framing techniques and leveraged the uneven impact of the Financial Crisis to appeal to the public's sense of fairness. As will be discussed in greater detail in Chapter 4, these transnational activist groups utilised new strategies and forms of online communication to expand on an existing base of anti-globalisation protestors. These movements shed light on the challenges of taxing multinational corporations and helped to increase the exposure of the work being undertaken by specific tax justice groups. The accounts of transnational advocacy networks and social movements rallying against inequality in the global capitalist system squared with those provided by tax activists, both of which highlighted the perceived unfair nature of the global corporate tax system.

Tax activists have successfully launched a vocal campaign against the injustice of the global financial system that has taken the debate around corporate tax from a limited and technical arena to one in which the media, publics, governments and activists themselves are actively participating. Thus it is evident that a new politics of corporate taxation has emerged in the period since the FC. Evidence of this opening up of the debate is present in public debates about fairness, the taxation burden and reform to the global corporate tax system that include a wide variety of voices. Section 3.7 illustrates the effectiveness of the campaign through content analysis of major progressive newspapers in the UK and US. Here, it is shown that very little public discussion of tax avoidance or tax havens took place prior to 2000, and it was not until the FC that the issue gained salience in the minds of the public.

The chapter concludes that the campaign waged by civil society against corporate tax avoidance has been slow to gain momentum. However, the onset of the FC provided transnational activists with a political opportunity to draw attention to the inequalities arising from the global corporate tax system. Not only has the debate around tax opened up as a result of this campaign, but this new politics has the potential to enable new forms of governance, including the private and voluntary systems of governance explored elsewhere in this volume.

REFERENCES

Carroll, P. and A. Kellow (2011), *The OECD: A Study of Organisational Adaptation*, Cheltenham, UK and Northampton, MA, USA: Edward Elgar Publishing.

Christian Aid (2005), *The Shirts Off Their Backs: How Tax Policies Fleece the Poor*, available at http://www.taxjustice.net/cms/upload/pdf/CA_the_shirts_of_their_backs_SEP-2005.pdf (accessed 19 June 2018).

Christians, A. (2013), 'Tax Activism and the Global Movement for Development through Transparency', in M. Stewart and Y. Brauner (eds), *Tax, Law and Development*, Cheltenham, UK and Northampton, MA, USA: Edward Elgar Publishing, pp. 288–315.

Citizens for Tax Justice (2017), 'About CTJ', available at http://www.ctj.org/about/ (accessed 16 July 2017).

Clark, I. (2003), 'Legitimacy in a Global Order', *Review of International Studies* **29**, 75–95.

Cooper, C. (2016), 'Local Councils Should Vet Suppliers for Tax Avoidance, Charity Says', *Independent*, available at http://www.independent.co.uk/news/uk/politics/local-councils-should-vet-suppliers-for-tax-avoidance-charity-says-a6799961.html (accessed 16 July 2017).

Culpepper, P.D. (2010), *Quiet Politics and Business Power: Corporate Control in Europe and Japan*, Cambridge: Cambridge University Press.

Dietsch, P. and T. Rixen (2016), 'Global Tax Governance: What It Is and Why It Matters', in T. Rixen and P. Dietsch (eds), *Global Tax Governance: What Is Wrong with It and How to Fix It*, Colchester: ECPR Press, pp. 1–24.

Earl, J., K. Kimport, G. Prieto, C. Rush and K. Reynoso (2010), 'Changing the World One Webpage at a Time: Conceptualizing and Explaining Internet Activism', *Mobilization: An International Quarterly* **15** (4), 425–446.

Eccleston, R. (2013), *The Dynamics of Global Economic Governance: The OECD, the Global Financial Crisis and the Transformation of International Tax Regulation*, Cheltenham, UK and Northampton, MA, USA: Edward Elgar Publishing.

Eccleston, R., A. Kellow and P. Carroll (2015), 'G20 Endorsement in Post Crisis Global Governance: More Than a Toothless Talking Shop?', *British Journal of Politics and International Relations* **17** (2), 298–317, doi:10.1111/1467-856x.1203.

Eden, L. and R.T. Kudrle (2005), 'Tax Havens: Renegade States in the International Tax Regime?', *Law and Policy*, **27**, 100–127.

Elliott, L. (2016), 'Gordon Brown Urges EU States to Unite against Tax Havens', *Guardian*, available at http://www.theguardian.com/world/2016/may/10/gordon-brown-urges-eu-states-to-unite-against-tax-havens (accessed 19 July 2017).

European Parliament (2018), 'Committees: End of Mandate PANA Committee', available at http://www.europarl.europa.eu/committees/en/pana/home.html (accessed 19 June 2018).

European Parliament Committees (2016), 'Highlights: Committees', available at http://www.europarl.europa.eu/committees/en/pana/home.html (accessed 15 July 2017).
Fitzgerald, S.T. (2015), 'Is Equality the Goal? Challenging Economic Inequality in the US and UK', in E. Avril and J.N. Neem (eds), *Democracy, Participation and Contestation: Civil Society, Governance and the Future of Liberal Democracy*, London: Routledge, pp. 51–66.
G7 Finance Ministers (1996), 'Lyon Summit Economic Communiqué: Making a Success of Globalization for the Benefit of All', available at http://europa.eu/rapid/press-release_DOC-96-5_en.htm (accessed 14 July 2017).
Gaby, S. and N. Caren (2012), 'Occupy Online: How Cute Old Men and Malcolm X Recruited 400,000 US Users to OWS on Facebook', *Social Movement Studies*, **11** (3–4), 367–374, doi:10.1080/14742837.2012.708858.
Goffman, E. (1974), *Frame Analysis: An Essay on the Organization of Experience*, Cambridge, MA: Harvard University Press.
Goodwin, J. and J.M. Jasper (2014), *The Social Movements Reader: Cases and Concepts*, Oxford: John Wiley & Sons.
Houlder, V. (2004), 'The Tax Avoidance Story as a Moral Tale,' *Financial Times Online*, published electronically 22 November, available at http://ezproxy.library.usyd.edu.au/login?url=http://search.proquest.com.ezproxy1.library.usyd.edu.au/docview/228832983?accountid=14757 (accessed 20 July 2017).
House of Commons Treasury Committee (2011), *Principles of Tax Policy: Eighth Report of Session 2010–11*, available at https://publications.parliament.uk/pa/cm201011/cmselect/cmtreasy/753/753.pdf (accessed 19 June 2018).
Karpf, D. (2010), 'Online Political Mobilization from the Advocacy Group's Perspective: Looking beyond Clicktivism', *Policy and Internet* **2** (4), 7–41, doi:10.2202/1944-2866.1098.
Mathiason, N. (2009), 'Obama Bid to Stamp Out Tax Havens', *Guardian*, published electronically 5 March, available at https://www.theguardian.com/business/2009/mar/04/obama-tax-haven-crackdown (accessed 22 July 2017).
O'Neill, P. (2001), 'Treasury Secretary O'Neill Statement on OECD Tax Havens', available at http://www.treasury.gov/press-center/press-releases/Pages/po366.aspx (accessed 23 July 2017).
OECD (1998), *Harmful Tax Competition: An Emerging Global Issue*, Paris: OECD Publishing, available at http://www.oecd.org/tax/transparency/44430243.pdf (accessed 22 July 2017).
Oxfam (2000), *Tax Havens: Releasing the Hidden Billions for Poverty Eradication*, available at http://policy-practice.oxfam.org.uk/publications/tax-havens-releasing-the-hidden-billions-for-poverty-eradication-114611 (accessed 20 July 2017).
Oxfam (2016a), 'After the Panama Papers, What Does Fair Tax Look Like?', available at https://www.oxfam.org/en/campaigns/even-it/after-panama-papers-what-does-fair-tax-look (accessed 15 July 2017).
Oxfam (2016b), 'It's Time to Even It Up!', available at https://www.oxfam.org/en/even-it/its-time-even-it (accessed 12 July 2017).
Palan, R. (1998), 'Trying to Have Your Cake and Eating It: How and Why the State System Has Created Offshore', *International Studies Quarterly* **42** (4), 625–643.
Picciotto, S. (1992), 'International Taxation and Intrafirm Pricing in Transnational Corporate Groups', *Accounting, Organizations and Society* **17** (8), 759–792.
Reguly, E. (2015), 'Social Justice Is in Her Blood: Winnie Byanyima, Executive Director of Oxfam International', *Globe and Mail*, published electronically 1

August, available at http://search.proquest.com.ezproxy1.library.usyd.edu.au/docview/1700443379?pq-origsite=summon (accessed 15 July 2017).
Rixen, T. (2008), *The Political Economy of International Tax Governance*, Basingstoke: Palgrave Macmillan, available at http://dx.doi.org/10.1057/9780230582651 (accessed 17 July 2017).
Seabrooke, L. and D. Wigan (2013), *Emergent Entrepreneurs in Transnational Advocacy Networks: Professional Mobilization in the Fight for Global Tax Justice*, Working Paper No. 41, GR:EEN, Global Reordering: Evolution through European Networks, FP7, available at http://pipesproject.eu/assets/GREEN41.pdf (accessed 1 November 2017).
Sharman, J.C. (2006), *Havens in a Storm: The Struggle for Global Tax Regulation*, Ithaca, NY: Cornell University Press.
Steger, M., J. Goodman and E.K. Wilson (2013), *Justice Globalism: Ideology, Crises, Policy*, London: Sage Publications.
Tanzi, V. (1995), *Taxation in an Integrating World*, Washington, DC: Brookings Institution Press.
Tarrow, S. (2005), *The New Transnational Activism*, New York: Cambridge University Press.
Tarrow, S. (2011), 'Why Occupy Wall Street Is Not the Tea Party of the Left: The United States' Long History of Protest', *Foreign Affairs*, published electronically 10 October, available at https://www.foreignaffairs.com/articles/north-america/2011-10-10/why-occupy-wall-street-not-tea-party-left (accessed 19 July 2017).
Tax Justice Network (2015), 'About Us – Our Goals', available at http://www.taxjustice.net/about/who-we-are/goals/ (accessed 21 July 2017).
Traywick, C. (2017), 'Trump Repeal of SEC Regulation Signals More to Come', *Bloomberg.com*, published electronically 15 February, available at https://www.bloomberg.com/news/articles/2017-02-14/trump-repeal-of-energy-anti-corruption-rule-signals-coming-wave (accessed 16 July 2017).
US Senate Committee on Homeland Security and Governmental Affairs (2006), *Tax Haven Abuses: The Enablers, The Tools and Secrecy*, available at http://www.hsgac.senate.gov/download/report-tax-haven-abuses-the-enablers-the-tools-and-secrecy (accessed 20 July 2017).
Webb, M. (2004), 'Defining the Boundaries of Legitimate State Practice: Norms, Transnational Actors and the OECD's Project on Harmful Tax Competition', *Review of International Political Economy* **11** (4), 787–827, doi:10.1080/0969229042000279801.

PART II

4. Tax justice activists in global wealth chains

Leonard Seabrooke and Duncan Wigan

4.1 INTRODUCTION

In the wake of the Financial Crisis (FC), questions of tax system design and tax justice increased in political salience as authorities recognised their decreased capacity to tax international capital. A seemingly urgent interest in filling and fixing the fiscal coffers emerged alongside concerns about addressing increased inequality. Austerity policies, labour's declining wage share, increased returns to capital, and marked uncertainty as to a political-economic recipe for sustainable recovery have propelled issues of taxation to centre stage. Unlike the 1980s, where talk was of taxation and inefficiency, this time the talk has been about inequality and effectiveness. Broad-based and innovative policy initiatives have resulted. The US moved first, flexing its muscles with extra-territorial and unilateral action in the form of the Foreign Account Tax Compliance Act (Eccleston and Gray 2014; Palan and Wigan 2014). The EU has re-tooled its armoury against tax evasion and avoidance, moving against some large multinational corporations through state aid investigations, improving transparency and increasing tax information requirements and sharing. As was noted in Chapter 2, the OECD completed its Base Erosion and Profit Shifting initiative in 2015, tightening up rules and instigating the automatic exchange of tax information between tax authorities and new reporting requirements for multinational corporations in the shape of country-by-country reporting (CbCR). More is in the pipeline.

At the same time, interstate tax competition continues unabated, with taxes on capital falling, and most recently the UK threatening to lower its corporate income tax rate below that of any OECD member state if its Brexit deal does not meet expectations of a soft landing, while on the other side of the Atlantic the Trump administration has secured Congressional support for sweeping corporate tax cuts (Seabrooke and Wigan 2017a). In this period of accelerated change, activists have played a prominent role, a role previously perceived as precluded by thick technocracy and construed complexity (Picciotto 2015; Christensen forthcoming; this volume, Chapter 3). Issue control of taxation prior to the FC lay with market and state actors. The policy space now includes a range of activists with clout, and some with more clout than others (Seabrooke and Wigan 2016).

The socio-political context is important to any explanation of increased issue salience and accelerated policy innovation. One aspect of this is the liquidity and mutability of forms of capital, with for instance asset and corporate form transcending fiscal systems designed for another era (Bryan et al. 2017). The post-crisis context fuelled radical change in various forms, most pointedly in the rise to prominence of nationalist and populist agendas in the United States and across a host of European countries. However, context alone does not define what issues shift up the salience index, or what content these issues are imbued with. Actors, organisations and organisation matter here. This chapter, drawing on more than a decade of participant observation and multiple elite interviews with tax justice activists, policy makers, private sector practitioners and other non-specialist non-governmental organisation (NGO) professionals, focuses on one organisation that has occupied the central position in propelling a tax justice agenda centre stage, the Tax Justice Network (TJN). In doing so, the chapter specifies the peculiar constellation of actor attributes, organisational form and organising that can help explain issue adoption, policy influence and accelerated policy innovation in what until recently has been a technical policy domain largely impervious to civil society activism.

The chapter is set out as follows. In section 4.2, we provide both a framework that furnishes an apparatus through which to conceive of the role of law, finance and accounting in defining who gets what from global economic activities, and a heuristic device to conceive of the policy space in which the 'global tax battles', which are the focus of this volume, unfold (Seabrooke and Wigan 2017b, 2018). Section 4.3 identifies the agency and mode of organising that have proved conducive to activating expertise in this case. Here, we show how certain forms of *agency* and *organising*, as opposed to organisational resources, empower disruptive expertise more than others. To illustrate the operation of activist expertise, section 4.4 explains how ideas are deployed in global tax battles to effect radical change on the policy agenda. The proliferation of a new corporate reporting standard in the guise of country-by-country reporting has raised the spectre of an account of global corporate activity that transcends the prioritisation of investors that to date has characterised corporate reporting. In consequence, corporate reporting now responds to a broader set of concerns and serves the priorities of a wider group of stakeholders. Section 4.5 shows how expert activists benchmark financial opacity and how benchmarks that seek to effect transformative change are successfully pushed centre stage. The Financial Secrecy Index (FSI) is now widely deployed in tracking the transgression of international norms and shining light on jurisdictions perceived to be standing in the way of tax justice (Seabrooke and Wigan 2015). The FSI as a revolutionary benchmark also seeks to transform the extant normative order and how it is perceived. We return in conclusion to consider how these cases and the organisational and professional dynamics add to an understanding of NGOs' and activists' transnational strategies (Cooley and Ron 2002; Stroup and Wong 2017) and the politics of global economic justice.

4.2 GLOBAL WEALTH CHAINS

Perhaps the most widely used heuristic device deployed in analysing globalising economic processes has been global value chains (GVCs) (Gereffi et al. 2005). GVC analysis has been applied to track the governance of transnational production processes and power relations attached to the journey of commodities from raw material to shop floor. To track these processes, GVC analyses have provided typologies reflecting an initial concern with the question of whether particular chains are driven by a lead buyer or a lead supplier, while more recent iterations have identified five distinct types of chains in order of transaction and coordination complexity: *market*, *modular*, *relational*, *captive* and *hierarchy*. These chains differ in complexity, ranging from *market* chains, where product complexity and information requirements are low and exchange is conducted at arm's length, to *hierarchy*, where product complexity and information requirements are high, leading to spatially dispersed production conducted in-house or subject to close coordination (Gereffi 1994; Gereffi et al. 2005). The focus here is on relationships between suppliers and buyers, particularly what information is needed for transactions to take place, and the relative capacities of various actors to add value in the chain and contribute to the finished product. Relative silence on issues of finance and law requires redress where finance occupies 'the top floor of the house of trade' (Arrighi 1994) and multinational firms rely as much upon regulatory machinations as efficiency in production for competitive advantage.

Global wealth chains (GWCs) can be conceived as the yin to the yang of global value chains. In seeking to contribute answers to the question of who gets what from global economic activity, GWC analyses focus on issues of accounting, finance and law. We have defined GWCs as 'transacted forms of capital operating multi-jurisdictionally for the purposes of wealth creation and protection' (Seabrooke and Wigan 2017b, p. 2). The upshot of this definition is a focus on asset strategies, whether the asset be a labour force, a structured finance product or profits accruing to firms or individual capital holders. In developing a typology of GWCs we draw directly on Gereffi et al. (2005), identifying five wealth chains delineated on three bases: the complexity of information and knowledge transfer with regard to the product or service being provided by the supplier to meet clients' requirements; the regulatory liability involved in transactions or the ease of multi-jurisdictional regulatory intervention; and the capabilities of suppliers to create solutions to mitigate challenges to the status of the product or service by regulators. The GWCs framework copies Gereffi et al. (2005) in positing market, modular, relational, captive and hierarchy chains. *Market* chains are simplest in having clear, non-personal supply and demand mechanisms. *Modular* chains offer limited customisation from suppliers to clients based on a standard basket of products. *Relational* chains are high-trust networks. *Captive* chains are where a few suppliers dominate service provision and associated information technologies. *Hierarchy* chains are where wealth and capital management is in-house in big firms and largely unknown to regulators (Seabrooke and Wigan 2017b).

Gereffi et al. (2005) differentiate value chains on the basis of the ability to codify transactions. We substitute regulatory liability for codification. Many activities in wealth chains are premised on the capacity to hide and obscure the nature of a transaction, with opacity highly prized for the shield it provides against regulatory intervention. Figure 4.1 shows our five types of wealth chain (these mirror those of Gereffi et al. (2005), although of course the dynamics at play are markedly different), with the lines between actors (suppliers, clients and regulators) denoting the degree of information asymmetry and consequent regulatory traction on wealth chain processes. By way of illustration we attach activities to chain types.

One crucial legal issue appertaining to asset strategies and wealth management is that of what proportion of private wealth is made public through systems of taxation. For a GWC perspective, the key question is how multi-jurisdictional transactions sever links between the location of value creation and the location, virtual and real, of profits and capital for tax purposes (this volume, Chapter 2). Now a key concern of international organisations, the issue has occupied the attention of international political economists for some time. The focus on issues of international taxation in international political economy has been on multilateral regulatory efforts to curb avoidance and evasion (Sharman 2006; Vlcek 2008; Eccleston 2012), the structural and institutional determinants of an 'offshore world' (Picciotto 1992; Palan 1998, 2003; Picciotto 2011) and an apparent imperative of tax competition given a system of sovereign states

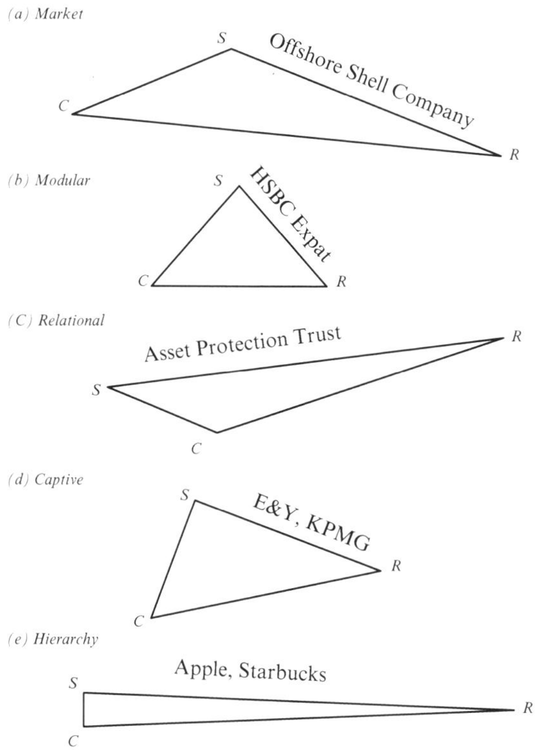

Notes: S = suppliers; C = clients; R = regulators.

Source: Seabrooke and Wigan (2017b, p. 14).

Figure 4.1 Information asymmetries in the governance of global wealth chains, with examples

with, second to a monopoly on the legitimate use of violence, a jurisdictional right to tax resident citizens and economic entities a defining feature (Rixen 2008; Hakelberg 2015). This chapter adds to this body of literature a focus on activists in global wealth chains. As was argued in Chapter 3, in the arena of international taxation activists have not until recently played a decisive role. As noted, the strong prerogative of the state in deciding on what to levy tax, how much to levy, where and when, combined with the perceived highly technical content of the issue, has militated against activist intervention. Notably, issue content, as well as being technical, is cross-disciplinary, with issue navigation requiring expertise in accounting, economics, political economy, law and public policy. Not surprisingly

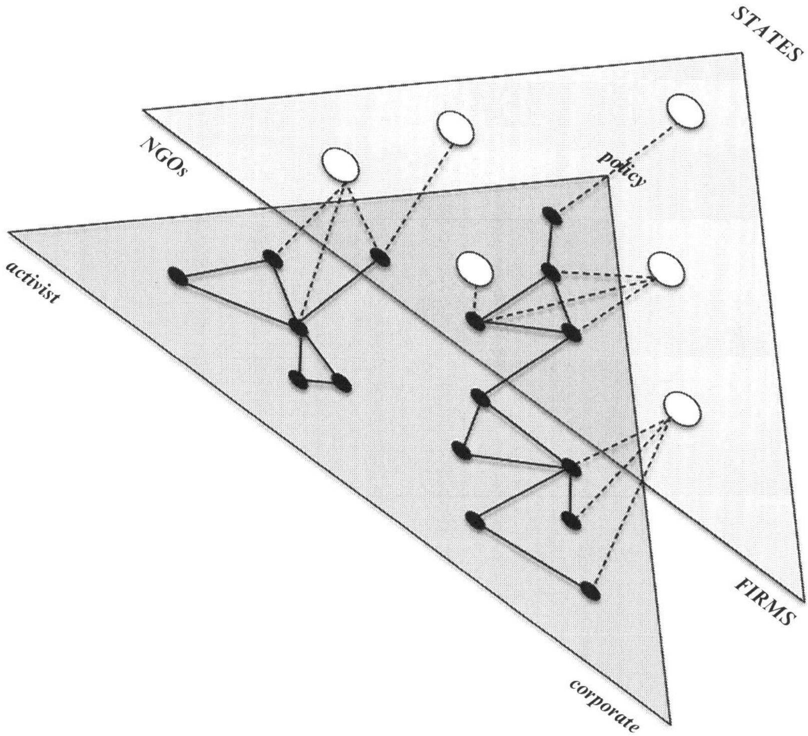

Source: Seabrooke and Wigan (2016, p. 359). For a range of cases following this framework see Seabrooke and Henriksen (2017).

Figure 4.2 Professional and organizational governance triangles

perhaps, activists have on the whole been locked out. In the wake of the Financial Crisis this has changed (see this volume, Chapter 3 for an account of the shift).

Figure 4.2 depicts the policy space where activists contest established practices and protest for radical reform. The figure adapts Abbott and Snidal's (2009) 'governance triangle', where organisations representing firms, states and non-governmental organisations occupy space and compete for supremacy.

In the case of international taxation, on the upper surface of Figure 4.2 states are represented by the Organisation for Economic Co-operation and Development (OECD), the European Commission, the African Union, the International Monetary Fund and the World Bank. Private sector organisations include the Institute of Chartered Accountants in England and Wales (ICAEW), the Business and Industry Advisory Committee (BIAC) to the OECD, Business Europe, the International Fiscal Association, the so-called Big Four accountancy firms, a host of multinational corporations, the International Bureau of Fiscal Documentation (IBFD) and the Heritage Foundation. The list of NGOs weighing in on the issues has exploded to include most prominently the Extractive Industries Transparency Initiative, Global Witness, World Development Movement, the European Network on Debt and Development, Save the Children, New Rules for Global Finance, Publish What You Pay, ActionAid, Oxfam, Christian Aid, the Global Alliance for Tax Justice, Citizens for Tax Justice and the Tax Justice Network. On the lower surface of Figure 4.2 are various professionals: lawyers, accountants, transfer pricing specialists, tax authority employees, economists, lobbyists and activists. These professionals compete for voice and authority on forms of knowledge deemed appropriate. Interactions on the lower surface impact organisational positions on the upper surface and define which organisations are situated to exercise issue control, or where the issue sits on the tax battlefield. Our analysis of the NGO field on the issue of taxation highlights the conditions for possible shifts in established positions within the triangle.

4.3 ACTIVATING EXPERTISE

The Tax Justice Network (TJN) is by the standards of internationally active NGOs rather small fry, with a budget that pales into insignificance when compared to that of more established and prominent organisations. Without an office to operate from and with threadbare administrative support, it has since its establishment in 2003 punched well above its weight. Policy tools now in play such as country-by-country reporting for multinational companies, the automatic exchange of tax information between public authorities and transparency on the beneficial ownership of trusts and companies are now either in the pipeline, on the statutes or subject to heated political debates. These policy tools have been pushed by TJN since its inception. At the time of that inception these tools were widely considered outlandish. NGOs with 'a polished image, well-known experts, and large budgets, are more likely to gain access to decision-makers' (Bloodgood 2011, p. 114). Given TJN's minimal resources, understanding policy impact in this case must lie outside resource-based explanations. Until 2007 TJN's sole employee was its director, and on only a part-time salary.

For TJN the harnessing of human resources has been critical. The core team in TJN is composed of professionals employed or formerly employed in finance, accounting, business, government and academia. The organisation's director until 2017, John Christensen, is a Jersey native, who worked on the island selling financial services for a major UK provider to firms and individuals eager to reduce contributions to the public exchequer. He then served as chief economic adviser to the States of Jersey. Another key figure, Richard Murphy, is a UK chartered accountant trained at what is now KPMG and is a serial entrepreneur. Prem Sikka has been a leading figure in academia, until recently professor of accounting at the University of Essex, and previously worked for an oil major in the City of London. Sol Picciotto is an emeritus professor at the Onati Institute, Spain and formerly a professor of law at a UK university. His training included the Chicago School of Law, where he attended as Commonwealth Fellow. In 2012 *The Economist* reported global private wealth held offshore as standing between $21 trillion and $33 trillion, or 18 to 25 per cent of all global financial assets, a figure subsequently referred to by the US Permanent Subcommittee. The figure was the work of James Henry, TJN's big hitter in the United States. Henry is the managing director of a private equity venture, served as a consultant and chief economist at McKinsey & Co and was business development manager in Jack Welch's office at General Electric. He is also the author of five monographs.

The key point here is that these core actors are not typical activists, whose commitment to a cause is prior to experience. All have spent time at the coal face, and in combination this core team has the expertise to traverse the complex issues constituting international taxation. Insiders turned outsiders are more able to campaign on the highly technical and trans-disciplinary issue of taxation and in doing so penetrate what is undoubtedly an arcane world normally reserved for a few deemed suitably qualified. Carpenter (2011) suggests the senior management of orthodox NGOs dedicate time to vetting which issues can be campaigned on. Highly technical issues, such as international taxation, are likely to be avoided, since these require considerable in-house expertise or the sourcing of expensive expertise outside the organisation (Seabrooke and Wigan 2015). Since large, well-resourced NGOs tend to be highly bureaucratic, they are consequently less flexible and ready to adopt a complex issue as required by a changing political climate. Indeed, when an issue is fast-moving, as tax has recently been, large NGOs may be simply unable to keep pace because of the gap between the speed of legitimate organisational decision-making procedures and that of issue evolution. At the core of TJN are a team of expert activists with the experience and knowledge to voice on international taxation. Voice that commands attention is backed by inter-disciplinary knowledge traversing and integrating diverse specialisms. Capacity in terms of expertise and knowledge is a precondition for impact. Moral authority in itself is not enough. Impact requires that knowledge and expertise are activated effectively in the right social domains (Seabrooke and Wigan 2013) and with the right ideational weapons.

4.4 IDEAS AS WEAPONS

Corporate reports address the performance of firms in relation to chosen criteria and provide a basis on which to compare that performance with other firms. Such reports may address environmental impact, gender equality, labour rights or corporate social responsibility. The dominant form of corporate report is the annual report. Annual reports provide a consolidated view of a firm's financial performance and primarily target investors as the chief stakeholder. Thus, their form facilitates evaluation in terms of future capital market performance. Since tax positions are constructed on past activity, established international accounting standards are inadequate (Murphy and Sikka 2015). Consolidated accounts provide a performance overview that, for MNCs, amalgamates the contributions of multiple entities within a group and across jurisdictions. This is a long-established practice. Investors receive a wealth of information in the annual report, including cash flow, turnover, employee numbers, borrowings, assets and profits. These numbers, however, are bundled together so that a stakeholder interested in reviewing the performance of a firm in a particular country would be unable to do so on the basis of an annual report. This matters for tax purposes. One reason why, identified in Chapter 2, is transfer pricing practice.

Estimates of the proportion of international trade accounted for by intra-firm trade, where constituent parts of the same multinational company buy and sell inputs from each other, vary enormously. At the top end, the OECD issued a report asserting that transfer pricing accounted for up to 60 per cent of the total (Neighbour 2002). A firm may choose to set transfer prices at a tax-advantaged level. For instance, a firm may choose to charge a subsidiary in high-tax Canada a disproportionate sum for an input to a production process. The receiving entity in turn may be located in a low-tax offshore financial centre such as Bermuda. The impact of the transaction in consequence is to move profits from a high-tax jurisdiction to a low-tax jurisdiction. The potential to actively construct a favourable tax position in this way has only increased with the advent of the 'intangible economy' where the assets of firms and inputs to production processes increasingly take abstract form. In abstract form, assets are eminently transferable (it is easier to move a server than a tractor) and difficult to price with a high degree of certainty. Given that the dominant 'arm's length' method for transfer pricing stipulates that transfer prices should ideally reflect a comparable price that would hold in a market transaction between unrelated parties, that intangible assets are predominantly intellectual property only exacerbates the potential problem (Bryan et al. 2017). Almost by definition no comparable prices exist for intellectual property.

Country-by-country reporting offers a potential solution to tax-motivated transfer (mis)pricing, providing transparency regarding how far a firm's activities in a particular jurisdiction tally with the level of activity in that jurisdiction. In requiring reports that provide comprehensive financial information on a country-by-country basis, opportunities for firms to allocate profits and losses in tax-advantaged ways via internal transactions are severely curtailed. For instance, where a firm reports considerable profit in a low-tax jurisdiction but has insignificant levels of sales, investment, assets, turnover and employees in that jurisdiction, tax authorities and civil society will be empowered to question that basis of a transfer price. Thus country-by-country reporting is an idea that vastly increases regulatory traction in captive and hierarchy wealth chains, where complexity militates against regulatory traction.

Corporate reporting has long been dominated by the International Accounting Standards Board (IASB), an organisation that 'closely aligns its organizational tasks with the expertise of its professionals, who are mainly accountants, economists and other capital market actors' (Seabrooke and Wigan 2016, p. 365; see also Leblond 2011, p. 449). IASB standards allow for geographical disclosures via IFRS 8 on 'operating segments', but here 'geographical segments' are not defined at the country level but as 'North America' or 'Asia-Pacific'. Therefore, when a company chooses to report financial information by geographical segment, the International Financial Reporting Standards framework does not require a breakdown by country. International accounting standards for geographical disclosures furnish investors with useful information but do not permit insight into the impact of tax arbitrage between national tax systems.

Templating here becomes a lever with which to prise open an entrenched issue. A key tactic used by the expert activists associated with TJN is the creation of treatments for complex technical issues on global tax reform. This tactic relies on gaining access from experience in the scientific and corporate domains, especially professional networks that assist in understanding technically complex issues. Activation points then follow in the policy and activist network domains, where templates are released to guide policy thinking, design and implementation. The template for the country-by-country reporting standard was drafted early in the history of TJN when the director, Christensen, asked Murphy what would be the single most important policy change necessary to promote greater tax equity. Murphy drafted the standard in response within three days.

The narrative of the expansion of CbCR as a policy tool bears witness to the power of ideas when carried forward by expert activists. The earliest example of a reporting framework mandating country-level disclosures was the Extractive Industries Transparency Initiative (EITI), which is examined in greater detail in Chapter 9. It was launched in 2002 by UK prime minister Tony Blair after a push forward from Publish What You Pay (PWYP), a transnational advocacy group of 650 members. PWYP at first understood its mission in terms of tackling the sources of corruption in developing countries, by tracing discrepancies between payments to governments and levels of investment and extraction. PWYP, however, did not have the expertise to move forward on the issue as primarily a corporate transfer pricing concern.

PWYP picked up the concept of CbCR in 2005 after Global Witness, a lead organisation in the network, published a report on the extractive industries that explicitly called for a new international financial reporting standard. This was drafted by TJN's Murphy. By 2005, PWYP began demanding that International Financial Reporting Standard 6 incorporate CbCR for the extractive sectors, and subsequently pushed for its inclusion in International Financial Reporting Standard 8.

While setting up a sub-group on the topic, the IASB, the private standard-setting body, took a largely obstructive stance with regard to the demands of PWYP. The IASB had been asked to consider adding country-by-country reporting requirements to its agenda. Feedback from the 2011 agenda consultation strongly and consistently highlighted that this should not be a priority for the IASB (IASB 2013, p. 22). However, by allying itself with PWYP and grafting a tax justice agenda on to this network's narrower corruption agenda, it allowed CbCR to become a readily available tool for tackling tax avoidance. TJN's CbCR template then sparked interest from the European Commission, and in 2010 a Directive was put forward to apply the financial reporting standard either to all companies or to extractives (Baden and Wigan 2017). TJN played a critical consulting role in providing the template for applying CbCR to the extractives industry, with TJN associate Richard Murphy noting that 'NGOs just don't get accounting'.

Once the CbCR template was active in European policy it was noted by the Big Four accountancy firms and the larger professional service firms. PricewaterhouseCoopers, for example, issued a report on CbCR in late 2013 discussing how a more minimal form of CbCR had become a new standard in the EITI framework, in Dodd–Frank legislation in the US, in the EU Accounting Directive, and in the Capital Requirements Directive

(CRD) IV, which is critical to the Basel III international regulatory regime for banking within Europe (see Lesage and Kaçar 2013 for the distinction between 'maximalist' and 'minimalist' CbCR). PricewaterhouseCoopers' report explicitly acknowledges TJN as the founder of CbCR and uses the TJN designation of what constitutes CbCR as the basis for comparison between regulatory regimes. CbCR has been incorporated into multiple national fiscal systems in the wake of the OECD's Base Erosion and Profit Shifting initiative (OECD 2015). The key section of BEPS related to transfer pricing, Action 13, provides a model for CbCR.

Thus TJN's role in providing policy templates to the activist and policy network domains has also had a significant impact on how the biggest private players in tax, finance and accounting are treating global tax justice issues.

> There is a new emphasis on CbCR as technology that can ease the rift between the state and international capital. As a form of corporate financial reporting, CbCR fuses technical expertise with claims to how firms should pay taxes. Prior to the emergence of CbCR, accounting standards served a constituency perceived solely in terms of investors. That has changed, with NGOs providing an active voice on accounting issues, provided they have the right professionals to power their ideas with expertise. Crucially, what was at first promoted as a limited purpose technology, combatting corruption, has been inflated to become an all-purpose technology available for policy-makers. (Seabrooke and Wigan 2016, p. 368)

4.5 BATTLING WITH BENCHMARKS

Benchmarks provide a means to track performance and adjudicate on the quality of actor behaviour. Gauging this performance on a uniform measure, benchmarks have become a powerful tool in global governance policing a variety of actors on issues ranging across human rights protection, innovation levels, climate change performance and degree of state failure (Broome and Quirk 2015). Issues addressed by benchmarks such as the Fragile/Failed States Index are often plagued by indeterminacy. This indeterminacy calls for authoritative adjudication if a benchmark is to gain traction and have impact. This is where claims to expertise matter. A benchmark, given intrinsic indeterminacy, is likely to face resistance, and challenges must be fended off. The science informing benchmark composition is likely to be attacked (this volume, Chapter 11). These attacks must be rebuffed. Our work on benchmarking for global economic justice (Seabrooke and Wigan 2015) has traced the steps necessary to construct a benchmark that is revolutionary rather than reformist in intent. The development of benchmarks requires three elements: (1) salience, that the community of concern is aware of the issue and views it as important; (2) will, that activists and expert activists will carry the message forward; and (3) expertise, that benchmarks created can be defended as accurate representations of what is happening on the issue of concern. In terms of the menu of tactics we identify with TJN, benchmarking is a form of narrating. Narratives can be constructed to promote radical change or reform. Tests of salience, will and expertise differ accordingly.

Reformist benchmarks go with the flow and align with a widely-accepted normative order. These benchmarks chime with extant public and private concerns and therefore face lower barriers in meeting tests of salience, will and expertise. Reformist benchmarks are often mounted and sustained by larger NGOs, which, owing to bureaucratisation, corporatisation and reliance on funds from a broad support base, are likely to respond to organisational interests in maintaining the status quo (Hopgood 2006; Dauvergne and LeBaron 2014). Agenda vetting is important here, as some issues and lines of attack will likely threaten the interests of the larger organisation owing to complexity and ambiguity (Carpenter 2011). Larger NGOs seek to construct 'scale-free' networks that members join because of easily communicable issues with obvious political and moral salience. Such NGOs often cooperate closely with firms and other established organisations such as the World Bank or International Monetary Fund from which expertise can be sourced for benchmark creation. These collaborating organisations in turn will assist in ensuring sufficient political will. In sum, large established NGOs face incentives that push them to establish benchmarks that are easily incorporated into established normative orders. These organisations are less likely to push forward on a benchmark that mounts a challenge to the established order and promotes radical change.

An example of a reformist benchmark is Transparency International (TI)'s Corruption Perceptions Index (CPI). Established in 1993 by Peter Eigen, who had retired from the World Bank, Transparency International is a large NGO with over 100 national chapters. The CPI was launched in 1995 in a post-Cold War context where liberal internationalism included a commitment to democracy promotion. Wang and Rosenau argue that the CPI would more likely succeed 'if it does not contradict the interests of powerful actors' (2001, p. 41). The Organisation for Economic Co-operation and Development was already pushing forward an anti-corruption agenda with its members in 1997 agreeing to criminalise the paying of bribes to foreign officials. Powerful states and corporations shared an interest in reducing corruption in capital importing states. The CPI in consequence fell on fertile ground and is now widely used across the public and private sector. The World Bank, the International Monetary Fund, the Bank for International Settlements and the Organisation for

Economic Co-operation and Development have, for instance, incorporated the CPI into governance indicators.

To distinguish revolutionary from reformist benchmarks it is worth noting the composition of the index. The CPI indexes countries on a scale of 1 to 100, with a score of 100 positive and 0 negative. It draws on polls and surveys from political risk firms, other civil society organisations, business schools and international organisations including the World Bank. Transparency International itself makes no claim to strong legal expertise, and instead index creation relies on extant analyses and expertise drawn from outside. Importantly, the index emphasises 'institutional quality, public officials' proclivity to demand bribes, and the dependence of business performance on corrupt transactions. The CPI does not provide a full picture of corruption in a given jurisdiction, but focuses on political and administrative corruption' (Seabrooke and Wigan 2015, p. 895). Deploying a narrow concept of corruption has led to some criticism of the index on the basis of its neglect of the supply side of corruption and its lack of focus on private actors (Cobham 2013). In 2016 Switzerland, Germany, the Netherlands, Singapore and Luxembourg held positions in the top ten of the index, indicating that these countries hosted little to no corruption. Importantly, these countries are depicted as central to tax injustice in the revolutionary benchmark now addressed.

While reformist benchmarks draw on established external expertise including public and private actors and organisations already committed to the ideal the benchmarks seek to police and impose, revolutionary benchmarks face markedly different conditions. External experts may not be inclined to lend resources to the effort of benchmark construction; this means that actors must be persuaded that issue salience needs to be created, rather than assume it will be generated automatically. Revolutionary benchmarks swim against the tide in aspiring to construct narratives where analysis confronts an existing orthodoxy and units in the system under scrutiny must be re-defined, meaning that organisations leading on benchmark creation must be able to successfully push uphill. Larger, established non-governmental organisations may not be able to. The creation of TJN's Financial Secrecy Index highlights the distinctive inputs that reformist and revolutionary benchmarking demand and provides insights into how NGOs may be able to precipitate more revolutionary change to the international tax regime.

The FSI ranks countries and jurisdictions by the level of opacity provided by their financial systems. This is indexed on the basis of two factors, the level of transparency provided by law and regulation and the size of the financial sector in terms of external business. Legal and regulatory opacity is weighted by footprint in global finance. A jurisdiction that flagrantly disregards international norms and explicitly seeks to attract business from elsewhere on the basis of severe regulatory laxity may, if not a significant global player, not be identified as a leading transgressor. Conversely, a jurisdiction, such as the United States, that fares better in terms of regulatory and legal standards, but accounts for a large proportion of international capital market activity, will, by design, be ranked poorly. The logic here is that it is not only what you do but how much you do that matters in the promotion of global economic justice. The revolutionary intent of the FSI includes aspirations to transform how the issues of corruption and 'harmful tax competition' (OECD 1998) are seen and who the chief culprits are. All this might well rub powerful interests up the wrong way.

In consequence revolutionary benchmarking follows a distinctive path. Rather than issue selection being a function of passing internal gatekeepers charged with policing the bounds of political acceptability and vetting agendas for how they might play with a broad, financially critical support base, expert activists select issues and move straight to benchmark creation. For TJN, consultation with external stakeholders is minimal, and expertise is internal. This increases the vulnerability of the index to challenge later, when such challenges are mounted on methodological grounds. If a benchmark confronts established expertise and expert consensus, external actors may choose to simply ignore the index or choose to actively defend territory. Reacting to the FSI in 2012 the head of tax policy and administration at the OECD, Pascal Saint-Amans (2012, p. 27), stated:

> I wish that their financial secrecy index would be a bit more robust. They have a secrecy index that built on a number of criteria that are disputable and based on information that is outdated. [. . .] They came up with a financial secrecy level made up of a mathematical formula to get countries they want on the top of the list to be on the top of the list. That's disingenuous, it's not fair, it's not good and it sends the wrong message.

The FSI has faced similar challenges from implicated jurisdictions and economists contracted to question methodology. In light of these challenges the expert activists in TJN have to step in to defend the index. Despite challenges, and in the absence of 'open ears', the FSI is now well established in the broader non-governmental organisation world, with ActionAid and Christian Aid incorporating it in campaign materials and the Center for Global Development using it as one component of its own Commitment to Development Index, measuring the developmental value of OECD country policies. In the private sector the FSI is used by sustainability rating agencies, and the Basel Institute on Governance uses the index in compiling the Basel Anti-Money Laundering Index (Seabrooke and Wigan 2015, p. 902). Despite opposition from well-resourced established and authoritative players, TJN has sustained a radical narration of global economic injustice, deploying internal expertise based on corporate and scientific experience to spark action in the policy and activist domains.

Non-governmental organisations use benchmarks to push agendas and provide leverage points on issues of choice. Large organisations may find it difficult to launch indexes which are complex, politically sensitive, transformative and untested. This is where looser organisations with high levels of internal expertise such as TJN have a crucial role to play, deploying this internal expertise in high-risk, high-reward strategies. Revolutionary benchmarks must persuade non-governmental organisations to buy in; opposition from established actors who may have an interest in suppressing the upstart index must be met and quashed; push-back from political authorities must be overcome. Bolstering reform with an established normative order meets lower hurdles, but, if pushing to change that normative order, the demands are high.

4.6 CONCLUSION

This chapter has addressed questions of how NGOs can impact on corporate tax reform and the governance of global wealth chains to promote greater global economic justice. A key aspect of economic justice is taxation, or who pays what, where and when towards the provision of public goods. Issues of taxation are complex and multi-faceted, calling for expertise in accounting, law, finance and economics if intervention is to be effective. Many NGOs are replete with moral authority and populated by NGO professionals, with low levels of experience in technical policy arenas outside the activist domain. These NGOs may also be constrained in adopting issues which are difficult to communicate, politically sensitive, and likely to divide opinion in a supporter base that is crucial to an organisation's financial sustainability. Particularly where the policy environment is fast-changing, large NGOs may be hindered by bureaucratic procedures from striking while the iron is hot. Catalysing an effective intervention from civil society on such issues and in such fast-changing environments requires multiple and highly developed disciplinary and professional skills. Our analysis of the Tax Justice Network suggests that in this context, smaller organisations may pack a bigger punch.

The cases addressed here suggest that work on NGOs in international politics and the international political economy might develop sensitivity to issue and organisational specificity to distinguish when and how impact is mounted with more or less success. The chapter encourages engagement with strategic and tactical range in the non-governmental arena and asks us to pay careful attention to agency and agent knowledge. It also suggests that the analyses of change in networks and change driven by networks can be usefully augmented with a focus on organising as opposed to assuming characteristics based on the type of organisation. While we note the peculiarities of taxation as a campaign issue, it may be that effecting change in other areas of global economic activity is subject to similar conditions of possibility.

REFERENCES

Abbott, K. and D. Snidal (2009), 'The Governance Triangle: Regulatory Standards, Institutions and the Shadow of the State', in W. Mattli and N. Woods (eds), *The Politics of Global Regulation*, Princeton, NJ: Princeton University Press, pp. 44–88.

Arrighi, G. (1994), *The Long Twentieth Century: Money, Power, and the Origins of Our Times*, London: Verso.

Baden, A. and D. Wigan (2017), 'Professional Activists on Tax Transparency', in L. Seabrooke and L. Folke Henriksen (eds), *Professional Networks in Transnational Governance*, Cambridge: Cambridge University Press, pp. 130–146.

Bloodgood, E. (2011), 'The Interest Group Analogy: International Non-Governmental Advocacy Organizations in International Politics', *Review of International Studies* **37** (1), 93–120.

Broome, A. and J. Quirk (eds) (2015), 'The Politics of Numbers: The Normative Agendas of Global Benchmarking', *Review of International Studies* **41** (5), 813–1010.

Bryan, D., M. Rafferty and D. Wigan (2017), 'Capital Unchained: Finance, Intangible Assets and the Double Life of Capital in the Offshore World', *Review of International Political Economy* **24** (1), 56–86.

Carpenter, C. (2011), 'Vetting the Advocacy Agenda: Networks, Centrality and the Paradox of Weapons Norms', *International Organization* **65** (1), 69–102.

Christensen, R. (forthcoming), 'Technical Battles for Corporate Tax Transparency', in L. Seabrooke and D. Wigan (eds), *Global Wealth Chains: Asset Strategies in the World Economy*, Oxford: Oxford University Press.

Cobham, A. (2013), 'Corrupting Perceptions: Why Transparency International's Flagship Corruption Index Falls Short', *Foreign Policy*, published electronically 22 July, available at http://foreignpolicy.com/2013/07/22/corrupting-perceptions/ (accessed 19 June 2018).

Cooley, A. and J. Ron (2002), 'The NGO Scramble: Organizational Insecurity and the Political Economy of Transnational Action', *International Security* **27** (1), 5–39.

Dauvergne, P. and G. LeBaron (2014), *Protest Inc.: The Corporatization of Activism*, Cambridge: Polity Press.

Eccleston, R. (2012), *The Dynamics of Global Economic Governance: The Financial Crisis, the OECD and the Politics of International Tax Cooperation*, Cheltenham, UK and Northampton, MA, USA: Edward Elgar Publishing.

Eccleston, R. and F. Gray (2014), 'Foreign Accounts Tax Compliance Act and American Leadership in the Campaign against International Tax Evasion: Revolution or False Dawn?', *Global Policy* **5** (3), 321–333.
Gereffi, G. (1994), 'The Organisation of Buyer-Driven Global Commodity Chains: How US Retailers Shape Overseas Production Networks', in G. Gereffi and M. Korzeniewicz (eds), *Commodity Chains and Global Capitalism*, Westport, CT: Praeger, pp. 95–122.
Gereffi, G., J. Humphrey and T. Sturgeon (2005), 'The Governance of Global Value Chains', *Review of International Political Economy* **12** (1), 78–104.
Hakelberg, L. (2015), 'The Power Politics of International Tax Cooperation: Luxembourg, Austria and the Automatic Exchange of Tax Information', *Journal of European Public Policy* **22** (3), 409–428.
Hopgood, S. (2006), *Keepers of the Flame: Understanding Amnesty International*, Ithaca, NY: Cornell University Press.
IASB (International Accounting Standards Board) (2013), *Discussion Forum – Financial Reporting Disclosure: Feedback Statement*, London: IASB.
Leblond, P. (2011), 'EU, US and International Accounting Standards: A Delicate Balancing Act in Governing Global Finance', *Journal of European Public Policy* **18** (3), 443–461.
Lesage, D. and Y. Kaçar (2013), 'Tax Justice through Country-by-Country Reporting: An Analysis of the Idea's Political Journey', in J. Leaman and A. Waris (eds), *Tax Justice and the Political Economy of Global Capitalism, 1945 to the Present*, New York: Berghahn Books, pp. 262–282.
Murphy, R. and P. Sikka (2015), *Unitary Taxation: Tax Base and the Role of Accounting*, Working Paper No. 34, Brighton: International Centre for Tax and Development, Institute of Development Studies.
Neighbour, J. (2002), 'Transfer Pricing: Keeping It at Arm's Length', *OECD Observer*, Paris: OECD Publishing.
OECD (Organisation for Economic Co-operation and Development) (1998), *Harmful Tax Competition: An Emerging Global Issue*, Paris: OECD Publishing.
OECD (Organisation for Economic Co-operation and Development) (2015) *BEPS 2015 Final Reports*, Paris: OECD Publishing, available at http://www.oecd.org/tax/beps-2015-final-reports.htm (accessed 20 October 2017).
Palan, R. (1998), 'Trying to Have Your Cake and Eating It: How and Why the State System Has Created Offshore', *International Studies Quarterly* **42**, 625–644.
Palan, R. (2003), *The Offshore World: Virtual Spaces and the Commercialization of Sovereignty*, Ithaca, NY: Cornell University Press.
Palan, R. and D. Wigan (2014), 'Herding Cats and Taming Tax Havens: The US Strategy of "Not in My Backyard"', *Global Policy* **5** (3), 334–343.
Picciotto, S. (1992), *International Business Taxation: A Study in the Internationalization of Business Regulation*, Cambridge: Cambridge University Press.
Picciotto, S. (2011), *Regulating Global Corporate Capitalism*, Cambridge: Cambridge University Press.
Picciotto, S. (2015), 'Indeterminacy, Complexity, Technocracy and the Reform of International Corporate Taxation', *Social and Legal Studies* **24** (2), 165–184.
Rixen, T. (2008), *The Political Economy of International Tax Governance: Transformation of the State*, Basingstoke: Palgrave Macmillan.
Saint-Amans, P. (2012), 'Pascal Saint-Amans Finds His Stride in Owens's Shoes', *International Tax Review* **23** (1), 27.

Seabrooke, L. and L.F. Henriksen (eds) (2017), *Professional Networks in Transnational Governance*, Cambridge: Cambridge University Press.
Seabrooke, L. and D. Wigan (2013), *Emergent Entrepreneurs in Transnational Advocacy Networks: Professional Mobilization in the Fight for Global Tax Justice*, Working Paper No. 41, GR:EEN, Global Reordering: Evolution through European Networks, FP7, available at http://pipesproject.eu/assets/GREEN41.pdf (accessed 1 November 2017).
Seabrooke, L. and D. Wigan (2015), 'How Activists Use Benchmarks: Reformist and Revolutionary Benchmarks for Global Economic Justice', *Review of International Studies* **41** (5), 887–904.
Seabrooke, L. and D. Wigan (2016), 'Powering Ideas through Expertise: Switchmen in Global Tax Battles', *Journal of European Public Policy* **23** (3), 357–374.
Seabrooke, L. and D. Wigan (2017a), 'Brexit and Global Wealth Chains', *Globalizations* **14** (6), 820–829.
Seabrooke, L. and D. Wigan (2017b), 'The Governance of Global Wealth Chains', *Review of International Political Economy* **24** (1), 1–26.
Seabrooke, L. and D. Wigan (2018), *Global Tax Battles: The Fight to Govern Corporate and Elite Wealth*, Oxford: Oxford University Press.
Sharman, J.C. (2006), *Havens in a Storm: The Struggle for Global Tax Regulation*, Ithaca, NY: Cornell University Press.
Stroup, S.S. and W.H. Wong (2017), *The Authority Trap: Strategic Choices of International NGOs*, Ithaca, NY: Cornell University Press.
Vlcek, W. (2008), 'Development vs. Terrorism: Money Transfers and EU Financial Regulations in the UK', *British Journal of Politics and International Relations* **10** (2), 286–302.
Wang, H. and J. Rosenau (2001), 'Transparency International and Corruption as an Issue of Global Governance', *Global Governance* **7** (1), 25–49.

5. Private regulatory approaches and international tax policy

Aynsley Kellow

5.1 INTRODUCTION

The 2003 G8 summit was hosted by France in Évian-les-Bains, a spa town on the southern shores of Lake Geneva. Évian had the advantage of displacing most of the security risks on to Switzerland, as the nearest airport capable of receiving the jets of the leaders and their entourages was Geneva, across the lake. French security dealt readily with the risk of protests from anti-globalisation activists, who were seemingly more prevalent at the turn of the millennium than now, but were simply displaced to Switzerland, where they did considerable damage to banks and other businesses in Geneva and as far away as Vevey, where the Nestlé headquarters are located.

The burghers of Geneva anticipated trouble and took various actions. The WTO remained closed, and many businesses covered their shopfronts with industrial ply. A few rather courageously eschewed the plywood in favour of displaying the rainbow flag used in various forms by numerous groups including the International Cooperative Alliance and the Peace Movement, the latter often overlaid with the Italian *PACE*. The intention was clearly to express some solidarity with the protestors and thus receive a free pass.

It worked – to an extent. But the protestors included some hardened anarchists, who displayed no sympathy with such expressions of commitment and smashed some of the windows regardless.

This story is something of a metaphor for private governance regimes that seek to improve outcomes using various forms of certification, which commenced with Fairtrade in 1988. Critics have suggested that certification schemes amount to an 'extortion racket' (Wilson 2011), but they are – like the G8 example above – perhaps more akin to secular versions of Passover. Corporations have come under increasing scrutiny from political campaigns (Manheim 2001; this volume, Chapter 3), all the way from the nature of products and process methods to overall corporate social responsibility (CSR), and, while some have attacked CSR as a needless distraction from the responsibility of corporations to obey the law while maximising returns to shareholders (Henderson 2009), most corporations have to some extent sought to engage with such issues, which are broadly referred to as their 'social licence'.

After widespread disappointment at attempts to prevent international taxation competition eroding the revenue base of governments (such as the Harmful Tax Competition initiative in the OECD – see this volume, Chapters 1 and 2), there has been a focus on whether multinational corporations in particular are 'paying their fair share', particularly in the UK, where post-FC austerity measures (see this volume, Chapter 3) have caused many, from the charity Christian Aid to the more spontaneously formed UK Uncut, to seek voluntary governance remedies outside of formal governance institutions. It should be noted that perceptions that large corporations are not paying enough tax are not always sustained by evidence. In Australia, for example, a study found that 'Larger corporate tax payers face, ceteris paribus, a higher tax burden than do smaller corporate tax payers' (Davidson and Heaney 2012, p. 102).

A corporation certification scheme, the Fair Tax Mark (FTM), was established in February 2014. As Chapter 10 describes in detail, FTM uses a set of metrics to assess companies on their transparency and tax conduct, with those meeting a minimum of 13 criteria out of 20 awarded certification. The aim is to highlight those companies that are paying the right amount of tax, rather than to sanction those that are not. Two years on, only ten corporations, mostly smaller regional or national companies in the UK, had achieved certification. Only Lush Cosmetics was a multinational corporation likely to have much opportunity for profit shifting, although the sole FT100 company, SSE plc, did have an Irish subsidiary with a project in the Netherlands.

It is too early to ascertain whether Fair Tax Mark will certify large numbers of corporations, especially those with the opportunity to minimise tax. While the founders of the FTM are satisfied with progress to date there are grounds for pessimism. This is because the scheme requires a positive change in consumer and investor preferences to favour the virtuous, and a limited list of certified corporations, mostly domestic players, is unlikely to make much impact on international tax practice. There is no certified product as such, so consumers will have to select products of certified companies.

This chapter examines the prospects for voluntary tax governance in the international tax arena by first reflecting on some aspects of tax as a policy problem that inform a subsequent discussion about the nature and limits of certification schemes. It concludes that we should not be too sanguine about the prospects of FTM (or any other tax certification schemes) and suggests that the issues should be best addressed by nation-states and international instruments, although it also notes that it has been questionable whether sufficient political support exists in some domestic jurisdictions, particularly in Switzerland and the European Union (especially Ireland, Luxembourg and the Netherlands), to address the issues at stake. While reforms such as unitary reporting or the harmonisation of tax rates and instruments such as international tax credits might be worth exploring, the prospects for the necessary international agreement are not good.

The chapter concludes that the characteristics of the tax policy problem do not make it amenable to action through a private governance regime. It involves at its core intangibles, rather than 'brandable' products, including profits that can be shifted between jurisdictions; unlike product certification schemes, there are no economic interests that might support civil society campaigns and counter the pernicious effects of 'beggar-thy-neighbour' tax competition; and there are numerous administrative problems. All this suggests that NGOs would do better to press for policy action at the level of nation-states.

5.2 SOME REFLECTIONS ON TAX AS A POLICY PROBLEM

Taxes serve two purposes: a means of raising revenue, but often also a means to alter behaviour. A carbon tax is not intended to raise revenue, but to reduce emissions. Such taxes are regulatory, although they often come to be seen as sources of revenue, and the dilemma for governments is often that their original purpose can become lost.

Some taxes are a little different again, being effectively charges to recover costs for goods and services provided. Such taxes range from airport arrival taxes to taxes or charges to recover the costs of providing public roads. But taxes are frequently seen primarily, if not only, in redistributive terms, and corporate taxation is almost always seen in redistributive terms, but taxing company profits prior to distribution depends for its redistributive impact upon the ownership structure of the company in question: it is clearly redistributive with a single private owner, but less clearly so if it is owned by a large number of union pension funds, but the perception of redistribution drives much of the rhetoric behind attempts by social movements to develop private governance tax regimes.

The likely success of private governance regimes (and, indeed, government regimes) depends crucially on some of the characteristics of their targets, and it is to these characteristics the discussion now turns.

Tangibles and Intangibles

With company tax at around 5 per cent of GDP, Australia was considered by its Treasury to have a robust corporate tax base, with its strength derived from some of the characteristics of its economy (Kellow and Carroll 2017). For example, a large proportion of Australia's exports are tangible, consisting of commodities such as iron ore, coal, LNG, aluminium and other processed resources. Such tangibles are more easily taxed than intangibles. It is infinitely easier to address issues such as transfer pricing when exports are carried in 200 000 dwt bulk carriers than when dealing with intangibles, and the London Metal Exchange sets prices against which contract sales might be assessed. Additionally, iron ore producers such as BHP Billiton and Rio Tinto have, over the past decade, tended to favour the spot market to long-term contract sales, and so – even if they have been using marketing hubs in Singapore where taxes are lower – there is some accountability in terms of pricing.

The distinction between tangibles and intangibles is an important one for taxation, and for our broader understanding of business politics, as are distinctions between the resources sector and more 'footloose' industries. Stephen Krasner pointed out that the structural power of business varies from one sector to another. A mineral exploitation company needs access to territory where deposits are located, but a clothing manufacturer can operate anywhere there is cheap labour and transportation, so the state has more leverage over natural resource developers than clothing manufacturers. 'Oil, gold, copper, and tin do not migrate across international boundaries. Multinational corporations cannot develop these resources without permission from the state' (Krasner 1995, p. 272).

Krasner's point, while valid, should be treated with caution. While resources are immobile, capital is mobile (as are profits), and, if there are multiple opportunities for resource development, the structural power of business can still be substantial, as was the case with a resource rent tax proposal in Australia (Kellow 2016). The tangible/intangible issue is exacerbated by the centrality of intellectual property rights issues and international transactions. All tax regimes were established before we had e-commerce (see Chapter 1 for a historical overview), and e-commerce in general gives rise to problems with consumption taxes, sales taxes and value-added taxes – but how are royalty payments for intellectual property to be treated?

The problem is readily apparent with Google and Apple. Google's core business is communication of information and revenue from pay-per-click advertising. Apple is also overwhelmingly an intellectual property enterprise: the manufactured cost of an iPhone 6 was about $200; most of the rest was intellectual property (Luckerson 2014). Apple makes its money primarily by designing and selling desirable hardware and the operating systems and applications that run on it. The iPhones, iPads, MacBooks and iMacs are tangible, but the rest is intangible and difficult to place a value on. It is important, however, that we note the differences between companies such as Apple and Google.

Apple has booked offshore profits of $181.1 billion, the largest of any US company, and has paid effectively only a 2.3 per cent tax rate on its offshore profits, largely by booking its profits in Ireland (European Commission 2014; McIntyre et al. 2015, p. 12; European Commission 2016b). It uses three tax haven subsidiaries. Google (now Alphabet Inc) has booked $47.4 billion, and uses only two tax haven subsidiaries. But Apple and Google have exhibited contrasting behaviour, despite both being essentially 'growth plays' for their shareholders, not paying dividends for many years. Google stock, for example, appreciated tenfold over the decade to 2015. This is important, because dividends would be taxable in the hands of the shareholders – with about two-thirds of its stock held by institutions. (The role of shareholders should not be overlooked.)

Apple started paying a meaningful dividend of about 2 per cent, under pressure from shareholders to return its significant pile of cash, which has now reached perhaps $150 billion. Unlike Google, Apple does not invest much in R&D, so the problem for it is what it might do with the cash. It is thought that its strategy is to wait for a tax holiday or significant corporate tax cuts before repatriating its profits to the US, something which has occurred in the past and is likely with the passage of the Trump administration's Tax Cuts and Jobs Act in December 2017.

Google, on the other hand, has never paid a dividend, as it invests heavily in R&D and wants to have the capacity to make large corporate acquisitions (like YouTube in 2006) or fund the development of something like Google Fiber, with a potential investment in tens of billions, or driverless cars. Generally, dividends are seen by many technology and growth companies as indicating they are unable to make a return from reinvesting profits in their own business. Amazon has been able to reinvest *all* of its earnings into its growth, so has a very small cash position relative to others.

Reinvesting in R&D is generally tax deductible, but whether it is treated as a capitalised expense, amortised over many years or is an operating expense is a complex matter. Repatriation of offshore profits is taxable, so there is a strong incentive not to pay dividends back to shareholders, as the company would pay the US corporate tax on them and then shareholders would have to pay dividend tax. Both Apple and Alphabet make the majority of their profits overseas.

The relationship between shareholders and management is also important. Holding a 'fortress' of cash helps management maintain their independence, as do voting structures that often prevent shareholders from affecting senior management other than by selling the stock and putting price pressure on them.

Intellectual property plays a central role in the avoidance of corporate tax by Starbucks, along with some deft use of jurisdictional boundaries and differential tax rates (Jolly 2014; Worstall 2014; Alderman 2015). Starbucks reportedly paid only £8.6 million in corporation tax in the UK over 14 years, despite generating over £3 billion in sales – and no tax payments on £1.3 billion of sales in the three years prior to 2012. The UK branch of Starbucks pays high licensing fees, causing it to declare losses. The UK subsidiary pays patent fees to the US subsidiary and the Netherlands subsidiary (where corporation tax is lower than in the UK), and the Swiss subsidiary provides other 'miscellaneous services'.

Responsibility for this lies with the Netherlands government, which granted a special tax rate to Starbucks' European headquarters, but also the tax law of the Netherlands, alone in the EU, permits companies to transfer royalties collected from other countries to tax havens without incurring taxes. The coffee served to UK consumers is purchased from the subsidiary in Switzerland, but never touches the ground there, although quality assurance is conducted there.

Green coffee beans are bought from a Swiss subsidiary (a Lausanne-based firm, Starbucks Coffee Trading Co) and then sold at a 20 per cent mark-up to the roasting subsidiary in Amsterdam, which then sells the roasted beans to Starbucks outlets. In 2008, tax authorities in the Netherlands issued a new tax ruling for Starbucks, which resulted in the coffee roasting subsidiary sending large royalty payments to a mysterious company called Alki for use of a bean roasting recipe, which the European Commission in October 2015 stated to be grossly inflated.

The recipe was essentially a set of instructions and the temperature at which to roast the beans, but counting it as intellectual property allowed Starbucks' roasting unit to shift most of its profit to Alki in the form of royalties, practically wiping out the Dutch tax bill. The EC noted that no other Starbucks companies or roasters paid royalties for the same information. Intellectual property, in other words, is hard to tax. The Irish, French and German subsidiaries are also either owned by or indebted to the Dutch subsidiary, which charges them higher interest rates than the group pays to borrow.

Starbucks is doing nothing illegal, and the matter has been somewhat exaggerated: it is the laws of the Netherlands and Switzerland (and those of their host countries) that permit what is happening – including transactions for royalties and interest payments at other than market rates. At parliamentary hearings on tax avoidance in Britain in 2012, executives of Google, Amazon and Starbucks maintained their tax policies were legal because EU law lets companies based in one member state operate across the 28-country bloc (Jolly 2014; this volume, Chapter 7). Moreover, the tax saved by Starbucks using the Dutch arrangement is minimal, estimated by the Commission at a mere €20 million over a decade (in a global turnover of about $US14 billion per annum). The Commission also found that the royalty payments were not excessive. Starbucks both operates its own outlets as subsidiaries and licenses franchises, and charges both the same price (Worstall 2014).

Addressing such matters should not be beyond the capacity of sovereign states, and the United Kingdom had some recent success with the £130 million payment by Google, although EU law has not always been helpful. For example, the European Court of Justice in 2002 in *Lankhorst-Hohorst GmbH v Finanzamt Steinfurt* ruled that German thin capitalisation laws were contrary to EU law, leading to a review of such laws in Germany, France and the UK. The Commission has recently demonstrated increased vigour, however, pursuing McDonald's, Fiat and Amazon in Luxembourg, with a probe into the possibility that the Grand Duchy may have approved hundreds of tax deals for multinational corporations (European Commission 2015a, 2015b, 2015c, 2016a). Leaked documents revealed in 2014 that more than 340 companies such as PepsiCo Inc, Ikea Group and FedEx Corp transferred profits to the country through 'creative' tax arrangements (Sebag and Bodoni 2015).

The EC has also recently cracked down on a tax scheme in Belgium, in place since 2005, that allowed certain corporations to reduce their tax base by between 50 and 90 per cent to discount for so-called excess profits allegedly resulting from being part of a multinational group. The ruling (subject to appeal) would affect mainly European multinationals: of the €700 million in back taxes to be repaid, €500 million would come from European companies (European Commission 2016a; Fairless 2016).

Intellectual property also impacts the politics of regulation, especially international regulation. Patents are limited monopolies allowing the developers of inventions to recoup their costs of development and make excess profits for a limited time. Patents impact substantially on international regulation of products such as chemicals. Copyright is rather more insidious, and typically extends for much longer – which might be acceptable for authors, artists and composers – but, as the Starbucks example shows, can allow some questionable control to be exerted. Is the value of the Starbucks brand really worth what the UK subsidiary is paying to use it? Does the price charged to licensees set a valid market price for the price paid by its subsidiaries? Copyright allows control and sometimes dubious restrictions to be placed on competitors.

Profits and Shareholders

One unusual feature of the Australian taxation regime diminishes the scope for profit shifting: the dividend imputation system (introduced in 1987) provides an incentive for business to recognise profits, since resident shareholders receive a tax credit for company tax already paid – often at 100 per cent of the 30 per cent company tax paid. This lowers the tax on dividend income substantially (to zero for some) and creates pressure from shareholders for companies to generate the credits by paying company tax: should they avoid paying Australian company tax, the benefits of dividend imputation will be similarly diminished. The way in which income is treated for imputation purposes is a matter of debate, and the treatment of foreign income can affect investment patterns by Australian-owned companies (ANZ 2015). New Zealand has a similar system, and the UK introduced imputation in 1973, but abolished this provision in 1999.

This encourages companies to pay tax where their shareholders are resident, but it depends for its full impact upon co-location of taxable earnings and shareholders, and will not work as well with globally dispersed earnings or globally dispersed shareholding. But this draws attention to the need to consider jurisdictional boundaries and the distribution of ownership, corporate location and earnings in considering the issue of corporate taxation – and to consider the nature of the enterprise in question, as the point about intangibles highlights. The US grants credit for taxes paid offshore, but, since a major problem is the failure of corporations to repatriate *any* profits, this does not come into play. President Trump's 2017 reforms reduced the rate for repatriated profits to 8–15 per cent.

Again, the nature and size of taxes on dividend income are likely to have effects on behaviour. The existence of dividend imputation is one factor, but so too is capital gains tax. Capital-intensive industries like mining are more likely to be growth stocks than yield stocks, and this difference is likely to be amplified if revenue is drawn internationally so that it qualifies very little for franking credits and capital gains taxes present opportunities for minimisation. Australia, Canada and others offer a 50 per cent discount on capital gains liabilities for stocks held for longer than 12 months. Capital gains on stocks held until an individual's taxable income is low (or zero) are thus likely to be taxed lightly.

The trend towards self-funded retirement benefits systems in some jurisdictions has altered the redistributive politics of corporate taxes, both income and capital gains. Taxpayers on modest incomes are increasingly dependent on the earnings of pension funds that are at least partly invested in stocks, and taxes will reduce their future earnings. To give but one example, the Ontario Teachers' Pension Fund is a global investor, with a diverse portfolio. Increasingly ordinary people are an important cohort who benefit from corporate profits. Such funds have limited capacity to use various international tax minimisation strategies.

With the international dimension to tax policy, we are dealing with a different set of issues to those with global regulation. Business wants harmonised regulatory standards so that it can sell products in as many markets as possible meeting a common regulatory standard, but tax avoidance thrives on a lack of harmonisation. If all corporate tax rates were harmonised, there would be no advantage in profit shifting. To give an example, the Tim Hortons–Burger King merger depended on the existence of a substantial differential between US and Canadian corporate tax rates. The new entity was located in Canada, where the rate of corporate tax was 15 per cent, 20 per cent lower than in the US. If both rates were harmonised at, say, 25 per cent, there would be no incentive to locate in Canada. President Trump's 2017 reforms have narrowed the gap by reducing corporates' rates to 21 per cent.

One corollary of this is that what might be called 'the politics of envy' can be counterproductive. If rates are driven higher by populist politics, the result may well be *lower*, not higher, total revenue collections from corporate taxation. The Tim Hortons–Burger King arrangement depends upon political support for a high rate in the US, and the solution lies in harmonisation and therefore the lowering of US rates – or the raising of Canada's.

Competition and Races to the Bottom

Competition between states should not always be seen as driving regulatory standards down, however. The common fear is that international competition will drive down environmental regulatory standards through states attempting to attract investment by creating 'pollution havens' or states being reluctant to adopt strong regulatory standards for fear of producing 'industrial flight'. The empirical evidence in support of these mechanisms is weak (Leonard 2006). Indeed, there is evidence of a 'race to the top', with rising standards providing advantage for businesses within vanguard jurisdictions (Vogel 1995). Regulations can serve as a certificate of superior product quality that is rewarded by the market. Then, high levels of regulation may create a competitive advantage for those firms subject to them, and result in competitive pressures on other governments to raise their own levels of regulation (Scharpf 1997, p. 523).

German automobile safety standards, for example, enhance the market for their cars.

Competition is significant in areas such as taxation, especially taxation of mobile factors of production, but less so in product-related environmental and health regulation, but with process-related regulation of this kind it might be so, especially where capital is mobile (Scharpf 1997, p. 526). Clark (1993) described how there were forces driving a 'race to the top' in the global mining industry because the global nature of the industry means that the reputation of firms has a great bearing on the granting of their 'social licence to operate' by governments. To some extent, all transnational enterprises could be said to require a licence to operate, but the case of the mining industry (Prno and Slocombe 2012) illustrates an important point: that the characteristics of the industry impact upon the politics surrounding regulatory policy. Business usually exerts greatest structural power over governments by promising to make investments or threatening to relocate elsewhere (Levy and Egan 1998; Kellow 2002), because government revenue flows and the jobs through which voters secure their income depend upon the profitability of business.

Taxation of company profits is therefore a difficult problem for policymakers, and corporate profits and income for wealthy individuals are intangible and highly mobile. The ability of governments to collect revenue is hampered by the rising importance of intellectual property to many of the most successful companies. Harmonisation, difficult enough to achieve in other regulatory domains, is something the tax minimisation industry and its clients do not desire. There are few or no features that might result in a 'race to the top', and there is much to gain from 'beggar-thy-neighbour' approaches, not just by Third World tax havens, but by national governments in quite affluent jurisdictions such as the Netherlands, Luxembourg and Switzerland. The default position is a lack of harmonisation in tax policy, upon which the tax minimisation industry thrives.

These characteristics also militate against the probable success for private regulatory regimes initiated. Labelling is unlikely to provide much 'purchase' to NGOs, as profits are mobile and creative use of intellectual property facilitates profit shifting. It is difficult to see how 'fair tax' certification schemes might exert sufficient upward pressure to counter the 'beggar-thy-neighbour' policies of tax havens, especially given disclosures that weaken the moral claim of social movement campaigns such as the revelation in the 'Paradise Papers' in 2017 that Bono, founder of the campaigning group ONE and a campaigner for tax justice, had himself been using tax havens.

Administrative Problems

There are arguments that corporate profits should not be subject to taxation – that only income in the hands of their owners should be taxed – so that the issue should be seen as one of addressing tax minimisation by income earners or the beneficiaries of capital gains. Even if we were to accept this, we would still be left with the problems of the wealthy arranging their financial affairs across national jurisdictions. And if the income and/or corporate taxation base is eroded, greater pressure falls upon other sources of revenue, such as consumption taxes, which are regressive (although they at least charge the rich for consumption even if they can minimise income tax).

The final features of tax systems that should be noted are administrative problems noted by Christopher Hood in his *The Limits of Administration* (1976). *Inter alia*, Hood noted that it was not possible to tax diamonds, because they were too easily hidden and could not be identified and traced to particular sources. Technology changes, and laser identification now makes it possible for diamonds to be etched with a diamond identification number. This allowed rapid action against 'conflict' or 'blood' diamonds after a campaign by Global Witness in 1998, with the adoption of UN Security Council Resolutions 1173 (1998) and 1295 (2000) and the Kimberley Process Certification Scheme (2003), initiated by the diamond producing nations themselves. Laser etching, in short, altered diamonds in a practical sense, from effectively being 'intangibles' to identifiable, traceable items. In other words, technological change changes regulatory possibilities.

Hood (1976)'s second point worth noting was that taxation agencies are constantly in a contest with the tax minimisation industry (this volume, Chapter 6), and are always at a disadvantage, because they train tax officers only to see them recruited by the industry, which was usually able to pay higher salaries and whose employees were usually better trained with more expertise than those tasked with countering them. There has been an increase in 'tax planning', which has been pushed from the corporate level to the retail level: agencies consider tax offices around the world should be targeting the promoters of such schemes. But avoidance is a relatively small part of the factors driving tax policy. Tax agencies recognise that corporate tax shelters must always adapt their products to circumvent anti-avoidance measures, and will always have to react to innovation. Together with Hood's point about recruitment, this suggests tax authorities will always to some extent be playing 'catch-up'.

5.3 WHAT IS TO BE DONE?

The obvious remedies to global tax minimisation are relatively easy to state, though perhaps more difficult to attain. Some form of effective international instrument might emerge from the OECD's BEPS initiative, though it would need to cover the European OECD members profiting from profit shifting (Luxembourg, the Netherlands and Switzerland), which are likely to stand in the way of mutual agreement within the OECD (see this volume, Chapter 2 and Carroll and Kellow, 2011). The EU is also a promising venue, especially given its recent activism in addressing Apple's tax practices in Ireland (see this volume, Chapter 11), but would not cover the case of Switzerland. The developing country tax havens would remain, and would necessitate successful and effective action within the UN system, which is not a prospect about which one can be overly sanguine. As one diplomat put it when contemplating possible alternative venues to the OECD to progress the Harmful Tax Competition initiative, 'There's always the UN – but only if one wanted to kill it' (Kellow and Carroll 2017, p. 229).

The prospects for international success are not promising, but domestic measures such as the UK threat of a 'Google tax' yielded some results (see this volume, Chapter 12), although it is perhaps understandable given the previous history that those hoping for improved revenue collections have turned to some kind of certification schemes or other social movement action to address shortfalls in revenue. Certification schemes have been developed by social movements for industries such as forestry, fishing and aquaculture and for 'fair trade' (see Gale forthcoming), and NGOs have developed this model for application to tax issues (Elbra forthcoming; this volume, Chapter 11).

One problem is 'slacktivism' – the passive support for noble causes that does little to address problems. In the development issue area, Hartmut Elsenhans (2005, p. 21) has criticised many NGOs as selling 'certificates of good conscience' to ignorant buyers and claiming 'Potemkin-like successes'. Where such factors influence consumer choices, the passivity of the action is perhaps unimportant, although the effectiveness of the certification scheme is still problematic. Certainly, the effectiveness of Fairtrade coffee certification in assisting growers has been called into question (Beuchelt and Zeller 2011), and so the claim of 'Potemkin-like successes' should be taken seriously.

Consumption of certified products is a public act – a public display of virtue, a new kind of conspicuous consumption. By choosing Fairtrade coffee, FSC-compliant furniture or MSC-certified seafood, consumers make a public statement of support for a particular cause. This public display of virtue reinforces compliance. A germane question is whether certification would be effective with a relatively private act such as using an internet browser, in the case of Google, or would be sufficient to sway purchasers of smartphones. Is Gen X, Y or Z sufficiently concerned about the tax affairs of Apple for this issue to over-ride the 'cool' of its products (or the disadvantages of a Samsung Note 7)? There are grounds for deep pessimism, to say the least. Halal or kosher certification works precisely because of the commitment of a large number of consumers, and this commitment might not be matched with tax.

A further problem is that of multiple certificates. There might be a market for Fairtrade organic, de-caff, responsible soy latte with two Better Sugar Initiative certified sugars, made with Water Round Table approved water, but the value of each additional label is diminished in this example. It is inevitable that the effectiveness of certification and labelling will be diminished with the addition of further labels. And what if there are inconsistencies between the objectives of each certification scheme? This seems to be one of the problems with Fairtrade organic coffee, because the organic certification in particular drives up costs to the point where the price premium concerned consumers are willing to pay is not sufficient to outweigh the additional costs of meeting standards required for organic certification (Beuchelt and Zeller 2011). It cannot be assumed that every issue supported by consumers in Berkeley is necessarily compatible with all others when it comes to their impact on Third World producers. Regardless, there are more general questions as to whether Fairtrade actually delivers benefits for those it seeks to help (Cramer et al. 2014; FTEPR 2014).

There is an issue, too, with the existence of multiple groups that might not all deliver on the promise of an absence of oppositional campaigns that is inherent in the mechanism of certification. A Tasmanian aquaculture company that went through a WWF certification process was nevertheless in 2016 attacked over its environmental standards. Wilson (2011) has identified the use of 'good cop, bad cop' strategies against corporate targets, and the Tax Justice campaign has something of this structure, with the campaign of Christian Aid (highlighting the problem) being followed at short notice by the solution, the establishment of the Fair Tax Mark (providing the solution). But, unless their campaigns are in fact coordinated, the presence of multiple groups with multiple perspectives and objectives is likely to undermine the effectiveness of labelling regimes.

Then there is the problem that many regulatory regimes – state imposed or voluntary – are supported by influential interests, often producers that can spread compliance costs across larger markets and will be advantaged relative to smaller competitors. It is not coincidental that the MSC was initiated by Unilever, or that the ICMM was formed by the larger transnational mining companies and adopted voluntary standards that raise the regulatory bar. Such measures raise entry costs and favour those players with global reputations to defend and economies of scale or technological advantage that others cannot match. Bruce Yandle (1983) drew attention to the importance of 'bootlegger and Baptist coalitions' – tacit coalitions and confluences of those who derive economic benefits from regulation and those who seek regulation because they consider some act to be morally wrong (and thus make it respectable to channel support and resources to the interest-based cause).

The Kimberley Process Certification Scheme was initiated and supported by the legitimate diamond producing nations, which had an interest in protecting their market from cheaper conflict diamonds. It is difficult to see from where such a 'bootlegger' interest might emerge to support the adoption and implementation of a certification system for taxation. The Kimberley Process Certification Scheme, it should be noted, failed to halt the trade in blood diamonds, and proponents such as Global Witness withdrew their support for the scheme in 2011 because of its failings, which stemmed from governance failures in diamond producing countries, where certification could be arranged by bribing officials (BBC 2011).

It is also worth emphasising that the model for standard setting and certification was a private self-regulatory regime. Responsible Care was launched by the Chemistry Industry Association of Canada in 1985, as a defensive measure against campaigns against chemical products by environmental groups such as Greenpeace. Responsible Care was then spread internationally after being adopted by the International Council of Chemical Associations, and now covers more than 50 countries, and its member companies account for almost 90 per cent of chemical production. Can the Fair Tax Mark succeed without corporate backing? Certification regimes such as FSC were adopted because of a perceived failure of global policy. Failure is evident with global tax policy, but FTM has been backed mostly by smaller companies largely based in a single jurisdiction, and by very few MNCs that are actually likely to engage in profit shifting. Thus FTM would seem to lack sufficient legitimacy to be effective.

This suggests that the Fair Tax Mark is unlikely to succeed in addressing the issues of profit shifting it seeks to remedy. David Vogel (2008), surveying civil regulation generally, concluded it addresses but does not resolve the challenge of making global firms and markets more effectively and democratically governed, and the factors discussed here suggest that tax justice might be even less amenable to a civil society regulatory regime.

There is less conspicuous virtue in favouring corporations that are certified as paying tax, rather than consuming particular products, and no obvious economic interests that might support the scheme, which will doubtless become popular among the largely national players that have been the first to seek certification, but receive little take-up among the multinationals that have been targeted by the Tax Justice campaign. Product certification has a chequered history anyway, but the factors that produced some of the successful outcomes are patently not present with tax.

The voluntary governance approach seems simple by comparison to the OECD's BEPS programme (see this volume, Chapter 2), although it must be noted that policy initiatives developed and promoted by tax justice activists such as country-by-country reporting have subsequently been incorporated into OECD standards. Given the significant barriers to developing either an effective private governance regime or broad-based international agreement it would seem that domestic action represents the most viable approach to corporate tax reform. It has been argued that the most comprehensive solution to ending the use of tax havens in the US would be to not allow US multinational corporations to defer indefinitely paying US taxes on profits attributed to foreign subsidiaries, so companies pay taxes on their foreign income at the same rate and time they pay them on their domestic income. Paying US taxes on overseas income would not constitute 'double taxation', because US MNCs already subtract any foreign taxes paid from their US tax bill, and that would not change. It was estimated by the Congressional Joint Committee on Taxation and the US Treasury Department that ending 'deferral' would potentially raise nearly $900 billion over ten years (McIntyre et al. 2015, p. 18).

There would also seem to be potential – being realised at least partially – for action within the EU, which is being pursued primarily by the directorate-general responsible for competition. And, as Margrethe Vestager, the EU's competition chief, pointed out, many of these problems arise from the conversion of bilateral double taxation agreements into double non-taxation agreements. There would appear to be considerable scope for the exit from such treaties by parties that are being undermined by the major tax havens – Ireland, the Netherlands, Luxembourg, Switzerland, Singapore and Hong Kong.

While multilateral, or even plurilateral, action might have a remote chance of succeeding, there appears to be substantial scope for action by national governments (if persuaded to act), and this is likely to be more effective than any private certification scheme. The threat of losing taxation revenue to EU members has led to concern in the US and lies behind the proposal for a reduced corporate tax rate that would lessen the incentive for keeping profits offshore (US Department of the Treasury 2016).

It is arguable that better outcomes are likely to result from the tax justice movement bringing pressure to bear to support national and international measures such as the BEPS programme. Even international measures will require domestic political action, and NGOs would perhaps do best to act as a principled issue network (Keck and Sikkink 1998) and work to bring pressure to bear on the recalcitrant governments of the OECD and the other tax havens. For Ireland, Luxembourg and the Netherlands, action in the European Union might also be fruitful. Much was made of the election to the presidency of the EC of Jean-Claude Juncker, opposed by the United Kingdom, and the subject of an attempt at an early censure motion in the European Parliament. The Tax Justice Network has drawn attention to Juncker's role in establishing Luxembourg as a tax haven from the time of his appointment as minister of finance in 1989 or as prime minister in 1995. On one view, this could indicate that the European Commission might run cold on tax reform. An alternative view could be that Juncker might be vulnerable to attack on the issue and therefore might not stand in the way of reform – and this appears to be borne out by recent activity.

5.4 CONCLUSION

The Tax Justice Network might do better to bring pressure to bear on the governments of Ireland, Luxembourg, the Netherlands and Switzerland as well as the European Commission, and in any other arena that might be helpful in addressing the incidence of 'double non-taxation'. A private certification scheme of corporations, rather than products, which expects support rather than boycott, is unlikely to be particularly effective, because it lacks most of the elements that have made other product certification schemes effective, albeit only to a limited extent.

The solutions to the tax justice issue are likely to lie in effective multilevel approaches to policy. And 'solutions', rather than 'a solution', are needed: silver buckshot rather than a silver bullet. Measures such as 'Google taxes' or similar policies, refinement of bilateral tax conventions, or measures in the EU, OECD and (if one can dream) the UN might provide elements that counter base erosion and profit shifting. The EU has seen a good start, perhaps stimulated by BEPS; it has certainly stimulated a concern in the US that it might miss out on revenue collected in Europe when (and if) the profits of US corporations are repatriated. Harmonisation of rates, perhaps lower than the US rate, and measures that reduce the incentives for avoidance are likely to be more effective than the Fair Tax Mark. However, as other contributors to this volume have argued, it could be that elements of private standards such as FTM are subsequently incorporated into domestic legislation and international agreements. In terms of domestic reforms, would international dividend imputation create sufficient shareholder demand, for example, for franking certificates that might reduce the tax liability for shareholders as well as US corporations, individual or institutional? One suspects that this kind of certificate would be more effective than private standards that are essentially gold stars awarded to the virtuous, though measures would also be needed to counter aggressive tax planning by shareholders.

But there is a dilemma here. The move to lower corporate tax rates in the US is not likely to win popular support, and nor would crediting taxpayers for tax already paid somewhere else by the corporation they partly own. However, it is precisely the high rate of effective taxation that creates the incentive for tax havens to operate and taxpayers to use them. Political support for high rates of taxation clearly can have the effect of increasing the incentive for aggressive tax planning, reducing revenue.

Tax, especially corporate tax, is a complex matter and not readily amenable to social movement politics. The tax justice movement is more likely to be effective in supplying good policy analysis and support as a principled issue network, and that means, in the first instance, countering policies in Ireland, Luxembourg, the Netherlands and Switzerland and countering the stances of these countries in blocking action beyond the nation-state.

REFERENCES

Alderman, L. (2015), 'European Inquiry Focuses on a Mysterious Starbucks Business', *New York Times*, published electronically 21 October, available at http://www.nytimes.com/2015/10/22/business/international/european-inquiry-focuses-on-a-mysterious-starbucks-business.html?_r=0 (accessed 23 January 2016).

ANZ (2015), 'Winning the Away Game: Australia-Based Global Companies and the Economy', *ANZ Insight* 7, August.

BBC (2011), 'Global Witness Leaves Kimberley Process Diamond Scheme', published electronically 5 December, available at http://www.bbc.com/news/business-16027011 (accessed 16 June 2015).

Beuchelt, T.D. and M. Zeller (2011), 'Profits and Poverty: Certification's Troubled Link for Nicaragua's Organic and Fairtrade Coffee Producers', *Ecological Economics* **70** (7), 1316–1324.

Carroll, P. and A. Kellow (2011), *The OECD: A Study of Organisational Adaptation*, Cheltenham, UK and Northampton, MA, USA: Edward Elgar Publishing.

Clark, G. (1993), 'Global Competition and the Environmental Performance of Australian Mineral Companies: Is the "Race to the Bottom" Inevitable?', *International Environmental Affairs* **5** (3), 147–172.

Cramer, C., D. Johnston, B. Mueller, C. Oya and J. Sender (2014), 'How to Do (and How Not to Do) Fieldwork on Fair Trade and Rural Poverty', *Canadian Journal of Development Studies* **35** (1), 170–185.

Davidson, S. and R. Heaney (2012), 'Effective Tax Rates and the Political Cost

Hypothesis: A Re-evaluation of Australian Evidence', *Australian Tax Forum* **27** (1), 79–105.

Elbra, A. (forthcoming), 'The Rise of Tax Justice NGOs and the New Politics of Corporate Taxation', in A. Kellow and H. Murphy-Gregory (eds), *Research Handbook on NGOs*, Cheltenham, UK and Northampton, MA, USA: Edward Elgar Publishing.

Elsenhans, H. (2005), 'Equality, Market, Profit, Growth: Small-Scale Industry and the Expansion of Mass Markets with Reference to an Empirical Research in Algeria', Paper presented to the Annual Conference of Verein für Socialpolitik: Research Committee Development Economics, Kiel Institute for the World Economy, 8–9 July.

European Commission (2014), *Alleged Aid to Apple*, Commission Decision COMP/SA.38373, 2014 O.J. C 369/22.

European Commission (2015a), *Alleged Aid to Amazon*, Commission Decision COMP/SA.38944, 2015 O.J. C 44/13.

European Commission (2015b), *State Aid Implemented by the Netherlands to Starbucks*, Commission Decision COMP/SA.38374, 21 October.

European Commission (2015c), *State Aid Which Luxembourg Granted to Fiat*, Commission Decision COMP/SA.38375, 21 October.

European Commission (2016a), 'State Aid: Commission Concludes Belgian "Excess Profit" Tax Scheme Illegal: Around €700 Million to Be Recovered from 35 Multinational Companies', Press Release No. IP/16/42, 11 January, available at http://europa.eu/rapid/press-release_IP-16-42_en.htm (accessed 10 January 2018).

European Commission (2016b), 'State Aid: Ireland Gave Illegal Tax Benefits to Apple Worth up to €13 Billion', Press Release No. IP/16/2923, 30 August, available at http://europa.eu/rapid/press-release_IP-16-2923_en.htm (accessed 10 January 2018).

Fairless, T. (2016), 'EU Announces Ruling on Illegal Tax Breaks in Belgium; EU Orders Belgium to Recover over $760 Million from 35 Multinationals', *Wall Street Journal*, published electronically 11 January, available at http://www.wsj.com/articles/eu-to-rule-on-illegal-tax-breaks-for-multinationals-1452506740 (accessed 14 January 2018).

FTEPR (2014), *Fairtrade, Employment and Poverty Reduction in Ethiopia and Uganda*, Final Report to DFID, April.

Gale, F. (forthcoming), 'NGOs and Private Governance/Certification Challenges', in A. Kellow and H. Murphy-Gregory (eds), *Research Handbook on NGOs*, Cheltenham, UK and Northampton, MA, USA: Edward Elgar Publishing.

Henderson, D. (2009), 'Misguided Corporate Virtue: The Case against CSR, and the True Role of Business Today', *Economic Affairs* **29** (4), 11–15.

Hood, C. (1976), *The Limits of Administration*, London: Wiley.

Jolly, D. (2014), 'Criticized on Taxes, Starbucks Will Move European Offices to London', *New York Times*, published electronically 16 April, available at http://www.nytimes.com/2014/04/17/business/international/starbucks-to-move-european-offices-to-london.html (accessed 12 January 2018).

Keck, M. and K. Sikkink (1998), *Activists beyond Borders: Transnational Activist Networks in International Politics*, Ithaca, NY: Cornell University Press.

Kellow, A. (2002), 'Comparing Business and Public Interest Associability at the International Level', *International Political Science Review* **23** (2), 175–186.

Kellow, A. (2016), 'Learning from the RSPT Mistakes: Is Reform Still Possible?', *Australian Journal of Political Science* **51** (1), 134–149.

Kellow, A. and P. Carroll (2017), *Middle Powers and International Organisations: Australia and the OECD*, Cheltenham, UK and Northampton, MA, USA: Edward Elgar Publishing.

Krasner, S.D. (1995), 'Power Politics, Institutions, and Transnational Relations', in T. Risse-Kappen (ed.), *Bringing Transnational Relations Back In: Non-State Actors, Domestic Structures and International Institutions*, Cambridge: Cambridge University Press, pp. 257–279.

Lankhorst-Hohorst GmbH v Finanzamt Steinfurt [2002] ECR I-11779.

Leonard, H.J. (2006), *Pollution and the Struggle for the World Product: Multinational Corporations, Environment, and International Comparative Advantage*, Cambridge: Cambridge University Press.

Levy, D.L. and D. Egan (1998), 'Capital Contests: National and Transnational Channels of Corporate Influence on the Climate Change Negotiations', *Politics and Society* **26** (3), 337–361.

Luckerson, V. (2014), 'Apple's $649 iPhone 6 Reportedly Costs $200 to Make', *TIME Magazine*, published electronically 24 September, available at http://time.com/3426087/apple-iphone-6-cost/ (accessed 19 June 2018).

Manheim, J.B. (2001), *The Death of a Thousand Cuts: Corporate Campaigns and the Attack on the Corporation*, Mahwah, NJ: Lawrence Erlbaum.

McIntyre, R.S., R. Phillips and P. Baxandall (2015), *Offshore Shell Games 2015: The Use of Offshore Tax Havens by Fortune 500 Companies*, Washington, DC: U.S. Public Interest Research Group Education Fund and Citizens for Tax Justice.

Prno, J. and D.S. Slocombe (2012), 'Exploring the Origins of "Social License to Operate" in the Mining Sector: Perspectives from Governance and Sustainability Theories', *Resources Policy* **37** (3), 346–357.

Scharpf, F.W. (1997), 'Introduction: The Problem-Solving Capacity of Multi-Level Governance', *Journal of European Public Policy* **4** (4), 520–538.

Sebag, G. and S. Bodoni (2015), 'McDonald's Faces EU Probe over Luxembourg Sweetheart Tax Deals', *Bloomberg Business*, published electronically 3 December, available at http://www.bloomberg.com/news/articles/2015-12-03/mcdonald-s-faces-eu-probe-over-luxembourg-sweetheart-tax-deals (accessed 12 January 2018).

Tax Justice Network (2015), 'The Share of Tax Havens in U.S. Corporate Profits Made Abroad', available at http://www.taxjustice.net/wp-content/uploads/2015/04/Juncker-Luxembourg.jpg (accessed 19 June 2015).

US Department of the Treasury (2016), *The European Commission's Recent State Aid Investigations of Transfer Pricing Rulings*, White Paper, 24 August.

Vogel, D. (1995), *Trading Up: Consumer and Environmental Regulation in a Global Economy*, Cambridge, MA: Harvard University Press.

Vogel, D. (2008), 'Private Global Business Regulation', *Annual Review of Political Science* **11**, 261–282.

Wilson, T. (2011), *Naked Extortion? Environmental NGOs Imposing (In)voluntary Regulations on Consumers and Business*, Melbourne: Institute of Public Affairs.

Worstall, T. (2014), 'Starbucks and the EU Tax Investigation: Pretty Trivial Really, Hardly Any Money in It at All', *Forbes*, published electronically 14 November, available at http://onforb.es/1pZYnD1 (accessed 15 November 2014).

Yandle, B. (1983), 'Bootleggers and Baptists: The Education of a Regulatory Economist', *Regulation* **7**, May/June, 12.

6. Large accounting firms and tax planning in a 'fair tax' era

Lyne Latulippe[1]

6.1 INTRODUCTION

The highly complex and technical nature of international corporate taxation has insulated it from public scrutiny for many years (this volume, Chapter 3). Yet the work of activists and journalists, combined with major economic events ranging from the collapse of large corporations in the early 2000s to the 2008–09 Financial Crisis (FC), has driven growing public interest in the tax strategies of multinational corporations (MNCs). This exposure has been a watershed moment for the corporate tax planning industry, and has prompted attempts by MNCs to address fairness and transparency concerns.

Tax professionals are important and influential actors in the international tax regime, and their expertise and global networks have allowed them to gain more control as taxation has become increasingly transnational (Cross and Davis 2013, p. 140, referring to Tsingou 2003). More specifically, a small number of large global accounting firms, often referred to as the 'Big Four' firms of Deloitte, Ernst & Young, KPMG and PwC, dominate the tax services industry worldwide, and are particularly active in providing tax policy advice to governments and firms alike.

Recently, tax professionals' involvement in the tax planning industry has attracted significant public scrutiny, forcing them to justify the impact of the services they provide before a significantly larger audience. More specifically, large accounting firms have been targeted for developing and selling aggressive tax planning strategies to their clients, including audit clients. Recent criticism has also highlighted the shortcomings, and potential dangers, of overreliance on their expertise in tax policymaking (Sikka and Hampton 2005). Indeed, the UK Parliamentary Public Accounts Committee (PAC) has questioned the probity of allowing the four large accounting firms to advise government on the drafting of tax legislation, while subsequently advising their clients on how to manipulate loopholes in those very same provisions to minimize their tax liabilities (UK

Committee of Public Accounts 2013). Large accounting firms have reacted by publishing reports or articles on topics related to fairness, transparency and risk, and have also been compelled to appear before parliamentary or senate committees on tax avoidance in countries such as the United Kingdom, the United States, Canada and Australia to explain and justify their positions on these issues.

This chapter analyses the positions of the Big Four accounting firms as expressed in their official publications, but also in their testimony at public hearings and inquiries. The analysis focuses on how they have responded to recent developments requiring greater financial and tax transparency and an emphasis on fairness in the tax practices of their clients. The conclusions drawn contribute to an understanding of their position in the public debate on international tax issues, and the consequent implications for the fair tax debate and the politics of tax justice. Section 6.2 provides an overview of the evolution of tax specialists' monopoly of expertise over many years. Section 6.3 explains the focus on large accounting firms, owing to their central role in the tax field (particularly in international taxation) and their relatively similar tax practices, as well as their common involvement in the development of tax policy. Following this, section 6.4 outlines three interrelated developments that have thrown the spotlight on to the tax planning industry and increased the pressure on large accounting firms. These developments are the fall of Enron, the growing momentum of country-by-country reporting (CbCR), and the wider rise in tax activism documented in this volume. This section also examines some initial responses from the large accounting firms, as evidenced in their official public documents as well as testimony before public committees and inquiries. Section 6.5 expands the analysis to discuss large accounting firms' assessments of tax planning from a legal perspective, and the resulting challenges of reconciling arguments of tax morality versus tax legality. It also explains how large accounting firms confine discussions of fairness and transparency issues within discourses and processes of risk management. The conclusion (section 6.6) explores large accounting firms' expected influence in the short term, and the implications for debates about fair tax issues and policy proposals explored elsewhere in this volume.

6.2 THE GENERAL EVOLUTION OF TAX PRACTICE AND TAX POLICY ADVICE

The discussion of MNC tax practices has evolved from a narrow focus on compliance and litigation services to incorporate tax planning and advice. It is now widely recognized that the practices of tax professionals have the potential to weaken tax regimes, because their planning services may reduce the effectiveness of tax legislation, allowing their clients to exploit loopholes that policymakers must then attempt to close. Policymakers are thus frequently one step behind firms, responding to existing problems and fighting fires rather than developing innovative new strategies. Further, since tax professionals are the gatekeepers of tax compliance, and are perceived as experts in the field, their opinions carry significant weight in policy development and implementation processes.

Tax Practice

The growing scope and complexity of income tax systems spawned demand for tax services from professionals with tax-specific expertise, specifically accountants and lawyers. Tax laws create legal obligations that can be disputed, and costs that must be accounted for. By the mid-1950s, each profession had gained control over a specific sub-market – lawyers over tax litigation, and accountants over tax compliance. In time, however, both professions came to be involved in a larger, integrated market as the tax planning industry emerged and their services started to overlap.

To increase their scope and worldwide reach and to take advantage of the integration and liberalization of markets, multinationals have gradually adapted their organizational structures. In particular, MNCs have developed complex networks of subsidiaries in multiple countries, and a business model that required multiple transactions among these entities. From the 1990s onwards, governments, businesses and professionals struggled to apply tax policies and tools to this new global corporate environment (see this volume, Chapter 2). Although significant efforts have been made to adapt tax policies to multinational corporations' structures and transactions, MNCs have been able to take advantage of legal fictions (such as the creation of legal entities in any jurisdiction or the legal qualification of transactions with no economic substance) to manipulate the rules and avoid taxation (Rixen 2008; Picciotto 2011; see also this volume, Chapters 1 and 2), frequently with the help of tax professionals (Sikka and Hampton 2005).

The history of large accounting firms is intertwined with that of multinationals. As Aharoni argues, 'When US multinationals expanded abroad, their auditing firms followed them. Offering an ever-widening range of auditing and tax services, they gradually increased their size and developed into professional behemoths' (1999, p. 20). Multinationals sought national lawyers and accountants for advice in implementing specific tax strategies (Picciotto 1995), eventually creating a market for tax planning, including international tax strategies, which tax professionals offered to these corporations (Braithwaite 2005). By their practice and, more importantly, through the development of the tax planning industry, tax professionals influenced the development of the international tax regime, both nationally and internationally. Just as the industrialization era created a need for professional services to protect property and rights, the rapid pace of globalization throughout the 1980s opened up a market for specific professional services, including international tax planning.

Regulation of the tax profession varies around the world, from comprehensive regulation to an exclusive practice profession or reserved title. From one country to another, the rules differ significantly, and it can be difficult to draw common formal guidelines that apply to the tax profession generally, and to tax planning services more specifically (CFE Professional Affairs Committee 2013). The lack of specific rules and codes of conduct for tax practices has blurred the tax professional's obligations to act in the public interest, and the dominance of the market has weakened professionalism by reducing it to only one of its components: expertise.

A complex market for tax planning has developed over the years, and a neoliberal logic has lured professional service providers away from some codes of conduct traditionally associated with professionalism. The abandonment by professionals of 'professional goals, such as transparent and accurate reporting, in favour of becoming sales people for tax shelters' significantly affects the tax system (Steuerle 2008, p. 30). Professionals influence the structure of the current system through their use and interpretation of the rules. Through their practice, tax professionals construct the norms and the problems (Edelman et al. 1992) that need to be solved in the international tax system. In other words, tax practitioners are ideational entrepreneurs who create the environment to which tax policy must be adapted. For example, although it may be legal to create an intermediary legal entity in country C to obtain a tax benefit for a transaction between an entity in country A and another in country B, the institutionalization of this practice, called 'treaty shopping', has impelled countries to try to devise policies for controlling it.

Tax professionals have thus become knowledge brokers (Hasseldine et al. 2011) with a product to sell: expertise and knowledge in the area of tax planning, including international tax planning. Referring to professionals as a whole, Larson contends that, 'at the core of the professional project, we find the fusion of antithetical ideological structures and a potential for permanent tension between "civilizing function" and market orientation, between the "protection of society" and the securing of a market, between intrinsic and extrinsic values of work' (2013, p. 63).

According to Picciotto (1995, p. 26),

> not only do these corporate professionals compete for business in the markets for their services, it is important to understand that they themselves help to construct those markets. Their business and corporate clients operate in markets which by their nature are regulated, and professionals play a key role in the mediation of such regulation, by structuring their clients' transactions.

This is also supported by Braithwaite's (2005) study of the market for tax planning, which he identifies as a supply and demand market. Taxpayers go to tax professionals to benefit from advice on the implementation of tax planning. However, tax professionals, particularly from large accounting firms, are often proactive in contacting potential clients to sell tax planning ideas. For example, one of the four large accounting firms had more than 20 per cent of its global revenues from tax services, notably the sale of 'tax products'. Highlighting this pervasive phenomenon, Sikka (2010) observed that 'The organizational structure included a "Tax Innovation Centre" which functioned as a profit centre and was solely dedicated to developing new products' (Sikka 2010, p. 159). Another firm was identified as having crafted a number of tax avoidance schemes in the UK (Sikka and Hampton 2005).

Policy Advice

Understanding the impact of the international tax system's rules on multinational businesses requires technical knowledge and practical experience. The expertise of tax professionals can contribute to the development of tax policy, but simultaneously their practice adversely affects the tax policy environment by creating conditions that must be managed by policies. In short, tax professionals influence the design, implementation and effectiveness of tax policy.

The participation and influence of tax professionals in the policy process is facilitated by their unique expertise and knowledge, and by the dominant discourse of economic liberalization, which constrains tax policy choices. International tax professionals are members of global firms or global networks, which gives them an edge over national officials with regard to international tax knowledge. These firms need to understand (or have easy access to people who understand) the tax systems of many countries and the international norms associated with these systems. '[T]ransnational professionals are increasingly prominent and . . . policy networks are ever more centred in those who can demonstrate that their professional skills and professionalization are transnational rather than remaining within a national system' (Seabrooke 2014, p. 55). Government officials' knowledge of other countries' tax regimes is limited, as is the ongoing exchange between officials. Although some cooperation does exist, these governmental networks are very different from those that benefit tax professionals.

Furthermore, given the dominant paradigm of economic liberalization and the notion that countries address international tax policy through the lens of competitiveness, tax professionals' advice is more likely to be seen as credible and actually influence policy decisions (Latulippe 2016). Representing their firms, their professional associations or clients in the policy process, tax professionals tend to put forward recommendations amenable to business and business competitiveness that fit well with the advice governments are seeking or that are useful to justify policies. Also, the technical nature of tax professionals' advice depoliticizes the issues and facilitates policy adoption.

Essentially, the practice of tax advice has moved on from the dual perspectives of compliance (accountants) and litigation (lawyers) to a tax planning-driven industry. The market for tax planning has evolved alongside the development of a perception of MNCs' tax departments as 'profit centres' (Slemrod 2004). Furthermore, as tax rules have become more complex, the knowledge of tax professionals has exerted increasing influence over the policymaking process embedded in a global liberalization discourse. This is the background that undergirds the analysis undertaken in this chapter. The next section accounts for the emphasis on large accounting firms.

6.3 LARGE ACCOUNTING FIRMS AND TAX SERVICES

Homogeneity in Tax Practice

Although law and accounting firms differ in their tax practice as well as their organization (Bankman 2001), their practices are intertwined, as discussed above. Moreover, large accounting firms hire lawyers to work in their tax departments (Rostain 2006), or create their own global network of law firms to work in tax litigation or provide legal advice on tax matters (Aharoni 1999). International tax professionals are generally members of a few large firms (mainly accounting firms or associated law firms) with expertise in international taxation. In this context, as was noted above, the Big Four accounting firms are ranked in the first tier of most countries' tax practitioners (*International Tax Review* 2016). Although the number of accounting firms that have globalized in recent decades outstrips the number of law firms, some law firms in several different countries have recently globalized as well. Nevertheless, even the largest law firms operate only a fraction of the number of offices and employees that the large accounting firms do.

For the purposes of this chapter, large accounting firms are considered as a collective, homogeneous community rather than as discrete individual actors, because, as Ramirez (2012) contends, 'shared knowledge and values produced by complex socialization systems that are transformed into shared expertise, common interests and jointly-run projects are enough to define the Big Firms as a community, or at any rate a community that is different from any other community within the accounting profession' (Ramirez 2012, p. 49). In other words, they all provide similar audit, advisory and tax services to a client base that includes MNCs. Each earns a large portion of its revenues from tax services, and each is involved in tax policy advice to some degree.[2] Each has a global website with sub-national sites and publishes similar types of reports and information related to taxation and tax policy. Each large accounting firm also offers legal services, directly or through partnerships with boutique law firms. In at least four countries (Canada, the US, the UK and Australia), each firm has been asked to appear before parliamentary committees investigating tax planning issues because they had been identified as key actors in this area. The Big Four accounting firms have also recently been shown to pursue very similar strategies regarding tax haven use compared with other, smaller accounting firms. Research has demonstrated a strong positive correlation between engaging the services of a Big Four accounting firm and operating a large network of subsidiaries in tax haven jurisdictions. Furthermore, these links can be shown to illustrate causation, with networks of tax haven subsidiaries growing almost 3 per cent faster after becoming a client of the Big Four compared with beforehand, and compared with observably similar firms engaging other accounting firms. Interestingly, the observed correlation is present not only in firms that receive tax consultancy services from Big Four accounting firms, but also in audit clients (Jones et al. 2018, p. 178).

It must be noted that there may be intra-firm variations in tax practice and involvement between offices in different countries. Nevertheless, an analysis of the firms' many hearings and reports shows that their remarks, assessments and critiques are sufficiently similar to warrant considering the firms as a unified actor in global tax governance. As will be discussed further in this chapter, the Big Four frequently experience the same problems and espouse the same solutions, and circulate similar ideas and critiques of the tax system locally or internationally.

Tax Policy Advice

Though the Big Four's representatives may not be explicitly coordinating their involvement in tax policymaking, each firm has a global tax policy leader, and their tax policy advice is based on largely similar ideas. Commonalities in the advice they dispense in different countries could be due to their professional culture and expertise, and their relationships with clients. They generally favour lower taxes to some extent, and, at the national level, they promote systems favouring tax planning for residents who invest abroad. They advocate reductions in compliance costs by simplifying rules and compliance requirements (Latulippe 2016).

Tax professionals in large accounting firms are actively involved in the policy process, and policymakers often defer to their expertise. They '[contribute] to the public debate by writing articles, participating in seminars and conferences, and acting as consultants to the Department of Finance' (Kerr et al. 2012, 3:22). Governments do seek the participation of tax professionals in the development of international taxation policies. For example, in Australia and Canada tax professionals have been appointed to bodies responsible for conducting a consultation on international tax policy, many of whom were professionals from the Big Four firms (Latulippe 2016). Seabrooke (2014) notes that these professionals make claims about the type of knowledge that is valuable in tax policy. Additionally, the control they exert over this knowledge provides them with powerful expertise that then influences international tax policy. They disseminate and promote this knowledge in tax policy development, as indicated in the following statement on the website of one of the Big Four accounting firms: 'As the nation's largest tax practice, Deloitte is committed to shaping tax policy that will create a globally competitive and innovation-friendly economy.'[3]

Large accounting firms contribute comments during domestic consultation processes, are involved in the submissions prepared by professional associations, and help clients provide input. As an example of involvement through professional associations, the Joint Committee on Taxation of the Canadian Bar Association and the Canadian Institute of Chartered Accountants

> focuses on assisting the federal government in producing practical tax legislation and in preventing mistakes. This focus wins the respect of government officials and allows the committee to exert ongoing influence on the tax policy process. However, the Joint Committee's contributions are limited largely to technical issues and do not generally extend to broad tax policy concerns. (Kerr et al. 2012, 3:23)

Chairs and members of this committee include representatives from the Big Four firms and their associated law firms. At the international level, the OECD and other international organizations recruit tax professionals, often from large accounting firms, to join or advise specific committees that study international tax policy issues, conduct seminars or technical training, or participate in large consultation processes as experts who develop standards or recommendations.

At some point, tax professionals may even choose the level at which they wish to influence the policy process, either domestic or international. For example, if asked by the government of a country to comment on a proposal to eliminate treaty shopping, they could choose to indicate that this issue should be dealt with at the international level and recommend that a country should not act unilaterally to close the door on this kind of planning. This may be a rational position for these professionals when either the tools offered at the international level are less restrictive or there seems to be no possible international consensus on a single solution to end such strategies. This practice is a form of forum shopping, as tax professionals can select the forum in which they want to voice their opinions about international tax policy (this volume, Chapters 2 and 4).

Additionally, by providing tax policy advice in multiple countries, global professional firms can maintain a climate of competitiveness, because each country separately asks for their expertise in making its domestic tax systems more competitive. This in turn contributes to the maintenance of a tax policy environment favourable to international tax planning. As Picciotto (2011) notes, tax law experts are most likely not working to facilitate global tax policy harmonization, but rather wish to hinder the emergence of formal global regulation. Their business relies on designing tax planning strategies which take advantage of differences in tax systems and their lack of harmonization, and their interests are thus antithetical to those of policymakers aiming to eliminate the potential for double non-taxation. In summary, large accounting firms are sufficiently homogeneous in their practice and involvement in tax policy processes to warrant consideration as a collective actor.

6.4 RECENT DEVELOPMENTS AFFECTING TAX PRACTICE

As has been noted in Part I of this volume, since the early 2000s, developments in financial transparency and growing demands for 'fair' taxation have placed aggressive tax practices under increasing scrutiny and public pressure, forcing large accounting firms to respond. Along with a brief description of these developments, this section will detail the initial reactions of professionals and large accounting firms. Although the following three episodes concerning tax transparency and fairness issues are presented separately, they are highly interrelated and their stories overlap.

The Emergence of Tax Transparency Ideas: Enron's Fall

The external shock created by the fall of Enron (Teather 2003) had serious repercussions for the accounting profession. Enron's auditing and accounting firm, Arthur Andersen (one of the larger firms of the time), was dissolved following the turmoil. Arthur Andersen was criticized for not having adequately audited Enron's financial statements to provide an accurate picture of its financial situation. Investors, the public and governments subsequently questioned the reliability and transparency of Enron's financial statements, as they appeared to provide misleading information on the earnings, value and risks of the firm. The Enron case raised a wide range of issues, including several key problems related to taxation (Gravelle 2003). Evidence from the Enron collapse indicated that its accounting profit had been manipulated to show a better return on investment than was actually the case, but also that the corporation relied on a variety of aggressive tax planning strategies to reduce its taxable income without lowering its book income. Unsurprisingly, to combat the serious damage to its reputation, the accounting profession agreed to a series of measures it hoped would restore the credibility of its audit work and the reliability of financial statements.

As problems emerged following the case of Enron (and of other corporations), solutions were proffered from various quarters (Gravelle 2003). Among these, the Sarbanes–Oxley Act, adopted in the US in 2002, enhanced auditors' independence by restricting the services that a firm could provide to an audit client. However, it did not contain any general restrictions with regard to tax services. Audit firms could continue to provide tax services to an audit client if approved by the audit committee, an operating committee of the corporation's board of directors.

After Enron's collapse, large accounting firms began to discuss 'corporate tax governance'. In one of the first publications from one of the large accounting firms addressing this topic, KPMG stated that

> tax has changed dramatically in recent years. Its public profile has become much more conspicuous, it has acquired moral, ethical and social dimensions that have never been discussed before and, for these reasons, the business management issues associated with tax have become more complicated, more subtle, more steeped in risk and much more challenging. (KPMG 2004, p. 1)

Additionally, in response to the financial transparency problems that dogged the tax planning industry after the Enron case, the Financial

Accounting Standards Board (FASB), the body responsible for US accounting norms, issued an accounting standard on uncertain tax positions in 2006 (FIN48).

This standard provided a more systematic method for reporting benefits associated with uncertain tax positions in financial statements. By so doing, it was driving a major change in the computation of a provision for income taxes in financial statements. Before FIN48, US accounting principles did not provide specific rules on how to account for the tax risks associated with tax planning. Investors and other users of financial statements had very little information on the financial risks incurred owing to the potential refusal of aggressive tax planning strategies by the tax authorities. Under this new accounting standard, however, companies producing their financial statements in accordance with US accounting principles were forced to account for each uncertain tax position. The accounting standard states that a reserve must be calculated on the basis of the financial risk associated with the possibility that the tax position might be successfully rejected by a tax authority. Although the components of the reserve are not detailed in the financial statement, the auditor must prepare a worksheet explaining the calculation of the amount recorded. This document contains information on the level of risk incurred by the company for each uncertain tax position that it holds, including tax planning strategies. This worksheet is not publicly available, but tax professionals argue it could become a 'road map' if used for tax audit purposes (Dolan, quoted in Kroll 2011).

Many experts, academics and professionals believed the new norm would be a 'game-changer' in tax planning, marking 'the most significant change in accounting for income taxes over the past decade' (Blouin and Robinson 2011, p. 2). Many anticipated that, in addition to increasing transparency, this norm would moderate aggressive tax planning, because a high-level reserve (i.e. considerable funds being put aside in the financial statement, resulting in a lower profit until the benefit of the tax planning was certain enough to be recognized) could have a negative impact on a corporation's value. In 2010 the Internal Revenue Service (IRS), recognizing the value of the information on uncertain tax positions prepared for financial statement purposes, required that corporations file a specific schedule (Schedule UTP) with their tax return to provide these details (Harvey 2010). It is also noteworthy that other countries have followed suit, implementing similar disclosure standards for uncertain tax positions (Branson 2012). The adoption of this norm has created an incentive for tax professionals, especially accountants, to consider transparency issues and risks associated with tax planning for their clients.

Increased Global Pressure for Tax Transparency: Country-by-Country Reporting

While the Enron episode affected accountants' practice in a general way, other scandals documented elsewhere in this volume, like those related to Starbucks and Google, have raised global public awareness of tax avoidance, and resulted in increased pressure on tax advisers by directly targeting them as facilitators of these aggressive tax strategies. The pressure on MNCs to be more transparent about their tax affairs has also affected tax advisers indirectly. By disclosing information about cases of aggressive tax planning, tax activists have influenced public opinion and highlighted the need for tax transparency to assess whether corporations are paying their fair share of tax. In the same vein, tax activists also promoted the idea of public CbCR and unitary taxation with formula apportionment (this volume, Chapter 2). While the original idea propounded by the Tax Justice Network was to develop an accounting norm for CbCR (Murphy 2003; Seabrooke and Wigan 2013), a lack of support from accountants and their professional associations initially prevented the idea from being adopted as such.

Recognizing that information is critical to the development and implementation of effective tax policy (Eccleston 2013), governments and international organizations have been promoting exchange of tax information at the international level, particularly over the past 15 years. Asymmetries of information between taxpayers and governments make it hard to control evasion, as does 'legal' tax planning using other jurisdictions. While tax professionals hold valuable knowledge pertaining to compliance, their contribution is constrained by their reluctance to share information (Dabner and Burton 2009; Hasseldine et al. 2011). This reluctance can be explained by the fear that if they (or their clients) were to be totally transparent about tax issues, this could lead to the adoption of tax rules that would prevent the implementation of tax planning in the future or even compromise the current tax strategies employed by their clients.

In order to gather the necessary support for the adoption of CbCR and associated reforms, the OECD, an influential organization in the field of international taxation (Porter and Webb 2008; Lesage and Van de Graaf 2013), ensured it fitted with other ideas held by the organization and other actors, including governments and tax advisers. The organization combined CbCR with transfer pricing documentation requirements within the BEPS Action 13, fostering acceptance of this approach within the tax community (this volume, Chapter 2).

As was explained in Chapter 2, the application of the OECD's version of CbCR is significantly narrower than the original proposition. Under the OECD version, for instance, only the largest MNCs (with consolidated revenues of €750 million or more) are required to report. These companies are made to disclose only limited aggregated data for each country in which they operate. Moreover, this information is only provided to the tax authorities of the country in which the parent company is located, and limitations are placed on when and how information can be shared with other countries' tax authorities.

Nevertheless, large accounting firms were not entirely enthusiastic and supportive of the OECD CbCR requirement. Their practice and training are based on the idea that financial information and reporting are primarily relevant for investor purposes. Since the CbCR information is not seen as providing valuable information to investors, the norm does not fit well within this paradigm. Tax accountants criticized the idea as inefficient and costly for taxpayers, as well as posing confidentiality risks. Tax advisers and tax directors within MNCs argued for voluntary disclosure of some tax information instead. Furthermore, some tax professionals fear that CbCR is only the first step towards an international taxation system based on a formulary apportionment (see this volume, Chapter 2), which they do not support.

However, when the idea gathered sufficient support from governments and international organizations, tax accountants recognized that CbCR would likely be adopted, and they sought to turn it into an opportunity instead. They offered new services, and advised their clients not only on their new obligations but also on how to strategically address this complex data gathering exercise and its associated risks. Indeed, their businesses, which already included support services for the preparation of transfer pricing documentation, could now naturally be expanded to incorporate CbCR.

All of the large firms published newsletters or other documents to inform their clients about CbCR and outline the services they could offer to address this new issue. In the words of one of the firms, KPMG, 'The new requirements for disclosure, and for effective explanation, will bring significant operational challenges. But the strategic challenge is wider and more fundamental' (KPMG 2014). This firm mentioned the necessity for MNCs to develop a narrative around their corporate tax policy. Others also offered their services directly or indirectly to help their clients be ready for the challenges associated with CbCR (informational strategy, data gathering, auditing and reporting, and risk assessment).

By disentangling CbCR from the idea of paying a fair share of tax and promoting public transparency, the OECD made it more palatable to the international tax community and even to tax professionals, who eventually came to see this standard as inevitable and turned it into an opportunity for offering more services to their clients.

Tax Activism and the Fair Tax Issue

As discussed throughout this volume, the discourse around corporations having to pay their fair share was developed by tax activists and resonated strongly with public outrage at aggressive tax planning, particularly following the FC (see this volume, Chapter 3). Some argued for the development of a fair tax label targeting 'corporations wishing to distinguish themselves from tax avoiders in order to maintain or improve their reputations' (Fair Tax Mark, FTM; see also this volume, Chapter 10). Following the growing public awareness of tax issues in the early 2000s, tax professionals could not ignore the global debates around the notion of a fair tax share.

Tax professionals prefer to work with legal rules and ethical standards in applying these rules, particularly in the case of tax planning services, rather than from the perspective of a 'moral'[4] standard. Along with MNCs, they argue that tax planning is a legal issue, that tax planning is about legality and not morality, and that the advice they give clients should not be based on moral considerations but rather on maximizing efficiencies and shareholder returns. Tax morality claims are not clearly reflected in complex tax rules, particularly in the international tax arena. However, legality in tax planning remains an important grey area, because tax systems are based on legal fictions that can be manipulated for tax planning purposes (Latulippe 2018).

Another core group of actors in tax practice also agree on the predominance of legality over morality, particularly tax lawyers who reject the notion that there is a connection between morality and tax (Arnold 2015), instead arguing that legal advice should be based on the law rather than on contested moral considerations. Pascal Saint-Amans (2015), director of the OECD's Centre for Tax Policy and Administration, also rejects any connection between tax morality and international tax rules, suggesting that the rules need improvement and that tax compliance should not be based on moral considerations as a means of compensating for failures in the rules.

The fair tax debate also includes discussion of the idea of developing a fair tax certification. When the Institute of Chartered Accountants in England and Wales (ICAEW) expressed support for the development of a fair tax certification, it was criticized by many of its members (Stainforth 2014). Unsurprisingly, large firms were sceptical about the relevance and potential for success of such a certification. In the words of a representative of PwC, 'What we think is dangerous is the assertion of "fair" (or unfair) tax' (Bracco 2014). Deloitte's representative stated that 'it seems quite unlikely that we shall see many applicants' (Dodwell 2014). An EY representative framed the issue as a question of compliance rather than fairness, suggesting that the control of compliance should be left to the tax authorities. These statements dismiss any discussion of substantive 'fair tax' issues and overshadow their potential relationship to tax planning.

The response of tax professionals and large accounting firms to public claims for more tax transparency and fairness concerning corporations has generally been dismissive, but there is some evidence of a strategic shift in response to mounting political pressure. While some of their initial responses have been presented in this section, the next section analyses more broadly their arguments relating to tax planning strategies within the fair tax debate and the strategies they have adopted in the face of growing public scrutiny.

6.5 LARGE ACCOUNTING FIRMS' REACTIONS TO THE FAIR TAX DEBATE

Large accounting firms have refrained from entering the fair tax debate by framing their support of tax planning in terms of legality, and by responding to pressures on the tax planning services industry by addressing it primarily as a risk management issue.

Responses Concerning Tax Planning Activities

Large accounting firms have framed the debate on tax avoidance and tax evasion as a question of legality. Contrary to tax evasion, tax avoidance can be 'rationalized' by the assertion that aggressive tax planning strategies are not only legal but required by MNCs in order to remain competitive. In a variety of parliamentary committee hearings (in the UK, the US and Canada), tax professionals have argued that they are involved in applying the law, and that the tax planning that they promote or help implement is 'supportable in law' or is 'supported by a credible basis in tax law' (PwC 2017).

Anchoring their argument in discourses of legality prevents tax professionals from having to take an active role in the discussion of fairness in tax issues. International taxation experts are thoroughly knowledgeable about the impact of national and international tax rules on MNCs. Unlike those in some other policy fields (Tsingou 2003), tax professionals use an approach to tax policy that tends to be driven by rules rather than by standards (Bankman 2001). Therefore, by adopting a disputable interpretation of the rules, tax professionals can find ways to create and justify aggressive tax planning strategies, many of which seem excessive from a tax administration standpoint. The identification and use of loopholes in the law have created the need for new and more complex rules which also get circumvented, further complicating tax systems. For example, tax systems include many specific anti-avoidance measures that have been added to prevent taxpayers from accessing benefits from planning strategies developed by tax professionals. Loopholes in international tax systems are even more difficult to resolve, because states must cooperate to adopt efficient rules, a policy problem discussed in more detail in Chapter 2. Whereas a standards approach might slow down the tax planning industry, a rules-based approach reinforces it. Furthermore, the argument that complex transactions based on existing tax rules are legal, and therefore justifiable, creates a structural hole (Seabrooke 2014; this volume, Chapter 4) preventing the entry of tax activists' ideas in the regime. While activists' discourse based on the fair share imperative resonates well with public opinion, it is at odds with the ideas and interests of influential actors in the global tax regime.

The large accounting firms have more recently acknowledged that some legal tax planning may offend some people. For example, EY states that 'Institutional investors may also grow sceptical, concerned that certain tax planning strategies may be unsustainable contributors to profit' (Ernst & Young 2015). Scores of representatives have affirmed that some of the planning carried out in the past is no longer feasible, and that such activities, while legal, were carried out in a different time and context. For example, a KPMG representative at a parliamentary hearing in Canada said:

> There's a third element, and I call it a reputational lens, that has been developing I think over the last 12 to 13 years. Some of it is because of some of the pressures that taxpayers would be under, multinationals would be under, tax advisers like ourselves around the world would be under, but we've been following that pretty closely. That's part of the reason why, in 2009, we developed our global tax code of conduct to reflect this changing world, because it is a very different world. (Parliament of Canada Standing Committee on Finance 2016)

Acknowledging the importance of ensuring that their tax practice can sustain scrutiny, some firms have adjusted their codes of conduct. However, their principles continue to be rooted in the legality argument. Large accounting firms still refrain from entering into any discussion about tax morality, as expressed by a representative from PwC: 'Listen, if it becomes a matter of morality for us to know if we should act or not, we read the law. It is the legislator who writes them. Our role is to interpret them, that's all. Then the courts recognized that' (Parliament of Canada Standing Committee on Finance 2016, author's translation).

Furthermore, when asked if they would be inclined to change their practices after the UK PAC hearing investigating their involvement in tax planning, KPMG's representative responded: 'we had tax principles in place before the PAC hearing and we continue to operate according to them. We, and our clients, are however conscious of the increased risk of reputational damage and of course we take this into account when giving advice' (*International Tax Review* 2013).

They also argue that governments have adopted tax policies and signed tax treaties to make international planning possible and to foster a competitive environment. For example, Deloitte's representative at the hearings of the Commission parlementaire sur les paradis fiscaux (Quebec) justified certain planning strategies using the Mauritius tax treaty network by arguing that it was the government of Mauritius that decided to sign these numerous tax treaties.

Large accounting firms invite clients to address the issue through a risk assessment process that more specifically evaluates potential risks for reputation as expressed in numerous publications or public statements (Deloitte 2014; KPMG 2015). Public testimony and publications from these firms show that criticisms about the tax planning industry are taken seriously. However, they dismiss the discussion on morality or fairness, and they transpose the criticisms into a risk management issue for their clients.

Are Legal and Moral Arguments Irreconcilable?

Based on analysis of publications, reports and testimony from large accounting firms and their representatives, it is argued here that justifications put forward in support of the tax planning activities by large accounting firms and those of fair tax proponents can conceptually be represented as two distinct scales of acceptability which are difficult to reconcile.

The concept of fair tax as applied to assessing the acceptability of tax planning amounts to these strategies being analysed from a moral perspective. It also includes analysis at the domestic as well as the international level, because, while it could be conceded that an MNC does not legally owe tax in a specific country, the idea that it does not pay tax anywhere, even in the other jurisdictions where it operates, may be unacceptable from a moral standpoint. When adopting a fair tax discourse, the acceptability of tax planning and tax avoidance are measured on the same scale as tax evasion. This approach therefore results in considering overly aggressive tax planning as tantamount to tax evasion. The application of a morality test for tax planning is exemplified by the quote from Margaret Hodge, chair of the UK PAC committee in 2012, when addressing MNCs' representatives, 'We are not accusing you of being illegal, we are accusing you of being immoral' (UK Committee of Public Accounts 2013). Also, a survey from Oxfam shows that public opinion on tax avoidance is not based on legality, with 85 per cent of respondents indicating a belief that tax avoidance is morally wrong even if legal (Oxfam Australia 2016).

The wider importance of morality is also evident in the words of members of parliamentary committees who asked, in interviews with tax professionals, about the basis upon which determinations were made regarding the minimum level of confidence required in a tax strategy before it would be implemented. For example, members of parliament in the Quebec commission asked if large accounting firms would recommend a tax planning strategy that had a low probability of being legal. This question refers to tax strategies that ostensibly abide by the law, but interpret the law in such a way that their strategies might be challenged for not respecting its spirit, and therefore have a certain probability of being found to constitute abusive tax avoidance. However, framing the question in this way combines evasion and avoidance on the same scale and offers the opportunity for large accounting firms to dismiss the question, answering that they don't recommend illegal strategies at all. Figure 6.1 illustrates the tax morality scale used to assess the acceptability of tax planning strategies, tax avoidance and tax evasion.

The grouping of these notions on the same scale does not resonate well with the structure of taxation laws. Within tax systems, tax evasion is generally treated as entirely distinct from tax avoidance, with different burdens of proof and widely varying consequences. Tax professionals' arguments about the legality of tax planning have their roots in a strict view of the tax rules themselves. Professionals repeatedly base their claims to legality on a different scale (see Figure 6.2), according to which tax planning activities never end up in evasion because of the principals' goal to abide by the law.

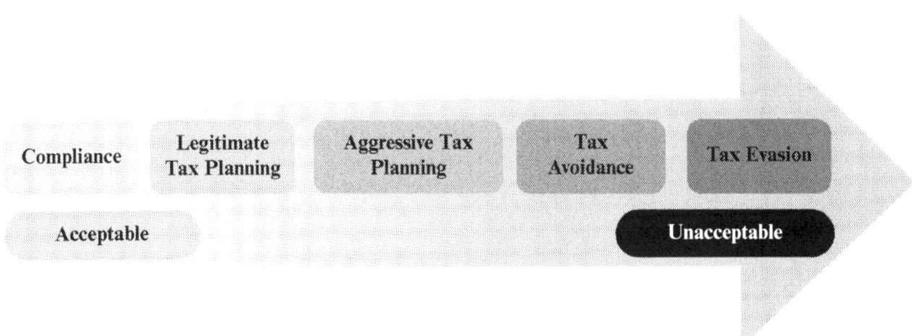

Figure 6.1 The tax morality scale

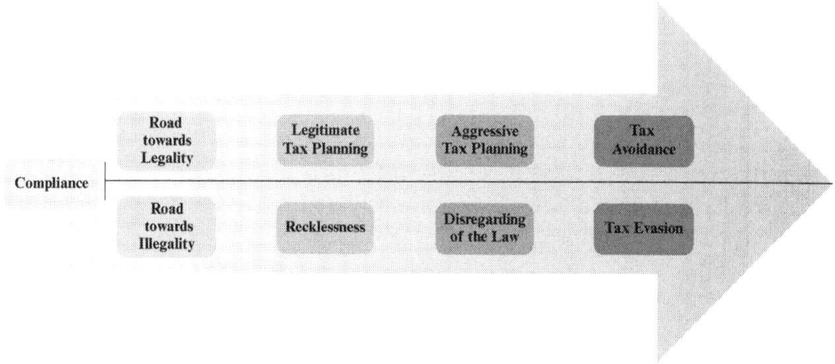

Figure 6.2 The tax legality scale

This other scale features a breaking point, or a fork at which a road must be chosen: either the taxpayer decides to respect the law (which is broadly the case for MNCs), albeit by working under an interpretation of the law that makes it possible to minimize their tax liabilities, from legitimate tax planning to abusive tax avoidance, or the taxpayer decides to disregard the law completely, commit fraud and evade tax. Figure 6.2 illustrates the tax legality scale.

Not all tax planning activities survive the scrutiny of the tax authorities or the courts, but even the most aggressive tax planning and abusive tax avoidance schemes might rely on some plausible (although sometimes weak) interpretation of the law and are not based on an intent to disregard the law, as is the case with evasion. If taxpayers choose the tax planning option, they look at planning opportunities, often with the help of tax professionals. Once on that road, tax planning could become more creative and more aggressive, and ultimately even be considered abusive, in which case it could be successfully challenged by the tax authorities. However, even in this extreme case, nobody would be sued or convicted for tax evasion.

The legality scale also allows tax professionals to rationalize their actions by arguing that governments have adopted certain tax rules, and, if the results are not acceptable, the onus is on government to change the law. This argument would not be sustained on a tax morality continuum, where such planning activities would be considered to be as offensive as evasion.

The above two-tiered continuum circumscribes the debate on legality at the national level. Since each country establishes its tax policy domestically (with some adjustments through international bilateral agreements), some arguments claim that international tax strategies are established to reduce taxes on income earned abroad and therefore are of no concern to specific countries. The tax morality scale may lead to an assessment of international tax planning as unacceptable when corporations pay taxes nowhere or, as was argued in Chapter 2, tax planning facilitates the 'poaching' of the revenue base of one jurisdiction by another. When an argument is based on the tax legality scale, however, the assessment of the application of the law is necessarily restricted to a national analysis, because domestic tax rules are considered distinctively and the global impact for an MNC is disregarded. Therefore, international tax planning strategies can be supported by a tax legality scale even if an MNC pays taxes nowhere.

From a tax morality perspective, placing tax planning on a continuum leading to tax evasion makes sense because of its end effect – the unacceptability of abusive tax avoidance strategies. On the other hand, framing tax planning issues in a discourse based on legality, as firms often do in public hearings, allows them to justify their actions and to avoid taking a stand on the morality of tax planning.

Fair Tax Framed as a Risk Management Issue

Persistent public scrutiny from a tax morality perspective has placed ongoing pressure on large accounting firms with regard to tax planning. Their representatives continue to justify tax planning from a legal perspective, but, as discussed earlier, they have reacted to these pressures by recognizing that, while some tax planning may be legal, it could nevertheless offend the sensibilities of some stakeholders. Tax planning has therefore acquired a risk management element, particularly concerning the risk of reputational damage.

Following the inclusion of tax issues under the rubric of corporate governance after the collapse of Enron, all Big Four accounting firms have published extensively on the concept of tax risk management, with an emphasis on the reputational risks associated with tax planning. In their view, the tax morality issue does not need to be addressed specifically, but rather should be dealt with through risk assessment and risk management processes. According to this position, the decision to implement a tax strategy should take into account the possibility that this planning process could become publicly known, and may offend stakeholders.

This choice of strategy diverts tax professionals from the task of determining whether tax planning strategies are morally acceptable, and allows them instead to concentrate on stakeholders' possible perceptions of the planning, including how these viewpoints can affect risk for their clients. Furthermore, by framing the problem as one of risk management, large accounting firms have created the opportunity to offer risk management support services while not necessarily constraining the tax planning industry. This reaction was also explained by Hasseldine et al. (2011, p. 49), who noted that 'accounting firms have a tendency to exaggerate risks in order to validate and secure future assignments'. Publications, reports and transcripts from testimony by the large accounting firms all show a clear trend over the last decade of briefly acknowledging pressures from tax activists and the media, and then explaining to clients the need to be ready to voluntarily disclose tax information to some degree, develop a tax narrative to justify their tax strategy, and manage tax risk.

6.6 CONCLUSION

The analysis of large accounting firms' publications, reports and testimony in public hearings in this chapter shows that large accounting firms have restricted their involvement in the fair tax debate, and reacted more directly to related issues of tax transparency. So far, their reactions have centred on tax risk management and tax governance. While continuing to use the legality argument in relation to tax planning, they have nevertheless conceded that some strategies, although ostensibly legal, could be considered potentially unacceptable or immoral by stakeholders and thus expose clients to reputational risk.

Tax professionals have an interest in the survival of an international tax policy regime that requires sophisticated planning, thereby securing an ongoing market for their services and expertise. Professionals may thus be reluctant to provide specific advice for the development of tax rules (and even more so a tax standard) that could create further uncertainty for their tax planning activities. Given the preferences of tax professionals regarding tax planning opportunities, it is unlikely that they will provide significant valuable input and expertise to design policies or standards that could interfere with their actual current or anticipated tax planning activities. More specifically, in the short term it seems unlikely that tax professionals would support fundamental reform of the international tax regime such as the adoption of a unitary tax regime for corporate income (this volume, Chapter 2). Tax professionals are most likely to support policies that continue to be based on legal fictions, thereby providing them with some leeway in the tax planning industry. They will likely maintain the argument that governments should simply implement clear policies that outlaw specific strategies if and when they consider these strategies to be exploitative, even though they may be legal. Furthermore, as long as

MNCs consider taxation to be a cost that needs to be reduced as much as possible, substantive involvement from accounting firms in defining what is a fair share in the taxation area is unlikely.

The traditional influence of tax professionals on policy could be explained by the fact that learning and persuasion are more likely to be effective within a 'less politicized' and more 'insulated' setting (Checkel 2001, p. 563), and when 'the parties are dealing with highly technical issues' (Johnston 2001, p. 499), characteristics which describe the context for the involvement of large accounting firms. While corporate taxation might have been insulated from public scrutiny in the past because of its complex language and technical rules, scandals have raised public awareness of fairness issues over the past decade (this volume, Chapter 3). Now that tax planning is under the microscope, it remains to be seen whether tax professionals' expertise will continue to be influential in a more politicized setting, and whether this trend will be maintained or even intensify.

Some conditions, such as increasing public pressure on their own, as well as their clients', reputations, might lead large accounting firms to decide that it is in their interests to take a more active role in discussions around what constitutes a fair tax burden for an MNC. Additionally, if concerns over corporate social responsibility become more prevalent among MNCs, large accounting firms may increasingly need to become involved in helping their clients address such issues beyond the narrow context of risk management. Provided that external pressures to develop a label are strong, tax professionals who do not necessarily agree with the 'fair share' concept may nevertheless wish to take part in the development of a certification. Arguing for the need to provide certainty for businesses at minimal cost, they are then likely to support a label if criteria are clear and unambiguous, and based on a legal assessment of what is fair.

Lastly, some conditions may also reinforce the capacity of large accounting firms to influence the fair tax debate at the international level. The development of criteria for determining fairness must take into account how the gamut of domestic rules and international rules and treaties is to be used, providing large accounting firms with an ongoing incentive to promote their expertise as objective knowledge. Furthermore, global firms can continue to effectively lobby their domestic and international counterparts, while large accounting firms would be expected to provide support by sharing recommendations globally and thus giving their ideas more power.

Will fair tax ideas persist and lead to less aggressive tax practices? Over the last decade or so, large accounting firms' positions have remained based on arguments rooted in a legalistic discourse. However, they have also increasingly been forced to consider the potential tax risks associated with abusive tax planning. Nevertheless, unless some tax information is to be made available publicly, it will remain difficult for the public and actors within civil society to assess the acceptability of tax planning on a 'morality' scale. While large accounting firms recognize the need for MNCs to be ready to provide more information about their tax strategy, they continue to assert that, as long as their tax planning is legal, MNCs should develop a narrative supporting their tax strategy. If this narrative is based in very technical terms, tax professionals will continue to be able to control the debate. In addition, even if every MNC publishes detailed tax information and this information shows that all have availed themselves of legal tax planning, the public may still come to accept these behaviours unless tax activists, particularly tax experts within this network, can continue to spark broader debate on these issues.

NOTES

1. The author expresses her sincere thanks to the Chaire de recherche en fiscalité et en finances publiques, to Anthony Sylvain for research assistance in preparing this chapter, to participants on the 'Paying a Fair Share? Activism, Business and Tax Justice' panel at the International Conference on Public Policy, Milan, 1–4 July 2015 and the 'Paying Their Fair Share: Business, Civil Society and the Campaign against Corporate Tax Evasion' workshop at the University of Tasmania, Hobart, 2–3 February 2016 for comments on previous versions of this chapter, and to other reviewers of this volume.
2. Global revenue from tax practice for 2011–12: US$7944 million for PwC, US$5900 million for Deloitte, US$6011 million for EY and US$4860 million for KPMG (UK Committee of Public Accounts 2013, p. 8).
3. This statement appeared on Deloitte's Canadian website and in letters submitted to the Finance Ministry with regard to consultation on tax matters (Deloitte 2014).
4. The words 'moral' and 'morality' are used here to highlight the arguments expressed in relation to acceptable tax planning strategies and fair tax. It is nonetheless important to note that there are moral values embedded more broadly in tax policymaking, tax rules, tax practices and so on. Other research could focus on the ethics of tax professionals or tax as a business ethic matter or a corporate social responsibility issue, which is not the purpose of this chapter. Therefore, the opposition between 'moral' and 'legal' in this chapter serves the purpose of illustrating the debate which takes place regarding tax planning activities even if it certainly understates the underlying moral dimension in relation to tax in general.

REFERENCES

Aharoni, Y. (1999), 'Internationalization of Professional Services', in D.M. Brock, M.J. Powell and C.R. Hinings (eds), *Restructuring the Professional Organization: Accounting, Health Care and Law*, London: Routledge, pp. 20–40.
Arnold, B.J. (2015), 'Morality and Taxation', Speech at TaxCOOP conference,

Montreal, 3 November, available at http://www.taxcoop-conference.com/wp-content/uploads/2015/12/Brian_Arnold.ppt (accessed 15 February 2017).

Bankman, J. (2001), 'The Business Purpose Doctrine and the Sociology of Tax', *SMU Law Review* **54**, 149–158.

Blouin, J.L. and L.A. Robinson (2011), *Academic Research on FIN48: What Have We Learned?*, Report prepared for the Financial Accounting Foundations' Post-Implementation Review of Financial Accounting Standards Board Interpretation No. 48, available at https://papers.ssrn.com/sol3/papers.cfm?abstract_id=2191137 (accessed 15 February 2017).

Bracco, G. (2014), 'Tax Transparency: What Is Fair Tax?', *PwC Tax Blog*, published electronically 12 March, available at http://pwc.blogs.com/tax/2014/03/tax-transparency-what-is-fair-tax.html (accessed 27 June 2018).

Braithwaite, J. (2005), *Markets in Vice, Markets in Virtue*, Oxford: Oxford University Press.

Branson, C.C. (2012), 'Reportable Tax Positions: A Recent Innovation by the ATO', *Taxation in Australia* **46** (7), 296–300.

CFE Professional Affairs Committee (2013), *European Professional Affairs Handbook for Tax Advisers*, ed. R. Reibel, Brussels: IBFD Publishing.

Checkel, J.T. (2001), 'Why Comply? Social Learning and European Identity Change', *International Organization* **55** (3), 553–588.

Cross, M. and K. Davis (2013), 'Rethinking Epistemic Communities Twenty Years Later', *Review of International Studies* **39** (1), 137–160.

Dabner, J. and M. Burton (2009), 'Lessons for Tax Administrators in Adopting the OECD's "Enhanced Relationship Model": Australia and New Zealand's Experiences', *Bulletin for International Taxation*, **63** (7), 316–326.

Deloitte (2014), 'Risk Angles: Five Questions on the Impact of Tax Risk', available at https://www2.deloitte.com/content/dam/Deloitte/global/Documents/Governance-Risk-Compliance/gx_grc_Deloitte%20Risk%20Angles-Impact%20of%20tax%20risk.pdf (accessed 12 February 2017).

Dodwell, B. (2014), 'The Fair Tax Mark for Multinationals', *Tax Journal*, published electronically 11 July, available at https://www.taxpublications.deloitte.co.uk/tis/dtp.nsf/0/12A13B5144180EAC80257D120063CE53?OpenDocument (accessed 17 November 2016).

Eccleston, R. (2013), *The Dynamics of Global Economic Governance: The OECD, the Global Financial Crisis and the Transformation of International Tax Regulation*, Cheltenham, UK and Northampton, MA, USA: Edward Elgar Publishing.

Edelman, L.B., S.E. Abraham and H.S. Erlanger (1992), 'Professional Construction of Law: The Inflated Threat of Wrongful Discharge', *Law and Society Review* **26** (1), 47–83.

Ernst & Young (2015), 'A New Mountain to Climb: Tax Reputation Risk, Growing Transparency Demands and the Importance of Data Readiness', available at http://www.ey.com/Publication/vwLUAssets/ey-managing-tax-transparency-and-reputation-risk/$FILE/ey-managing-tax-transparency-and-reputation-risk.pdf (accessed 11 February 2017).

Gravelle, J.G. (2003), *The Enron Debacle: Lessons for Tax Policy*, Discussion Paper No. 6, Washington, DC: Urban–Brookings Tax Policy Center, available at http://webarchive.urban.org/UploadedPDF/310622_Enron.pdf (accessed 12 February 2017).

Harvey, R.J. (2010), 'Schedule UTP: An Insider's Summary of the Background,

Key Concepts, and Major Issues', *DePaul Business and Commercial Law Journal* **9** (3), 349.
Hasseldine, J., K. Holland and P. van der Rijt (2011), 'The Market for Corporate Tax Knowledge', *Critical Perspectives on Accounting* **22** (1), 39–52.
International Tax Review (2013), 'UK Big Four Tax Partners', available at http://www.internationaltaxreview.com/Article/3288226/UK-Big-4-tax-partners.html (accessed 12 February 2017).
International Tax Review (2016), 'Welcome to World Tax 2018', available at www.itrworldtax.com (accessed 17 February 2017).
Johnston, A.I. (2001), 'Treating International Institutions as Social Environments', *International Studies Quarterly* **45** (4), 487–515.
Jones, C., Y. Temouri and A. Cobham (2018), 'Tax Haven Networks and the Role of the Big 4 Accounting Firms', *Journal of World Business* 53 (2), 177–193.
Kerr, H.I., K.J. McKenzie and J.M. Mintz (eds) (2012), *Tax Policy in Canada*, Toronto: Canadian Tax Foundation.
KPMG (2004), *Tax in the Boardroom: A Discussion Paper*, available at http://www.kpmg.com.au/aci/docs/tax-boardroom.pdf (accessed 13 February 2017).
KPMG (2014), 'Country-by-Country Reporting', *KPMG Insights*, September, available at https://home.kpmg.com/xx/en/home/insights/2014/09/country-by-country-reporting.html (accessed 17 November 2016).
KPMG (2015), 'Reputational Risk: Boards Need to Focus on Tax', available at https://home.kpmg.com/au/en/home/insights/2015/12/reputational-risk-impact-on-tax.html (accessed 12 February 2017).
Kroll, K.M. (2011), 'Dealing with the IRS on Uncertain Tax Positions', *CIO*, available at https://www.cio.com/article/2411503/finance/dealing-with-the-irs-ruling-on-uncertain-tax-positions.html (accessed 26 June 2018).
Larson, M.S. (2013), *The Rise of Professionalism: Monopolies of Competence and Sheltered Markets*, Piscataway, NJ: Transaction Publishers.
Latulippe, L. (2016), 'Tax Competition: An Internalized Policy Goal', in T. Rixen and P. Dietsch (eds), *Global Tax Governance: What Is Wrong with It and How to Fix It*, Colchester: ECPR Press, pp. 77–100.
Latulippe, L. (2018), 'Taxing Multinationals in a Globalised World', in B. Alepin, L. Otis and B.M. Dodson (eds), *Winning the Tax Wars: Tax Competition and Cooperation*, Series on International Taxation, Alphen aan den Rijn: Wolters Kluwer, pp. 47–58.
Lesage, D. and T. Van de Graaf (2013), 'Thriving in Complexity? The OECD System's Role in Energy and Taxation', *Global Governance: A Review of Multilateralism and International Organizations* **19** (1), 83–92.
Murphy, R. (2003), 'A Proposed International Accounting Standard Reporting Turnover and Tax by Location', available at http://www.taxjustice.net/cms/upload/pdf/new_int._Account_Standard.pdf (accessed 16 February 2017).
Oxfam Australia (2016), 'The Hidden Billions: How Tax Havens Impact Lives at Home and Abroad', available at https://www.oxfam.org.au/wp-content/uploads/2016/06/OXF003-Tax-Havens-Report-FA2-WEB.pdf (accessed 14 February 2017).
Parliament of Canada Standing Committee on Finance (2016), 'Comprehensive Review of Canada's Tax System', available at http://www.ourcommons.ca/Committees/en/FINA/StudyActivity?studyActivityId=9323214 (accessed 11 February 2017).

Picciotto, S. (1995), 'The Construction of International Taxation', in Y. Dezalay and D. Sugarman (eds), *Professional Competition and Professional Power: Lawyers, Accountants and the Social Construction of Markets*, London: Routledge, pp. 25–50.
Picciotto, S. (2011), *Regulating Global Corporate Capitalism*, Cambridge: Cambridge University Press.
Porter, T. and M. Webb (2008), 'The Role of the OECD in the Orchestration of Global Knowledge Networks', in R. Mahon and S. McBride (eds), *The OECD and Transnational Governance*, Vancouver: UBC Press, pp. 43–59.
PwC (2017), 'What We Stand For', available at https://www.pwc.com/gx/en/tax/assets/pwc-global-tax-code-of-conduct-2017.pdf (accessed 27 June 2018).
Ramirez, C. (2012), 'How Big Four Audit Firms Control Standard-Setting in Accounting and Auditing', in I. Huault and C. Richard (eds), *Finance: The Discreet Regulator*, Basingstoke: Palgrave Macmillan, pp. 40–58.
Rixen, T. (2008), *The Political Economy of International Tax Governance*, London: Palgrave Macmillan.
Rostain, T. (2006), 'Travails in Tax: KPMG and the Tax-Shelter Controversy', in D.L. Rhode and D.J. Luban (eds), *Legal Ethics: Law Stories*, New York: Foundation Press, pp. 5–25.
Saint-Amans, P. (2015), 'The OECD'S BEPS Project', Speech at TaxCOOP conference, Montreal, 3 November.
Seabrooke, L. (2014), 'Epistemic Arbitrage: Transnational Professional Knowledge in Action', *Journal of Professions and Organization* **1** (1), 49–64.
Seabrooke, L. and D. Wigan (2013), *Emergent Entrepreneurs in Transnational Advocacy Networks: Professional Mobilization in the Fight for Global Tax Justice*, Working Paper No. 41, GR:EEN, Global Reordering: Evolution through European Networks, FP7, available at http://pipesproject.eu/assets/GREEN41.pdf (accessed 1 November 2017).
Sikka, P. (2010), 'Smoke and Mirrors: Corporate Social Responsibility and Tax Avoidance', *Accounting Forum* **34** (3–4), 153–168.
Sikka, P. and M.P. Hampton (2005), 'The Role of Accountancy Firms in Tax Avoidance: Some Evidence and Issues', *Accounting Forum* **29** (3), 325–343.
Slemrod, J. (2004), *The Economics of Corporate Tax Selfishness*, Working Paper No. w10858, Cambridge, MA: National Bureau of Economic Research, available at http://www.bus.umich.edu/otpr/WP2004-8.pdf (accessed 12 February 2017).
Stainforth, P. (2014), 'Mixed Reaction to ICAEW Support of Fair Tax Mark', *Tax Journal* **1207**, available at https://www.taxjournal.com/articles/mixed-reaction-icaew-support-fair-tax-mark-06032014 (accessed 27 June 2018).
Steuerle, C.E. (2008), *Contemporary US Tax Policy*, Washington, DC: Urban Institute Press.
Teather, D. (2003), 'Scandal of Crashed Company's Tax Evasion', *Guardian*, published electronically 14 February, available at https://www.theguardian.com/business/2003/feb/14/corporatefraud.enron1 (accessed 11 February 2017).
Tsingou, E. (2003), *Transnational Policy Communities and Financial Governance: The Role of Private Actors in Derivatives Regulation*, CSGR Working Paper No. 111/03, Coventry: Centre for the Study of Globalisation and Regionalisation, University of Warwick, available at http://citeseerx.ist.psu.edu/viewdoc/download?doi=10.1.1.412.3624&rep=rep1&type=pdf (accessed 17 February 2017).
UK Committee of Public Accounts (2013), *Tax Avoidance: The Role of Large*

Accountancy Firms: Forty-fourth Report of Session 2012–13: Report, together with Formal Minutes, Oral and Written Evidence, available at https://publications.parliament.uk/pa/cm201213/cmselect/cmpubacc/870/870.pdf (accessed 14 February 2017).

7. Paying a 'fair share': multinational corporations' perspectives on taxation

John Mikler and Ainsley Elbra

7.1 INTRODUCTION

Multinational corporations (MNCs) can take advantage of opportunities to reduce or eliminate their taxation obligations in the states where they earn much of their revenue. These opportunities arise as states use tax concessions to compete for corporate investment. However, since the Financial Crisis (FC) many governments have been beset by slow economic growth and unsustainable public debt levels. In response to these twin challenges, they have sought to regain fiscal control by searching for ways to increase government revenue whilst reducing spending, often on social services. Clearly, there are contradictions in tax competition between states and governments' goals of fiscal consolidation. It is no wonder the ability of MNCs to avoid paying their 'fair share' of tax, combined with austerity measures being endured by citizens, has led to the campaign waged by tax justice activists, international non-government organisations and the media, detailed in Chapter 3 of this volume. The campaign has been highly critical of the actions of MNCs, painting corporate tax avoidance as a failure of democratic governance, an issue that reflects a growing dissatisfaction with the distribution of power and wealth in society (e.g. see Oxfam America 2016). Our point in this chapter is that this campaign has impacted MNCs' legitimacy, with the dismissive responses of many corporations to the claims that they are not paying their 'fair share' of tax galvanising public opinion against corporate tax avoidance.

In section 7.2 we consider the ideological and structural context in which MNCs operate. While the bailouts and fiscal stimulus measures the FC necessitated seemed to presage the end of neoliberal globalisation, eight years later they appear to have been temporary measures designed to get national and global economies back 'on track' (e.g. see Wade 2010). As states seek to pay off the public debt they incurred, neoliberal ideology has been re-embedded rather than undermined, with power retained or increased by MNCs, and with the burden for picking up the costs falling on society (e.g. see Crouch 2011; Blyth 2013). This is the starting point for our analysis, and it might seem commensurate with critical accounts of neoliberal globalisation (e.g. see Teeple and McBride 2011). However, we demonstrate that, rather than global markets being free, competitive and globally diffuse, their economic and geographical concentration in the hands of a small number of MNCs headquartered in a small number of powerful states, particularly the US, is the contemporary reality. The power these MNCs wield, in both political and economic terms, underlies the potential for systematic tax avoidance as they notionally shift the jurisdictions in which they earn profits.

In section 7.3 we consider the likelihood of MNCs participating in emerging private governance regimes and voluntarily paying tax. It can be argued that their taxation strategies affect brand value, and therefore that their legitimacy is potentially damaged by being seen to aggressively minimise tax payments. If corporations view their reputations as precious assets that may be jeopardised, then their desire to be seen as good corporate citizens may mitigate their efforts to minimise taxes paid. However, we contrast these theoretical arguments with data on how corporate leaders themselves judge corporate reputation. Focusing on the US-based MNCs most publicly attacked for aggressive tax avoidance strategies, we demonstrate that their perceptions of legitimacy are at odds with their social responsibility to pay a fair share of tax. This suggests that this group of powerful firms are unlikely to feel motivated to voluntarily do so.

In section 7.4 we turn to how corporations themselves have discursively shaped their legitimacy in respect of their tax obligations in light of the criticisms they have faced. We consider the cases of Google and Apple as two of the world's most visible corporations in terms of their brand value and their efforts to minimise tax by profit shifting. Using statements made to government inquiries, we demonstrate that they have adopted an approach of highlighting how their tax strategies are designed to meet their legal obligations rather than paying a socially desirable amount of tax (this volume, Chapter 6), and declaring that their actions should be seen as legitimate in this light.

We conclude that, despite what might be perceived as risk to brand value, MNCs' strategies to minimise tax are not being conducted with any sense of shame, but are being pursued proactively and defended proudly. However, we suggest that the result is that corporate leaders are promoting the crisis of legitimacy they should seek to avoid. In stressing that their corporations' actions are legal, reasonable and even the fault of governments they have increased the likelihood of ceding power to regulators, over whom they have previously sought the discursive leverage that has underpinned claims of good citizenship. In regarding social concern as largely irrelevant in the face of what is most important to their reputations (financial performance and shareholder value) it may be that they have unintentionally provided the most compelling argument for the need for international agreements to mitigate the tax minimisation opportunities they have seized.

7.2 GLOBALISATION AND THE 'BUSINESS OF BUSINESS'

MNCs are usually conceived of as market actors (e.g. see Broome 2014, pp. 92–111). Therefore, material returns are 'naturally' seen as their prime focus, evidenced through measures such as their profitability, share price, shareholder value, competitiveness and market share. There is much robust debate between those in favour of this conception and more critical voices of it (e.g. see Micklethwait and Wooldridge 2003), but there is neither the space nor the need to review the vast literature around neoliberal globalisation here. It suffices to say that Milton Friedman's (1970) declaration that 'the social responsibility of business is to increase its profits', while the collective, public good is the responsibility of governments, is problematic in the context of a globalised economy. Given the reality of markets and market actors that are no longer territorially defined, versus states and their governments which are, the political options for states seem reduced to either neoliberalism or shared sovereignty for global governance (e.g. see Martell 2007).

Yet the global economy is neither as deterritorialised nor as diffuse as is often claimed. Wealthy, industrialised countries still account for 80 per cent of world output and 70 per cent of international trade, and make up to 90 per cent of foreign direct investments (Chang 2008, p. 32). To be more accurate, it is the corporations from these countries that do so. Table 7.1 demonstrates that 84 per cent of FT Global 500 corporations[1] are headquartered in just ten states, with the US alone accounting for nearly half of them. Even with the rapid emergence of China and India as economic powers, 'a statistical profile for the current corporation indicates that it is predominantly Anglo-American' (Harrod 2006, p. 27). Between 1990 and 2013, 81 per cent of the value of mergers and acquisitions (M&A) purchases were carried out by corporations from developed states, with those from the US and Europe alone accounting for 67 per cent of total corporations. The top two states from which the purchasers came were the US (17 per cent) and the UK (14 per cent) (UNCTAD 2014a). It is also the case

Table 7.1 The top ten headquarters of FT Global 500 corporations, 2015

Country	Number of corporations	Percentage
US	208	42
China[a]	55	11
Japan	35	7
UK	27	5
France	24	5
Canada	19	4
Germany	18	4
India	13	3
Switzerland	11	2
Sweden	10	2
Total	420	84

Note: [a] The FT Global 500 lists China and Hong Kong separately, but they have been combined here.

Source: *Financial Times* (2015).

that over the same period the US and Europe accounted for 73 per cent of M&A sales – i.e. a similar percentage to M&A purchases – again with the top two states being the US (25 per cent) and UK (16 per cent) (UNCTAD 2014b). Rather than global diffusion in MNCs' operations, the dominant corporations from the world's economically dominant states have been buying each other, further entrenching the geographical concentration of their operations. Yet ironically while corporate power is increasingly concentrated the offshore system which evolved over the second half of the twentieth century, the system has also allowed MNCs to use an array of small offshore centres to minimise their global tax liabilities.

It is also the case that all the world's major industries are controlled by five corporations at most, and 28 per cent have one corporation accounting for more than 40 per cent of global sales (Harrod 2006, p. 25; see also Fuchs 2007). The world's major corporations, based in the world's largest economies, control trade and investment flows and do so because they dominate the markets for their products. In dominating these markets, they do so from the states in which they are headquartered. Although the world's 100 largest corporations ranked by foreign assets have an average Transnationality Index (TNI) of 60,[2] suggesting a high degree of independence from their home base, many are in fact bi-national or regional rather than global (e.g. see Rugman and Verbeke 2009), and the average TNI of US MNCs is 51. On average, these well-established MNCs from the world's most powerful industrialised state retain half their sales, assets and employment at home, even though they have had the most time to 'go global' (UNCTAD 2014c).

Studies have also demonstrated that corporations' headquarters remain of strategic importance to them (Rugman and Oh 2010; Buckley 2011). It is not just that individual firms have different ways of organising their operations, but that 'the basic institutional structures of MNCs may be influenced or even determined by the characteristics of states' (Pauly and Reich 1997, p. 5). If 'national boundaries demarcate the nationally specific systems of education, finance, corporate management, and government that generate social conventions, norms, and laws' (Wade 1996, p. 85), then corporate structures and strategies must also be substantially influenced by the national institutional contexts of their operations. The importance of this concept is clear in the example of the United States, which is often taken as the exemplar of liberal market shareholder capitalism (e.g. see Hall and Soskice 2001; Jackson and Deeg 2008). This has significant implications not just for corporations' actual material interests, but for how they *perceive* the achievement of them; namely, from a liberal market perspective.

Therefore, MNCs like Google, Apple, Amazon and Starbucks that have been widely criticised for minimising their tax payments may perhaps be better conceived as US corporations that control the markets in which they operate at home and abroad. Their desire to minimise the tax they pay, in pursuit of short-term profitability and shareholder value, is a reflection of their home state's institutional preferences. That is, they have an institutional and strategic predisposition to primarily focus on the bottom line in terms of production and sales, as well as related financial indicators of market performance such as share price and ability to pay dividends (e.g. see Lazonick 2014). Furthermore, US-based corporations are more likely to seek to impose their form of capitalism globally as 'best practice', given that they face pressure from their shareholders to deliver value regardless of the location of their operations. By comparison, those from state-guided or coordinated economies are more inclined to share their decisions with a range of other stakeholders (e.g. see Geppert and Dörrenbächer 2011). Being accustomed to a more collaborative form of capitalism in their home states, theirs by definition cannot be a global model.

However, it may also be the case that all corporations, regardless of the institutional and organisational preferences of their headquarters, have incentives to seek low-tax jurisdictions when they invest and operate abroad. Thus, competition for business location choice inevitably gives rise to tax competition by states seeking to attract business operations. In fact, surveys such as Deloitte's (2014)[3] demonstrate that low levels of corporate taxation and 'transfer pricing issues' were regarded as of 'extreme importance' in making foreign direct investment choices. As was noted in Chapter 2, transfer pricing is a prominent tax minimisation practice, involving lowering the profits of a corporation's division located in a state with higher taxes by reporting the profits in another jurisdiction that has low (or no) tax. But transfer pricing also means that corporations may not have to move their operations at all. They may stay 'at home', or locate in jurisdictions where they have business interests, whether these be productive assets, sales or skilled employees, and pay tax elsewhere. If they can do business in one jurisdiction while notionally and legally shifting the jurisdiction in which they pay tax, then national institutional variations and the strategic preferences that flow from these may effectively be retained while for tax purposes they are irrelevant.

In addition to the liberal institutional foundations of most of the world's major MNCs, those that are most global in their operations would seem to have an interest in choosing to exercise the option of paying minimal taxes in jurisdictions that are outside both the geographical focus of their market interests and the location of the majority of their operations. Either way, it is states that should be central to understanding MNCs' strategies, because it is the lack of coordination between national tax regimes that enables MNCs to act on their interests. In short, either their liberal institutional embedding in their home state (for the dominant US MNCs) or the tax competition evident between states (for all MNCs) explains the corporate motivation and ability to engage in tax minimisation strategies.

7.3 CORPORATE REPUTATION

Although MNCs may be conceived as instrumentally motivated global pursuers of profits, with those from the US also driven by an institutional preference for liberal market shareholder capitalism due to their headquarters, nevertheless they also have an interest in ensuring their reputations are not tarnished by their actions. This is because, while they can minimise tax by shifting the jurisdiction in which they pay it without necessarily shifting their operations, normative questions of whether it is 'right' or 'wrong' for them to do so are important in the sense that if they do not use their power in ways that are regarded as socially responsible they risk losing it. Lawrence et al. (2005, p. 47; originally Davis and Blomstrom 1966) call this 'the iron law of responsibility', and it has led international business scholars to claim that, given the power they possess, corporations understand they must 'proactively build reputational capital for strategic advantage' (Jackson 2004, p. 3). In essence, the argument is that corporate leaders realise that, while shareholders are interested in profitable businesses, they also expect firms to mitigate both market and regulatory risks by adhering to socially accepted norms of business behaviour.

The result is that corporate reputations may be regarded as 'exceedingly valuable commodities' (O'Callaghan 2007, p. 114) or even intangible assets (e.g. see Gotsi and Wilson 2001). The ability of NGO campaigns and other forms of societal pressure to promote or undermine corporate reputation potentially functions as a self-regulatory mechanism to constrain socially negative aspects of corporate behaviour. This has given rise to the widespread embrace of corporate social responsibility (CSR) programmes. Beyond traditional notions of philanthropy and charity, CSR suggests an active concern for stakeholders very broadly defined, and a willingness to take action to mitigate the negative consequences of all business activities. In acting as a self-regulatory mechanism, CSR programmes that enhance corporate reputation may be used as leverage to avoid government regulation while enhancing profitability. For example, a 2001 review of the international business literature found that 68 per cent of studies identified a positive correlation between socially responsible firms and profitability, while just 15 per cent found a negative correlation (Margolis and Walsh 2001). More pragmatically, Vogel (2006, p. 17) argues that although 'there is no evidence that behaving more virtuously makes firms more profitable . . . conversely the fact that CSR does not make firms *less* profitable means that it is possible for a firm to commit resources to CSR without becoming less competitive'. It makes sense for companies to engage in CSR programmes, as they either increase or have little to no effect on profitability, while the enhanced corporate reputation they confer may well convince others that self-regulatory mechanisms are effective in enhancing social outcomes.

The pioneering corporate reputation study is the annual Fortune 500 World's Most Admired Companies list (Ponzi et al. 2011). The list is based on questionnaires provided to corporate representatives and takes place in two rounds (Melo and Garrido-Morgado 2012). In the 2015 study, respondents from 668 firms across 29 countries were first asked to rank their industry peers across nine criteria, one of which was community responsibility. Secondly, the industry leaders who responded to the first round of industry surveys (4104 in total in 2015) were asked to select their ten most admired corporations overall. The results are presented in Table 7.2 for the top five most admired corporations, and their ranking by criteria if in the top ten for each of these. What is notable is that *none* of the top five corporations judged by their peers as most admired are ranked in the top five for the criterion of community responsibility. In fact, they do not even rank in the top ten. This suggests that these firms' ranking

Table 7.2 Fortune 500 World's Most Admired Companies ranked by key attributes, 2015

Most admired	Community responsibility	Management quality	Quality of products/ services offered	Innova-tiveness	Value as a long-term investment	Soundness of financial position	Ability to attract, develop and retain talent	Wise use of corporate assets	Effectiveness of conducting a global business
1 Apple	–	–	4	1	7	3	5	9	3
2 Google	–	6	5	2	3	1	2	–	5
3 Berkshire Hathaway	–	–	–		10	–	–	–	–
4 Amazon	–	–	3	4	–	–	10	–	–
5 Starbucks	–	9	–	8	–	–	–	–	–

Note: '–' signifies that the corporation was not ranked in the top ten.

Sources: http://fortune.com/worlds-most-admired-companies/2015/ (accessed 2 May 2016); http://fortune.com/2015/02/19/wmac-ranked-by-key-attribute/ (accessed 2 May 2016).

as 'most admired' is derived mostly from the other criteria, particularly management quality, quality of products/services offered, innovativeness, and soundness of financial position.

Because the Fortune 500 World's Most Admired Companies list represents the view of 'business insiders' from the world's largest, most well-known firms, it has been criticised for only presenting their views rather than the views of those whose judgement actually confers or undermines the reputations corporations seek (e.g. see Brown and Perry 1994; Fryxell and Wang 1994). But what corporate representatives value in judging corporate reputation has implications for corporate tax strategies. Four of the top five most admired firms – Apple, Google, Amazon and Starbucks – have faced the most high-profile public criticism for their complicated global corporate taxation structures. The importance of factors other than community responsibility for them suggests CSR is unlikely to be a primary driver in considering their taxation obligations. This is supported by studies such as Davis et al. (2016), who find that corporations with the most extensive CSR programmes are those with the most aggressive tax minimisation efforts. They conclude not only that 'the payment of taxes is not viewed as an important socially responsible activity' but also that 'CSR and taxes act as substitutes rather than complements' (Davis et al. 2016, p. 65). It takes no great leap of logic to conclude, as they do, that CSR activities are primarily intended to offset negative perceptions arising from aggressive tax avoidance strategies.

7.4 DISCURSIVE POWER AND LEGITIMACY

The prediction that business should be able to leverage the growing interconnectedness associated with globalisation to demand business-friendly policies was highlighted by the likes of Fukuyama (1992), Strange (1997, p. 184) and Friedman (2000), who declared that states were retreating in the face of MNCs, for which they would increasingly serve as mere 'handmaidens'. The importance of corporate reputation should make this a problematic prediction, yet because corporate leaders rank community responsibility below other factors, the 'race to the bottom' thesis that characterises so much of the globalisation literature would seem to hold weight – i.e. states competing to bid down taxes and standards to attract corporate investment. However, if corporations' reputations come under attack as a result of their CSR efforts being seen for what they really are, namely 'window-dressing' their real agenda of underpinning brand value through financial performance, then this weakens their position.

Generally speaking, 'whoever sets the terms of discourse will almost always determine the outcome' (Lowi 2001, p. 131). Therefore, if MNCs lose the ability to do this on the basis of their reputations then they are in a diminished position to make widely accepted claims as to their social responsibility. In technical terms, they lose discursive power. This refers to the ability to use communicative practices to shape the preferences of others, to actively promote norms of behaviour that become the accepted 'rules of the game'. Essentially, it is the ability to create 'truths' that are accepted by other political actors including policy-makers (Lukes 1974). As Elbra (2014, p. 247) puts it, 'interests do not need to be pursued if they can be created', and thus, if corporations are able to develop a high level of perceived legitimacy, they can promote the 'projection of a particular set of interests as the general interest' (Levy and Newell 2002, p. 87). If they lose the ability to do this, they risk being in a position where their claims are more easily 'dismissed by a skeptical and cynical public' (Tienhaara 2014, p. 167).

Fuchs (2007) outlines a three-faces-of-power framework for global businesses, which includes instrumental and structural in addition to discursive forms of power. According to her framework, instrumental power is the most basic form of power MNCs wield. It entails them directly influencing the policy process through staffing governments with industry supporters, and influencing government decision-makers through campaign contributions and lobbying (Lukes 1974; Hacker and Pierson 2002). This type of power is relatively weak owing to its high visibility if exercised publicly, or because of the relational networks required in order for it to be exercised covertly (e.g. see Culpepper 2011). Whether more overt or covert, it means that business agendas must be pursued through the expenditure of considerable time and resources in order to influence policy-makers who may be more inclined for political reasons to respond to social concerns. Structural power refers to corporations' size and economic dominance. Their geographical and market concentration referred to previously gives MNCs leverage to organise issues 'in' and 'out' of politics, and have their interests served without explicitly making the case for this (e.g. see Bachrach and Baratz 1962). For example, they can punish or reward countries for the provision of favourable investment conditions by implicitly threatening to relocate their operations (e.g. see Frank 1978; Cox 1987).

What we are suggesting here is that MNCs risk having to fall back on the instrumental and structural power they possess if they lose discursive power in defending and justifying their tax minimisation strategies. Up to now, they have not had to risk doing so, because they have been able to rely on the glacial progress of global corporate tax reform. As was noted in Chapter 1, over two decades ago the G7 Finance Ministers (1996) noted the following: '[G]lobalization is creating new challenges in the field of tax policy. Tax schemes aimed at attracting financial and other geographically mobile activities can create harmful tax competition between States, carrying risks of distorting trade and investment and could lead to the erosion of national tax bases.' Yet, despite public commitments made to tackle the problem, there have been few tangible outcomes. Frustrating the process of reform has been wavering support from member states such as the US, whose commitment and participation are seen as crucial to effective reform efforts. The most recent of these, the OECD's Base Erosion and Profit Shifting (BEPS) initiative, promises reform of global tax norms and has been undertaken through extensive multilateral negotiations. However, as discussed in Chapter 2 of this volume, the BEPS initiative's success hinges on sustaining international cooperation in the context of the divergent interests of participating states (Palan and Wigan 2014).

The lack of an international agreement has served the interests of MNCs, not just for the tax minimisation opportunities that flow from states' competition in taxation rates, but also in the sense that it allows their motivations to be obscured. As J.K. Galbraith (2001 [1979], p. 121) opined on the operations of American corporations prior to what we now call globalisation:

> The service of the accepted image of economic life to the political needs of the business firm – the large corporation in particular – is, in fact, breathtaking. In broad concept it removes from the corporation the power to do wrong, leaves with it only the power to do right. Are prices too high? The corporation is blameless. Prices are set by the market. Are products deficient in safety, durability and design? Are they really needed? They only reflect the will of the sovereign consumer. . . . One sees how great are the political and social advantages of this image of economic life.

However advantageous it may be, seeing MNCs as simply operating on the basis of global market forces, obeying the imperatives of consumers and shareholders, and essentially being mechanisms of profit maximisation while obeying legal requirements, is now under attack as a legitimate vision of them and their responsibilities. Instead, they are increasingly seen as what they are in reality: powerful economic entities exploiting the opportunities afforded them by an inadequate and antiquated state-based corporate tax regime. The cases of Apple and Google illustrate how MNCs have used the arbitrage opportunities afforded through their negotiations with, and the differing national regulatory contexts of, the states in which they operate (i.e. instrumental power), coupled with their national and global economic dominance (i.e. their structural power) to dramatically minimise their tax payments. The dissatisfaction of citizens of states in which these firms operate but pay little or no tax has led to governments undertaking a series of inquiries and, in the case of the UK, embarking on a unilateral attempt to tax 'diverted profits' (Callaghan 2015). Corporate attempts to defend their strategies when challenged by policy-makers suggest that they are in danger of losing discursive power and thence legitimacy in respect of their operations.

Apple

Apple is headquartered in the US, with a 2015 market capitalisation of US$416 billion. In 2014 the firm's global operations recorded turnover of US$182.7 billion and net profit of US$39.5 billion (Apple Inc 2015). With a TNI of 59.6, it has the majority of its sales, assets and employees abroad (61, 58 and 60 per cent respectively), and so it may be thought of as a global corporation (UNCTAD 2014c). The company has been the focus of much attention regarding corporate tax minimisation, including the recent European Commission 'state aid' ruling (subject to appeal proceedings at the time of publication) demanding that Apple repay €13 billion in back taxes to a reluctant Irish government, which was concerned that this might damage its competitiveness as a low-tax jurisdiction (Campbell 2016). Apple's key tax minimisation strategy was the creation of three subsidiaries incorporated in Ireland but which were effectively not registered as tax residents of any country. In essence, Apple pays taxes in the US but is legally able to claim that most of its profits are earned in other jurisdictions. These jurisdictions, in turn, do not regard these profits as taxable. Apple's subsidiaries collect dividends from most of Apple's offshore affiliates and pay little to no tax on these. In fact, they would seem to exist primarily for this purpose. One of them, Apple Operations International, receives dividends from most of Apple's offshore affiliates but has no employees and no physical presence. Another, Apple Sales International, contracts manufacturers in China to make Apple products, which it then sells to Apple Distribution International, which pays as little as 2 per cent tax on its profits, having negotiated this 'special' rate with the Irish government (Schwartz and Duhigg 2013). It is this complex tax avoidance strategy that attracted the attention of the European Commission (EC). The Irish government's decision to appeal against the ruling, alongside Apple, reflects the strategic nature of tax competition for attracting foreign investment.

The result is not just that Apple pays less tax in the US, but also that it pays less tax in other states in which it conducts business. This is because until recently Irish tax law asserted jurisdiction only over companies managed and controlled in Ireland, but as Apple is managed and controlled from its US headquarters this arrangement allowed Apple to escape both US and Irish taxation. The US has consistently criticised the use of sweetheart tax deals by Ireland (despite the US itself being considered a tax haven by many analysts), as it seeks to maximise the share of Apple's taxation payments directed to the US government (Bowers 2016). In this sense, the US remains less interested in Apple and other MNCs' tax avoidance strategies than it is in other sovereign states asserting their rights to tax American-headquartered companies. Indeed, the US Treasury Department's main concern at the time of the EC's decision was that 'the EU was trying to become some kind of global tax authority' (Cellan-Jones 2016).

In May 2013, the United States Senate Committee on Homeland Security and Governmental Affairs held a public inquiry into Apple's compliance with US tax laws to 'spotlight Apple's extensive tax-avoidance strategies' after finding evidence of tax avoidance and an 'unusual tax scheme' whereby its three Irish subsidiaries paid no tax in either Ireland or the US (US Senate Committee on Homeland Security and Governmental Affairs 2013). Among the most damning accusations were that in exploiting the gap between US and Irish tax jurisdictions Apple was able to pay *no* tax on income totalling US$30 billion over 2009–12 through Apple Operations International, and enjoyed a tax rate of 0.05 per cent on income of US$74 billion over the same period through Apple Sales International (US Senate Committee on Homeland Security and Governmental Affairs 2013). Senator Levin argued that 'Apple wasn't satisfied with shifting its profits to a low-tax offshore tax haven' but instead 'created offshore entities holding tens of billions of dollars, while claiming to be a tax resident nowhere' (US Senate Committee on Homeland Security and Governmental Affairs 2013). Senator McCain noted that while 'Apple claims to be the largest US corporate taxpayer . . . it is also among America's largest tax avoiders' (US Senate Committee on Homeland Security and Governmental Affairs 2013). The inquiry focused on the following three tax practices: using a cost sharing agreement to transfer valuable intellectual property overseas, thereby moving profits into a tax haven jurisdiction; using loopholes to disregard offshore subsidiaries in order to shed billions of dollars in income that would otherwise be taxable in the US; and negotiating a tax rate of less than 2 per cent with the government of Ireland. This rate is significantly lower than the nation's 12 per cent statutory rate, and having negotiated it Apple used Ireland as the base for its extensive network of overseas subsidiaries (US Senate Committee on Homeland Security and Governmental Affairs 2013).

In addition to a written submission, Apple sent its chief executive officer, Tim Cook, and chief financial officer, Peter Oppenheimer, to represent the company at the inquiry's hearing. In his opening statement, Cook highlighted the company's decision to keep its product design and development staff (approximately 50000 employees) in the US, with the jobs created by companies in Apple's US supply chain, and pointed out that Apple is the largest corporate taxpayer in the US. This was based on the company paying US$6 billion, or an effective tax rate of 30.5 per cent, in the US (Cook 2013). Although Senator McCain noted that this disregarded revenue the firm had moved offshore to be effectively outside the reach of *any* tax authorities, Cook (2013, p. 3) stated that Apple pays all the taxes it owes, complies with the spirit and letter of the laws, and does not 'stash money on some Caribbean Island'. Cook (2013, p. 4) concluded:

> Apple has always believed in the simple, not the complex. You can see it in our products and the way we conduct ourselves. It is in this spirit that we recommend a dramatic simplification of the corporate tax code. This reform should be revenue neutral, eliminate all corporate tax expenditures, lower corporate income tax rates and implement a reasonable tax on foreign earnings that allows the free flow of capital back to the US. We make this recommendation with our eyes wide open, realising this would likely increase Apple's US taxes. But we strongly believe such comprehensive reform would be fair to all taxpayers, would keep America globally competitive and would promote US economic growth.

In other words, Apple would be prepared to negotiate paying more tax in the US as long as its offshore arrangements are left alone, but blames the US government for its tax arrangements rather than accepting responsibility for them.

In April 2015, the Australian Senate also held an inquiry into corporate tax avoidance, at which senior Google and Apple representatives appeared. At this inquiry Tony King, Apple's Australia and New Zealand managing director, stated in a similar vein that his company 'pays all the taxes it owes in accordance with Australian law' and that its effective tax rate in Australia was above 30 per cent (*Official Committee Hansard* 2015, p. 42). When asked about the company's seemingly low gross profit and its use of tax minimisation strategies, he reiterated that Apple pays tax in accordance with Australian tax law (*Official Committee Hansard* 2015, p. 45). When it was put to King that, of the $600 retail price of an iPad in Australia, $550 is shifted to Ireland, of which approximately $220 is never taxed anywhere in the world, and that while this may be lawful it would nevertheless constitute avoiding tax, he replied: 'We do not avoid tax. We pay all of our taxes that are due in the Australian market in accordance with the law' (*Official Committee Hansard* 2015, p. 48).

Google

Google is also a US-based firm. Its market capitalisation is US$530.7 billion. In 2014, it recorded global revenues of US$66 billion and net profit of US$14 billion (Google Inc 2015). Estimates of the company's market share suggest that approximately 65 per cent of the world's internet searches are undertaken using Google, while in 2013 it attracted 33 per cent of the world's digital advertising revenue (Efrati 2013). However, Google has a TNI of just 41.9, and it is only in sales that it has a majority of its operations abroad (55 per cent). Only 37 per cent of its assets and 34 per cent of its employees are outside its home state (UNCTAD 2014c). Unlike Apple, Google may therefore be thought of as a US corporation with international interests. Regardless of the difference in the profile of its operations, Google has also relied on profit shifting to reduce its taxable income. In 2011, the company moved 80 per cent of its pre-tax profits from international subsidiaries to Bermuda, where a corporate tax rate of zero applies to the company (Allard 2014). Google's profit shifting, use of complex tax manoeuvres through Ireland and the Netherlands, and routeing of sales through them to the low-tax jurisdiction of Bermuda mean that the company pays as little as 2.4 per cent tax on its non-US revenues (Johnston 2014).

Inquiries into Google's taxation strategies were held in the UK in 2012 and 2013. The terms of the 2013 inquiry noted that, in order to avoid corporate tax, 'Google relies on the deeply unconvincing argument that its sales to UK clients take place in Ireland, despite clear evidence that the vast majority of sales activity takes place in the UK' (UK Public Accounts Committee on Tax Avoidance 2015). At both of these inquiries the company was represented by its vice-president for sales and operations, Matt Brittin. When questioned about the company's claim that Google conducts the bulk of its European business from its low-tax-jurisdiction Dublin offices, Brittin (2013) noted that 'any advertiser in the UK, Germany, France or any European country contracts with Google in Ireland, because that is where they have the rights to sell Google advertising'. The parliamentary committee repeatedly presented evidence, including sales job advertisements for positions located in London, as well as that provided by whistle-blowers, suggesting a significant portion of Google's sales activities take place in the UK, where the company paid just £10 million in tax on 2006–11 revenues of £11.5 billion (Syal 2013). Despite the evidence, Google's official position was that 99 per cent of its European sales take place in Ireland, hence the legitimacy of the company's tax structure. When pressed on the specific actions of Google, Brittin declined to elaborate further, saying 'I am not a tax or a legal expert' and declaring: 'Obviously, what I cannot do is talk specifically about Google's affairs.' However, he eventually acknowledged that 'the lower tax regime was one factor in establishing us in Ireland' (Brittin 2013).

A similar position was taken by Google Australia at the Australian

Senate inquiry into corporate taxation, represented by managing director Maile Carnegie. Agreeing with her Apple counterpart that global taxation requires overhauling, Carnegie stated that, in relation to taxation, 'Google believes international cooperation at the OECD level is essential' (*Official Committee Hansard* 2015, p. 43). Carnegie went on to respond to questions about profit shifting from Google Australia to the low-tax jurisdiction of Singapore, saying that 'the products and services we sell to Australian customers are sold by our Singapore group', leading to the following breakdown in profits from sales in Australia: '$2 billion in software products and services revenue booked in Singapore and a little over $100 million of consulting services booked in Australia' (*Official Committee Hansard* 2015 p. 51).

Carnegie and Brittin's positions are consistent with public statements made by Google's chairman, Eric Schmidt, who has declared that 'we pay lots of taxes; we pay them in the legally prescribed ways', and that he is 'very proud of the structure that we set up. We did it based on the incentives that the governments offered us to operate' (Womack 2012). As with Apple the clear implication is that the fault lies with governments if they engage in tax competition and choose not to close opportunities for tax minimisation. Far from shying away from what others may regard as corporate obligations to pay a fair share, Schmidt proudly stated: 'It's called capitalism. . . .We are proudly capitalistic. . . .I'm not confused about this' (Womack 2012).

Implications

There is clearly an expression of a liberal ideological belief in free markets in the corporate taxation strategies of Apple and Google and the justifications offered in respect of them. Whether this is due to the national institutional context of their home state or the opportunities afforded them as a result of tax competition among states is debatable. However, the justifications offered by Apple and Google's corporate leaders for their companies' strategies undermine any claims that they are socially responsible when it comes to paying tax. Their representatives consistently explain their tax strategies with reference to legal requirements, and even declare their pride in the way in which they have structured their tax affairs. This is more than simply revealing of their attitudes and corporate motivations. From a discursive power and legitimacy perspective it is strategically cavalier. In claiming their position as a legitimate one, and in the process shifting blame to governments for the opportunities afforded them, they are inviting and politically enabling the response they least desire. Through their responses to inquiries when presented with evidence of the strategies they have employed, in the context of demands that they pay their fair share of tax, they have helped to confirm that their corporations cannot be part of the solution to global tax avoidance.

7.5 CONCLUSION

Regardless of the CSR literature on the potential for self-regulation to enhance corporate reputation, what appears to matter most to corporate leaders is traditional financial and market performance metrics. These, above community responsibility, are what confer the reputation that matters to business leaders. Therefore, it is unsurprising that the comments of corporate leaders presented above amount to a disregard for tax minimisation concerns expressed by tax justice groups. Instead, like tax professionals (this volume, Chapter 6), they stress their firms' lawful behaviour. They have a point. They are not breaking any laws and they are not evading tax. They are minimising it. If the public believes them to be acting legitimately and that the outcomes produced are desirable, then they remain in a politically-powerful position to arrange their tax affairs as they see fit, with the help of the states that allow them to do so.

The problem for both is that increasingly this seems to be no longer the case. Part of the reason for this is their responses to the criticisms they have faced on their tax affairs (see this volume, Chapter 3). Power that is believed to be exercised responsibly comes to be regarded, at the very least, as 'tolerable' (Wilks 2013, p. 177). It therefore endures and institutionally re-embeds itself rather than having to be continually asserted and imposed. The latter condition, wherein power and authority must be constantly reiterated, now afflicts many corporations as they try to explain their strategies with reference to the law, and even declare their pride in the way they have structured their tax affairs. As they stress this, they are undermining their legitimacy in the eyes of the public, and therefore undermining their discursive power. In claiming their positions as legitimate, and in the process shifting blame to governments for the opportunities afforded them, they are inviting and politically enabling the response they least desire: global regulation. At the same time, they are strengthening the arm of states that wish to put in place greater tax demands while working towards the necessary global reforms to undermine the strategies of tax havens like Ireland.

We only considered the examples of Google and Apple and cannot claim that they represent all MNCs' perspectives. Similarly, we primarily focused on US MNCs owing to their dominant positions by comparison to those of other nationalities, and in debates surrounding corporate tax avoidance.

Space constraints preclude a comparative analysis, but future studies could consider the extent to which MNCs of other nationalities perceive their interests in similar terms. Even so, we suggest that a concern for shareholder value and financial drivers are likely to be more globally generalisable than other forms of capitalism. If corporations do not primarily judge their standing and brand value on the basis of social responsibility, being less concerned with an obligation to society than to shareholders, then they are unlikely to be voluntary payers of tax. In failing to pay a fair share, claiming their position as a legitimate one, and in the process shifting blame to governments for the opportunities afforded them, they are not only weakening their position and inviting and enabling the regulatory response they least desire. They have also demonstrated that global corporate tax avoidance is primarily the result of tax competition between states. The solution to the problem therefore cannot reside with the MNCs that have benefited from the opportunities states have afforded them. It must reside with states themselves.

NOTES

1. The world's top 500 companies on the basis of their stock market capitalisation.
2. The United Nations Conference on Trade and Development's TNI is a simple composite average of foreign assets, sales and employment to total assets, sales and employment. The figure of 60 is derived as the simple average of their TNIs. If the top 100 corporations are treated as a group, calculating their transnationality in total based on the sum of their assets, sales and employment yields an average TNI of 59 (i.e. slightly less).
3. This survey involved 800 corporate executives in 20 jurisdictions across the Asia Pacific region.

REFERENCES

Allard, T. (2014), 'Global Tax Avoidance: A Trillion Dollar Evil', *Sydney Morning Herald*, published electronically 21 February, available at http://www.smh.com.au/business/global-tax-avoidance--a-trillion-dollar-evil-20140221-337u1.html (accessed 14 May 2015).

Apple Inc (2015), 'Apple: Investor Relations', available at http://investor.apple.com/financials.cfm (accessed 8 May 2015).

Bachrach, P. and M. Baratz (1962), 'Two Faces of Power', *American Political Science Review* **56** (4), 947–952.

Blyth, M. (2013), *Austerity: The History of a Dangerous Idea*, Oxford: Oxford University Press.

Bowers, S. (2016), 'The Apple Tax Ruling – What This Means for Ireland, Tax and Multinationals', *Guardian*, published electronically 30 August, available at https://www.theguardian.com/business/2016/aug/30/eu-apple-ireland-tax-ruling-q-and-a (accessed 20 September 2016).

Brittin, M. (2013), 'Statement to the Public Accounts Committee on Tax

Avoidance – Google', available at http://www.publications.parliament.uk/pa/cm201314/cmselect/cmpubacc/112/130516.htm (accessed 22 May 2015).
Broome, A. (2014), *Issues and Actors in the Global Political Economy*, Houndmills, Basingstoke: Palgrave Macmillan.
Brown, B. and S. Perry (1994), 'Removing the Financial Performance Halo from Fortune's "Most Admired" Companies', *Academy of Management Journal* **37** (5), 1347–1359.
Buckley, P.J. (2011), 'International Integration and Coordination in the Global Factory', *Management International Review* **51** (2), 269–283.
Callaghan, M. (2015), 'Why a "Google Tax" Is Not the Answer to Corporate Tax Avoidance', *Lowy Interpreter*, available at http://www.lowyinterpreter.org/post/2015/04/13/Why-the-UK-Google-tax-is-not-the-answer-to-corporate-tax-avoidance.aspx?COLLCC=3861547897& (accessed 22 May 2015).
Campbell, J. (2016), 'Apple Tax Ruling "a Serious Blow" to Irish Investment', *BBC News*, published electronically 30 August, available at http://www.bbc.com/news/uknorthernireland37219372 (accessed 31 August 2016).
Cellan-Jones, R. (2016), 'EU Takes on Apple, Ireland and the United States', *BBC Technology*, published electronically 30 August, available at http://www.bbc.com/news/technology37218692 (accessed 31 August 2016).
Chang, H. (2008), *Bad Samaritans: The Myth of Free Trade and the Secret History of Capitalism*, New York: Bloomsbury Press.
Cook, T. (2013), Opening Statement of Tim Cook, Chief Executive Officer Apple Inc. before the Permanent Subcommittee on Investigations US Senate, available at https://www.apple.com/pr/pdf/timcookopeningstatement.pdf (accessed 21 May 2015).
Cox, R.W. (1987), *Production, Power and World Order: Social Forces in the Making of History*, New York: Columbia University Press.
Crouch, C. (2011), *The Strange Non-Death of Neoliberalism*, Cambridge: Polity Press.
Culpepper, P. (2011), *Quiet Politics and Business Power: Corporate Control in Europe and Japan*, Cambridge: Cambridge University Press.
Davis, A.K., D.A. Guenther, L.K. Krull and B.M. Williams (2016), 'Do Socially Responsible Firms Pay More Taxes?', *Accounting Review* **91** (1), 47–68.
Davis, K. and R. Blomstrom (1966), *Business and Its Environment*, New York: McGraw-Hill.
Deloitte (2014), *Risk, Uncertainty and Opportunity in a Changing Landscape: 2014 Asia Pacific Tax Complexity Survey*, available at http://www2.deloitte.com/content/dam/Deloitte/cn/Documents/tax/deloitte-cn-tax-2014asiapacific-tax-complexity-en-220414.pdf (accessed 21 January 2016).
Efrati, A. (2013), 'In Online Ads, There's Google – And Then Everybody Else', *Wall Street Journal*, published electronically 13 June, available at http://blogs.wsj.com/digits/2013/06/13/in-online-ads-theres-google-and-then-everybody-else/ (accessed 14 May 2015).
Elbra, A. (2014), 'Interests Need Not Be Pursued If They Can Be Created: Private Governance in African Gold Mining', *Business and Politics* **16** (2), 247–266.
Financial Times (2015), 'FT Global 500 2015', available at www.ft.com/ft500 (accessed 5 November 2015).
Frank, A.G. (1978), *Dependent Accumulation and Underdevelopment*, London: Macmillan.
Friedman, M. (1970), 'The Social Responsibility of Business Is to Increase Its Profits', *New York Times Magazine*, 13 September, 122–126.

Friedman, T. (2000), *The Lexus and the Olive Tree*, revised edition, London: HarperCollins.
Fryxell, G.E. and J. Wang (1994), 'The Fortune Corporate "Reputation" Index: Reputation for What?', *Journal of Management* **20** (1), 1–14.
Fuchs, D. (2007), *Business Power in Global Governance*, Boulder, CO: Lynne Rienner.
Fukuyama, F. (1992), *The End of History and the Last Man*, New York: Avon Books.
G7 Finance Ministers (1996), 'Lyon Summit: Economic Communiqué: Making a Success of Globalization for the Benefit of All', *European Commission Press Release Database*, available at http://europa.eu/rapid/press-release_DOC-96-5_en.htm (accessed 14 May 2016).
Galbraith, J.K. (2001 [1979]), 'The Valid Image of the Modern Economy', in *The Essential Galbraith*, ed. A.D. Williams, Boston, MA: Houghton Mifflin Company, pp. 118–133.
Geppert, M. and C. Dörrenbächer (2011), 'Politics and Power in the Multinational Corporation: An Introduction', in C. Dörrenbächer and M. Geppert (eds), *Politics and Power in the Multinational Corporation: The Role of Institutions, Interests and Identities*, Cambridge: Cambridge University Press, pp. 3–40.
Google Inc (2015), 'Google: Investor Relations', available at https://investor.google.com/financial/tables.html (accessed 21 May 2015).
Gotsi, M. and A.M. Wilson (2001), 'Corporate Reputation: Seeking a Definition', *Corporate Communications: An International Journal* **6** (1), 24–30.
Hacker, J.S. and P. Pierson (2002), 'Business Power and Social Policy: Employers and the Formation of the American Welfare State', *Politics and Society* **30** (2), 277–325.
Hall, P.A. and D. Soskice (2001), *Varieties of Capitalism: The Institutional Foundations of Comparative Advantage*, Oxford: Oxford University Press.
Harrod, J. (2006), 'The Century of the Corporation', in C. May (ed.), *Global Corporate Power*, Boulder, CO: Lynne Rienner, pp. 23–46.
Jackson, G. and R. Deeg (2008), 'From Comparing Capitalisms to the Politics of Institutional Change', *Review of International Political Economy* **15** (4), 680–709.
Jackson, K.T. (2004), *Building Reputational Capital: Strategies for Integrity and Fair Play That Improve the Bottom Line*, Oxford: Oxford University Press.
Johnston, D.C. (2014), 'How Google and Apple Make Their Taxes Disappear', *Newsweek*, published electronically 14 December, available at http://www.newsweek.com/2014/12/26/how-google-and-apple-make-their-taxes-disappear-291571.html (accessed 15 May 2015).
Lawrence, A.T., J. Weber and J.E. Post (2005), *Business and Society: Stakeholders, Ethics, Public Policy*, 11th edition, New York: McGraw Hill.
Lazonick, W. (2014), 'Profits without Prosperity', *Harvard Business Review* **92** (9), 46–55.
Levy, D.L. and P.J. Newell (2002), 'Business Strategy and International Environmental Governance: Towards a Neo-Gramscian Synthesis', *Global Environmental Politics* **2** (4), 84–101.
Lowi, T.J. (2001), 'Our Millennium: Political Science Confronts the Global Corporate Economy', *International Political Science Review* **22** (2), 131–150.
Lukes, S. (1974), *Power: A Radical View*, London: Palgrave Macmillan.
Margolis, J.D. and J.P. Walsh (2001), *People and Profits? The Search for a Link*

between a Company's Social and Financial Performance, Mahwah, NJ: Lawrence Erlbaum.
Martell, L. (2007), 'The Third Wave in Globalization Theory', *International Studies Review* **9** (2), 173–196.
Melo, T. and A. Garrido-Morgado (2012), 'Corporate Reputation: A Combination of Social Responsibility and Industry', *Corporate Social Responsibility and Environmental Management* **19** (1), 11–31.
Micklethwait, J. and A. Wooldridge (2003), *The Company: A Short History of a Revolutionary Idea*, London: Phoenix.
O'Callaghan, T. (2007), 'Disciplining Multinational Enterprises: The Regulatory Power of Reputation Risk', *Global Society* **21** (1), 95–117.
Official Committee Hansard (2015), 'Senate Economic References Committee: Corporate Tax Avoidance', 8 April, available at http://parlinfo.aph.gov.au/parlInfo/download/committees/commsen/b59a2852-c505-4494-b974-d5972c67447f/toc_pdf/Economics%20References%20Committee_2015_04_08_3366_Official.pdf;fileType=application%2Fpdf#search=%22committees/commsen/b59a2852-c505-4494-b974-d5972c67447f/0000%22 (accessed 9 November 2017).
Oxfam America (2016), *Broken at the Top: How America's Dysfunctional Tax System Costs Billions in Corporate Tax Dodging*, available at http://www.oxfamamerica.org/static/media/files/Broken_at_the_Top_FINAL_EMBARGOED_4.12.2016.pdf (accessed 11 May 2016).
Palan, R. and D. Wigan (2014), 'Herding Cats and Taming Tax Havens: The US Strategy of "Not in My Backyard"', *Global Policy* **5** (3), 334–343.
Pauly, L.W. and S. Reich (1997), 'National Structures and Multinational Corporate Behaviour: Enduring Differences in the Age of Globalisation', *International Organization* **51** (1), 1–30.
Ponzi, L.J., C.J. Fombrun and N.A. Gardberg (2011), 'RepTrak™ Pulse: Conceptualizing and Validating a Short-Form Measure of Corporate Reputation', *Corporate Reputation Review* **14** (1), 15–35.
Rugman, A.M. and C.H. Oh (2010), 'Does the Regional Nature of Multinationals Affect the Multinationality and Performance Relationship?', *International Business Review* **19** (5), 479–488.
Rugman, A. and A. Verbeke (2009), 'Location, Competitiveness, and the Multinational Enterprise', in A. Rugman (ed.), *The Oxford Handbook of International Business*, 2nd edition, Oxford: Oxford University Press, pp. 146–180.
Schwartz, N.D. and C. Duhigg (2013), 'Apple's International Structure', *New York Times*, published electronically 20 May, available at http://www.nytimes.com/interactive/2013/05/21/business/apples-international-structure.html?ref=business&_r=0 (accessed 14 May 2015).
Strange, S. (1997), 'The Future of Global Capitalism; Or, Will Divergence Persist Forever?', in C. Crouch and W. Streeck (eds), *Political Economy of Modern Capitalism: Mapping Convergence and Diversity*, London: Sage Publications, pp. 182–191.
Syal, R. (2013), 'MPs Recommend Comprehensive Inquiry into Google's "Unconvincing" Tax Affairs', *Guardian*, published electronically13 June, available at http://www.theguardian.com/technology/2013/jun/13/google-face-tax-inquiry-mps (accessed 22 May 2015).
Teeple, G. and S. McBride (2011), *Relations of Global Power: Neoliberal Order and Disorder*, Toronto: University of Toronto Press.
Tienhaara, K. (2014), 'Corporations: Business and Industrial Influence', in P.G.

Harris (ed.), *Routledge Handbook of Global Environmental Politics*, Abingdon: Routledge, pp. 164–175.
UK Public Accounts Committee on Tax Avoidance (2015), 'Public Accounts Committee Ninth Report: Tax Avoidance – Google', available at http://www.publications.parliament.uk/pa/cm201314/cmselect/cmpubacc/112/11202.htm (accessed 22 May 2015).
UNCTAD (2014a), *World Investment Report 2014*, Web Table 10: Value of Cross-Border M&As by Region/Economy of Purchaser 1990–2013, available at http://unctad.org/Sections/dite_dir/docs/WIR2014/WIR14_tab10.xls (accessed 20 October 2015).
UNCTAD (2014b), *World Investment Report 2014*, Web Table 9: Value of Cross-Border M&As by Region/Economy of Seller 1990–2013, available at http://unctad.org/Sections/dite_dir/docs/WIR2014/WIR14_tab09.xls (accessed 20 October 2015).
UNCTAD (2014c), *World Investment Report 2014*, Web Table 28: The World's Top 100 Non-Financial TNCs, Ranked by Foreign Assets 2013, available at http://unctad.org/Sections/dite_dir/docs/WIR2014/WIR14_tab28.xls (accessed 20 October 2015).
US Senate Committee on Homeland Security and Governmental Affairs (2013), 'Subcommittee to Examine Offshore Profit Shifting and Tax Avoidance by Apple Inc.', available at http://www.hsgac.senate.gov/subcommittees/investigations/media/subcommittee-to-examine-offshore-profit-shifting-and-tax-avoidance-by-apple-inc (accessed 21 May 2015).
Vogel, D. (2006), *The Market for Virtue: The Potential and Limits of Corporate Social Responsibility*, Washington, DC: Brookings Institution Press.
Wade, R. (1996), 'Globalisation and Its Limits: Reports of the Death of the National Economy Are Greatly Exaggerated', in S. Berger and R. Dore (eds), *National Diversity and Global Capitalism*, Ithaca, NY: Cornell University Press, pp. 60–88.
Wade, R. (2010), 'Is the Globalisation Consensus Dead?', *Antipode* **41** (1), 141–165.
Wilks, S. (2013), *The Political Power of the Business Corporation*, Cheltenham, UK and Northampton, MA, USA: Edward Elgar Publishing.
Womack, B. (2012), 'Google Chairman Says Android Winning Mobile War with Apple: Tech', *Bloomberg*, available at http://www.bloomberg.com/apps/news?pid=webport_news&tkr=ALGT:US,CMG:US,GOOG:US&tkr2=GOOG:US&sid=abGe62AIVPwg (accessed 28 April 2015).

PART III

8. The role of private actors in the international tax policy process: towards a conceptual framework

Tony Porter and Karsten Ronit

8.1 INTRODUCTION

The formation and sustainability of states have been intrinsically linked to their capacity to collect customs and taxes (Tilly 1992),[1] and thus private or non-state actors have often been seen as peripheral to the implementation and enforcement of tax collection. This is especially the case for business actors, which are typically assumed to always want to minimize taxes and maximize tax avoidance (this volume, Chapter 7). In this chapter, we challenge these views. As is argued in other contributions to this volume, we argue that civil society actors have played a key role in advocating for more socially-just tax policies. We also argue that there is potential for increasing the role played by business in preventing tax evasion and aggressive tax avoidance but only if public authorities alter the incentives for business actors to do this: forms of self-regulation that are initiated by business, while effective in some contexts, are alone unlikely to be effective in the area of global taxation. In making this argument we highlight the importance of the wider structural context, or meta-governance framework, in which particular self-regulation initiatives are embedded and how these contextual factors influence the success or otherwise of the regime.

It is important to go beyond analysing forms of private action that have already proven to be effective in contributing to fairer and more sustainable outcomes in taxation and other policy areas, to imagine how new forms of governance might be developed in response to the significant challenges facing the international tax regime. For example, would private actors be able to assume roles that only public actors might previously have played? Today it is common and well-recognized that effective global governance can involve informal coordination of relatively decentralized implementation at the national level by states and by private firms rather than vesting strong capacity in conventional international organizations.

In this chapter, we consider examples of such practices, not necessarily as evidence of already established organizational configurations, but rather to assist in imagining how such practices might be modified and adopted.

The potential for the involvement of private actors in any area of public policy, including taxation, can be obscured if differences across the policy process are not recognized. We therefore examine the roles of public, business and civil society actors across the five well-recognized stages of the policy process which determine whether public or private policies succeed or fail: agenda setting, policy formulation, decision making, implementation and evaluation. This can include, for instance, agenda-setting activities that seek to change government policy, as with businesses that seek to minimize taxes or civil society organizations that seek to have MNCs pay a larger share. It can include private sector roles in tax collection, at the implementation stage, as when retail stores collect sales taxes or employers collect income taxes. We are especially interested in the independent contribution that business actors can make to foster stronger implementation and enforcement of tax policy globally. This includes elements of self-regulation, which we define as processes in which business groups exercise a significant degree of autonomy and discretion in the creation or implementation of rules. At the same time, we acknowledge that business will interact with other actors in its environment, such as public authorities and civil society organizations, to develop and implement self-regulation.

In the remainder of the chapter we examine potential roles for both civil society and business actors for each stage of the policy process. We start by examining these intersections for the role of self-regulation in general, and then we consider them more specifically with regard to taxation at the global level.

8.2 NEW AND EMERGING ROLES FOR DIFFERENT ACTORS IN SELF-REGULATION

Public Authority

For centuries, the nation state has provided the type of stability that is a pre-condition for self-regulation and the sustainability of market-based capitalism more generally. This includes defining and enforcing property rights and contracts, as well as the provision of public goods, such as military security, education and infrastructure, for which business and markets have traditionally been poorly suited.

In recent decades, the benefits of hierarchical organization and bureaucratic administration have been called into question, as is evident in the widespread displacement of the term 'government' by 'governance', which emphasizes the perceived value of more horizontal and informal networks (Bevir 2012). Greater involvement of business and self-regulatory arrangements in governance was often seen as enabling more decentralized, open and flexible forms of organization. However, these changes also enhanced the power of business, allowing it to remove or forestall meaningful regulation and to promote forms of self-regulation that appear to be effective while being anything but in practice. We need to be particularly cognizant of the risks associated with self-regulation in the international tax arena, given the lengths to which many major corporations have gone to minimize their tax obligations.

In highlighting the role played by public authorities in self-regulation it is useful to look in turn at each of the stages of public policy making that traditionally have been identified: agenda setting, policy formulation, decision making, implementation and evaluation (Ronit and Porter 2015). In the agenda-setting, policy formulation and decision stages, public authorities often take initiatives that create or incorporate self-regulatory arrangements. The character of this relationship between public authorities and self-regulation can be crucial to the success or failure of policy implementation. When there are conflicts between business interests and the public interest the former can win out if too much discretion is left to business. However, the public interest can suffer if policies fail to consider the contribution that business organization can make to policy implementation. At all stages, there is a continuum of possible relations between public authorities and business, ranging from cases where public authorities retain full control and use threats of stringent public regulation to force business organizations to agree to take some responsibility for ensuring the compliance of their members, to cases where the initiative originates entirely from the eagerness of business to solve problems it has identified, and business is soliciting support from the public authorities.

Business itself has more capacity to effectively implement self-regulation and incentivize or coerce individual firms than is often assumed. For instance, powerful firms or business associations can impose various regulatory requirements, and reputational risks, such as those associated with corporate tax avoidance, can be a powerful motivation for compliance independent of public authority. Nevertheless, public authorities can, in innumerable ways, underwrite or reinforce self-regulation, including by making national court systems available for enforcing the contracts that codify self-regulation, requiring compliance as a condition of receiving a licence to operate, imposing regulatory penalties on firms that are non-compliant, or assisting with monitoring for non-compliance.

These activities at different stages of the policy process can be summarized in the following way. First, public authorities have the capacity to set frameworks and incentivize self-regulation in ways that conform with public goals, but they must be very pro-active to steer such processes. Second, governments and international organizations can examine various opportunities for self-regulation and weigh up the pros and cons, often in a dialogue with potential private regulators. Third, the decision to adopt a programme will usually depend on what business and other parties can offer and what public authorities will and can endorse. Fourth, if self-regulation is delegated by public institutions or tacitly accepted it may be difficult for public authorities to maintain a central role in implementation, but implementation can be shared between public and private organizations. Fifth, public authorities need to follow developments in self-regulation closely, but, once regulation is surrendered to private actors, in whole or in part, evaluation may become difficult.

In general, public and private elements are often so closely integrated in regulatory arrangements that it is hard to tell which is dominant. However, there are a variety of approaches that seek to assess the relative strength of each through careful analysis of particular arrangements (Cafaggi 2012; Liss and Sharman 2015; Porter and Ronit 2015). As we shall see below, paying closer attention to the complementarities between public policy, business self-regulation and civil society advocacy can be important for more effective and just tax governance globally.

Organized Business

Business is subject to many forms of governance to regulate competition and exchange with actors in and beyond markets (Greif 2005). These include formal associations of firms that leverage government or regulate their own industries. They also include business practices internal to the firm that contribute to governance by conforming to professional norms and interacting with practices in other firms. Furthermore, there are many self-regulatory professional codes, such as accounting standards and certifications, that govern the individual conduct of professionals and thereby contribute to governance in business.

Although we find examples of self-regulation spanning industry sectors, most examples of self-regulation occur within specific industry sectors and product groups, that is, relatively narrow areas where firms are active in the same markets and face a number of identical challenges (Hale and Held 2011). Indeed, a plethora of international industry associations are available for such tasks, whilst there are rather few international peak associations that can speak for ‘business’ in general – a factor which explains why peak business associations have not generally been involved in international tax negotiations.[2]

As noted above, it is useful to consider the self-regulatory roles that business can play across all stages of the policy process, often with a significant degree of autonomy and discretion relative to governmental actors (Porter and Ronit 2006; this volume, Chapter 7). Contrary to a common tendency to see self-regulatory functions as appearing together within private 'self-regulatory organizations' such as stock exchanges, we argue that the different functions that are associated with the policy stages and that are required for policies to be developed and implemented can be supplied by diverse actors in different organizations (Porter and Ronit 2015). First, it is useful for business to set agendas that define a self-regulatory problem in ways that are relevant and manageable for business and match up with business practices, preferences and norms. Indeed, as is highlighted throughout this volume, high-profile international tax rulings against specific firms such as Apple have triggered significant changes to corporate tax strategy. Second, further scrutiny and negotiation are necessary to find an appropriate design for policy in general, and business needs to harness available knowledge when building proposals for self-regulation. Third, the relevant parties must be involved in decision making to define the concrete objectives of self-regulation and to agree on the necessary measures to achieve these goals. Fourth, rules are not always complied with, and different forms of monitoring are required to follow the behaviour of firms, identify cases of non-compliance and install mechanisms for sanctioning. Fifth, systematic work must be launched to gather information, evaluate current practices and disseminate this information to different interested parties to enhance learning and adjust the rules and norms behind self-regulation.

Because business self-regulation is found in many areas, experiences vary considerably (Braithwaite and Drahos 2000). However, a common critique is that self-regulation is vulnerable when it comes to implementation (Gunningham 2010).[3] There can be disagreement with the interpretation of rules, insufficient resources and expert knowledge to police firms, lack of corporate support and significant free-riding, and lack of appropriate sanctions to correct behaviour and deter future non-compliance. Despite this, there are numerous international examples of successful implementation of self-regulation carried out with minimal governmental involvement, often by a diverse set of business actors, such as the arbitration processes managed by the International Chamber of Commerce (Porter and Ronit 2015).

Civil Society

Increasing scholarly interest has been directed toward analysing the many and diverse forms of civil society action in private regulation, often manifested through formal non-governmental organizations but including a host of other forms of cooperation which are difficult to classify. Civil society often leverages states and intergovernmental organizations, but civil society is also a countervailing power in relation to business, and efforts are made to make business change practices in the market (Ronit 2006). For civil society groups, traditional public policy adopted by states and intergovernmental organizations is usually seen as more legitimate and effective than rules adopted in the business community. However, as was argued in Part I of this book, there is an undersupply of public regulation in many areas of global policy (Reinicke 1998),[4] and in a number of cases civil society groups promote and are engaged in self-regulation.[5] As noted below and in other chapters of this book this is becoming increasingly evident in relation to international taxation and is being actively promoted by the tax justice movement.

As with business, civil society can be involved in different stages of the policy process. First, civil society has a capacity to set agendas and launch campaigns to change the behaviour of business and encourage self-regulation (this volume, Chapter 4). Second, civil society may, alone or together with expert groups and professions, hold important knowledge essential in developing relevant proposals (this volume, Chapter 6). Third, civil society groups adopt schemes which business can voluntarily join, but it is also possible that business and other actors invite civil society to negotiate and adopt rules. Fourth, civil society even becomes involved in administering self-regulation and thus plays an active role in monitoring corporate behaviour, identifying cases of non-compliance and contributing to sanctioning. Fifth, civil society may be so involved in running a particular scheme that it can also have a role in the evaluation of its strengths and weaknesses, and civil society bands with expert groups and forms various alliances with third parties to pool knowledge (Stone 2013; this volume, Chapter 4).

Most forms of self-regulation with civil society participation are found in relation to industries where special knowledge is needed to enter into, and maintain, a dialogue with business. It may be easier to mobilize collective action around issues that target specific areas of business, but civil society is also involved in schemes applied to a variety of industries and products, such as fair trade principles or human rights. It is always a question, however, who civil society groups actually represent. In general, the engagement of civil society groups tends to be seen as an element in democratic development and helpful in correcting business power and public authority, but further scrutiny is needed (Gourevitch et al. 2012).

8.3 IMPLICATIONS FOR TAX POLICY

Public Authority

Reflecting the 'new' high-profile politics of international taxation outlined in Chapter 3 there are now significant numbers of international initiatives by public authorities to improve tax compliance and important national schemes that have global implications. The major initiatives of public authorities, detailed in other contributions to this volume, include the Base Erosion and Profit Shifting (BEPS) project at the OECD, US Foreign Account Tax Compliance Act (FATCA), the EU's Directive on Administrative Cooperation in the Field of Taxation and its prohibition of state aid designed to gain competitive advantage rather than economic development, and the creation of the Global Forum on Transparency and Exchange of Information for Tax Purposes (Global Forum). Additionally, the UN Committee of Experts on International Cooperation in Tax Matters has formulated strategies to address certain aspects of tax avoidance (though it has a broader agenda and is highly focused on developing countries). The public aspects of these have been discussed elsewhere (Rixen 2008; Eccleston 2013), and our focus here is on the role of business (plus civil society) in arrangements such as these. The typical international tax model has involved states negotiating with one another about how to share information and the revenues from taxation of international activities, and only in the background are there often unexamined but conventional assumptions about the role of private institutions. Business action has especially focused on national governments during the implementation phase (Eccleston 2013).

Yet there are numerous roles played by private actors in domestic tax governance that are worth considering for their possible international relevance. While taxation is often seen to involve interactions between only public authorities and business, the actual relationship between these two types of actors in the area of taxation is far more complex, because most taxes, such as sales and income taxes, are collected by businesses and then passed along to government (Mehrotra 2010), and they operate in a quasi-automatic way (Lederman 2007). Tax intermediaries that assist private actors with tax preparation and payments, including accounting firms, law firms and the tax departments of large corporations, also play a significant independent role (OECD 2008; this volume, Chapter 6).

A key question, then, is whether global tax regulation can be redesigned by incorporating private actors in new ways so that its 'structural systems' become more effective. Since there is no single global tax authority, this would, for instance, involve encouraging forms of private governance across multiple jurisdictions by getting governments to multilaterally agree to such initiatives, by individual powerful states extraterritorially promoting such strategies by requiring them of multinational firms that wish to operate on that state's territory, or by governmental encouragement of global business associations or other entities to promote such reforms. A prominent example which is central to the campaign against corporate tax avoidance is the ongoing implementation of the commitment of OECD and G20 member states to require 'country-by-country' (CbC) reports for each jurisdiction in which a multinational corporation does business (OECD 2013).

Another powerful example of such a structural redesign of particular relevance to taxation is the anti-money laundering and terrorist financing regime organized around the Financial Action Task Force (FATF). FATF was created by the G7 in 1989 with a secretariat hosted at the OECD. Since then, it has developed 49 Recommendations that have been widely accepted as desirable. A wide variety of firms, including banks, insurance companies, investment dealers, casinos, accountants, lawyers, precious metal traders and others, have been required to exercise due diligence in identifying customers and detecting suspicious transactions, and to report these to the authorities (mostly independent financial intelligence units which collaborate in the Egmont Group). However, more generally the FATF regime illustrates how business self-regulation can be enlisted in global regulatory initiatives.

Some firms and industry associations are very actively involved in devising and implementing procedures to ensure that they are in compliance with anti-money laundering activities. For instance, the private Investment Industry Regulatory Organization of Canada (IIROC) provides specific detailed guidance (IIROC 2010), and a majority of US and EU banks rely on commercial risk assessment software which is provided by transnational firms, especially World-Check, and the standardized training provided by the Association of Certified Anti-Money Laundering Specialists (ACAMS) (Liss and Sharman 2015). These private activities standardize and reinforce compliance. The anti-money laundering (AML) regime is especially relevant to global taxation because both involve regulation of relatively intangible flows of capital initiated by actors that have an interest in concealing them from the authorities. The effective incorporation of private actors into AML regulation and governance is more advanced and widely recognized than in the case of taxation, and can provide a model for taxation.

There have also been domestic efforts to enhance the role of private actors in tax collection, which may be relevant to international efforts. For instance, the US Internal Revenue Service (IRS) only seriously began studying and increasing regulatory oversight of paid preparers from 2009,[6] and this type of regulation could enhance professional self-regulation, for instance through certification systems and codes of conduct (Allen 2004). Similarly, as Johnson highlights in Chapter 12, the US has experimented with using whistleblower protections and rewards as a form of regulation (Broderick 2007; Tett 2015).

While there has been considerable interest in 'tax farming' and tax 'bounty hunting', where private actors are delegated the task of collecting taxes, there is substantial evidence that there are problems with this form of private participation (Stella 1993). These have generally turned out to be more costly or otherwise less effective than reliance on government employees (Resnick 2005).

A key question is the degree to which the principles of 'responsive regulation' can be applied as an alternative to more traditional 'command and control' enforcement (Ayres and Braithwaite 1992). Responsive regulation involves a more collaborative relationship between regulators and regulatees, where the latter are induced to participate in regulation and an enforcement pyramid provides an escalating series of monitoring and sanctions for those who are deemed to have a higher probability of resistance and non-compliance. In the 1990s, the Australian Taxation Office (ATO) launched an initiative to replace adversarial relationships between tax authorities and tax advisers with a partnership model, and a similar model was initiated in New Zealand and has been suggested for the US (Ventry 2008). However, there are 'emanations of adversarialism within the partnership model which threaten to destabilize that model and undermine the efficiency gains that simplistic depictions of the model might suggest' (Burton and Dabner 2008, p. 137), and in the UK the Institute of Chartered Accountants in England and Wales (ICAEW) noted that the '[t]ax industry "cannot be trusted" to self regulate' in response to Big Four perceived complicity with tax avoidance schemes (Griffin 2015; this volume, Chapter 6).

Overall, public authorities can involve elements of business self-regulation in all stages of tax administration. First, at the agenda-setting stage, public authorities can encourage self-regulation by promoting domestic and international norms relating to paying tax, since there is experimental evidence that norms matter in increasing tax compliance (Lederman 2003). Tax evasion can be linked normatively to other crimes such as money laundering or corruption, to delegitimize it and to make it amenable to inclusion in strict rules for controlling those crimes, as with the FATF example.

Second, at the stage of policy formulation, a key challenge for public authorities is to find business allies who will support greater business involvement. For instance, if governments wish to involve professionals it will be important to consider carefully how such proposals interact with existing professional practices. For example, it would be easier to enlist tax intermediaries in preventing tax evasion, which is illegal, than tax avoidance, which may be unjust but is nevertheless legal and beneficial to a firm and its shareholders. Some professionals may see ethical behaviour as a valuable reputational benefit which clients will value for its capacity to enhance their own reputation, while other professionals, as we have noted, may sell themselves through their ability to find loopholes in the law (Chapter 6, this volume).

Third, at the decision stage, business and civil society have not been formal parties to the various agreements and conventions adopted to hinder tax avoidance – and, as will be discussed in the next subsection, they have only marginally been written into the programmes. The major role has clearly been taken by a few intergovernmental agencies, in particular the OECD and its member states.

Fourth, the examples provided in this subsection show how business self-regulation is most closely associated with the implementation stage. Self-regulatory elements can be included in tax administration, but their costs and benefits depend on the organizational configuration within which they are embedded.

Fifth, there is already a system in place to evaluate the implementation of agreements, and especially the exchange of information, through the Global Forum and its secretariat, as well as the BEPS peer review process. Participation is from member countries and intergovernmental agencies, but private involvement in implementation may spill over into the evaluation process, where private actors offer various services at the global level.

Organized Business

Some problems of tax avoidance are clearly associated with the globalization of business and the emergence of new corporate practices that are difficult to control by individual governments. Therefore, business tends to be seen as *the* problem, but business has an input in the formation of global tax policy as managed by intergovernmental organizations, and contributes to various forms of self-regulation. The BEPS project, initiated by the OECD and endorsed by the G20 in 2015, seeks to restrict the aggressive tax planning of MNCs (this volume, Chapter 2). Interestingly, stakeholders, including organized business, have been deeply involved in the development of the BEPS package at a more general level, and it is expected that 'the follow-up work as well as the work to monitor and support the effective implementation of the measures agreed upon in the course of the BEPS Project will benefit greatly from stakeholders' input' (OECD 2013). This involvement suggests that global business is in a position to assume different roles in the policy process, although the different projects do not refer to self-regulation as such.

Tax policy is a policy field that is of relevance to all sectors of business. Therefore, there is a demand for organizations that represent and formulate a coordinated strategy and address the pertinent issue of tax avoidance. Some forms of self-regulation are based on a kind of certification where firms can voluntarily join a scheme, and where leading roles are often taken by forces outside business, an issue we will return to in the next subsection (Auld et al. 2015). Other forms involve a stronger role for business where initiatives tend to be launched by formal organizations, such as associations, that coerce members to follow the rules and norms agreed upon.

Only a handful of global business associations represent global business in a very broad sense and could be candidates as self-regulators in the business community. Organizations such as the International Chamber of Commerce (ICC), the Business and Industry Advisory Committee to the OECD (BIAC) and the B20 Coalition are all engaged in various tax issues (B20 2017; ICC 2017), with the goal of making sure that international regulation does not hinder competition and free trade. They also belong to the stakeholders referred to by the OECD. The ICC has a stronger administrative capacity than BIAC and the B20 Coalition to become potentially involved in self-regulation (Mattli and Dietz 2014), but BIAC has very close relations with the OECD and has taken various initiatives to step up cooperation in relation to the formulation and implementation of BEPS (BIAC 2013). However, BIAC identifies important administrative deficits in governments that are unable to utilize all the information supplied by business, and it sees itself as having a special status as a contributor to the development of international tax policy. In other words, global tax policy is viewed as an issue best handled in an intergovernmental framework but with key roles assigned to business. We must remember that self-regulation is not always desirable for business associations, and that in a controversial issue such as tax avoidance, clear reputational risks are at stake.

The potential of the business community is not limited to general and representative business associations. Associations in specific industries also possess relevant resources and expert knowledge. For instance, the International Banking Federation (IBFed) is involved in combating financial crime, and its 'working group acts as a forum for national banking associations to discuss the development of national industry guidance for banks to promote effective self-regulation and the sharing of international good practice' (IBFed 2015). In other words, self-regulation is an important element in the strategy of organized banks and, in principle, it can also be advanced to combat tax avoidance. At the same time, unsurprisingly, international financial associations work against tax reform.[7]

We further find that relevant private actors that assist in the implementation of rules on a commercial basis, such as specialized firms, are involved in the prevention and investigation of crimes (Liss and Sharman 2015). These actors do not necessarily engage in the creation of self-regulatory schemes but may together with other private actors combine activities and constitute a kind of self-regulation. ACAMS has adopted its own professional self-regulatory code, and other third parties service business on a broader scale, for example the Global Accounting Alliance (GAA) and the International Federation of Accountants (IFAC). These actors are obliged to follow rules on confidentiality in giving tax advice, and are therefore accountable to their clients, but they have capacities to establish and police rules, perform certain auxiliary functions and thus assist in avoiding non-compliance. However, there are inherent dangers in relying on such actors if their basic goal lies in helping business with tax evasion (Mitchell and Sikka 2011).

Summing up, organized business has different roles across the policy process. First, a few trans-industry business associations are involved in agenda setting, and professional groups contribute with special perspectives. Organized business mainly focuses on governments and their coordinated efforts rather than running or supporting self-regulatory systems. The key concern expressed in these agenda-setting activities is the consequences for business of fragmented and different tax regimes and to a lesser extent the economic and social importance of minimizing taxes.[8]

Second, some associations and professional organizations have specialized entities to examine certain aspects of tax policy. Today intergovernmental organizations need input from various stakeholders to adopt strategies to combat tax avoidance, as this is a growing concern in many countries. This makes it relevant for organized business to follow these developments and provide relevant knowledge in consultations.

Third, some business associations have adopted rules to self-regulate – but not in relation to tax policy, where members may have different interests and reputations. Business associations must be very careful and not infringe on the discretionary power of firms – the target of much tax avoidance policy. Although they seek to portray their members as responsible corporations, this is not always successful.

Fourth, organized business is to a limited degree engaged in self-regulation of tax compliance, but it is possible to monitor the correct implementation of agreements. Some professional bodies or large firms that provide tax intermediary services, such as multinational accounting firms, value their reputation for integrity, since that is a central source of the value they bring to clients, although, as we have noted (this volume, Chapter 6), large international accounting firms remain a key source of tax planning advice and schemes. Therefore there is some as yet unrealized potential for these business actors to work to reduce tax avoidance, either from fear that they will be sanctioned by public authorities or lose clients if they are seen as unethical, or because they see attestation of high standards as a valuable selling point for their own business.

Fifth, evaluation of self-regulation in the field of tax policy, and more concretely tax evasion, is an exercise in which business associations and other private actors are not systematically active, but there is some potential here as well. Some associations take an interest in following and contributing to the general experiences with the evaluation of the implementation of public policy and the work of intergovernmental agencies.

Civil Society

A central theme of this book is the rise of civil society organizations to become the prominent actors in setting new agendas in global tax policy. Over the last decades, a number of civic groups have emerged and have specialized in addressing tax avoidance as an overriding global concern (Christians 2013). Compared to many other policy areas where policies aim to provide key global public goods, such as defending universal human rights or halting climate change, where there is a long history of civil society activism, the groups in tax policy cannot build on strong traditions (Grabosky 2012; this volume, Chapter 4).

Recent agreements, schemes and standards to combat tax avoidance, such as BEPS, have to some extent acknowledged the contributions of civil society. For instance, the non-profit Global Policy Forum and the BEPS Monitoring Group have both produced a detailed analysis of BEPS, and comments have also been provided by experts associated with the European Network on Debt and Development (Eurodad) (Murphy 2014; Global Policy Forum 2015). It is characteristic of these processes, however, that consultations are on an ad hoc basis, and that there is no real mention of self-regulation – with or without civil society involvement.

Other factors may complicate the role of civil society organizations. Most self-regulatory arrangements try to enhance the reputation of firms in relation to particular products made available to end-consumers, for instance fair trade products, and civil society organizations involved in such schemes help consumers make an informed choice and offer alternatives to conventional products. However, the various civic groups engaged in tax policy represent general citizen interests. If firms could be certified by tax-related programmes, created by or involving civil society organizations, certification might enhance the reputation of firms and signal responsible behaviour (this volume, Chapter 10). This could, of course, incentivize consumers and make them prefer responsible corporations but not in relation to their purchase of certified products, and thus civil society organizations engaged in shaping self-regulation in such a general field face more complex challenges.

Experiments are being conducted with fair tax arrangements at domestic levels, however. The most prominent example is the Fair Tax Mark in the UK (as discussed in greater detail in Chapter 10) and the application of a certification scheme. Such experiences are helpful and may be considered in other jurisdictions and at the global level. However, it is not certain that such schemes will be welcomed in other contexts where expectations are that tax policy should be administered by governments with a strong sanctioning potential rather than by private actors. Furthermore, if such schemes are adopted and joined by corporations in other jurisdictions and at the global level, the question is whether civil society has sufficient resources to monitor and evaluate their correct implementation. The complexity of implementation will also increase once addressing tax avoidance at multiple levels, demanding different capacities and tools. However, there is also evidence that, over time, private standards may be incorporated into public regulation, again demonstrating the complex relationship between public and private authority.

Much civil society activity is today concentrated in the Global Alliance for Tax Justice (GATJ), which builds on regional tax justice organizations. A leading role is assumed by the general Tax Justice Network (TJN), formed in 2003 (GATJ 2017). The Independent Commission for the Reform of International Corporate Taxation (ICRICT) held its first meeting in 2015, and it was initiated by a coalition of civil society and labour organizations, including the GATJ and the TJN. It brings together recognized experts on global tax justice issues to comment on evolving issues (ICRICT 2017). Interestingly, it is a strong proponent of intergovernmental solutions and advocates a specific UN body to handle these issues.

It is important to note that the GATJ and the TJN are global actors with members and partners in many countries, and they seek to expand and become representative as global countervailing powers. They work to promote better standards and norms and watch development in the field closely. Although the TJN cannot be dismissed as a 'Northern' or 'Western' civil society organization, its stronghold is clearly in the affluent parts of the world where 'tax activist groups' are strongest. As such, it is not very different from many other global civil society initiatives, but the GATJ and the TJN are aware that they suffer from some deficits in the representation of interests and are consequently working to embrace weakly-represented regions and countries as well.

As Seabrooke and Wigan argue in Chapter 4, the TJN is engaged in a variety of tax policy issues. A major goal is to avoid or at least to reduce tax evasion by hindering capital flight from the Global South to the Global North (Knobel and Meinzer 2014). Indeed, capital flight makes the building of state capacity difficult in developing countries and ultimately affects the creation of democratic institutions. However, tax evasion not only involves a North–South dimension but is also a serious problem for countries with advanced tax systems and competent tax authorities in place. Wealth generated in some countries is by means of tax evasion transferred to a number of tax havens.

Other entities are also seeking to shape global tax policy with some important initiatives linked to transparency. A prominent civil society initiative is represented by the International Consortium of Investigative Journalists (ICIJ) (see this volume, Chapter 12), a US-based organization involving journalists and media in different countries. Though not specializing in tax affairs, it has recently embraced the issue of tax avoidance and has established its own rules of conduct. The ICIJ played a central role in leaking the Panama Papers in early 2016 and is an example of institutionalized whistleblowing, a tool of monitoring increasingly applied in many sectors. Where other instances of whistleblowing in tax matters have been related to a single or few jurisdictions, this leak was global in scope. Additionally, Transparency International, an equally general actor in civil society, embraces tax policy and links this with other issues such as corruption (Transparency International 2015). Such initiatives are important in raising public awareness and triggering political and administrative actions. At the same time, this shows that it is, indeed, possible for civil society actors to bring issues on to the public agenda. While whistleblowing has mostly been fashioned in an ad hoc style, it has become increasingly frequent and influential (as discussed in Chapter 12), and its character as a regulatory instrument is becoming more clearly identified and disseminated globally (Yeoh 2014; Andrade 2015; Lewis and Vandekerckhove 2015; Porter and Ronit 2016; White 2016).

To analyse the capacity and performance of civil society we can analyse the different stages of self-regulation. This highlights the central role played by civil society organizations in agenda setting, which might be obscured if this stage is underestimated owing to a focus on the problem of implementation. Civil society actors have helped set the agenda of public authorities, but also of business actors for whom a reputation for tax avoidance may have become more damaging to their branding, although interestingly, to date, the GATJ and the TJN have not been strong proponents of formal arrangements with individual firms or industries (OECD 2014). Civil society can set and maintain agendas, and refine or correct them – especially because the OECD as a major actor is usually seen as favouring rich countries over poor countries. UN efforts are an additional option. When addressing tax evasion, the GATJ emphasizes that 'to solve this problem, we need to develop a new set of rules and to ensure that the voices of all countries are heard during the process', and it is primarily hinting at solutions through public regulation (GATJ 2017).

Second, the TJN has developed significant knowledge through cooperation with other parties in building activism and knowledge together. This capacity is insignificant compared to the resources held by governments and by business, but it may play a role when drafting and adopting international agreements. In particular, this analytical capacity may benefit developing countries where governments do not have sufficient resources to develop policies and instruments to control international business.

Third, civil society organizations have so far not been engaged in creating or certifying rules that business must comply with, as has been the case in other issue areas such as in food and environment policies. In taxation, rule building is mainly an issue for public regulation. Global civil society organizations still stand outside the key decision-making forums of governments and intergovernmental organizations. However, there is potential for further engagement by civil society with certification that firms are meeting private tax compliance standards.

Fourth, the behaviour of the regulated market actors needs to be closely monitored to verify compliance, and, in order not to erode self-regulation, measures have to be developed to sanction cases of non-compliance. Other actors, such as accounting firms and government agencies, may provide civil society organizations with information and assist in implementation, but a huge problem is the disclosure of private and confidential information.

Fifth, important tasks are carried out in the evaluation of self-regulation. If civil society has not been involved in the former stages of self-regulation, it is hardly realistic that it can assume a major role in evaluation, and currently experiences are limited. If rules are established by civil society or at least involve civil society, and firms and industries join and become certified as 'paying a fair share of tax', there is a possibility that a role is granted to civil society organizations.

8.4 CONCLUSION

There has been a growing interest in self-regulation as a mechanism of governance to replace or complement traditional top-down regulation, and this has been installed in many industries in recent decades. It is applied in many global contexts, but there is a strong institutional variation and many models exist, involving different public authorities, organizations in the business community and a plethora of civil society actors. The question is whether these experiences can be applied to the complex field of an emerging global tax policy. In attempting to answer this question great caution is needed. The lessons for the theory of self-regulation are that multiple barriers exist and, in some respects, international tax policy is an extreme case. What hinders self-regulation is that it is difficult for public authority to surrender tasks intrinsically connected with the classical exercise of power, for business to coordinate in an area where interests are split and where traditional efforts have centred on lowering taxes, and for civil society to develop collective action in a policy field of such general concern.

Nevertheless, there are some opportunities for strengthening the self-regulatory elements in global tax policy. It is useful to identify how these opportunities vary across the stages of the policy processes. In contrast to some other issue areas, our findings show that this strengthening of self-regulation is mainly likely to occur in response to initiatives taken by public authorities, although there are some examples, such as the development of CbC reporting, where new policies have been developed by civil society actors before being adopted and implemented by public authorities. Table 8.1 illustrates the variation in the profoundness and consistency of public and private engagement across the different stages. Although public institutions have been comparatively more active, this does not suggest, however, that serious and timely interventions have always been made, or that decisive solutions have been found to date.

Table 8.1 Stages and actors in the emerging global tax policy to combat tax evasion

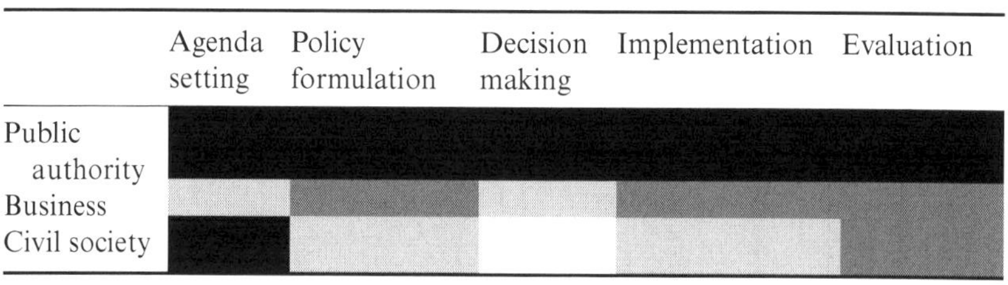

At the agenda-setting, policy formulation and decision stages the initiative in global tax policy has been taken by public authorities through multilateral initiatives such as the BEPS project, initiated by the OECD and endorsed by the G20, and more unilateral measures such as the US FATCA. Typically, business on its own will tend to resist a strengthening of tax collection capacities, and the agenda-setting, policy formulation and decision stages will be driven by public authorities, with the private sector making more incremental adjustments, such as providing valuable advice on the negative consequences of an overly blunt or burdensome public mechanism or cases of tax evasion that will jeopardize the financial system and delegitimize business. Likewise, relevant groups in civil society have played a key role in putting more effective global tax policy on to the agenda, but they have favoured public regulation, because it is seen as better able to police behaviour and sanction non-compliance in business. Overall, in the early stages of global tax policy, business and civil society are both active, but primarily in advocating or responding to initiatives driven by public authorities.

In the implementation and evaluation stages public authority remains central in global tax policy. The implementation and enforcement of international tax standards, as for national tax policy, primarily remain the responsibility of states. However, the self-regulatory roles of business are more evident in these stages than in the earlier agenda-setting, policy formulation and decision stages. In domestic tax policy, variations in the way that business organizations are incorporated in tax collection processes have had significant impacts on the degree of tax compliance, and it is important to consider this aspect of tax policy when reforming global tax policy as well. Combined with a general interest in bringing business actors and practices more directly into public administration, there have been experiments at the national level and new tools have been created. These results have been mixed, and this points to the importance of having an appropriate mix of public and private elements when bringing self-regulatory elements into global tax policy. The example of the very strong self-regulatory elements in the enforcement regime for money laundering and terrorist financing organized around the Financial Action Task Force suggests that there is additional opportunity for strengthening these elements in the global tax regime as well. Overall, though, it is clear that public authorities will continue to be the driving force in global tax policy, with business and civil society playing important but secondary roles, although for different reasons.

NOTES

1. It should be noted that there is also a long recorded history, stretching back more than three millennia to ancient Mesopotamia, of delegating certain of these functions to private actors. See Webber and Wildavsky (1986) and Stella (1993).
2. It may be disputed whether there is an undersupply of global peak associations, but there are, indeed, a relatively small number of them. See Kellow (2002).
3. A particularly critical issue in self-regulation studies has always been the implementation of rules and (the lack of) compliance. See Gunningham (2010).
4. To characterize these imbalances, we may refer to the gaps between 'economic' and 'political' geographies, and the difficulties for public authorities to catch up with economic processes. See Reinicke (1998).
5. Different concepts circulate to characterize civil society engagement, for instance 'civil regulation' (Vogel 2008) or 'multi-stakeholder arrangements' (Fransen and Kolk 2007).
6. Afield (2014, p.319) notes that, 'despite increased use of paid preparers, the IRS has historically known surprisingly little about who these preparers are and what their level of expertise is'.
7. The Institute of International Finance (IIF) is an important association of the financial industry and is heavily involved in global bank regulation, but is surprisingly not very involved with tax issues. An exception is the IIF's Council on Asset and Investment Management participation in the production of a 2013 position paper on the proposed EU financial transaction tax (IIF 2017).
8. To some extent the lack of engagement in agenda setting can be seen as a case of non-decision making on the part of organized business (Bachrach and Baratz 1963).

REFERENCES

Afield, W.E. (2014), 'A Market for Tax Compliance', *Cleveland State Law Review* **62** (2), 315–342.

Allen, W.T. (2004), 'Corporate Governance and a Business Lawyer's Duty of Independence', *Suffolk University Law Review* **38** (1), 1–16.

Andrade, J.A. (2015), 'Reconceptualising Whistleblowing in a Complex World', *Journal of Business Ethics* **128**, 321–335, available at https://doi.org/10.1007/s10551-014-2105-z (accessed 25 March 2017).

Auld, G., S. Renckens and B. Cashore (2015), 'Transnational Private Governance between the Logics of Empowerment and Control', *Regulation and Governance* **9** (2), 108–124, doi:10.1111/rego.12075.

Ayres, I. and J. Braithwaite (1992), *Responsive Regulation: Transcending the Deregulation Debate*, Oxford: Oxford University Press.

B20 (2017), 'Global Leaders to Tackle Profit Shifting and Tax Evasion', available at http://www.b20coalition.org/coalition-activities/communiques/global-leaders-to-tackle-profit-shifting-and-tax-evasion#sthash.KvB5WQQS.dpuf (accessed 23 March 2017).

Bachrach, P. and M.S. Baratz (1963), 'Two Faces of Power', *American Political Science Review* **56** (4), 947–952.

Bevir, M. (2012), *Governance: A Very Short Introduction*, Oxford: Oxford University Press.

BIAC (Business and Industry Advisory Committee) (2013), *Business Dialogue with the OECD on Base Erosion and Profit Shifting (BEPS)*, available at http://biac.

org/wp-content/uploads/2014/05/04-24_October_2013_BIAC_Letter_to_OECD_on_BEPS.pdf (accessed 26 June 2018).

Braithwaite, J. and P. Drahos (2000), *Global Business Regulation*, Cambridge: Cambridge University Press.

Broderick, C.O. (2007), 'Qui Tam Provisions and the Public Interest: An Empirical Analysis', *Columbia Law Review* **107** (4), 949–1001.

Burton, M. and J. Dabner (2008), 'The Partnership Model of the Relationship between Tax Administrators and Tax Practitioners: Drivers, Challenges and Prospects', *Journal of Australian Taxation* **11** (2), 108–137.

Cafaggi, F. (ed.) (2012), *Enforcement of Transnational Regulation: Ensuring Compliance in a Global World*, Cheltenham, UK and Northampton, MA, USA: Edward Elgar Publishing.

Christians, A. (2013), 'Tax Activism and the Global Movement for Development through Transparency', in M. Stewart and Y. Brauner (eds), *Tax, Law and Development*, Cheltenham, UK and Northampton, MA, USA: Edward Elgar Publishing, pp. 288–315.

Eccleston, R. (2013), *The Dynamics of Global Economic Governance: The Financial Crisis, the OECD and the Politics of International Tax Cooperation*, Cheltenham, UK and Northampton, MA, USA: Edward Elgar Publishing.

Fransen, L.W. and A. Kolk (2007), 'Global Rule-Setting for Business: A Critical Analysis of Multi-Stakeholder Standards', *Organization* **14** (5), 667–684.

GATJ (Global Alliance for Tax Justice) (2017), 'About Us', available at https://www.globaltaxjustice.org/en (accessed 25 March 2017).

Global Policy Forum (2015), *Overall Evaluation of the G20/OECD Base Erosion and Profit Shifting (BEPS) Project*, BEPS Monitoring Group, published electronically 7 October, available at https://www.globalpolicy.org/home/272-general/52817-overall-evaluation-of-the-g20oecd-base-erosion-and-profit-shifting-beps-project.html (accessed 20 March 2017).

Gourevitch, P.A., D.A. Lake and J.G. Stein (eds) (2012), *The Credibility of Transnational NGOs: When Virtue Is Not Enough*, Cambridge: Cambridge University Press.

Grabosky, P.N. (2012), 'Beyond Responsive Regulation: The Expanding Role of Non-State Actors in the Regulatory Process', *Regulation and Governance* **7** (1), 114–123, doi:10.1111/j.1748-5991.2012.01147.x.

Greif, A. (2005), 'Commitment, Coercion and Markets: The Nature and Dynamics of Institutions Supporting Exchange', in C. Ménard and M.M. Shirley (eds), *The Handbook of New Institutional Economics*, Amsterdam: Springer, pp. 727–788.

Griffin, O. (2015), 'PAC: Tax Industry "Cannot Be Trusted" to Self-Regulate', *Economia*, published electronically 6 February, available at http://economia.icaew.com/news/february-2015/pac-tax-industry-cannot-be-trusted-to-self-regulate (accessed 21 March 2017).

Gunningham, N. (2010), 'Enforcement and Compliance Strategies', in R. Baldwin, M. Cave and M. Lodge (eds), *The Oxford Handbook of Regulation*, Oxford: Oxford University Press, pp. 120–145.

Hale, T.N. and D. Held (eds) (2011), *Handbook of Innovations in Transnational Governance*, Cambridge: Polity Press.

IBFed (International Banking Federation) (2015), 'About IBFed', available at http://www.ibfed.org/about-ibfed (accessed 22 March 2017).

ICC (International Chamber of Commerce) (2017), 'Taxation', available at http://

www.iccwbo.org/about-icc/policy-commissions/taxation/ (accessed 22 March 2017).
ICRICT (Independent Commission for the Reform of International Corporate Taxation) (2017), 'About ICRICT', available at http://www.icrict.org/ (accessed 19 March 2017).
IIF (Institute of International Finance) (2017), 'IIF CAIM Raises Concerns That Proposed EU Financial Transaction Tax Could Hurt Savers and Pensioners', available at https://www.iif.com/press/iif-caim-raises-concerns-proposed-eu-financial-transaction-tax-could-hurt-savers-and-0 (accessed 20 March 2017).
IIROC (Investment Industry Regulatory Organization of Canada) (2010), *Anti-Money Laundering Compliance Guidance*, available at https://docs.iiroc.ca/DisplayDocument.aspx?DocumentID=6279890DECD84244A8E38F8A23E80E4A&Language=en (accessed 26 June 2018).
Kellow, A. (2002), 'Comparing Business and Public Interest Associability at the International Level', *International Political Science Review* **23** (2), 175–186.
Knobel, A. and M. Meinzer (2014), '"The End of Bank Secrecy?" Bridging the Gap to Effective Automatic Information Exchange: An Evaluation of OECD's Common Reporting Standard (CRS) and Its Alternatives', Tax Justice Network, available at http://www.taxjustice.net/wp-content/uploads/2013/04/TJN-141124-CRS-AIE-End-of-Banking-Secrecy.pdf (accessed 24 March 2017).
Lederman, L. (2003), 'The Interplay between Norms and Enforcement in Tax Compliance', *Ohio State Law Journal* **64** (6), 1453–1514.
Lederman, L. (2007), 'Statutory Speed Bumps: The Roles That Third Parties Play in Tax Compliance', *Stanford Law Review* **60** (3), 695–744.
Lewis, D. and W. Vandekerckhove (eds) (2015), *Developments in Whistleblowing Research 2015*, e-book, published by the International Whistleblowing Network.
Liss, C. and J.C. Sharman (2015), 'Global Corporate Crime Fighters: Private Transnational Responses to Piracy and Money Laundering', *Review of International Political Economy* **22** (4), 693–718.
Mattli, W. and T. Dietz (2014), 'Mapping and Assessing the Rise of International Commercial Arbitration in the Globalization Era: An Introduction', in W. Mattli and T. Dietz (eds), *International Arbitration and Global Governance*, Oxford: Oxford University Press, pp. 1–21.
Mehrotra, A.K. (2010), 'Capitalism, and the Institutional Foundations of the Modern Income Tax', *Law and Contemporary Problems* **73** (1), 25–62.
Mitchell, A. and P. Sikka (2011), *The Pin-Stripe Mafia: How Accountancy Firms Destroy Societies*, Association for Accountancy and Business Affairs, available at http://visar.csustan.edu/aaba/PINSTRIPEMAFIA.pdf (accessed 25 March 2017).
Murphy, R. (2014), 'Thoughts on the OECD BEPS Process: An NGO Perspective', *Tax Research UK: Richard Murphy on Tax and Economics*, available at http://www.taxresearch.org.uk/Blog/2014/09/20/thoughts-on-the-oecd-beps-process/ (accessed 21 March 2017).
OECD (2008), 'Study into the Role of Tax Intermediaries', OECD Forum on Tax Administration, available at http://www.oecd.org/tax/administration/studyintotheroleoftaxintermediaries.htm (accessed 19 March 2017).
OECD (2013), 'Country-by-Country Reporting', available at http://www.oecd.org/tax/beps/country-by-country-reporting.htm (accessed 25 March 2017).
OECD (2014), *Standard for Automatic Exchange of Financial Account Information in Tax Matters*, Paris: OECD Publishing.

Porter, T. and K. Ronit (2006), 'Self-Regulation as Policy Process: The Multiple and Criss-Crossing Stages of Private Rule-Making', *Policy Sciences* **39** (1), 41–72, doi:10.1007/s11077-006-9008-5.

Porter, T. and K. Ronit (2015), 'Implementation in International Business Self-Regulation: The Importance of Sequences and Their Linkages', *Journal of Law and Society* **42** (3), 413–433.

Porter, T. and K. Ronit (2016), 'The Institutionalization of Whistleblowing in Global Regulation: The Case of Taxation', Paper presented to the International Political Science Association Congress, Poznan, available at http://paperroom.ipsa.org/papers/paper_50176.pdf (accessed 22 March 2017).

Reinicke, W.C. (1998), *Global Public Policy: Governing without Government?*, Washington, DC: Brookings Institution Press.

Resnick, M.T. (2005), 'Outsourcing Federal Tax Collection', *Houston Business and Tax Law Journal* **5**, 128–204.

Rixen, T. (2008), *The Political Economy of International Tax Governance*, Basingstoke: Palgrave Macmillan.

Ronit, K. (2006), 'Introduction: Global Public Policy – The New Policy Arrangements of Business and Countervailing Groups', in Karsten Ronit (ed.), *Global Public Policy: Business and the Countervailing Powers of Civil Society*, London: Routledge, pp. 1–42.

Ronit, K. and T. Porter (2015), 'Harold D. Lasswell, *The Decision Process: Seven Categories of Functional Analysis*', in S.J. Bala, M. Lodge and E.C. Page (eds), *Oxford Handbook of Classics in Public Policy and Administration*, Oxford: Oxford University Press, pp. 54–68.

Stella, P. (1993), 'Tax Farming: A Radical Solution for Developing Country Tax Problems?', *IMF Staff Papers* **40** (1), 217–225.

Stone, D. (2013), *Knowledge Actors and Transnational Governance: The Private–Public Nexus in Policy Making in the Global Agora*, Basingstoke: Palgrave Macmillan.

Tett, G. (2015), 'Finance Must Blow the Whistle on Foul Play', *Financial Times*, published electronically 28 May, available at https://www.ft.com/content/f2c60908-047c-11e5-95ad-00144feabdc0 (accessed 19 March 2017).

Tilly, C. (1992), *Coercion, Capital and European States, A.D. 990–1992*, Hoboken, NJ: Wiley-Blackwell.

Transparency International (2015), *Tax Systems: A Channel for Corruption – Or a Way to Fight It?*, Working Paper No. 03/2015, Berlin: Transparency International, available at http://files.transparency.org/content/download/1939/12767/file/2015_WorkingPaper3_TaxSystems_EN.pdf (accessed 20 March 2017).

Ventry, D.J. (2008), 'Cooperative Tax Regulation', *Connecticut Law Review* **41** (2), 431–491.

Vogel, D. (2008), 'Private Global Business Regulation', *Annual Review of Political Science* **11**, 262–282, doi:10.1146/annurev.polisci.11.053106.141706.

Webber, C. and A. Wildavsky (1986), *A History of Taxation and Expenditure in the Western World*, New York: Simon & Schuster.

White, Micah (2016), 'The Panama Papers: Leaktivism's Coming of Age', *Guardian*, published electronically 5 April, available at http://www.theguardian.com/news/commentisfree/2016/apr/05/panama-papers-leak-activism-leaktivism (accessed 24 March 2017).

Yeoh, P. (2014), 'Whistleblowing: Motivations, Corporate Self-Regulation, and the Law', *International Journal of Law and Management* **56** (6), 459–474.

9. The EITI and fair taxation: exploring the linkages

James Van Alstine and Laura Smith

9.1 INTRODUCTION

Voluntary codes and standards have flourished within the extractive industries since the late 1990s, when the sector's contribution to sustainable development and transparency in oil, gas and mining projects became increasingly scrutinized (Van Alstine 2014). The global commodities super-cycle in the 2000s has driven foreign direct investment into some of the world's poorest economies, providing significant opportunities for development, but also the risk of failure due to corruption and mismanagement of revenues. Transparency in resource governance has thus risen up the political agenda in recent years, and was a key theme along with corporate tax avoidance and trade at the June 2013 G8 summit, hosted by the UK government.

International and national debates on corporate tax evasion and avoidance as well as illicit financial flows have converged to raise the profile of tax integrity as a core development challenge. This is because tax avoidance is estimated to cost developing countries between US$70 billion and US$120 billion per annum (UNCTAD 2015). According to the 2015 United Nations Economic Commission for Africa (UNECA 2015) report on illicit financial flows, Africa alone loses at least US$50 billion a year in illicit financial flows, through illegal activities such as trade mispricing, tax evasion, money laundering, bribery and corruption. African countries reliant upon the extractive industries for revenue and export earnings are particularly prone to illicit financial flows and opaque natural resource deals. Kofi Annan, head of the Africa Progress Panel, has called for greater transparency as a way for African countries to manage their resource wealth for positive transformation rather than squandering it (Annan 2013).

In this chapter we explore the linkages between fair taxation and transparency in the natural resource sector through the lens of the Extractive Industries Transparency Initiative (EITI). The EITI is a well-established global standard that promotes revenue transparency and accountability in the oil, gas and mineral resource sectors. Payment discrepancies identified through the EITI have led to scrutiny of taxation rates and audit processes in a variety of countries which have implemented the EITI Standard. Exploring the linkages between the EITI and fair taxation provides a framework for assessing the potential for the spread of tax transparency norms and private corporate tax standards beyond the resources sector.

We begin with a discussion of the origins and evolution of transparency in resource governance, and then discuss the design, scope and evolution of the EITI. We go on to highlight critiques of the EITI, followed by a discussion of the linkages between the EITI and emerging public and private forms of tax governance. While the EITI was not originally designed or intended to be a tax integrity initiative, there are a number of areas of synergy between the EITI's evolving mandate and debates on fair taxation, including changing regulatory regimes, country-by-country reporting (CbCR), unitary taxation and registers of beneficial ownership. We conclude with observations on the tensions between public and private forms of governance within the fields of transparency in resource governance and private corporate tax governance.

9.2 ORIGINS AND EVOLUTION OF TRANSPARENCY IN RESOURCE GOVERNANCE

The origins of the EITI lie in the turn to transparency in resource governance which occurred in the late 1990s and early 2000s (Gupta 2010). Four broad trends around this time influenced the rise of the transparency agenda.

First, the development challenges associated with natural resource wealth came to the attention of scholars and policy makers during this time. A link was identified between natural resource extraction and poor development outcomes: a phenomenon commonly termed 'the resource curse'. The resource curse denotes the paradoxical relationship between natural resource wealth and poverty, growing inequalities and conflict, which saw many resource-rich developing countries slip to the bottom of HDI rankings. Trends were identified in several resource-dependent developing countries, which varied in terms of size and diversity of population, wealth level and system of government (Auty 1993; Karl 1997; Sachs and Warner 2001).

Second, the resource curse began to be framed as a political and governance challenge. Rather than it being seen as an inevitable outcome of resource extraction, the literature focused on the ways resource wealth was managed, and the quality of national-level institutions as a determining factor (Ross 1999; Mehlum et al. 2006; Humphreys et al. 2007; Ross 2012). This resonated with wider debates about 'good governance' in development, which replaced the Washington Consensus and the largely discredited structural adjustment approach to development.

Third, sustainability, human rights, corruption and MNC conduct emerged as important issues for the international community (Jenkins 2005). The influence and reach of western-based non-governmental organizations grew significantly during this time, and they played an instrumental role in bringing these issues into the public sphere. More recently, the same NGOs have also attempted to draw attention to harmful tax practices by MNCs, which represents a continuation of this campaign to highlight MNC misconduct (this volume, Chapters 3 and 4).

Fourth, this coincided with a wider crisis of legitimacy within the extractives sector, which received sustained criticism for its poor environmental and human rights record, as well as for other unscrupulous conduct. As western-based MNCs became increasingly brand sensitive, the 'business as usual' approach was no longer tenable (Frynas 2009). In an example of how civil society organizations can set the international policy agenda, the role of corruption was placed at the centre of the debate by an influential report by activist NGO Global Witness in 1999. This report highlighted corruption at the highest levels of the Angolan state and the complicity of oil and banking companies in the direct impoverishment of the country through the hollowing out of state assets during Angola's civil war (Global Witness 1999). Demands for improved transparency and accountability in the extractives sector soon followed, driven by a global coalition of NGOs under the Publish What You Pay (PWYP) banner, which aimed to ensure that citizens would benefit from their nation's natural resource wealth.

The rise of the transparency agenda must also be understood in relation to two other initiatives – the Extractive Industries Review of the World Bank, and the Mining, Minerals and Sustainable Development (MMSD) project of the International Council on Mining and Minerals – both of which sought to align the sector with the goals of sustainable development and achieve greater transparency of information in the extractives value chain (World Bank 2003; Buxton 2012).

The MMSD was a two-year project between 2000 and 2002 initiated by nine major mining companies in the run-up to the World Summit on Sustainable Development in Johannesburg. It sought to align the sector to the goals of sustainable development. Although criticized by some activist groups for not having gone far enough, the initiative marked the start of an ongoing dialogue that focused on the contribution of the extractive industries to sustainable development and greater transparency in information production and dissemination throughout the extractive industries' project cycle (MMSD 2002; Bebbington et al. 2008; Buxton 2012).

The Extractives Industries Review of the World Bank, carried out between 2001 and 2004, provides further insight into the institutionalization of the revenue transparency agenda. The Review evaluated the Bank's role in oil, gas and mining, in light of its overall mandate to reduce poverty and promote sustainable development (World Bank 2003, 2004). The report, titled *Striking a Better Balance*, concluded that there was a continued role for the Bank in these sectors only if certain conditions were in place, including pro-poor public and corporate governance, more effective social and environmental policies, and respect for human rights.

Although many of the recommendations were either watered down or not implemented, the Review was significant in that it marked a substantial shift in thinking (Pegg 2006). Revenue transparency was one of the few issues that could be agreed upon by NGOs, mining companies and governments (van Oranje and Parham 2009). Bank officials required revenue transparency 'as a condition for new investments in the extractive industries sector' (World Bank 2004, p. 4). And, unlike in the taxation arena, mining firms actively sought greater transparency in an effort to reduce the amount of revenue they were paying to governments and their officials in the form of corrupt payments. The Review supported the EITI and voluntary host country approaches to revenue transparency over Washington Consensus donor conditionality and mandatory private sector rules.

9.3 THE DESIGN, SCOPE AND EVOLUTION OF THE EITI

The origins of the EITI represented a compromise negotiated by the UK government between what activist NGOs wanted and what companies resisted: mandatory reporting and public disclosure of payments and revenues in the extractives sector. It further sought to provide equal transparency from governments and companies (Rich and Moberg 2015). The idea of the EITI was originally outlined in a speech intended to be given by then UK prime minister Tony Blair at the World Summit on Sustainable Development in 2002. After the speech was made public and the UK Department for International Development convened a group of relevant stakeholders, momentum grew. The EITI was formally established in June 2003 at its first conference in London, when the 12 EITI Principles were agreed.

A unique feature of the EITI Standard is that, although it was driven by NGOs and industry, it is implemented by governments. The EITI is based on two key mechanisms – company reporting of the payments they make to governments, and governments reporting the amounts they receive from companies, thus making the information on payments and revenues received open and available for monitoring by citizens. Any discrepancies between monies paid and monies received are made public. Key to the success of EITI is the role of civil society in oversight, monitoring and public debate. This is important in ensuring that greater transparency can lead to greater accountability (EITI 2017b).

To be considered as an EITI candidate country, a government must complete five sign-up steps, which relate to government commitment, company engagement, civil society engagement, the establishment of a multi-stakeholder group (MSG) and agreement of an EITI work plan (EITI 2016). The initiative is governed by a board, a secretariat based in Oslo, and a global conference and members' meeting which is held at least every three years to, among other things, further the objectives of the EITI and appoint the board. A country's first EITI report must be published within 18 months of the date of acceptance as an EITI candidate. Then, over the next two and a half years, the country must complete the EITI validation process, which includes reporting and governance requirements that are reviewed and confirmed by an independent validator appointed by the EITI (EITI 2016).

A pilot phase of the EITI was implemented in Nigeria, Azerbaijan, Ghana and the Kyrgyz Republic. Although the initial focus of EITI was on countries in the global south, OECD countries gradually became EITI candidates: first Norway, which committed to implement the EITI in 2006 (becoming compliant in 2011), followed by the USA and the UK committing to implement in 2013, and Germany in 2016. Germany, the United Kingdom and the United States have adopted voluntary implementation, while Norway has made corporate participation in the EITI mandatory through a regulation aligned with the country's Petroleum Act (GIZ and D-EITI 2016). The addition of OECD countries is significant, because the EITI is no longer an initiative driven by countries in the global north for developing countries to implement. It is a truly global initiative, which holds countries to the same global standard (Rich and Moberg 2015). As of July 2017, there were 52 EITI countries. Of these, 47 were EITI compliant, three were suspended owing to inadequate progress, and two were suspended owing to political instability in the country.

Since its inception in 2003, the EITI has grown from an initiative narrowly focused on revenue collection into an international standard which aims to address the wider governance of extractive resources. It reflects an ongoing process of negotiation and consensus building to achieve better management of natural resources (Rich and Moberg 2015). The EITI has not remained static – while the original EITI Principles remain, the criteria for implementation and validation have evolved. The set of requirements known as the EITI Rules, first published in 2009, and revised in 2011, were replaced by the EITI Standard in 2013. The EITI board adopted a new 2016 EITI Standard, which included several refinements to better align the Standard with the extractive industries value chain, as will be discussed below.

9.4 EITI CRITIQUE

While the EITI may be the leading international standard on extractives governance, there are a number of critiques of the Standard that have relevance to the field of fair taxation (see e.g. Van Alstine 2017). First, the EITI is critiqued for being voluntary, and thus non-binding on both governments and companies. Governments and companies can report selectively, and despite auditing requirements the quality and integrity of data are not guaranteed (Gillies 2010; Dykstra 2011). The voluntary nature of the Standard also means that it has limited reach and therefore effect. A large portion of global production by the extractive industries remains outside its remit, particularly many state-owned companies (UNCTAD 2014). This discretion may allow companies the space to avoid corporate taxation (Otusanya 2011), and governments the secrecy and opaqueness necessary to pursue rent seeking and patronage (Kolstad and Soreide 2009). Many corruption, good governance and human development indicators have not improved significantly in EITI participating countries, suggesting that greater transparency has failed to address the resource curse in these countries (Wilson and Van Alstine 2014).

Second, while the reconciliation of government and company payments highlights incidences of corruption and poor administrative capacity in producing countries, it does little to inform what the tax burden of MNCs in the extractives sector ought to be (UNCTAD 2014). As was highlighted in Chapter 2, this challenge is common to many of the proposed transparency-based solutions to corporate tax avoidance – simply publishing the effective tax rate of a firm relies on further judgement as to what an appropriate amount of taxation should be and provides few insights as to strategies aimed at increasing the amount of tax firms pay.

Furthermore, translating transparency into accountability has been a persistent challenge for the EITI, as has demonstrating the ways that payment/revenue disclosure can lead to reductions in corruption (Idemudia 2013). In many EITI reporting countries, civil society cannot operate freely, and drawing attention to corruption within governments is simply not possible. Also, the EITI's limited mandate has, until recently, failed to address illicit financial flows and how revenues are actually spent. The 2013 and 2016 Standards have sought to address some of these gaps by making EITI reports more relevant and accurate and by extending the EITI to address issues of, for example, beneficial ownership. The disclosure of taxes and other payments by extractive firms to governments may provide the political impetus needed for reforming tax and ownership regimes. If this is possible, the EITI can then be viewed as an international norm that may influence multiple policy spaces beyond anti-corruption.

Third, the quality, timeliness and usefulness of EITI data have been problematic (Van Alstine 2014). Access to complete and reliable data is an issue that has dogged the EITI since its inception, as it has other campaigns designed to promote corporate tax justice (Ravat and Ufer 2010; Dykstra 2011; Gillies 2011). The 2013 and 2016 reforms of the Standard have sought to make improvements in this area. The 2013 Standard significantly broadened the scope of the reporting obligations. It required disclosure of payment information by project, and aligned to the US Dodd–Frank Act and the EU's Accounting and Transparency Directives. It also provided greater autonomy to MSGs to set objectives and tailor the Standard to the local context, and encouraged implementing countries to publish data in open and accessible formats. The Natural Resource Governance Institute (NRGI 2015) analysed the first 22 reports prepared under the 2013 Standard and found that, while the new reports were more comprehensive and informative, there were still significant shortcomings, including:

- Timeliness: the new reports generally contained data that was two years old.
- Openness: only ten countries published data in a machine-readable format, which limits its usefulness.
- Projects: the new reports generally did not report on a project-by-project basis; aggregation hides important information for end-users.
- Subnational revenues: most countries did not include subnational resource revenue transfers, which limits usefulness for local communities directly impacted by resource extraction.

The 2016 Standard aims to further strengthen EITI beyond a narrow focus on revenue transparency, to make the disclosure process throughout the extractive industries value chain more effective and efficient (EITI 2016). Countries with already robust systems are permitted to make use of existing reporting mechanisms for EITI data and make the results transparent at source. This is thought to increase government ownership of the process and reduce the manipulation of data. As discussed below, one of the most relevant changes for issues of tax avoidance and evasion is steps taken to disclose beneficial owners of companies that bid for, operate or invest in extractive projects (EITI 2017a). As of July 2017, the majority of countries were yet to be assessed against the 2016 Standard.

Fourth, when mismatches are found in EITI data, there is no clear course of action that should be taken (UNCTAD 2014). The MSGs are tasked with explaining, investigating and 'if necessary' addressing discrepancies identified in EITI reports (EITI 2016). The pathway from report outcomes to policy and/or governance impact will vary significantly by country. Some have argued that a key reason for the successes and longevity of the EITI initiative is its consensus-based and multi-partnered approach (O'Sullivan 2013); yet others, such as PWYP coalition, continue to push for mandatory disclosure, and to broaden the EITI's remit to engage more directly with areas beyond revenue transparency, including revenue expenditure, contract transparency and fair taxation.

The reports can be used to identify who is paying tax and who is not, and, compared against contracts, production figures and the tax regimes, these discrepancies can lead to governance impact (Rich 2013). For example, the Nigerian Extractive Industries Transparency Initiative's (NEITI) second report, published in 2009, identified major financial inconsistencies, tax discrepancies and system inefficiencies (Keblusek 2010). As a result, Nigeria launched a value-for-money audit to investigate whether reconciled payments nevertheless hide corruption. This is perhaps evidence of a shift towards more proactive tackling of corruption in the country stimulated by EITI, though Nigeria still languishes at the lower end of the Corruption Perceptions Index.

Finally, the key to the success of the EITI moving from outcomes to impact is the empowerment and capacity of civil society. Significant power imbalances remain between EITI stakeholders, and CSOs operate under restrictive and repressive conditions in many countries which have signed up to EITI (Wilson and Van Alstine 2014). Given the lack of political will and/or civic space, the link between transparency and accountability is tenuous in many contexts. To address this issue, the 2013 EITI Standard introduced a Civil Society Protocol, which provided guidelines to ensure that civil society has space to effectively carry out its oversight role. A revised Civil Society Protocol is included in the 2016 EITI Standard, which makes an assessment of civil society engagement in accordance with the protocol a requirement.

The above discussion demonstrates that persistent problems hamper the EITI regime's ability to provide adequate private tax governance and also limit the potential for transparency to increase accountability in fulfilment of broader sustainable development goals. Nevertheless, the Standard has been spurred along by its supporters and critics, which seek continual improvement, albeit in incremental stages.

9.5 EITI AND FAIR TAXATION

As outlined above, despite some progress there are significant limitations for EITI to act as a catalyst for fair corporate taxation, and a model for future private taxation regimes. By design, EITI in its original form is an anti-corruption measure rather than a tax integrity initiative. Nevertheless, there are important policy developments emerging from where EITI implementation overlaps significantly with debates on fair taxation and private corporate governance. With examples from sub-Saharan Africa, we discuss the EITI within the context of changing regulatory regimes, country-by-country reporting and beneficial ownership.

Changing Regulatory Regimes

As discussed above, a key role of EITI reports is to identify discrepancies in payments governments receive from domestic and foreign companies. While these discrepancies can lead to audits and greater accountability measures, they can also highlight debates about how much tax the extractives sector should be paying. From a regulatory perspective, the EITI can help catalyse efforts to strengthen tax and fiscal regimes to reduce concessions and respond to changing market conditions. EITI report data provide the opportunity to compare tax regimes between countries to raise awareness and debate and potentially lead to reform that will increase investment, job creation, economic development and ultimately government revenues (Rich 2013).

There has been a movement during the commodity super-cycle for African countries to renegotiate and revise tax rates, which is strongly linked to a discourse of resource nationalism and the rise of the African developmental state as highlighted in the African Mining Vision. For example, Liberia has used its EITI process to undertake a 'should-be-paid' audit (Rich 2013), and EITI data have been used to create debate on what royalty rates Areva should pay in Niger (Aidara 2014). A number of EITI implementing countries have introduced new tax rates, leading to significant increases in government revenue, for example Ghana, Zambia, Tanzania and Zimbabwe.

In 2010, Ghana's EITI (GHEITI's) reports highlighted a range of royalties between 3 and 6 per cent, with most companies paying at the lower level of the band (UNCTAD 2014). Mining companies in Ghana were expected to increase royalty payments if world market prices for minerals increased; however, in practice this had not occurred even though gold prices had increased significantly (Asiamah 2010). In an effort to gain more revenue from its mining sector, Ghana revised its royalty rate to 5 per cent in 2011 and changed its corporate tax rate from 25 to 35 per cent in 2012 (UNCTAD 2014).

In Zambia, there has also been ongoing debate on revising the fiscal regime for its mining sector. Revenues from Zambia's mining sector fell by 9 per cent from 2014 to 2015 owing to lower commodity prices and less production, exacerbated by lower demand for copper by China. Reported in the 2015 Zambia EITI (ZEITI) report, the government has gone through a process of adjusting the tax regime to commodity prices. In 2014, the government shifted to a 'royalty only' tax regime, with the aim of maximizing revenue during the early stages of production. In 2015, after external market conditions changed, Zambia shifted back to a dual system, which includes a royalty rate of 9 per cent and corporate income tax of 30 per cent (EITI Secretariat 2017b), and more recently, in 2016, the government changed the fiscal regime again to a sliding mineral royalty rate dependent on metal prices on the London Metal Stock Exchange (PWYP Zambia 2017). The government has been keen to protect investment in the mining sector during times of declining copper prices and slackening demand from China. The PWYP coalition in Zambia has raised concerns about this new fiscal regime, but the extent to which the ZEITI MSG has participated in and/or influenced government debates on a tax regime for the mining sector deserves further investigation (PWYP Zambia 2017).

During the commodity super-cycle a wave of resource nationalism started to emerge in Sub-Saharan Africa. Zambia introduced a 25 per cent windfall tax in 2008, and Ghana planned to introduce a 10 per cent windfall tax in 2012. However, Zambia's windfall tax was repealed in 2009 after a fall in global copper prices, and the government of Ghana dropped its planned windfall tax after threats by mining companies to lay off workers. MNCs often resist the proposed changes to the fiscal regime for the extractives sector. They may warn about redundancies, mine closures, reductions in investment or even legal action, but in practice the private sector rarely follows through on threats to leave a country (UNCTAD 2014). The structural power of MNCs outlined above is one of the key barriers to converting transparency measures (such as the EITI) to increased taxation rates, and therefore greater revenue for governments of resource-rich states.

Country-by-Country Reporting

Another key area of overlap between the EITI and fair taxation is country-by-country reporting. Country-by-country reporting occurs within the extractives sector when companies report what they pay to host governments, usually project by project. There is an important distinction between mandatory and voluntary approaches.

Since the Financial Crisis of 2008–09, the G8 and G20 have sought to reform the financial system, and have been supportive of mandatory country-by-country reporting (UNCTAD 2014). In 2010, the US took the lead in spurring new regulations for increased transparency in the extractive industries through section 1504 of the Dodd–Frank Act, which requires all US-listed companies to disclose project-by-project tax, royalty and other payments to governments when reporting annually to the US Securities and Exchange Commission (SEC). In June 2016, after lengthy deliberation and legal battles, the SEC announced that it had finally adopted the Dodd–Frank rules, and that reporting would begin in 2018 (US SEC 2016). However, in February 2017 President Trump signed a Congressional bill that effectively eliminated the extractives sector disclosure requirements in Dodd–Frank. Uncertainty remains over whether the SEC will redraft the rule or if Dodd–Frank will be repealed or amended (EITI Secretariat 2017a).

Following the US Dodd–Frank Act, in 2013 the EU approved its revised Accounting and Transparency Directives, which require all extractive firms (oil and gas, mining and logging of primary forests) listed on EU stock exchanges to disclose payments to government in the countries in which they operate. The EU Accounting Directive came into force in 2016, and the first reports were lodged in that year (EC 2018). Norway and Canada, among others, have made further national legislative commitments to greater transparency through mandatory country-by-country reporting. In this sense the extractive industries are at the forefront of the global push towards country-by-country reporting described in Chapter 2.

Some companies have sought to pre-empt these new rules, by disclosing a significant amount of tax-related information in voluntary sustainability reports. Companies that have voluntarily published details of profits and total taxes collected and borne on a country-by-country basis include Tullow Oil, Rio Tinto, BHP Billiton, Shell, Statoil and Newmont. As Tullow's chair, Simon Thompson, said when they published all tax, royalty and other payments to governments in their 2012 CSR report, they welcomed the legislation and argued that full project-by-project disclosure was the way forward, because it 'created an absolute level playing field so that . . . there are no commercial sensitivity issues as a result' (Rich

2013). Yet, outside of leading firms within the extractives sector, there has been widespread opposition to mandatory country-by-country reporting by business leaders such as the Confederation of British Industry and even by US transnational oil companies led by the American Petroleum Institute (Deloitte 2013). There are concerns that state-owned companies and domestic firms may be able to avoid these emerging forms of extra-territorial legislation, making an uneven playing field.

There are a number of themes that emerge between EITI and mandatory country-by-country reporting. First, the EITI is still *voluntary*, and falls short of the stringency required by these emerging mandatory disclosure rules. For example, the American Petroleum Institute, in their argument against the US Dodd–Frank Act, cited the EITI as a preferable alternative to mandatory country-by-country reporting, largely because it would allow firms discretion as to whether or not to participate. Nevertheless, as noted elsewhere in this volume, NGOs such as PWYP and Oxfam America continue to campaign for mandatory disclosure rules and the continual improvement of the EITI Standard. Second, the EITI is *complementary* to these modes of extra-territorial legislation. This wave of mandatory country-by-country reporting rules does not require disclosure by governments, whereas the EITI does. While the EITI is not intended to be a tax integrity initiative, wider adoption of its principles through either national legislation or voluntary firm adoption would likely lead to a reduction in corruption and stronger debates around what constitutes a fair amount of tax.

Beneficial Ownership

One of the most ground-breaking changes included in the 2016 EITI Standard is the steps taken towards disclosing beneficial owners of companies that bid for, operate or invest in extractive projects (EITI 2017a). In addition, 'politically exposed' persons who own extractive assets will be identified and disclosed. This is an important extension of the EITI, related to not only corruption but also tax avoidance and tax evasion. The updated 2016 Standard mandated that country-level MSGs develop beneficial ownership 'roadmaps' outlining how they will pursue such disclosures, the first of which were published in December 2016. By 2020 the identities of companies and individuals who own and profit from extractive industries must be disclosed by participating countries (EITI 2016).

The 2013 *Africa Progress Report* highlighted large-scale revenue losses from the privatization of extractive assets over the last decade. For example, in the DRC between 2010 and 2012 it is estimated that mining assets were significantly undervalued when sold to offshore shell companies, totalling losses of at least US$1.36 billion (Africa Progress Panel 2013, p. 56). Offshore companies are then able to secure very high profits during the onward sales of extractive assets. Losses in mining concessions' trading are symptomatic of opaque transactions throughout the extractive industry value chain – from secretive bidding processes, unpublished mining contracts, undervalued mining assets, and commercial secrecy of major mining companies, to a lack of transparency and accountability of state companies and government agencies to legislators (Africa Progress Panel 2013).

The new EITI rules on beneficial ownership are timely. Only a few months after the 2016 EITI Standard was adopted, the Panama Papers scandal broke in April 2016 (see this volume, Chapter 12). Comprising over 11.5 million leaked documents from a law firm in Panama, the leak highlighted the use of anonymous shell companies to hide or launder money (EITI 2017a). The Panama Papers have spurred increased scrutiny of illicit financial flows and tax evasion practices in Africa through identification of African elites connected to offshore companies (Fitzgibbon 2016). Countries around the world are investigating tax havens and legal loopholes that might drive tax evasion. For example, in the wake of the Panama Papers the US Treasury Department sought to make it more difficult for companies to move their tax residence overseas, and the Costa Rican finance minister mentioned the Panama Papers in his push to reform its tax system and prevent wealthy individuals evading tax (Zorrilla 2016).

In advance of the 2020 deadline, 20 countries have decided to establish public beneficial ownership registries with EITI assistance. There are a number of reasons EITI countries are pursuing beneficial ownership transparency, including: to assess the suitability of companies bidding and being granted rights for extractive assets; to prevent conflict of interest in public procurement and licence allocation processes; to prevent tax evasion and transfer mispricing; and to attract and diversify investment (EITI 2017a, pp. 12–13). As the EITI Secretariat stresses, the ownership registries have strong linkages with fair taxation because, once complete, 'information on the corporate structures of companies and their parent companies or subsidiaries will make it easier for tax authorities to understand which transactions are liable to taxation' (EITI 2017a, p. 11).

As a part of its incremental evolution the EITI has created the policy space for new beneficial ownership rules. In Cameroon, beneficial ownership provisions are now included in the mining code, and in Ghana the disclosure of beneficial ownership was included in regulations for the implementation of the 2016 Petroleum Exploration and Production Bill as well as an amendment to the Companies' Code (Energy Ghana 2017). The 2016 EITI Standard now extends beyond revenue to shed light on many of these links in the value chain, including beneficial ownership, but it will take political will, protection of civic space, and public demand to push reforms forward in countries plagued by opaque extractive deals such as the DRC.

9.6 CONCLUSION

In this chapter we have outlined the evolution of fiscal transparency in resource governance, focusing on the EITI and its unique form of voluntary private governance. We have demonstrated how the EITI has provided space for private actors to influence public and private sector tax governance, particularly within the areas of changing regulatory/fiscal regimes, country-by-country reporting and beneficial ownership.

This analysis has several implications for the possibility of private governance within the field of corporate taxation beyond the extractive industries. First, the link between private and public forms of governance in the extractive industries suggests potential for private governance to form the basis of formal public regulation in other sectors. The EITI is a partly firm-driven governance initiative, yet the principles behind this regime have gone on to be adopted as regulation by national governments. In this sense, voluntary governance by firms has led to mandatory modes of governance in a variety of country contexts. In the case of Nigeria, for example, Zainab Ahmed, Nigerian minister of budget and national planning, EITI board member and previous executive director of NEITI, at a recent call of the EITI board's Implementation Committee suggested that 'many of the changes and reforms the government is now pushing through are directly attributable to the work of NEITI' (EITI 2018). Yet the potential for firm-led regulation to be adopted by governments has been explored elsewhere (see Elbra 2017) and needs to be viewed cautiously, in the sense that private governance initiatives are not always best placed to meet the needs of developing states and instead can be used to usher in business-friendly policies (this volume, Chapter 8). In the taxation arena, this is evident in the push for the adoption of the EITI Principles (owing to their voluntary nature) without any binding agreement by firms to make disclosure mandatory.

This chapter also questions the extent to which lessons learned from the extractive industries, and in particular the EITI (i.e. its legitimacy and effectiveness), are applicable to other sectors. EITI has made a significant contribution to the governance of the extractives sector at the national and global level. 'Debates on transparency in the sector are unrecognisable from ten years ago, and the EITI is seen as being at the forefront of many frontier debates including beneficial ownership, commodity trading, and artisanal and small-scale mining' (EITI 2017a, p. 11). While change to governance in the extractives sector is evident, it remains questionable how much of this can be transferred to MNCs more generally, particularly in the arena of corporate taxation. As discussed elsewhere in this volume, MNCs have thus far been unwilling to take the lead on private taxation governance, and, without the impetus of the bribery and corruption that drove extractives firms to act, it remains unlikely that MNCs more generally will take the lead in tax transparency.

The EITI experience also suggests that civic space, or spaces of private authority and accountability, are critical within the 'new' politics of international taxation. This space is required in order to provide the catalyst for private forms of tax governance, which may then provide legitimacy and lead to mandatory approaches. However, as noted throughout this volume, there are challenges to engaging citizens in this arena as well as maintaining the political salience of the issue in the face of powerful firms. The EITI experience highlights the particular challenges faced by civil society actors in developing countries in particular.

While the debate on fair taxation is ongoing, it is important to see how the new EITI Standard is implemented in various countries, exploring the opportunities and challenges raised by such a technocratic process. Will it lead to more incremental change potentially legitimizing business as usual, or will it provide the impetus for more substantive pro-poor reform and inclusive development? The answers to these questions should inform future attempts at private tax governance.

Ultimately, exploring the links between the EITI and fair taxation provides a lens through which we can understand the drivers and constraints on policy development and change, and in particular private forms of governance. Private governance is not so much about firms self-regulating in this context, but it is a mix of normative pressures from host country commitments to international standards such as the EITI. In the arena of corporate taxation, we are witnessing a shift in expectations of business behaviour from the public and governments. What remains to be seen, however, is whether these expectations can converge on new norms and business practices that extend the progress made in extractives sector transparency to other sectors and in the critical field of corporate taxation.

REFERENCES

Africa Progress Panel (2013), *Equity in Extractives: Stewarding Africa's Natural Resources for All: Africa Progress Report 2013*, Geneva: Africa Progress Panel.

Aidara, I. (2014), 'Why Does AREVA Refuse to Pay a Fair Rate of Tax in Niger?', *African Arguments*, available at http://africanarguments.org/2014/02/20/why-does-areva-refuse-to-pay-a-fair-rate-of-tax-in-niger-by-dr-ibrahima-aidara/ (accessed 11 November 2017).

Annan, K. (2013), 'Stop the Plunder of Africa', *New York Times*, published electronically 9 May, available at http://www.nytimes.com/2013/05/10/opinion/global/stop-the-plunder-of-africa.html?_r=1& (accessed 13 November 2017).

Asiamah, F. (2010), 'Ghana: Country's EITI under Scrutiny', *AllAfrica*, available at http://allafrica.com/stories/201001150434.html (accessed 10 November 2017).

Auty, R.M. (1993), *Sustaining Development in Mineral Economies: The Resource Curse Thesis*, London: Routledge.

Bebbington, A., L. Hinojosa, D. Humphreys Bebbington, M.L. Burneo and X. Warnaars (2008), 'Contention and Ambiguity: Mining and the Possibilities of Development', *Development and Change* **39** (6), 887–914.

Buxton, A. (2012), *MMSD+10: Reflecting on a Decade of Mining and Sustainable Development*, IIED Discussion Paper, International Institute for Environment and Development (IIED), available at http://pubs.iied.org/16041IIED.html (accessed 12 November 2017).

Deloitte (2013), *Major Changes: International Tax Reform and Transparency*, available at https://www2.deloitte.com/content/dam/Deloitte/global/Documents/Tax/dttl-tax-indt-uk-tax-major-changes-in-tax.pdf (accessed 12 November 2017).

Dykstra, P. (2011), 'Learning from Success and Challenges', EITI 2011 Briefing, Revenue Watch Institute, available at https://resourcegovernance.org/sites/default/files/EITI_lessons_2011-02-23.pdf (accessed 10 November 2017).

EC (European Commission) (2018), 'Public Country-by-Country Reporting: Requirements for Extractive and Logging Industries', available at https://ec.europa.eu/info/business-economy-euro/company-reporting-and-auditing/company-reporting/public-country-country-reporting_en (accessed 26 June 2018).

EITI (Extractive Industries Transparency Initiative) (2016), *The EITI Standard 2016*, EITI International Secretariat, available at https://eiti.org/sites/default/files/migrated_files/english_eiti_standard_0.pdf (accessed 10 November 2017).

EITI (Extractive Industries Transparency Initiative) (2017a), *2017 Progress Report: Ending Company Anonymity*, available at https://eiti.org/document/eiti-progress-report-2017 (accessed 12 November 2017).

EITI (Extractive Industries Transparency Initiative) (2017b), 'The Extractive Industries Transparency Initiative', available at https://eiti.org/ (accessed 9 November 2017).

EITI (Extractive Industries Transparency Initiative) (2018), 'EITI: A Tool for Reformers', available at https://eiti.org/progress-report-2017/eiti-tool-for-reformers (accessed 26 June 2018).

EITI Secretariat (2017a), 'Statement from EITI Chair on Repeal of SEC's "Resource Extraction" Rule', available from https://eiti.org/news/statement-from-eiti-chair-on-repeal-of-secs-resource-extraction-rule (accessed 10 November 2017).

EITI Secretariat (2017b) 'Zambia: Fighting Corporate Tax Evasion with Data', available at https://eiti.org/news/zambia-fighting-corporate-tax-evasion-with-data (accessed 13 November 2017).

Elbra, A. (2017), *Governing African Goldmining: Private Governance and the Resource Curse*, London: Palgrave Macmillan.

Energy Ghana (2017), 'Ghana to Have Beneficial Ownership by End of Year –

Minister', available at http://www.energyghana.com/post.php?508c75c8507a2ae5223dfd2faeb98122=1500842450 (accessed 10 November 2017).

Fitzgibbon, W. (2016), 'Secret Offshore Deals Deprive Africa of Billions in Natural Resource Dollars', International Consortium of Investigative Journalists, available at https://panamapapers.icij.org/20160725-natural-resource-africa-offshore.html (accessed 11 November 2017).

Frynas, J.G. (2009), *Beyond Corporate Social Responsibility*, Cambridge: Cambridge University Press.

Gillies, A. (2010), 'Reputational Concerns and the Emergence of Oil Sector Transparency as an International Norm', *International Studies Quarterly* **54** (1), 103–126.

Gillies, A. (2011), 'What Do the Numbers Say? Analyzing Report Data', EITI 2011 Briefing, Revenue Watch Institute, available at https://resourcegovernance.org/sites/default/files/EITI_numbers_2011-02-23.pdf (accessed 9 November 2017).

GIZ and D-EITI (2016), *Implementation of the EITI in G7, EU and OECD Countries: Facts and Figures 15.02.2016*, Deutsche Gesellschaft für Internationale Zusammenarbeit (GIZ), available at https://eiti.org/sites/default/files/documents/study-on-eiti-implementation-in-oecd-countries.pdf (accessed 26 June 2018).

Global Witness (1999), *A Crude Awakening*, available at https://www.globalwitness.org/en/archive/crude-awakening/ (accessed 12 November 2017).

Gupta, A. (2010), 'Transparency in Global Environmental Governance: A Coming of Age?', *Global Environmental Politics* **10** (3), 1–9.

Humphreys, M., J.D. Sachs and J.E. Stiglitz (2007), *Escaping the Resource Curse*, New York: Columbia University Press.

Idemudia, U. (2013), 'The Extractive Industries Transparency Initiative and Corruption in Nigeria: Rethinking the Links between Transparency and Accountability', in F. Diallo and R. Calland (eds), *Access to Information in Africa: Law, Culture and Practice*, Leiden: Brill, pp. 127–148.

Jenkins, R. (2005), 'Globalization, Corporate Social Responsibility and Poverty', *International Affairs* **81** (3), 525–540.

Karl, T.L. (1997), *The Paradox of Plenty*, Berkeley: University of California Press.

Keblusek, M.E. (2010), 'Is EITI Really Helping Improve Global Good Governance? Examining the Resource Curse, Corruption, and Nigeria's EITI Implementation Experience', Niger Delta Professionals for Development, available at http://nidprodev.org/EITI%20-%20Nigeria%20Analysis.pdf (accessed 13 November 2017).

Kolstad, I. and T. Soreide (2009), 'Corruption in Natural Resource Management: Implications for Policy Makers', *Resources Policy* **34** (4), 214–226.

Mehlum, H., K. Moene and R. Torvik (2006), 'Institutions and the Resource Curse', *Economic Journal* **116** (508), 1–20.

MMSD (2002), *Breaking New Ground: The Report of the Mining, Minerals and Sustainable Development Project*, Earthscan, available at https://www.iied.org/mmsd-final-report (accessed 10 November 2017).

NRGI (Natural Resource Governance Institute) (2015), *From Reporting to Reform: Eleven Opportunities for Increasing EITI Impacts*, available at https://resourcegovernance.org/analysis-tools/publications/reporting-reform-eleven-opportunities-increasing-eiti-impacts (accessed 26 June 2018).

O'Sullivan, D. (2013), *What's the Point of Transparency?*, London: Open Society.

Oranje, M. van and H. Parham (2009), *Publishing What We Learned: An Assessment of the Publish What You Pay Coalition*, EITI, available at https://eiti.org/sites/

default/files/documents/Publishing%20What%20We%20Learned.pdf (accessed 8 November 2017).
Otusanya, O.J. (2011), 'The Role of Multinational Companies in Tax Evasion and Tax Avoidance: The Case of Nigeria', *Critical Perspectives on Accounting* **22** (3), 316–332.
Pegg, S. (2006), 'Mining and Poverty Reduction: Transforming Rhetoric into Reality', *Journal of Cleaner Production* **14** (3), 376–387.
PWYP Zambia (Publish What You Pay Zambia) (2017), 'Publish What You Pay Zambia 2015–2017 Narrative Report – June 2015 to June 2017', available at http://www.publishwhatyoupay.org/pwyp-resources/publish-what-you-pay-zambia-2015-2017-narrative-report/ (accessed 12 November 2017).
Ravat, A. and A. Ufer (2010), *Toward Strengthened EITI Reporting: Summary Report and Recommendations*, Extractive Industries for Development Series, World Bank Oil, Gas, and Mining Policy Division, available at https://openknowledge.worldbank.org/handle/10986/18281 (accessed 10 November 2017).
Rich, E. (2013), 'The Relationship between EITI and Tax Justice', EITI, available at http://eiti.org/blog/relationship-between-eiti-and-tax-justice# (accessed 11 November 2017).
Rich, E. and J. Moberg (2015), *Beyond Governments: Making Collective Governance Work*, Sheffield: Greenleaf Publishing.
Ross, M. (1999), 'The Political Economy of the Resource Curse', *World Politics* **51** (2), 297–322.
Ross, M. (2012), *The Oil Curse*, Princeton, NJ: Princeton University Press.
Sachs, J.D. and A.D. Warner (2001), 'Natural Resources and Economic Development: The Curse of Natural Resources', *European Economic Review* **45** (4), 827–838.
UNCTAD (United Nations Conference on Trade and Development) (2014), *Trade and Development Report, 2014: Global Governance and Policy Space for Development*, available at http://unctad.org/en/PublicationsLibrary/tdr2014_en.pdf (accessed 12 November 2017).
UNCTAD (United Nations Conference on Trade and Development) (2015), *World Investment Report 2015: Reforming International Investment Governance*, Geneva: United Nations.
UNECA (United Nations Economic Commission for Africa) (2015), *Illicit Financial Flows: Report of the High Level Panel on Illicit Financial Flows from Africa*, available at http://hdl.handle.net/10855/22695 (accessed 9 November 2017).
US SEC (US Securities and Exchange Commission) (2016), 'SEC Adopts Rules for Resource Extraction Issuers under Dodd–Frank Act', available at https://www.sec.gov/news/pressrelease/2016-132.html (accessed 12 November 2017).
Van Alstine, J. (2014), 'Transparency in Resource Governance: The Pitfalls and Potential of "New Oil" in Sub-Saharan Africa', *Global Environmental Politics* **14** (1), 20–39.
Van Alstine, J. (2017), 'Critical Reflections on 15 Years of the Extractive Industries Transparency Initiative (EITI)', *Extractive Industries and Society* **4**, 766–770.
Wilson, E. and J. Van Alstine (2014), *Localizing Transparency: Exploring EITI's Contribution to Sustainable Development*, International Institute for Environment and Development, available at http://pubs.iied.org/16555IIED.html (accessed 11 November 2017).
World Bank (2003), *Striking a Better Balance: The Extractive Industries Review*,

Washington, DC: World Bank Group, available at http://documents.worldbank.org/curated/en/961241468781797388/Striking-a-better-balance-the-World-Bank-Group-and-extractive-industries-the-final-report-of-the-extractive-industries-review (accessed 12 November 2017).
World Bank (2004), *Striking a Better Balance – The World Bank Group and Extractive Industries: The Final Report of the Extractive Industries Review*. The World Bank, Washington DC.
Zorrilla, R. (2016), 'After Panama Papers, a Focus on Tax Loopholes and Ownership Transparency', *Business News Americas*, available at http://www.bnamericas.com/en/news/insurance/after-panama-papers-a-focus-on-tax-loopholes-and-ownership-transparency/loopholes-and-ownership-transparency/ (accessed 9 November 2017).

10. Tax justice as social licence: the Fair Tax Mark

Allison Christians

10.1 INTRODUCTION

Tax justice advocates have spent the past decade building public consciousness about the tax planning practices of financial elites and large MNCs. They have approached this advocacy from a series of angles, from grassroots name-and-shame campaigns to documentary film making and political lobbying. Early successes focused on transparency in the resources sector, which led to broader efforts across industries and across countries, with multiple platforms around transparency and accountability (Christians 2013a; EITI 2017; this volume, Chapter 9). Inspired by the growing consumer response to tax justice campaigns (Christians 2013a), a group of tax justice advocates created a 'fair trade'-style branding and marketing strategy, called the Fair Tax Mark.

The goals of the Fair Tax Mark, like the wider ethical consumption movement, are multi-faceted. Their primary objective is to directly influence firm and consumer behaviours in the UK. By developing and promoting new standards of corporate tax reporting and transparency, the standard has the potential to influence tax policy and business practice both within and beyond the UK (Fair Tax Mark 2017a). This makes the Fair Tax Mark an emergent quasi-legal regime, which, if it replicates the success of fair trade, will reach well beyond the UK, with repercussions for consumers, firms and governments around the world (Klein 1997). Thus it is important to understand not only what the Fair Tax Mark is in terms of the 'rules' that make it a quasi-legal regime, but also how it might function as both a quasi-legal tax regime and a strategy for influencing consumer and corporate behaviour (Halliday and Carruthers 2007).

As has been noted earlier in this volume, perceived failures of the international tax regime gave rise to the civil society campaign for tax justice, including the creation of the Fair Tax Mark. That regime has undergone significant changes over the past several years, to some degree influenced by the efforts of those behind the Fair Tax Mark. The Mark is thus a new and discrete campaign in the wider tax justice movement that interacts with, influences and is in turn impacted by the ongoing evolution of policy in the international tax order. Understanding the Fair Tax Mark – its origins, its development, its impact and its prospects moving forward – may help explain some of the ways in which change in the international tax order comes about, and predict what might come next in the evolution of global tax policy. That is the purpose of this chapter.

Section 10.2 outlines the background conditions from which the Fair Tax Mark has emerged as a quasi-legal regime. Section 10.3 describes the Fair Tax Mark from the perspective of its law-like form and substance and examines it in the context of existing international tax standards. Section 10.4 analyses the proponents of the Fair Tax Mark and their foundational tenets in the context of the other actors, processes, norms and doctrines that constitute the contemporary international tax law order, and examines how the Fair Tax Mark interacts with rival standard setters, especially the Organisation for Economic Co-operation and Development (OECD) and the European Union (EU). The chapter concludes with a call for further study of the processes and mechanisms that drive evolution of the international tax law order.

10.2 (WHY) DOES THE WORLD NEED A FAIR TAX MARK?

The Fair Tax Mark was established in 2014 as the world was engaging in a deep discussion about the future of corporate income taxation, hosted by the ever-influential OECD. The OECD had in 2012 initiated a project seeking to address what it terms base erosion and profit shifting (BEPS), a moniker intended to convey a general sense of the relationship between multinational corporations and the states that seek to tax them (this volume, Chapter 2). The OECD was spurred to movement on this topic by political events taking place in several of its key member states (Christians 2013a; Homeland Security and Governmental Affairs 2013; Kaye 2014), as well as by a series of investigations into the tax strategies of member states by the European Commission. Understanding the Fair Tax Mark as a phenomenon requires situating it, as a form of private governance or a non-legal form of guidance or control, within the OECD's established role of developing and promoting policy on behalf of its member states, especially the EU and the United States.

Traditionally, civil society organizations, such as those described in Chapter 4, have sought to influence global tax by lobbying the OECD and its member states. This is because the OECD has successfully engaged a set of soft law methods to build an effective monopoly over global tax policy for the entirety of its existence. Its influence is partly explained by its institutional strength, featuring a permanent secretariat, consistent funding from the world's richest countries, and the ability, in effect, to mandate itself to formulate global policy, by leveraging its members' positions as key members of other intergovernmental networks (namely the G5, G7, G20, World Bank and IMF). Potential rival institutions, such as the United Nations, have lacked similar institutional support and professional network infrastructure for tax policy development.

Juxtaposed against the OECD, the Fair Tax Mark is an effort by a non-governmental organization (NGO) to directly influence tax policy by developing and promoting tax reporting standards using similar processes and mechanisms (TJN 2013). Tax justice advocates began by building their own epistemic community via transnational networks that involve a mix of tax and accounting professionals as well as others with skills and experience in consumer-oriented social justice movements (Seabrooke and Wigan 2013; this volume, Chapter 4). Just as the OECD develops policy by convening experts to undertake research and write reports, tax justice advocates spend time and effort developing unique research and publishing reports chronicling their analyses. Just as the OECD uses networks to develop common ground amongst stakeholders and articulate unified norms, tax justice advocates use networks to compare and disseminate their research and campaign goals, expand their membership and generate support for their norms. And, just as the OECD is influenced by the concerns and interests of its most powerful members, the world of tax justice advocacy is focused on addressing the issues and concerns raised by the individuals and organizations with the most power and visibility to direct attention to their efforts. Finally, just as the OECD uses peer review and monitoring to induce states to voluntarily comply with articulated goals and norms, tax justice advocates use social pressure to induce consumers and firms to act according to a different set of goals and norms (as well as, in the longer run, to induce lawmakers to accept policy changes by demonstrating that these goals and norms can be implemented).

In studying how individuals and groups influence the direction and shape of global tax policy, each of these parallels is worthy of attention. Yet, as events of the last several years have demonstrated, the last is of special interest. In a complex technical field defined by intergovernmental negotiations and dominated by the institutional juggernaut of the OECD and its member states, civil society's smaller, socially oriented and less doctrinally focused members might be expected to generate relatively little momentum. Instead, as earlier chapters have demonstrated, civil society groups have managed to generate a surprising amount of social pressure in the international tax sphere. Their success has simultaneously generated increasing power for this relatively small group of individuals (Schmitter 1985; Page 1986; Dezalay and Garth 1996). Accordingly, we can expect future attempts to replicate and expand these efforts.

A large part of these efforts involves convincing firms and consumers that paying a 'fair share' of taxation, as defined by the tax justice advocates, is a prerequisite for consumers and investors to accept the presence of firms in their communities. This makes the Fair Tax Mark part of a larger corporate social responsibility (CSR) movement (Freedman 2004, 2006). Indeed, many of the individuals who developed the Fair Tax Mark have a long history of campaigning to promote ethical business practices and consumer rights (Conley and Williams 2005; Beloe and Lye 2006). Some proponents of CSR hold that corporations operate in society not only owing to legal structures that make possible their existence as holders of property and rights, but also owing to social structures that accept them as valid actors entitled to conduct their business free from interference (Ostas 2001; Thomson and Boutilier 2011). This freedom is sometimes referred to as the company's 'social licence to operate' (Nelsen 2006; Cabezas 2014; Cullen-Knox et al. 2017).

Observers of the social licence to operate have noted that advocacy groups can impose real costs on businesses, holding their freedom to operate in abeyance until group standards are met (Gunningham et al. 2004; Ruggie 2013). An illustration of the intersecting efforts of tax justice advocates and national lawmakers can be found in the case of Starbucks, which was called 'the poster child for tax avoidance' when the details of its tax results spurred widespread calls for reform of the international tax system in 2012 (Davies 2015). Starbucks may be observed to have lost its social licence to operate in the UK after the public became aware that the company had failed to pay taxes in that country over the entire period of its existence (Christians 2013b; Cabezas 2014). The company's public commitment in 2013 to pay a set amount of tax to the UK – whether owed or not – appears to have been an attempt to regain its social licence.

Starbucks has avoided further social protest campaigns in respect of its tax situation since, but these events aligned with, and appear to have contributed to, further scrutiny by OECD member states. The European Commission (EC) investigated tax rulings granted to the company, and ultimately determined that the Netherlands had, through its tax ruling system, granted Starbucks impermissible subsidies in contravention of European anti-competition law (EC 2015). The EC called for a recovery of €20 million to €30 million, to be determined by the Dutch tax authorities as prescribed in the Commission decisions. At the same time, Starbucks, together with Google, Amazon and other companies whose tax planning had drawn similar attention, became the organizing factor driving the OECD's work on BEPS (*Economist* 2015). Finally, Starbucks seems to have contributed to a resurgence of interest in a previously abandoned plan for consolidating corporate tax systems across the EU (Garside 2016). The events of 2013 and the scrutiny that followed appear to have impacted Starbucks' overall approach to tax planning in part because civil society campaigns had a material impact on the company's UK operations in particular: subsequent restructuring decisions resulted in the company paying more tax in 2015 than in the previous 14 years combined (Davies 2015).

The events surrounding Starbucks' tax situation illustrate the complex interaction among tax justice advocates, national lawmakers, the EU and the OECD as each vies for control over tax policy design and outcomes. Even though taxation is fundamentally a creature of policy making, tax policy decisions both by firms (in terms of planning and compliance) and by governments (in terms of designing regulatory systems) are clearly influenced by effective campaigning and peer pressure. The success of the tax justice advocacy movement may be surprising, but it fundamentally mirrors the processes and mechanisms that have characterized the evolving international tax regime as developed by the OECD and its member states. The combination of these processes and mechanisms constitutes a pluralistic legal order, which actively facilitates the entry of a policy rival like the Fair Tax Mark. Thus, before examining the mechanisms of the Mark itself, it is useful to understand this legal order.

Transnational Tax Law Order

What we colloquially refer to as 'international tax law' is really more accurately described as a transnational legal order rather than an international legal regime (Halliday and Shaffer 2015). As autonomous entities, states generally behave with mutual respect for one another's sovereignty as the means of negotiating jurisdictional conflicts in the case of tax, as they do for other areas of law. Yet these borders are porous: money, goods, ideas, politics and social norms move around the globe with little restriction.

Tax jurisdictions therefore overlap in practice – that is, several countries may, according to generally accepted principles, claim the same taxpayer, the same transaction or the same activity. Outside of regional agreements like those of the European Union, states have not created a binding multilateral regime (such as a world tax organization) to resolve these overlaps. Instead, they have come to rely both on 'soft' methods for coordinating income taxation as a general policy matter and on negotiated agreements (treaties) with strategic partners as a means of sharing the tax jurisdiction on a case-by-case basis (Christians 2012a, 2012b). This regime derives from network-based collaboration, modelling, peer pressure, and emulation based on political, social and economic relationships among states (Braithwaite and Drahos 2000; Pagani 2002; OECD 2010).

Because of the importance of sovereign relationships and networking to work out tax conflicts, power struggles within existing relationships and pressure from without are both constants in international tax policy making (Biswas 2002; James 2002; Christians 2009). International tax law and policy act as a series of less and more powerful constraints on unilateral state behaviour, but there is no supranational authority to police the shared terrain of the global economy (Christians 2010a). The world's wealthiest countries have instead internationalized tax policy through their ongoing relationships. They have done so largely by creating an international architecture of transnational public and private sector institutions, first centred in the League of Nations and later in the OECD (this volume, Chapter 1). Through this 'soft law' system, a series of interrelated global tax trends have emerged and taken root.

Understanding the Fair Tax Mark as a phenomenon requires situating it, as a non-legal form of governance, against the OECD's more prevalent historical role as a non-legal form of guidance or control. The OECD is not in a general sense a tax lawmaking body. Instead, it uses 'dialogue, consensus, peer review and pressure' to develop international tax norms defining appropriate international tax practices (OECD 2017). OECD tax norms, presented as recommendations and guidelines, quickly disseminate within but also far beyond the member states of the OECD. The OECD method includes developing mandates for debate by selected members, gathering expert committees to debate the mandates and develop consensus positions, and then organizing monitoring and peer review mechanisms to review country practices. The OECD's recent project, addressing what it calls base erosion and profit shifting, provides a case study of this method (see this volume, Chapter 2).

Some international tax scholars have argued that the OECD is so important as a standard setter that certain forms of its guidance might constitute customary law (Christians 2010b). The emergence of rival policy frameworks like the Fair Tax Mark make clear why caution is necessary in assessing the weight to be accorded a self-appointed standard-setting body. Countries often do go along with OECD proclamations, but the OECD is careful to describe its own work product as non-legal in nature, thus denying the general legal obligation (*opinio juris*) associated with customary law (OECD 2013). It seems more likely that countries go along with OECD proclamations to gain benefits from coordination around an agreed standard or because cooperation has become a de facto prerequisite to full inclusion in the global economy (Christians and Shay 2017).

Accordingly, the degree to which a given state might cooperate with a particular OECD initiative likely depends on, among other factors, intuition about how much deviation might harm the country in the global economic order. For example, in recent discussions about the acquiescence or resistance of key states to the OECD's ongoing project on BEPS, various observers have suggested that the United States cannot ignore the OECD or go its own way, but also that the OECD needs US support for its own success in articulating international consensus (Brauner 2014; United States Senate Finance Committee 2015). There is probably no good way to measure whether and to what extent either of these statements is empirically true, though many observers suggest that the United States was responsible for effectively terminating the OECD's previous effort to curb BEPS (namely, the Harmful Tax Practices initiative) (Avi-Yonah 2009; Eccleston 2012).

The longstanding grip of OECD countries on international tax policy has inspired its members to make credible commitments to each other on key consensus points involving overlapping tax jurisdiction claims (Cockfield 2012). This consensus backed by power has inspired non-OECD members to acquiesce to the OECD for lack of any plausible alternative, even if such acquiescence might not be preferred as a domestic policy matter. Lack of plausible alternatives does not, however, eliminate the desire for plausible alternatives. Instead, it creates intense pressure for systemic or structural change.

Plausible Alternatives

Perhaps inevitably, the OECD's ability and propensity to lock out non-members from its policy-making infrastructure of working parties became the impetus for an alternative network to arise in the NGO community. This alternative network is most popularly associated with the Tax Justice Network (TJN), though other institutions have also been integral to building strength in policy consensus building beyond the OECD. Together, these justice-focused groups developed a loose consensus that tax policy ought not to be the prerogative solely of government and business representatives from rich countries, nor ought it to be based primarily on 'scientific', technical and economic rationalizing within epistemic communities that are closed to outside observation and participation.

The network of tax justice advocacy groups therefore seeks to alter the discourse around tax policy so as to focus on one central, driving theme: that of fairness. From the theme of fairness, the NGO community has articulated both institutional/process-based and substantive rule reforms.

With regard to the former, tax justice advocates have expressed the need for greater participation in decision making within the OECD and beyond it, for greater accountability of OECD decision-making processes, and for greater responsiveness by the OECD to the tax-related concerns faced by non-OECD members (TJN 2013; United Nations Department of Economic and Social Affairs 2013; Oxfam 2014; ADB 2015; GATJ 2017). With regard to the latter, tax justice advocates have focused on transparency as a key theme for realizing tax fairness (Kumar 2014; ActionAid UK 2017; Oxfam 2017).

The Fair Tax Mark emerges as one plank in the overall strategy of tax fairness being promoted as an alternative to the OECD's traditional tax policy rhetoric of high-level scientific inquiry. The Mark is most accurately described as a label or certification standard for firms to adopt in order to indicate their tax planning practices are 'fair' by the standards of the tax justice community (Fair Tax Mark 2017a). This label, like many private certification standards which have come before it such as a fair trade coffee label, denotes that a company has met a set of criteria indicating that it is not avoiding taxes in a manner that the designers of the Fair Tax Mark perceive to be unjust (Scott 2014; Fair Tax Mark 2017b).

Tax justice-focused NGOs seek both to establish themselves as independent sources of tax policy ideas and to influence the OECD's tax policy making. By developing and promoting a standard, the Tax Justice Network demonstrated the viability of concepts that could be adopted into public law and policy. For example, the OECD's adoption of the language of country-by-country reporting (CbCR) as a major plank in the BEPS initiative is directly traceable to the Tax Justice Network's efforts, even if the OECD's transparency regime differs in material respects, such as public disclosure, to the Tax Justice Network's version. One view is that the OECD's decision to adopt the moniker of country-by-country reporting signals its acquiescence to the policy goals of the Tax Justice Network, while another view is that the OECD has simply co-opted the language in order to foster consensus around the OECD's own distinct policy goals. Perhaps the reality lies somewhere in between, but it is incontrovertible that transference of language and ideas occurred between the Tax Justice Network and the OECD.

Indeed, the BEPS project as a whole was in fundamental ways prompted by the rise of the tax justice community (van Herksen 2013). In turn, the efforts of the tax justice movement seem to have contributed to the renewed interest in the taxation of multinationals at the level of the European Union, with efforts by the European Commission both to investigate ongoing state practices and to renew reform efforts. These developments provide evidence that tax justice advocacy cannot be ignored as a fringe social movement but rather expresses viable claims on the designers of tax policy consensus.

Accordingly, the emergence of the Fair Tax Mark as a new strategy by tax justice advocates should be taken seriously even if it is currently nascent and its impact is difficult to measure. This attention will be especially important if the Fair Tax Mark makes the transition from being a private standard to providing a viable framework for monitoring and peer review of national tax policies and, over time, providing a focal point for a new global tax policy consensus. Social movements may have been responsible for many national tax policy reforms in the past, but, as argued in recent chapters, they have not been active on the international stage until recently. Similarly, responsive regulation, in which industries engage in various forms of self-regulation beyond the obligations of formal law, may be familiar in other areas of law (Braithwaite and Drahos 2000) but is practically unheard of in international taxation (this volume, Chapter 8). The Fair Tax Mark arguably brings both of these phenomena to bear. Thus both the content and the procedures surrounding the Fair Tax Mark are worthy of closer attention.

10.3 FORM AND SUBSTANCE OF THE FAIR TAX MARK

Richard Murphy, an activist chartered accountant who co-founded the Tax Justice Network, is also the co-founder of the Fair Tax Mark and takes credit for its creation as a policy idea (Murphy 2014). His co-founder, Paul Monaghan, is a self-proclaimed consumer rights and corporate ethics activist and academic (Monaghan 2015). Together, Murphy and Monaghan, with support from *Ethical Consumer* magazine, created the Fair Tax Mark, establishing a small team to develop a new certification scheme whereby companies could be certified as paying their fair share of corporate taxes (Fair Tax Mark 2017a). This section examines the various components of the Fair Tax Mark system and assesses the extent to which it constitutes a quasi-legal order.

Code of Tax Ethics

The Fair Tax Mark team states that its mission is twofold: to 'outline a code of corporate ethics when it comes to tax' and to 'encourage and reward . . . the use of these principles when they are put into practice' (Fair Tax Mark 2014b). The reward and encouragement are reputational in nature: the organization asserts that its accreditation 'protects the company from both reputational and financial risk [by] projecting an image of openness, honesty and trustworthiness to consumers and investors' (Fair

Tax Mark 2017b). This social signalling is an important aspect of the Fair Tax Mark, and ties into its social licence roots. But it is the code that is of primary interest in understanding the Mark as an aspiring feature of the transnational tax law order. The Fair Tax Mark website explains the core guiding principles for this code:

> The basic premise of the Fair Tax Mark is that a Fair Tax Business: Has adopted a fair tax policy that suggests it is seeking to pay the right amount of tax (but no more) in the right place at the right time, where right means that the economic substance of the transactions undertaken coincides with the place and form in which they are reported for taxation purposes; Is transparent about who owns it, what it does and where it is; Provides sufficient accounting data to suggest that its fair tax policy has been put into practice. (Fair Tax Mark 2017b)

With this broad set of principles, the Fair Tax Mark seeks to articulate three ground rules for fairness in taxation which broadly align with the features of a 'fair' corporate tax system outlined in Chapter 2: (1) the word 'right' means 'corresponding to economic substance'; (2) fairness requires ownership transparency; and (3) fairness requires comprehensively descriptive accounting disclosure (Fair Tax Mark 2014a). Each of these is a claim about fairness that must be fleshed out in the details of the procedures by which a corporation can claim the title of a 'Fair Tax Business' and incorporate the logo into its branding and marketing (Fair Tax Mark 2017b).

The Fair Tax Mark therefore has more detailed documentation for companies. The first set applies to 'businesses that solely trade in the UK' and the second to 'UK-owned multinational businesses' (Fair Tax Mark 2017c, 2017d). In the documentation for each, the Fair Tax Mark lays out a set of four issue areas, together with recommended actions for Mark-adopting companies. For UK-headquartered companies, these categories are 'Transparency' (covering asset and entity ownership disclosure), 'Country-by-Country [CbC] Reporting' (covering global operations of these companies), 'Tax Policy, Implementation and Compliance' (covering mechanisms for documenting tax planning by the company, with a special focus on the use of 'tax havens'), and 'Tax Rate and Disclosure' (covering measuring issues relevant owing to book–tax accounting differences) (Fair Tax Mark 2017c, 2017d).

Scoring Compliance

The Fair Tax Mark's 'Fair Tax Scorecard' is instructive, as it provides a plain-language overview of the goals the Fair Tax Mark seeks to foster with the Fair Tax Mark brand, and purports to quantify what is in effect a qualitative analysis of a company's overall adherence to the Fair Tax Mark's articulated tax policy preferences (Fair Tax Mark 2013, 2014a, 2014b, 2014c). The Fair Tax Mark requires its applicants to achieve a minimum score of 29 points out of a possible 45 in order to receive Fair Tax Mark accreditation (Fair Tax Mark 2013, 2014a). Presumably, a company would review the point system and assess its chance for accreditation before seeking Fair Tax Mark approval. The procedure for discussing possible accreditation is not clear from the available materials, and suggests that self-selection is a feature of the system. However, Richard Murphy has stated that not all companies that have sought the Mark have received it, and that initial assessments have involved disagreements that were resolved through discussion among company representatives and the Fair Tax Mark assessors (Murphy 2015).

It is not clear what would happen if a company achieved the score one year, but later lost points sufficient to drop below the requisite 29. Richard Murphy has stated that the Fair Tax Mark is 'quite clear that we expect improvement not regression' and that the team has 'on occasion made our concern about limited progression clear to clients' (author's correspondence with Richard Murphy). This suggests that there is some internal, perhaps informal, discussion among the Fair Tax Mark team and its clients, and perhaps there is an ad hoc procedure under which a client could seek a second review of its progress after such an assessment. It appears to be the case that certification could be revoked, but it is not clear how revocation would be manifested or enforced – for example, whether clients would be given a grace period in which to cure defaults or remove Fair Tax Mark branding.

The Scorecard lays out each of the four categories discussed above and assigns points in each category. The 'Transparency' category assigns points for five types of financial account and shareholder ownership disclosures. These include publication of a 'full set of accounts', provision of clear evidence of 'what the company does either within its accounts or on an easily identifiable website', of 'a trading address (as opposed to a registered office address)' and of all 10 per cent or more 'ultimate beneficial owners', and a statement of the names and addresses of all company directors (Fair Tax Mark 2017a).

The 'Country-by-Country Reporting' category awards points for disclosures involving the structure and residence of corporate entities, the location and value of asset holdings, the nature of the trade of each company, consolidated income and loss statements, tax charges in each country for each entity, location and remuneration of employees, and company-wide business and trading data (Fair Tax Mark 2014d, 2017b). This category corresponds to the CbC reporting initiative promoted by Richard Murphy, who contributed to the development of the CbC reporting framework as an international accounting standard and further promoted it in the context of the Extractive Industries Transparency Initiative (this volume, Chapter 9).

The OECD has adopted the CbC terminology in BEPS but has altered its scope to mean government-to-government sharing of certain tax information without public disclosure (OECD 2014b). As a key mechanism to promote corporate accountability, public disclosure is central to Murphy's original vision of CbC reporting as an accounting standard and is an important feature of the EITI, and this is central to the Fair Tax Mark criteria. Accordingly, the OECD and the Fair Tax Mark are each currently promoting a regime they call 'CbC reporting', but each has distinct goals and parameters. Calls for public CbC reporting in Europe led the European Commission to adopt a proposal of a Directive requiring publication of CbC reports by specified entities (EC 2017). That Directive has now been passed in the European Parliament; if successfully implemented and enforced, it has the potential to shift the terrain for CbC reporting across the OECD and beyond.

The current debate about CbC standards parallels the debate about tax information exchange agreements (TIEAs) a decade earlier. Whereas the OECD, trying to maintain a consensus for reform, proposed a limited regime of information exchange on request, the tax justice movement argued that this was a weak standard. They therefore insisted that, in order to be effective, information exchange had to be comprehensive and automatic (Eccleston 2012). By 2014, and reflecting growing political concerns about offshore tax evasion facilitated by bank secrecy, the OECD had adopted the more ambitious standard of automatic information exchange as the global standard (OECD 2014a).

The Fair Tax Mark's 'Tax Policy, Implementation and Compliance' category takes a step further, attempting to glean a company's official policy toward tax planning (Fair Tax Mark 2017d, pp. 15–18). Points correspond to a company's issuance of public statements about its official policy toward taxation and the use of tax havens (as defined), as well as its identification of a specific individual responsible for the company's policies. This category reflects so-called self-regulation, by in effect allowing companies to self-assess and self-certify their eligibility for recognition as compliant with a given private legal order (Braithwaite 1982).

Apple Inc's appearance at a hearing convened by the US Senate Permanent Subcommittee on Investigations in 2013 serves as a useful example of some of the reasons that the Fair Tax Mark might have devised this self-regulation category within its code. At that hearing, Apple was asked to testify regarding its position on its own tax planning and on US corporate tax policy in general. CEO Tim Cook stated unequivocally that Apple does not 'move its intellectual property into offshore tax havens . . . to avoid US tax', 'hold money in a Caribbean island' or use 'tax gimmicks' (Cook 2013). Yet Apple has been at the centre of a major controversy involving Ireland, whose relationship with the company was subsequently investigated by the European Commission for possible violation of the EU treaty's anti-competition provisions respecting trade practices within the internal market (EC 2014; Christians 2015). The *Financial Times* reported in January 2016 that Apple CEO Tim Cook took it upon himself to personally visit the European commissioner Margrethe Vestager 'to lobby the EU's antitrust chief weeks before she [was] set to rule on a landmark case that could force the California-based technology company to pay billions in underpaid taxes to Ireland' (Oliver 2016). Despite receiving the public support of the United States Treasury in challenging the European Commission's intervention (Lew 2016; United States Treasury 2016), Cook's efforts, as outlined in Chapters 2 and 7, were unsuccessful, as the Commission issued a decision in 2016 finding that Ireland had improperly engaged in fiscal state aid in its dealings with Apple (EC 2016). Nevertheless, Cook continues to advocate reducing tax on US companies, including retroactively.

The mutually exclusive nature of Cook's positions seems to reflect the Fair Tax Mark's concerns that '[e]very company has a tax policy, even if it has never explicitly recorded it' (Fair Tax Mark 2014a). The issue to be resolved is that the absence of official articulations of policy allows too much latitude for inconsistent behaviour. The Fair Tax Mark notes that companies rarely state their policy toward tax explicitly and, as a result, 'few companies can explain fully their motivations for certain decisions nor can they be held to account' (Fair Tax Mark 2017d, p. 15). Consistent with this concern, Cook has never publicly acknowledged that seeking low US corporate rates for repatriated cash is advantageous to Apple precisely because of how it has organized its global affairs since the 1980s, with the help of Ireland. Neither does Cook indicate the normative justifications for either his dismissal of tax gimmickry or his embrace of very low taxation of corporate profits. The Fair Tax Mark criteria are designed to prevent companies from taking empty or inconsistent rhetorical positions.

Presumably, no Fair Tax Mark points ought to be awarded for simply stating that a company uses no tax gimmicks. In a legal regime, we would expect some evidence of coherence in the defined meanings of relevant terms. But, in a quasi-legal regime, voluntary certification is often accepted as a useful tool because companies will not want to risk exposing themselves to criticism if past promises or pledges are broken or even cleverly circumvented. The Fair Tax Mark materials thus seem to flesh out the concept of fairness by seeking certain undertakings or pledges in the company's stated tax policy.

Primary among these is a pledge not to use tax havens. Perhaps unsurprisingly, the Fair Tax Mark defines the term 'tax haven' by reference to the Tax Justice Network's own definition of the concept, which itself is assessed on the basis of a point system, using 15 'secrecy indicators', developed by the Tax Justice Network (TJN 2013). The exercise of defining terms is a key feature of any regulatory regime, whether public or private. Here, the Fair Tax Mark usefully employs terminology and criteria previously adopted by the Tax Justice Network, thus building upon an institutional credibility that each institution seeks to advance.

Finally, the 'Tax Rate and Disclosure' category addresses the book–tax accounting gap. The gap is a feature of public company tax filings, and it is responsible for some incoherence in public discourse about corporate taxation (Luppino 2003). The operable mechanism in this category is reconciliation between book and tax accounting in which the company makes its methods and decisions clear with detailed explanations. Again, the focus in this category appears to be clear: transparency of key financial information. With book–tax reconciliation, outside observers can (in theory) reconstruct the company's actual tax liability patterns and use cross-company comparisons to develop a picture of how the corporate income tax system actually works out for firms in the implementation of the law.

Its criteria thus laid out in a point system, it is evident that the Fair Tax Mark has a concrete vision of what fairness requires. Its code has been developed to articulate that vision. However, as is the case for any legal regime, the articulation of principles, standards and rules is only one node in the regulation of behaviour. Having articulated a code, the implementation and interpretation phase begins. In this phase, the defining role played by processes and procedures becomes clear.

In keeping with its theme that tax fairness requires transparency, the Fair Tax Mark has opted to be somewhat transparent about its own processes of making decisions and developing norms, though, as will be argued in more detail in Chapter 11, more clarity and third-party oversight would be advantageous. The Fair Tax Mark explains that its criteria were 'developed after more than a year of research and consultation', including a pilot study in 2013. The Fair Tax Mark website says that the research, consultation and study 'involved a broad range of stakeholders including civil society NGOs, business representatives and industry practitioners', as well as 'our group of independent technical advisers drawn from academia and the professions'. The Fair Tax Mark explains that '[d]eveloping the criteria is an evolving process of negotiation that responds to changes in the regulatory environment and is open to as many voices as possible' (Fair Tax Mark 2017b). These processes will be key to observing the interaction of the Fair Tax Mark with global tax policy standards, especially as they are quickly evolving as a result of the BEPS initiative.

Coordination with International Standards

As discussed above, the Fair Tax Mark regime is designed to impose standards that are not necessarily required in domestic law. However, these standards may also be inconsistent with standards currently being developed by the OECD in the context of the BEPS project, as well as by the EU as it develops and implements a series of new Directives. It is worth considering, for example, how the Fair Tax Mark's disclosure standards interact with those being discussed at the OECD and in the EU with respect to CbC reporting.

The OECD lays out its standard in *Action 13: Guidance on the Implementation of Transfer Pricing Documentation and Country-by-Country Reporting*, which provides for a three-part documentation regime for multinationals (OECD 2015). The first part is a 'master file', in which multinational enterprises are to provide tax administrations with information regarding their global business operations and transfer pricing policies. The master file is to be made available upon request to all relevant tax administrations in countries where the multinational does business, subject to certain conditions. Second, multinationals are to provide a 'local file' containing detailed transfer pricing documentation specific to each country. The local file will identify material related to party transactions, amounts involved in those transactions, and the company's analysis of the transfer pricing determinations they have made with regard to those transactions. Finally, large multinationals are required to file a country-by-country report that will provide annually and for each tax jurisdiction in which they do business the amount of revenue, profit before income tax, and income tax paid and accrued. It also requires multinationals to report their number of full-time-equivalent employees, stated capital, retained earnings and tangible assets in each tax jurisdiction, as well as to identify each entity within the group doing business in a particular tax jurisdiction and to provide an indication of the business activities in which each entity engages.

Countries participating in the OECD/G20 BEPS project agreed on the core elements of the implementation of transfer pricing documentation and country-by-country reporting. Peer review was set to be implemented for fiscal years beginning in 2016 and apply, subject to the 2020 review, to multinationals with annual consolidated group revenue equal to or exceeding €750 million. The OECD acknowledges that some jurisdictions will need more time to navigate the domestic legislative process in order to make necessary adjustments to the law.

This CbC reporting regime departs from the vision of tax justice advocates, including the Tax Justice Network and other civil society groups dedicated to transparency. The Financial Transparency Coalition, for example, noted with disappointment three areas of divergence in the OECD's CbC regime from the model put forth by the Tax Justice Network:

> First . . . there's no commitment to allow investors, analysts, journalists or activists the opportunity to hold multinationals accountable.
>
> Second . . . the OECD agreed . . . not to support individual tax authorities asking for CBCR from multinationals operating in their jurisdiction. [This means] that something tax authorities could have done unilaterally before the OECD got the CBCR mandate, would now be seen as counter to the international standards.
>
> Instead, tax authorities of host countries are expected to apply for the information to be provided by the tax authority of the home country – if the latter has it, if there is an information exchange protocol in place, if the host country has committed to confidentiality (no way back into public openness here). (Cobham 2015)

This critique suggests that companies seeking Fair Tax Mark accreditation are undertaking disclosure standards that run counter to, but are arguably more rigorous than, the internationally accepted standard articulated by the OECD. This is not fatal to the undertaking by a given company, since the Fair Tax Mark is a voluntary regime. Moreover, depending on how CbCR develops in Europe, the Fair Tax Mark may end up aligning with European law, forcing the OECD standard to yield. Even so, the current contrast between Fair Tax Mark ideals and the OECD standard puts the two regimes at odds in terms of defining a standard for acceptable tax management practices by firms. The Fair Tax Mark seeks public disclosure of items that are, for the moment, carefully protected by confidentiality in the OECD regime, even to the extent of denying countries access to information generated in CbC reporting.

A further question surrounds the use of information gleaned from CbC reporting under the two systems. Much of the data to be reported in each CbC regime would give countries the kind of information that would support using corporate tax accounting methods other than the arm's-length transfer pricing standard favoured by OECD countries. Specifically, CbC reporting would give countries data that might allow for 'combined reporting and formulary apportionment', that is, as described in Chapter 2, a method for allocating income across countries that involves aggregating income and expenses on a global basis and then dividing the profits according to a formulaic calculation. Formulary apportionment is favoured by some tax justice advocates, but is rejected as a policy choice by OECD countries. The OECD makes clear that information gleaned by CbC reporting is not to use formulary apportionment-type methods for allocating profits among countries (OECD 2015). This potentially creates an issue for a country that uses data gleaned from Fair Tax Mark-related disclosures for this purpose.

10.4 IMPACT OF THE FAIR TAX MARK ON THE EVOLUTION OF GLOBAL TAX LAW

In the course of introducing proposed legislation on a comprehensive general anti-avoidance regime in 2014, Danish lawmakers repeatedly referred to the Fair Tax Mark as an example of objective criteria that characterize the nature of a company's tax behaviour (Johansen 2014; Sorgenfri Kjær 2014). The proposed legislation, passed as Bill L167 on 21 April 2015 (Folketinget 2015; Rils and Hansen 2015a, 2015b), subjects all subsidiaries of Danish corporations within EU states to a test judging the 'genuine' nature of their measures that reduce tax (Folketinget 2015; Rils and Hansen 2015a, 2015b). Under this legislation, if the primary goal of a tax measure is the avoidance of taxes, the measure is considered abusive (*SKAT Online* 2014).

Does Denmark's acknowledgement of the Fair Tax Mark demonstrate the Mark's influence on political figures as lawmakers, seeking input on the appropriate design of tax policy instruments? Or does it demonstrate the Mark's influence on political figures as politicians, responding to social or cultural pressures with crowd-pleasing rhetoric? Perhaps the Fair Tax Mark has other functions, which may be less or more understood than other influences. Unpacking this question requires some attention to the evolving architecture of the international tax legal order, as nations begin to implement BEPS while, simultaneously, developments on corporate taxation in the European Union create additional and potentially inconsistent pressures on multinational firms.

That architecture is not a static form but can be aptly described as a constantly evolving regime in which governments continuously revisit their tax systems in response to economic, social and political forces from within and without their geographic territories. Domestic legislative processes involving national lawmakers may be the most obvious source of change in the tax system in any independent nation, but international events, institutions and individuals – while comparatively much less studied – are equally important contributors. Evolving political, social and economic relationships among states, institutions and individuals significantly impact the types of tax norms that arise internationally and take root nationally. These relationships involve intellectual, political and social ties among individuals and institutions that serve as vehicles for tax norm transmission (Halliday and Carruthers 2007).

In order to assess how the Fair Tax Mark might affect change in tax policy, we must revisit the idea that tax law is, like other forms of law, the product of politics, legislation, implementation and compliance. In a globalized world, it is also the case that tax law is regularly exposed to external pressure, which is economic, social, cultural and political in nature. Tax policy emerges through repeated interactions between lawmakers, tax experts, and affected parties in the public and private sector. These individuals are participants in the dynamic process of policy making and law enforcement that constitutes the tax 'rule of law'. As such, they are also agents of change, as they continually respond to each other.

National lawmakers and regulators may be ultimately responsible for recording tax law on the books – what scholars describe as 'formal law' (Halliday and Carruthers 2007) – in the form of statutes, regulations, treaties and interpretative guidance issued by government officials, through administrative and judicial interpretation. But they do not act in a vacuum: instead, they are shaped by contemporary events and the actions of individuals and institutions. In turn, their decisions induce response by a broad population of individuals, entities and groups. As those affected by the law react, they set in motion further policy development in the form of additional guidance, judicial decision making and legal reform. Figure 10.1 shows a contemporary sketch of the major players in the recursive cycle of international taxation as the BEPS project moves into implementation and the influence of the European Commission increases.

The relative import of each of the various actors and interactions depicted in Figure 10.1 will shift as the regime completes its current cycle. Depicted in the upper left quadrant are the initial designers of policy, which in tax are national legislators and regulatory authorities combined with the soft law institutions and processes they use to develop tax policy proposals. Currently, the OECD dominates this space, but the European Commission is increasing its role via fiscal state aid investigations under the EU treaty as well as via proposed EU Directives. With legal precepts in place, law's responders react: both by trying to influence a new cycle of policy making and by implementing the law on the books, as depicted on the right side of Figure 10.1. Those who implement the law by interpreting it, complying with it, planning around it and otherwise contending with it thereby inevitably expose weaknesses, inconsistencies and unresolved issues that in turn require further intervention by tax law authorities and

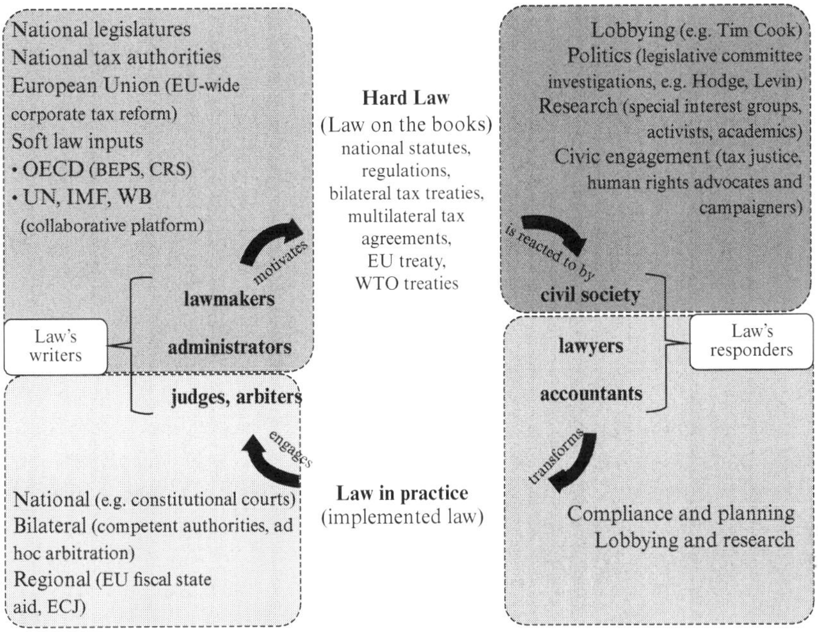

Figure 10.1 Evolution of tax law in the transnational legal order

judges. Thus a given cycle of tax law is completed and restarts with the engagement of judges and arbiters, who both clarify and add to the law on the books as well as induce lawmakers to respond further.

This sketch suggests that the Fair Tax Mark is but one idea or institution vying for policy space in a current iteration of an ongoing, recursive cycle of tax policy making. It seems possible to situate the Fair Tax Mark in a number of places along the path, but one likely entry point is an interjection at the legal interpretation stage. This stage involves the often strategic and future-oriented interpretation of tax law by tax compliance officers, in service to their clients. In other words, what tax professionals do is not simply review what clients are doing and guide them through applicable regulatory constraints (primarily an audit function), but also review the regulatory constraints for cost-saving opportunities, and present such opportunities to their clients under the mantle of tax planning.

Within this stage there exists a massive and sophisticated web of tax professionals and corporate clients (see this volume, Chapter 6), who both react to the law with strategic behavioural changes, and have professional reasons to collaboratively initiate and influence the next tax policy cycle by exercising political influence in various forms. As every tax practitioner and compliance officer is aware, some interpretation is in good faith and with legitimate motives, some is in bad faith and involves taking risks with respect to the expected level of legal enforcement, and much lies in a murky area between these poles. The calculations of obligation, ethics, risk and reward differ from nation to nation and within nations from practice to practice and from taxpayer to taxpayer. When the myriad decisions of hundreds, thousands or even millions of taxpayers are considered as a whole, those responsible for implementing the system, whether from the private sector, the academic community or the compliance and administrative sector, may observe that change is needed, and institute a new cycle of reform. Moreover, these individuals and actors often play dual roles by participating in international informal or soft law networks where they influence and are influenced by collaborations with their counterparts from other nations.

Those who create tax standards and rules and those who implement them thus may be conceptualized as nodes on the continuous cycle of tax reform, and the Fair Tax Mark is potentially relevant at more than one point within this cycle. Individual actors who play key roles typically operate within local, national and transnational professional settings, face multiple overlapping legal regimes, and have multi-faceted interests and agendas. Each individual works within various formal and informal networks, which overlap to various degrees in membership, goals and activities. Interests, activities, influence and alignments of institutions and networks change as individuals and issues respond to dynamic social, political and economic factors. These institutions and networks provide various forms of input and influence on the tax policy process and on the process of implementation in different contexts and over time.

The question yet to be answered is what role entrants like the Fair Tax Mark will play in changing the shape of tax policy moving forward, as the principal ideas are picked up, implemented, altered and adopted in other forms by other actors and institutions along the way. One possibility is that the Fair Tax Mark takes a place as another soft law contributor to the writing of law, in the upper left quadrant of Figure 10.1. In that position, tax justice advocates would negotiate directly with national and regional (EU) lawmakers as they formulate tax policy going forward. Some evidence that this is taking place may be found by observing the presence and vocal contributions of tax justice advocates at OECD meetings and consultations (as discussed in this volume, Chapter 4). On the other hand, the expressed sense of many tax practitioners seems to be that, while tax justice advocates were successful in bringing issues to public attention and prompting the OECD to develop the BEPS initiative, their subsequent engagement with the design and drafting of technical tax rules under

BEPS has been minimal. The presence of the BEPS monitoring group challenges that claim. Outside of revealed anecdotal impressions, it is difficult to either verify or debunk these perceptions, so it is not clear how to gauge the level and scope of tax justice advocacy in the negotiation of tax law reform.

An alternative (or additional) possibility to exerting direct influence on policy development is that proponents of the Fair Tax Mark may continue to act as responders to the law (upper right-hand quadrant of Figure 10.1), reacting with non-legal corporate social responsibility norms to address ongoing imperfections they perceive in the formal legal system. In other words, the Fair Tax Mark could consolidate its embryonic form of private governance. In that position, tax justice advocates would not negotiate directly with lawmakers to develop tax law reforms, but would continue in their role as outside agitators, engaging with the public in hopes of spurring political leaders to action in their preferred policy direction. The Fair Tax Mark would simultaneously engage with the implementers of law, namely lawyers and accountants. By thus influencing those who are tasked with implementing the law, the Fair Tax Mark would indirectly affect the continuation of the tax policy cycle. This does not necessarily indicate a lesser influence on the shape of the tax law going forward, but it is a less measurable form of influence. Of course, as will be outlined in the following chapter, these two processes are not mutually exclusive, as often private standards are incorporated into hard law, often at the behest of the corporations that have adopted private standards and want their competitors to be subjected to them (Vogel and Kagan 2004).

Accordingly, appreciating the full reach and impact of the Fair Tax Mark is a difficult if not impossible task. It is also important to note that the standard is embryonic and that successful environmental and trade-related certification regimes took over a decade to gain significant traction. The outcome of all of the interactions among actors and processes in the transnational tax order is a pluralistic, iterative landscape for tax lawmaking that creates challenges for predicting the main sources of input and influence for future tax reform. To better understand how national tax policy evolves would require a more comprehensive means of identifying the key participants, tracing their processes of information gathering, collaboration and decision-making activities, and exploring the influence of the various institutions, individuals and events on tax policy making. Otherwise, we can but observe that tax justice advocates have undoubtedly altered the landscape in the transnational tax law order. The extent and scope of that alteration are still unfolding. No doubt it will intrigue tax policy observers and invigorate efforts analogous to the Fair Tax Mark for years to come.

10.5 CONCLUSION

The past decade has witnessed the awakening of society to the difficulty of taxing firms that are globally dispersed, mobile, flexible, and well served by professional advisers around the world. Civil society actors, especially those who identify as tax justice advocates, have articulated widespread public frustration about the apparent lack of ability and will of governments to subject firms to a fair amount of tax, even in the case of the most visible, profitable and consumer-oriented companies. To some degree, as yet immeasurable, these advocates have inserted themselves in the channels of global tax policy making and altered the pathways to reform. The scrutiny brought to bear by tax justice advocates on multinational tax practices helped lead the world's most influential tax standard setter, the OECD, to adopt an ambitious project to reform the international tax regime. It also contributed to legislative reform proposals at the level of the European Union, which itself influenced the OECD's work.

The creators of the Fair Tax Mark have taken a step further than issue advocacy, developing an alternative tax standard based on their own conceptions of justice. They have done so by creating an independent set of acceptable parameters for tax planning and compliance, defined and measured by a point system that reduces taxpayer behaviour to an observable, quantitative measure. The Fair Tax Mark confronts the same challenges as any legal regime: regulating behaviour with words is an iterative project that involves complex interactions of discretion, interpretation, implementation, and subsequent monitoring for compliance. As would be the case for any legal regime, the Fair Tax Mark criteria involve principles, defined terms, exceptions, exemptions and discretionary application. Each familiar feature raises traditional legal questions about who gives exemptions, under what sort of discretionary authority, on what grounds they make decisions, and with what available appeals. As a quasi-legal regime, the Fair Tax Mark can be expected to expand to the extent it receives widespread adoption. A likely area of expansion involves appeals mechanisms and quasi-judicial or third-party oversight for interpreting standards and conflicting claims.

It remains to be seen whether this regime will become institutionalized as a new form of private governance within the international tax system, but there are also many normative questions to be asked about the attempt of any non-governmental body to intervene as a standard setter regarding what justice requires. These include the legitimacy of the purported standard setters in claiming this title, as well as their accountability in respect of the companies they seek to govern, the consumers whose decisions they seek to influence, and other stakeholders involved in the governance of the targeted companies. These questions are considered in more detail in the following chapter. As we ask these questions of the Fair Tax Mark, we may similarly continue to ask them about the actors, institutions and processes that currently dominate the transnational tax law order.

REFERENCES

ActionAid UK (2017), *Responsible Tax Practice by Companies*, available at http://www.actionaid.org.uk/sites/default/files/publications/responsible_tax_practice.pdf (accessed 12 September 2017).
ADB (African Development Bank) (2015), *African Economic Outlook 2015*, available at http://www.africaneconomicoutlook.org/en/outlook/regional-development-and-spatial-inclusion/ (accessed 16 September 2017).
Avi-Yonah, R. (2009), 'The OECD Harmful Tax Competition: A Retrospective after a Decade', *Brooklyn Journal of International Law* **34** (3), 783–796.
Beloe, S. and G. Lye (2006), *Taxing Issues: Responsible Business and Tax*, Report produced by SustainAbility, available at https://www.taxjustice.net/cms/upload/pdf/Sustainability_taxing_issues.pdf (accessed 15 September 2017).
Biswas, R. (2002), 'Introduction: Globalisation, Tax Competition and Economic Development', in R. Biswas (ed.), *International Tax Competition: Globalisation and Fiscal Sovereignty*, London: Commonwealth Secretariat, pp. 1–14.
Braithwaite, J. (1982), 'Enforced Self-Regulation: A New Strategy for Corporate Crime', *Michigan Law Review* **80** (7), 1466–1507.
Braithwaite, J. and P. Drahos (2000), *Global Business Regulation*, Cambridge: Cambridge University Press.
Brauner, Y. (2014), 'What the BEPS?', *Florida Tax Review* **16** (2), 55–115.
Cabezas, M. (2014), 'Tax Transparency and the Marketplace: A Pathway to State Sustainability', *McGill International Journal of Sustainable Development Law and Policy* **10** (2), 179–213.
Christians, A. (2009), 'Sovereignty, Taxation and Social Contract', *Minnesota Journal of International Law* **18** (1), 99–153.
Christians, A. (2010a), 'Global Trends and Constraints on Tax Policy in the Least Developed Countries', *UBC Law Review* **42** (2), 239–274.
Christians, A. (2010b), 'Taxation in a Time of Crisis: Policy Leadership from the OECD to the G20', *Northwestern Journal of Law and Social Policy* **5** (1), 19–40.
Christians, A. (2012a), 'Hard Law, Soft Law, and International Taxation', *Wisconsin International Law Journal* **25** (2), 325–334.
Christians, A. (2012b), 'How Nations Share', *Indiana Law Journal* **87** (4), 1407–1454.
Christians, A. (2013a), 'Activism and the Tax Transparency Movement', in Y. Brauner and M. Stewart (eds), *Tax, Law and Development*, Cheltenham, UK and Northampton, MA, USA: Edward Elgar Publishing, pp. 288–315.
Christians, A. (2013b), 'How Starbucks Lost Its Social License – And Paid £20 Million to Get It Back', *Tax Notes International* **71** (7), available at https://papers.ssrn.com/sol3/papers.cfm?abstract_id=2308921 (accessed 17 September 2017).
Christians, A. (2015), 'Friends with Tax Benefits: Apple's Cautionary Tale', *Tax*

Notes International **78** (11), 1031–1034, available at https://papers.ssrn.com/sol3/papers.cfm?abstract_id=2674335 (accessed 13 September 2017).

Christians, A. and S.E. Shay (2017), 'Assessing BEPS: Origins, Standards, and Responses', *IFA Cahiers de Droit Fiscal International* **102A**.

Cobham, A. (2015), 'OECD Country-by-Country Reporting: Only for the Strong?', Financial Transparency Coalition, published electronically 17 September, available at https://financialtransparency.org/oecd-country-by-country-reporting-only-for-the-strong/ (accessed 12 September 2017).

Cockfield, A.J. (2012), 'The Limits of the International Tax Regime as a Commitment Projector', *Virginia Tax Review* **33** (59), available at https://papers.ssrn.com/sol3/papers.cfm?abstract_id=2357961 (accessed 12 September 2017).

Conley, J.M. and C.A. Williams (2005), 'Engage, Embed, and Embellish: Theory versus Practice in the Corporate Social Responsibility Movement', *Journal of Corporation Law* **31** (1), 1–38.

Cook, T. (2013), 'Testimony of Apple Inc. before the Permanent Subcommittee on Investigations', available at http://www.hsgac.senate.gov/download/?id=E0A00AAA-F4A1-4FA0-B5B2-563B86A7588A (accessed 16 September 2017).

Cullen-Knox, C., R. Eccleston, M. Haward, E. Lester and J. Vince (2017), 'Contemporary Challenges in Environmental Governance: Technology, Governance and the Social Licence', *Environmental Policy and Governance* **27** (1), 3–13.

Davies, R. (2015), 'Starbucks Pays UK Corporation Tax of £8.1m', *Guardian*, published electronically 15 December, available at https://www.theguardian.com/business/2015/dec/15/starbucks-pays-uk-corporation-tax-8-million-pounds (accessed 14 September 2017).

Dezalay, Y. and B. Garth (1996), *Dealing in Virtue: International Commercial Arbitration and the Construction of a Transnational Legal Order*, Chicago, IL: University of Chicago Press.

EC (European Commission) (2014), 'State Aid SA.38373 (2014/C) (ex 2014/NN) (ex 2014/CP) – Ireland, Alleged Aid to Apple', available at http://ec.europa.eu/competition/state_aid/cases/253200/253200_1582634_87_2.pdf (accessed 15 September 2017).

EC (European Commission) (2015), 'Commission Decides Selective Tax Advantages for Fiat in Luxembourg and Starbucks in the Netherlands Are Illegal under EU State Aid Rules', published electronically 21 October, available at http://europa.eu/rapid/press-release_IP-15-5880_en.htm (accessed 17 September 2017).

EC (European Commission) (2016), 'State Aid: Ireland Gave Illegal Tax Benefits to Apple Worth up to €13 Billion', published electronically 30 August, available at http://europa.eu/rapid/press-release_IP-16-2923_en.htm (accessed 13 September 2017).

EC (European Commission) (2017), 'Public Country-by-Country Reporting: Corporate Tax Transparency', available at http://ec.europa.eu/finance/company-reporting/country-by-country-reporting/index_en.htm (accessed 16 September 2017).

Eccleston, R. (2012), *The Dynamics of Global Economic Governance: The Financial Crisis, the OECD and the Politics of International Tax Cooperation*, Cheltenham, UK and Northampton, MA, USA: Edward Elgar Publishing.

Economist (2015), 'New Rules, Same Old Paradigm', published electronically 15 October, available at http://www.economist.com/news/business/21672207-

plan-curb-multinationals-tax-avoidance-opportunity-missed-new-rules-same-old (accessed 15 September 2017).

EITI (Extractive Industries Transparency Initiative) (2017), *Publish What You Pay*, available at https://eiti.org/ (accessed 17 September 2017).

Fair Tax Mark (2013), 'The Fair Tax Mark: Company Name Assessment', available at http://www.fairtaxmark.net/wp-content/uploads/2014/02/Final-Company-Report-Template1.pdf (accessed 12 September 2017).

Fair Tax Mark (2014a), *The Fair Tax Mark: Fair Tax Mark Criteria Notes: UK-Based Multinationals 2014–2015*, available at http://www.fairtaxmark.net/wp-content/uploads/2014/10/MNC-Criteria-Notes-2014-15.pdf (accessed 15 September 2017).

Fair Tax Mark (2014b), *Fair Tax Mark Criteria Notes: Solely UK-Based Companies 2013–2014*, available at http://www.fairtaxmark.net/wp-content/uploads/2014/02/Criteria-notes_MASTER1.pdf (accessed 16 September 2017).

Fair Tax Mark (2014c), 'The Fair Tax Mark: Summary Scorecard', available at http://www.fairtaxmark.net/wp-content/uploads/2014/10/Multinational-Scorecard-.pdf (accessed 11 September 2017).

Fair Tax Mark (2014d), 'The Fair Tax Mark: What Is Country-by-Country Reporting?', available at http://www.fairtaxmark.net/wp-content/uploads/2014/01/Country-by-country-reporting.pdf (accessed 17 September 2017).

Fair Tax Mark (2017a), 'What's the Fair Tax Mark?', available at http://www.fairtaxmark.net/what-is-it/ (accessed 15 September 2017).

Fair Tax Mark (2017b), 'Fair Tax Mark Criteria', available at http://www.fairtax-mark.net/criteria/ (accessed 16 September 2017).

Fair Tax Mark (2017c), 'Solely UK-Based Businesses', available at http://www.fairtaxmark.net/criteria/solely-uk/ (accessed 16 September 2017).

Fair Tax Mark (2017d), 'UK-Based Multinationals', available at http://www.fairtaxmark.net/criteria/uk-multinationals/ (accessed 12 September 2017).

Folketinget (2015), 'L 167 Forslag til lov om ændring af ligningsloven, boafgiftsloven, fondsbeskatningsloven, skatteforvaltningsloven og forskellige andre love', *Skatteministeriet Online*, published electronically 29 April, available at http://www.ft.dk/samling/20141/lovforslag/L167/index.htm (accessed 13 September 2017).

Freedman, J. (2004), 'Defining Taxpayer Responsibility: In Support of a General Anti-Avoidance Principle', *British Tax Review* **2004** (4), 332–357.

Freedman, J. (2006), 'The Tax Avoidance Culture: Who Is Responsible? Governmental Influences and Corporate Social Responsibility', *Current Legal Problems* **59** (1), 359–390.

Garside, J. (2016), 'European Commission to Resurrect Overarching Corporate Tax Proposals', *Guardian*, published electronically 19 October, available at https://www.theguardian.com/world/2016/oct/19/european-commission-overarching-corporate-tax-proposals-profit-shifting (accessed 17 September 2017).

GATJ (Global Alliance for Tax Justice) (2017), *Asian Campaigners Demand the OECD's BEPS Process Do More for Developing Countries*, available at http://www.globaltaxjustice.org/asian-campaigners-demand-the-oecds-beps-process-do-more-for-developing-countries/ (accessed 15 September 2017).

Gunningham, N., R.A. Kagan and D. Thornton (2004), 'Social License and Environmental Protection: Why Businesses Go Beyond Compliance', *Law and Social Inquiry* **29** (2), 307–341.

Halliday, T.C. and B.G. Carruthers (2007), 'The Recursivity of Law: Global Norm

Making and National Lawmaking in the Globalization of Corporate Insolvency Regimes', *American Journal of Sociology* **112** (4), 1135–1202.
Halliday, T.C. and G. Shaffer (eds) (2015), *Transnational Legal Orders*, Cambridge: Cambridge University Press.
Herksen, M. van (2013), 'The OECD BEPS Report: The Story of the Elephant, the 800-Pound Gorilla and the Tiger', *BNA*, 12 July, available at http://www.bna.com/oecd-beps-report-n17179875162/ (accessed 13 September 2017).
Homeland Security and Governmental Affairs (2013), 'The Shifting of Profits Offshore by U.S. Multinational Corporations: Hearing before the Permanent Subcommittee on Investigations of the Subcommittee on Homeland Security and Governmental Affairs, 113th Cong. 2', available at https://www.gpo.gov/fdsys/pkg/CHRG-113shrg81657/pdf/CHRG-113shrg81657.pdf (accessed 16 September 2017).
James, V.E. (2002), 'Twenty-First Century Pirates of the Caribbean: How the Organization for Economic Cooperation and Development Robbed Fourteen CARICOM Countries of Their Tax and Economic Policy Sovereignty', *University of Miami Inter-American Law Review* **34** (1), 1–50.
Johansen, S. (2014), 'Ingen skattekroner i skattely: Det offentlige skal gå forrest i kampen mod skattesnyd', *IBIS Analyse*, available at http://ibis.dk/sites/default/files/media/pdf_global/analysis_pdf/ibis_analyse_ingen_skattekroner_i_skattely.pdf (accessed 14 September 2017).
Kaye, T.A. (2014), 'The Offshore Shell Game: U.S. Corporate Tax Avoidance through Profit Shifting', *Chapman Law Review* **18** (1), 185–190.
Klein, D.B. (ed.) (1997), *Reputation: Studies in the Voluntary Elicitation of Good Conduct*, Ann Arbor: University of Michigan Press.
Kumar, C. (2014), *Tax and Development: A Scoping Study of Funding Opportunities*, October, available at http://www.transparency-initiative.org/wp-content/uploads/2014/09/TAI_taxanddevelopment_FULL_OCT14.pdf (accessed 17 September 2017).
Lew, J.J. (2016), Letter of U.S. Treasury Secretary to European Commission President Jean-Claude Juncker, 11 February, available at https://www.treasury.gov/resource-center/tax-policy/treaties/Documents/Letter-State-Aid-Investigations.pdf (accessed 14 September 2017).
Luppino, A.J. (2003), 'Stopping the Enron End-Runs and Other Trick Plays: The Book–Tax Accounting Conformity Defense', *Columbia Business Law Review* **2003** (1), 35–190.
Monaghan, P. (2015), 'How to Stand Out from the Tax Dodgers and Avoiders', *Guardian*, published electronically 26 February, available at http://www.theguardian.com/sustainable-business/2015/feb/26/taxpayers-should-be-able-to-differentiate-themselves-from-tax-avoiders-and-dodgers (accessed 15 September 2017).
Murphy, R. (2014), 'Introducing the Fair Tax Mark', *International Tax Review*, published electronically 26 February, available at http://www.internationaltaxreview.com/Article/3311193/Latest-News-Archive/Introducing-the-Fair-Tax-Mark.html (accessed 13 September 2017).
Murphy, R. (2015), 'The Fair Tax Mark', Remarks at McGill University Tax Policy Colloquium, 2 November.
Nelsen, J.L. (2006), 'Social License to Operate', *International Journal of Mining, Reclamation and Environment* **20** (3), 161–162.
OECD (Organisation for Economic Co-operation and Development) (2010),

'OECD'S Current Tax Agenda', available at http://www.uscib.org/docs/CTPA_Brochure_June_2010.pdf (accessed 16 September 2017).
OECD (2013), *Addressing Base Erosion and Profit Shifting*, Paris: OECD Publishing.
OECD (Organisation for Economic Co-operation and Development) (2014a), 'Countries Commit to Automatic Exchange of Information in Tax Matters', available at http://www.oecd.org/ctp/exchange-of-tax-information/countries-commit-to-automatic-exchange-of-information-in-tax-matters.htm (accessed 12 September 2017).
OECD (Organisation for Economic Co-operation and Development) (2014b), *Public Consultation: Discussion Draft on Transfer Pricing Documentation and CbC Reporting*, available at http://www.oecd.org/ctp/transfer-pricing/discussion-draft-transfer-pricing-documentation.pdf (accessed 14 September 2017).
OECD (Organisation for Economic Co-operation and Development) (2015), *Action 13: Guidance on the Implementation of Transfer Pricing Documentation and Country-by-Country Reporting*, available at https://www.oecd.org/ctp/beps-action-13-guidance-implementation-tp-documentation-cbc-reporting.pdf (accessed 17 September 2017).
OECD (Organisation for Economic Co-operation and Development) (2017), 'About OECD', available at http://www.oecd.org/about/0,2337,en_2649_201185_1_1_1_1_1,00.html (accessed 12 September 2017).
Oliver, C. (2016), 'Apple's Cook Lobbies EU Antitrust Chief over Irish Back Taxes', *Financial Times*, published electronically 21 January, available at https://www.ft.com/content/4fbf2764-c063-11e5-846f-79b0e3d20eaf?mhq5j=e6 (accessed 16 September 2017).
Ostas, D.T. (2001), 'Deconstructing Corporate Social Responsibility: Insights from Legal and Economic Theory', *American Business Law Journal* **38** (2), 261–300.
Oxfam (2014), 'Reforming International Tax System Must Be Priority of G20', published electronically 10 February, available at https://www.oxfam.org/en/pressroom/pressreleases/2014-02-21/reforming-international-tax-system-must-be-priority-g20 (accessed 14 September 2017).
Oxfam (2017), 'Tax Transparency', available at https://www.oxfam.org/en/tags/tax-transparency (accessed 16 September 2017).
Pagani, F. (2002), *Peer Review: A Tool for Global Co-operation and Change*, OECD Observer No. 235, December, available at http://www.oecdobserver.org/news/fullstory.php/aid/881/Peer_review.html (accessed 17 September 2017).
Page, A.C. (1986), 'Self-Regulation: The Constitutional Dimension', *Modern Law Review* **49** (2), 141–167.
Rils, A. and O. Hansen (2015a), 'Danish Parliament Adopts General Anti-Abuse Provision', *Lexology Online*, published electronically 4 May, available at http://www.lexology.com/library/detail.aspx?G=4ec5d680-c395-462b-af0b-787aa62f2d38 (accessed 16 September 2017).
Rils, A. and O. Hansen (2015b), 'Denmark Introduces General Anti-Abuse Provision: Moving from SAAR to GAAR?', *Lexology Online*, published electronically 5 February, available at http://www.lexology.com/library/detail.aspx?G=4ec5d680-c395-462b-af0b-787aa62f2d38 (accessed 16 September 2017).
Ruggie, J.G. (2013), *Just Business: Multinational Corporations and Human Rights*, New York: Norton.
Schmitter, P.C. (1985), 'Neo-Corporatism and the State', in W. Grant (ed.), *The Political Economy of Corporatism*, London: Macmillan, pp. 32–62.

Scott, C. (2014), 'Fair Tax Mark to Reward Tax Justice', *Guardian*, 20 February, available at http://www.theguardian.com/sustainable-business/fair-tax-mark-to-reward tax-justice (accessed 12 September 2017).

Seabrooke, L. and D. Wigan (2013), *Emergent Entrepreneurs in Transnational Advocacy Networks: Professional Mobilization in the Fight for Global Tax Justice*, Working Paper No. 41, GR:EEN, Global Reordering: Evolution through European Networks, FP7, available at http://pipesproject.eu/assets/GREEN41.pdf (accessed 1 November 2017).

SKAT Online (2014), 'Tax in Denmark – An Introduction to the Danish Tax System for Non-Danish Speakers', available at http://www.nsi-center.dk/PDF/skatidanmark.Engelsk.pdf (accessed 15 September 2017).

Sorgenfri Kjær, J. (2014), 'Region Syd vil undgå handel med selskaber i skattely', *Politiken Online*, published electronically 25 November, available at http://politiken.dk/oekonomi/fokus_oekonomi/Luxembourg_laekage/ECE2465420/region-syd-vil-undgaa-handel-med-selskaber-i-skattely/ (accessed 11 September 2017).

Thomson, I. and R.G. Boutilier (2011), 'The Social License to Operate', in P. Darling (ed.), *SME Mining Engineering Handbook*, Englewood, CO: Society for Mining, Metallurgy and Exploration, pp. 1779–1796.

TJN (Tax Justice Network) (2013), 'Automatic Exchange of Information: An Opportunity for Developing Countries to Tackle Tax Evasion and Corruption', available at http://www.taxjustice.net/wp-content/uploads/2013/04/AIE-An-opportunity-for-developing-countries.pdf (accessed 13 September 2017).

United Nations Department of Economic and Social Affairs (2013), 'Financing for Development, Subcommittee on Base Erosion and Profit Shifting Issues for Developing Countries', available at http://www.un.org/esa/ffd/tax/BEPS_note.pdf (accessed 14 September 2017).

United States Senate Finance Committee (2015), 'Hatch, Ryan Call on Treasury to Engage Congress on OECD International Tax Project', Press release, available at http://www.finance.senate.gov/newsroom/chairman/release/?Id=ff0b1d06-c227-44be-8d5a-5f998771188b (accessed 16 September 2017).

United States Treasury (2016), *White Paper: The European Commission's Recent State Aid Investigations of Transfer Pricing Rulings*, 24 August, available at https://www.treasury.gov/resource-center/tax-policy/treaties/Documents/White-Paper-State-Aid.pdf (accessed 12 September 2017).

Vogel, D. and R. Kagan (2004), *Dynamics of Regulatory Change: How Globalisation Affects National Regulatory Policies*, Berkeley: University of California Press.

11. The legitimacy of private standards: lessons from fair trade and forestry for international tax governance

Fred Gale and Hannah Murphy-Gregory

11.1 INTRODUCTION

The intensification, speed and growing complexity of flows of finance, products, ideas and information in the twenty-first century have given rise to a myriad of global governance challenges (Held et al. 1999). Yet the formal governance arrangements spearheaded by nation-states and international organisations are uneven in coverage, vary widely in their compliance capacity, and sometimes conflict with each other in their intent. In efforts to rectify these intergovernmental limitations, a phenomenon known as global 'private' governance is proliferating (e.g. Cashore et al. 2004; Pattberg 2008; Gale and Haward 2011; Auld 2014; Green 2014). Proponents and protagonists – typically, but not always, from the civil society sector – see global private governance not only as a response to absent, piecemeal or ineffective formal arrangements, but also as an avenue to extract a higher standard of conduct from transnational actors, in particular corporations. While global private governance emerged to tackle social and ecological sustainability issues, initiatives have also emerged to govern economic issues such as corruption (Transparency International), investment (Equator Principles and UN Principles of Responsible Investment), trade (Extractive Industries Transparency Initiative) and taxation (Fair Tax Mark; this volume, Chapter 10). But what do these economic-focused global standards organisations (GSOs) offer? To what extent do they conform to, or differ from, established GSOs like the Forest Stewardship Council (FSC) and Fairtrade International (FI)? Most importantly, to what extent have they learned the hard lessons of pioneering GSOs of the importance of building organisational and scheme credibility and legitimacy?

In this chapter, we seek to provide some tentative answers to these questions using the lens of GSO legitimacy. Building on case studies of the FSC and FI, we examine how these two GSOs reformed themselves as they evolved to enhance their legitimacy and credibility, especially with external stakeholders and consumers. We identify four major strategies utilised: internal governance reform, formalisation of standards development processes, 'mainstreaming' of product availability, and global institution building. With regard to the latter, both organisations were founding members of the ISEAL Alliance, a global organisation 'whose mission is to strengthen sustainability standards systems' and whose 'membership is open to all multi-stakeholder sustainability standards and accreditation bodies that demonstrate their ability to meet the ISEAL Codes of Good Practice and accompanying requirements' (ISEAL Alliance 2016a). To assess whether the new GSOs are learning the lessons of their pioneering cousins, we conduct a desk study of a recently launched and fascinating new initiative described in the previous chapter, Fair Tax Mark (FTM), against the ISEAL Codes. Our study highlights that, despite its laudable intentions and noting that the standard is in its infancy, FTM currently falls significantly short of meeting the Codes' requirements, leading us to conclude that FTM will remain a 'niche' standard that will be unable to have the impact desired by its Tax Justice Network (TJN) founders until it evolves further and undergoes significant governance, standards development and outreach reforms.

The chapter is structured as follows. In section 11.2, we provide a brief account of global private governance and standards, prior to providing, in section 11.3, a review of the literature on GSO legitimacy as experienced by FSC and FI. In section 11.4, we examine the ISEAL Alliance, a joint initiative of GSOs to create greater consistency among them in standard setting. Drawing on the lessons learned from the FSC and FI experience and building on the ISEAL Alliance's Code of Good Practice in standard setting, we analyse the FTM in section 11.5, identifying several gaps in its governance arrangements, standards development processes and institutional structures. A short conclusion follows, which recapitulates our argument and analyses the implications for FTM in securing greater global tax justice.

11.2 GLOBAL PRIVATE GOVERNANCE AND STANDARDS

The emergence of global private governance can be traced back to the post-war period and the decision by national standard-setting bodies in the US, the UK and elsewhere to form the International Organization for Standardization (ISO). Launched in 1947, the ISO focused on the development of product standards to facilitate international trade and investment and minimise national standards acting as technical trade barriers (Heires 2008). In the 1980s, the ISO branched out into non-technical standards by negotiating the ISO 9001 Quality Assurance Standard, and further in the 1990s into the field of sustainable development with the negotiation of its ISO 14001 Environmental Management Standard. It subsequently negotiated the ISO 26000 Social Accountability guidelines, designed to improve the social responsibility of public and private sector organisations (Heires 2008, p. 365).

A range of other standards and guidelines emerged in the 1970s in response to increasing concerns over the impact that multinational corporations (MNCs) were having in developing countries. Two notable global standards emerged in 1977: the OECD Guidelines for Multinational Enterprises, and the Sullivan Principles. The former, negotiated by states, aimed at mollifying developing country concerns over 'unfair' global trading rules and demands for a New International Economic Order. The Sullivan Principles, developed in the US by Rev Leon Sullivan, focused in contrast on improving the performance of American MNCs operating in South Africa and required companies to commit to a variety of practices such as not segregating races when eating and drinking, increasing the representation of black people in management positions, and improving living conditions for black people beyond the workplace. They were updated in 1999 to the Global Sullivan Principles to make them more broadly applicable to investment anywhere in the world.

While these early global initiatives are relevant to the notion of 'paying one's fair share', it was really only in the 1980s that the idea of establishing fully fledged GSOs to govern the activities of corporations was formulated. In the shadow of state regulation following the devastating 1984 chemical leak at Union Carbide's Bhopal, India plant that killed and/or seriously injured an estimated 8000 people, the chemical industry launched its Responsible Care programme to improve industry practice (Prakash 2000). Responsible Care is a quality assurance programme managed by the International Council of Chemical Associations, whose members consist of national chemical associations. Although not all chemical companies within a country are obliged to become members of Responsible Care, some national chemical associations make joining the scheme a requirement of membership, rendering it mandatory. While there have been no subsequent 'Bhopals' following Responsible Care's establishment, the critics of Responsible Care, as an industry-sponsored quality assurance scheme that does not employ multi-stakeholder governance or binding standards, have branded it a weak, ineffectual marketing exercise (King and Lennox 2000; Gamper-Rabindran and Finger 2013).

In the 1980s, civil society organisations (CSOs) began to experiment with private governance systems, notably in the forestry sector, where the UK branch of Friends of the Earth (FoE-UK) launched a campaign to ban tropical timber imports that it argued contributed to significant levels of tropical deforestation and degradation. In developing its *Good Wood Guide* in 1986, FoE-UK sought to pressure British retailers to purchase timber from non-tropical sources, a strategy countered by tropical timber importers, which established a 'code of conduct' to reassure retailers and consumers that the harm claimed was not occurring. Together with the British government's Overseas Development Administration (ODA) programme, FoE-UK developed a proposal to investigate the feasibility of timber 'certification and labelling', but it caused such consternation at the newly formed International Tropical Timber Organization (ITTO) that it had to be completely reformulated, gutting its original intent (Gale 1998, pp. 159–161). However, following the failure to negotiate a Global Forestry Convention at the 1992 United Nations Conference on Environment and Development (UNCED), and in the wake of an influential consulting report that endorsed the potential of certification and labelling to contribute to improved tropical forest management, a group of CSOs, firms and individuals joined forces during 1991–93 to form what subsequently has become the icon of private global governance, the Forest Stewardship Council.

At around the same time, the growing group of alternative trading organisations that had been formed from the 1950s began to solidify into a more coherent network. In 1988, the first fair trade certification and labelling initiative was developed in the Netherlands: the Max Havelaar fair trade seal, which was initially used informally and regulated by national-level organisations. The development of the fair trade label facilitated the expansion of fair trade product availability by allowing such products to be purchased not just in speciality shops but in mainstream outlets accessible by a broader group of consumers. This development permitted the expansion of fair trade by, for example, effectively allowing any established brand-name coffee sold in mainstream outlets to utilise the fair trade label provided it met the conditions of fair trade: a fair price for producers, justifying the premium cost over conventional products.

In 1989, a peak umbrella fair trade advocacy group, the International Federation for Alternative Trade, was established as a network comprising 150 organisations in 47 countries. By the mid-1990s, a push by the European fair trade groups for greater formalisation was under way, with the aim of developing more consistent certification criteria and practices in the fair trade system. In 1997, the Fairtrade Labelling Organizations International, now Fairtrade International, was created to unite the proliferating number of national fair trade groups under one umbrella and to harmonise standards and certification. In 2002, FI launched an international fair trade certification mark – Fairtrade Mark – to improve visibility of the label on supermarket shelves, facilitate cross-border trade and simplify export procedures for fair trade producers and exporters. In 2004, the decision was made to separate the standard-setting side of the organisation from the assessment and verification processes in an effort to ensure the transparency and independence of the fair trade certification and labelling system. The organisation was thus divided in two and today consists of FI, which sets Fairtrade standards and provides producer support, and FLOCERT, which inspects and certifies producer organisations and audits traders.

The success of both the FSC and FI initiatives prompted other civil society groups to develop new schemes, with one of the major CSOs, World Wide Fund for Nature, often taking a leading role. In the late 1990s, this organisation in cooperation with the global food giant Unilever founded the Marine Stewardship Council (MSC); it was also a key initiator of the Roundtable on Sustainable Palm Oil (RSPO, 2003), the Roundtable on Responsible Soy (RTRS, 2006) and the Roundtable on Sustainable Biomaterials (RSB, 2007). CSO involvement in developing certification and labelling schemes is not always welcome, however, and competitor schemes have been established. One frequently cited example is the post-1993 emergence of a large number of national forest certification programmes to compete with the FSC, which subsequently combined to form a more business-friendly global umbrella scheme, the Programme for the Endorsement of Forest Certification.

11.3 LEGITIMACY AND STANDARD-SETTING ORGANISATIONS

To have significant influence in global markets, it is vital that GSOs are perceived to be credible and legitimate. In a ground-breaking study that built on Suchman's (1995) definition of legitimacy as 'a generalized perception or assumption that the actions of an entity are desirable, proper, or appropriate within some socially constructed system of norms, values, beliefs and definitions', Cashore et al. (2004) distinguished between 'pragmatic', 'moral' and 'cognitive' legitimacy based on the degree to which the norms promoted were internalised by relevant audiences. Pragmatic legitimacy is granted when a GSO's norms are not internalised but stakeholders nonetheless abide by the standard because of the benefits of doing so. Such pragmatic benefits may be positive and include meeting corporate social responsibility goals, or negative and involve not being excluded from key export markets. Moral legitimacy involves a deeper level of acceptance and is granted when actors come to share the GSO's normative objectives and view following the standard as 'the right thing to do'. The difference between pragmatic and moral legitimacy matters because, if only the former is granted, actors will continuously contest the need for the standard and will abandon it once it no longer delivers the anticipated benefits. Finally, at an even deeper level, 'cognitive' legitimacy is granted when the norms advocated by the GSO are so widely and deeply shared that they are regarded simply as the way things are done.

A key aspect of this 'output' approach to legitimacy is that it places considerable weight on the perceptions of internal and external 'audiences' to endow GSOs with legitimacy. In Cashore et al.'s (2004) study of forest certification, for example, forest companies are considered such an important legitimacy-granting audience that the mechanism they identify underpinning these schemes, 'non-state market-driven' governance, is derived from it. In this formulation, a GSO's success depends on it earning at least pragmatic legitimacy from business. A key focus of Cashore et al.'s (2004) study is then to examine the 'converting', 'conforming' and 'informing' strategies GSOs use to secure such legitimacy. In a converting strategy, a GSO encourages audiences to alter their perception of, and behaviour towards, a scheme by explaining and defending its rationale and outlining its pragmatic benefits and moral necessity. In contrast, in a conforming strategy, a GSO modifies its scheme to address specific audience concerns that are blocking implementation. Finally, in an informing strategy, a GSO provides facts and data about its standard, an approach targeted at scheme supporters. While the non-state market-driven governance literature appears to privilege what GSOs need to do to ensure legitimacy in the eyes of business, we view obtaining legitimacy as requiring striking a balance between economic, social and environmental audiences. From this perspective, conforming strategies that cede too much to corporations will alienate social and environmental stakeholders, an outcome that Schouten and Glasbergen (2011) observe in their study of the Roundtable on Sustainable Palm Oil. In summary, therefore, while a standard that lacks a degree of business backing is likely to be fatally flawed, a standard that concedes too much to business interests will also fail to achieve its objective. Striking a balance between competing audiences is difficult to achieve, and our two case studies below outline the strategies adopted by two GSOs to mediate the range of conflicting interests.

Seeking Legitimacy I: The Forest Stewardship Council Case

The Forest Stewardship Council today is a sprawling global network of certified companies and certifying bodies, closely coupled via national and regional offices to a corporate headquarters located in Bonn, Germany. With over 190 million hectares of forests certified and almost 31 000 chain of custody certificates issued, the organisation has become a key player in the world's $400 billion-plus timber market (UNEP 2013). Today, certification to its standard is increasingly perceived as a requirement for market entry in Europe, and companies that lack it can fail during international downturns (Gale and Haward 2011). FSC's mission is to promote 'environmentally appropriate, socially beneficial, and economically viable management of the world's forests' (FSC 2012, p. 7), which it achieves via a forest management standard consisting of 10 principles and 70 criteria spanning everything from legal compliance, indigenous peoples' rights and community consultation to the protection of high-conservation-value forests, forest management planning, and pesticide use and disposal.

FSC's current structure and operation represent a significant evolution from what they were at its 1993 founding. In 1993 it had developed only a single, draft forest management standard, whereas today there are a myriad of different standards covering, in addition to forest management, chain-of-custody certification, controlled wood, certification bodies, and use of the FSC logo. The organisational structure has also changed, with the original two 'chambers', representing environmental and social interests in the first and economic interests in the second, transforming into a three-chamber structure equally representing economic, social and environmental interests, with each chamber further equally divided into two sub-chambers to represent the interests of the global North and the global South. FSC's international board has also grown in size and altered in composition, from seven in the early years to nine and, more recently, 12 members. The larger board now enables all six sub-chambers to have equal representation in decision making. FSC has also put in place some robust dispute resolution mechanisms to manage a range of dispute types: those brought by stakeholders against (a) certificate holders, (b) decisions of a certification body, (c) violations of FSC's policy of association and (d) applications of an FSC normative document (FSC 2012).

One of the major changes since FSC's establishment has occurred in the procedures it uses to consult with stakeholders to develop new standards and revise existing ones. When it developed its original forest management standard in the early 1990s, a largely 'in-house' approach was taken that saw seven drafts of the standard written, circulated and revised within an increasingly large circle of FSC supporters (Synnott 2005). As greater experience was garnered from the standards development and revision process, however, several shortcomings were identified, including version control, date of coming into force, criteria intent, and stakeholder input. As the organisation evolved, the need became apparent to formalise and standardise the standards development process itself to ensure transparency, accountability, balance and clarity among other features. Today, FSC's standards are further elaborated in the form of glossaries of terms that clearly define the meaning of the words employed and guidance documents that explain what the purpose of a specific standard provision is.

FSC has also recognised the need for institutional evolution as a result of its experience of standard setting. When it became operational in 1995, it undertook two major functions: the setting of forest management and other standards for the FSC system and the accreditation of certification bodies to undertake audits to the FSC standards. However, not only did this arrangement not comply with international guidelines on standards development set by the International Organization for Standardization, which require certification bodies to be accredited by a separate and independent organisation, but it also provoked the concern that certification bodies might be pressured by FSC stakeholders and staff to unfairly deny or retract certification from companies on issues unrelated to their formal conformity to the FSC standard. Consequently, FSC explored a number of possible institutional reforms related to the separation of standards development from accreditation, ultimately opting to establish Accreditation Services International as a devolved company under the FSC umbrella to undertake the accreditation task. The reason for not undertaking a complete separation of the standards development and accreditation function was, as Wenban-Smith (2007, p. 2) explains, that 'differences in standards only deliver differences in performance if they are actually implemented' and 'decision makers need to have confidence in the reliability of whichever certificates of compliance are being issued if they are going to make purchasing or investment decisions based on them'. To ensure that decision makers interested in purchasing FSC certified products have such confidence, FSC retains a degree of involvement over all aspects of the system – setting global standards, monitoring their adaptation to national and regional jurisdictions, and ensuring that certification bodies are appropriately accredited via Accreditation Services International and do not engage in a 'race to the bottom' for certification business.

Seeking Legitimacy II: The Fairtrade International Case

The fair trade movement is a privately governed production and consumption regime administered by a complex array of local, national, regional and global fair trade CSOs. These CSOs serve as intermediaries between developing country producers and developed country consumers willing to pay a premium for socially and environmentally friendly products, most notably coffee, cocoa and handicrafts among many others. In 2013 sales of Fairtrade certified products reached US$7.3 billion worldwide (Fairtrade Australia New Zealand 2014), representing an increase of 15 per cent over sales in 2012. Fair trade products are sold in over 125 countries across the globe, whilst Fairtrade certified producers represent 75 countries (FI 2014). The main purpose of the fair trade system is to contest perceived inequitable global, regional and bilateral trade rules that disadvantage small producers in the developing world. It offers an alternative regime that endeavours to pay producers a fair wage, promote environmentally friendly production processes and reduce the diversion of producers' income to global commodity chain intermediaries – the 'middlemen'. Though in its early days (from the 1950s onwards) fair trade served as a symbolic counterpoint to the global trade regime, the creation of fair trade GSOs and their use of standard setting, labelling and certification through the 1990s and beyond have helped dramatically elevate sales in recent years. Several of the largest mainstream corporate players today, like Nestlé, Cadbury and Starbucks, are notable for signing up to the system and utilising fair trade labels, albeit controversially.

To govern this system, fair trade practitioners created Fairtrade International, a private governance organisation that provides overall coordination of Fairtrade labelling, including the development and setting of the international Fairtrade standards. The objectives of these standards are to ensure producers receive fair prices, invest in projects in developing countries that promote social, economic and environmental development, provide pre-financing to producers requesting it, develop long-term trading partnerships that involve greater producer control than in the mainstream market, and set clear criteria to ensure that the conditions of production and trade of certified products are fair and responsible (FI 2011a). FI also assists producers in gaining and maintaining certification and in capitalising on market opportunities within the fair trade market. Members of the organisation include three Fairtrade producers' networks (regional associations that Fairtrade certified producer organisations may join), and 25 national or regional Fairtrade organisations that promote the scheme to both business and consumers in the developed world, where such products are typically purchased (FI 2011b). The process of setting the Fairtrade standards is undertaken by the organisation's Standards Unit and Standards Committee, with a high level of consultation with internal and external stakeholders, including Fairtrade members, producer organisations, traders and external experts.

FI was split into two in 2004, with a new organisation, FLOCERT, formed to serve as the independent global certification organisation for the system. Today, FLOCERT essentially acts as an enforcement agency ensuring that FI's social and environmental standards are upheld by participating organisations (FLOCERT 2015). It seeks to ensure that producers and traders comply with the standards and that producers invest the benefits received through Fairtrade back into the system. FLOCERT follows the ISO standards for certification bodies, and in 2007 it became the first social certification body in the world to obtain an ISO 65/17065 accreditation for its Fairtrade certification services.[1] FLOCERT currently operates in more than 115 countries; it has around 90 employees, more than 100 auditors, and over 3300 customers across the world, ranging from small producers in developing nations to large global retailers (FLOCERT 2015).

The use of the Fairtrade Mark has evolved significantly, despite concerns about corporate co-option (Renard 2005, p.425). In the UK in late 2005, the Fairtrade Foundation granted use of the Fairtrade label to Nestlé, the globe's largest food multinational and top coffee trader, for a small range of coffee on British supermarket shelves (Tucker 2006, p.7). The coffee range, Partners, represented a fraction of 1 per cent of Nestlé's coffee purchases. Given Nestlé is a frequent target of CSOs, and the existence of long-running consumer boycotts of Nestlé products, this 'mainstreaming' of Fairtrade was a highly controversial decision that raised serious questions about how to avoid regulatory capture and maintain the integrity of the standards (see Jaffee and Howard 2010). A similar concern had been raised five years earlier, in 2000, when Starbucks was granted use of the Fairtrade label for only 1 per cent of its coffee sales, despite an earlier agreement that specified a minimum of 5 per cent of total sales. Whilst it can be regarded as positive that Nestlé, Starbucks and other large corporations are interested in signing up, signalling the relevance of the scheme and its label, the concern remains that mainstreaming Fairtrade undermines its original purpose and positions large corporate players to dilute the standard and thus the legitimacy of the system in the eyes of consumers. This is particularly so where only tiny proportions of a corporation's products are Fairtrade certified and its past practices have been controversial.

Another related source of tension within the fair trade movement is the practice of FLOCERT actively seeking out large corporate entities for Fairtrade licensing deals (Tucker 2006; Jaffee and Howard 2010). The lucrative nature of such deals for Fairtrade organisations has resulted in critics arguing that the current Fairtrade licensing fee structure compromises the independence of the system by acting as a disincentive to regulate high-volume licensees (Bahra 2009). Other critics see the alignment of FI with global certification and standards bodies such as the ISO as coming at the expense of linkages with small producers and farmers along with their associated concerns (see Mutersbaugh 2005). The underlying issue at the heart of these critics' concerns is their view that the purpose of fair trade is in stark counterpoint to the global trading system. Whilst the Fairtrade organisations see the mainstreaming of fair trade as a testament to the label's success, critics view such mainstreaming as a dilution of fair trade's original principles and ethos.

11.4 LEGITIMACY AND META-GOVERNANCE: THE ISEAL ALLIANCE

The larger number and greater formalisation of private governance systems in the 1990s, together with the prospect of new initiatives in sectors such as palm oil, soy, biofuels and farmed fish, created a renewed demand for GSO 'meta-standards' to distinguish 'credible' from 'non-credible' systems. The issue had become especially pressing as, following the establishment of the FSC, a range of national, industry- and government-sponsored competitor schemes for forest certification had been established in Canada, the United States, Finland, Germany and Indonesia (Gale 2004; Tollefson et al. 2008). These schemes became united under a single, industry-dominated umbrella in 1999 with the formation of the Programme for the Endorsement of Forest Certification (PEFC). From the perspective of many environmental and social CSOs, these industry–government schemes were not credible because they excluded, at the outset, important stakeholders from participation in governance arrangements and because the standards that emerged from them endorsed status quo practices which were viewed as part of the problem (e.g. TWS 2005). The solution was to establish an umbrella organisation that would set standards for how GSOs should be governed and how standards should be developed.

Formed as a loose alliance in 1992, the ISEAL Alliance was formally constituted in 2002 as the International Social and Environmental Accreditation and Labelling Alliance by a small number of founding members including FSC, MSC, FI and the International Federation of Organic Agriculture Movements (IFOAM) (Loconto and Fouilleux 2014, p. 170). The ISEAL Alliance aims to promote the credibility of GSOs like the FSC and FI as well as encourage greater inter-organisational collaboration and mutual recognition of members' standards. According to its website,

> ISEAL's mission is to strengthen sustainability standards systems for the benefit of people and the environment. ISEAL Alliance is the global membership

> association for credible sustainability standards, who work together to improve the impact and effectiveness of current and potential future members. We distinguish and promote credible standards and support cooperation among our members and other interested parties to shape an effective standards movement. By building a collaborative movement we aim to achieve a significant and increasing impact on the sustainability of products and services worldwide.

To achieve its objectives, the ISEAL Alliance has developed Codes of Good Practice for sustainability standards related to standard setting, impacts, assurance, and claims and labelling. For example, in 2014 it revised its Code of Good Practice for Setting Social and Environmental Standards (ISEAL Alliance 2016a), based on a set of recently negotiated principles of credibility: sustainability, improvement, relevance, rigour, engagement, impartiality, transparency, accessibility, truthfulness and efficiency. The standard-setting Code is structured as a hierarchy, the highest level being 'desired outcomes', which are further elaborated in the form of 'requirements'. Where there may be uncertainty with regard to meaning, the Code also provides explanations in the form of 'guidance'.

While the ISEAL Alliance's Code of Good Practice is a useful tool for GSOs to employ to assess the degree to which they are operating in conformity with industry best practice, its approach is not without fault. In a critique of the ISEAL Alliance's approach, Loconto and Fouilleux (2014) claim the Code is too process-oriented and that, despite the focus on promoting 'sustainability standards', no actual substantive definition of 'sustainability' is provided. They argue that a major reason for this is the increasing diversity of ISEAL Alliance members, which include not only first-generation GSOs like FI, FSC and MSC, but also more recently established ones that they view as having significantly weaker conceptions of sustainability such as GLOBALG.A.P. in agriculture, the RSPO and the RTRS. They note, further, that ISEAL Alliance's decision not to define 'sustainability', coupled with its process approach to code development, has led to the departure of an important founding member, IFOAM. According to IFOAM's executive director, 'we had to leave ISEAL. We stepped out because we could not actually ally with those people – too much greenwashing!' (quoted in Loconto and Fouilleux 2014, p. 170).[2]

11.5 LESSONS FOR THE FINANCE SECTOR: AN ASSESSMENT OF FAIR TAX MARK

What lessons might the tax justice movement learn from the FSC and FI experience and the ISEAL Alliance's approach to standard setting? In this section, we analyse the legitimacy of a new and intriguing financial sector initiative outlined in Chapter 10, Fair Tax Mark, and assess its approach against the ISEAL Alliance's Code of Good Practice for the setting of sustainability standards. The assessment reveals significant gaps in FTM's current structure and operation, suggesting that it, too, will need to evolve if it is to have the impact on the financial sector its supporters desire.

Fair Tax Mark

As noted in Chapter 10, FTM was officially launched in 2014 following the efforts of a group of British-based tax justice and consumer ethics campaigners, and consequently its scope is currently limited to UK-based companies despite the longer-term goal of scaling up to cover other jurisdictions. FTM's objective is to license businesses deemed to be practising transparent and 'fair' accounting, enabling qualifying companies to use FTM's kite-shaped logo on payment of a fee. The mission of FTM, and the broader TJN movement, is to '"change the weather" on a wide range of issues related to tax, tax havens and financial globalisation' and to 'push for systemic change' (TJN 2016). This activism has in turn been sparked by clear evidence of significant levels of tax avoidance, including by brand-name corporations like Google, Starbucks and Apple, and the associated public outrage that companies earning billions of dollars apparently pay very low – and sometimes no – tax on their profits in the jurisdictions in which they do a great deal of business (e.g. Lanis et al. 2015).

In seeking to 'change the weather' on corporate tax practices, TJN focuses on research and advocacy and draws on the expertise of its network of academics and experts in fields such as taxation, accounting, finance and law (TJN 2016; this volume, Chapter 4). Actual campaigns around tax justice themes are devolved to another body, the Global Alliance for Tax Justice (GATJ), which comprises five regional networks (in Asia–Australia, Latin America and Caribbean, Africa, Europe and North America) and which in turn receives support from some major development CSOs such as ActionAid, Christian Aid and Oxfam (TJN 2016). FTM can thus be viewed as an innovative element in TJN's strategy to improve tax transparency and ensure corporations are paying their 'fair' share. Ultimate success for FTM, however, will depend on its capacity to scale up and move beyond its UK-exclusive focus to encompass more companies in more jurisdictions, particularly in the European Union and North America. It also will need to manage the challenges being mounted to its legitimacy from external audiences linked to MNCs and their tax accountant and government defenders.

To determine which businesses qualify, FTM has developed two different standards: one for solely UK-based companies and another for

UK-based multinational corporations (FTM 2016a).[3] The standard for solely UK-based companies consists of two parts: one dealing with tax transparency and another with tax rate, tax avoidance and tax disclosure.

Criteria listed under 'transparency' include the requirement to publish a full set of tax accounts and clearly state the company's business, beneficial owners and corporate directors. FTM's focus on tax transparency reflects the broader history of the TJN, where transparency was perceived early on to be essential in generating relevant public information around which effective civil society campaigns could be mobilised (Christians 2013).

The second component of FTM's solely UK company standard focuses on the 'fairness' of the taxes actually paid. This is a more controversial and contestable issue, especially for tax accountants, for whom notions of fairness are very much in the eye of the beholder (this volume, Chapter 6). This point was made pointedly at a 2014 forum organised by the online magazine *Taxation* by a partner at the legal firm Pinsent Masons, who stated: 'You are putting forward a proposal that is introducing confusion, doubt and uncertainty in the minds of the general public who do not understand how tax works in this country. I don't think there is such a thing as a fair amount of tax' (quoted in Goodall 2014). The standard's methodology to assess fairness is to compare the average tax paid by the company to the average effective tax rate in the UK and to award points based on the degree to which the two deviate. To do this, companies are provided with a template to calculate the taxes paid in the previous four years, the annual difference between those taxes and the national effective tax rate, and the average tax paid and average effective tax rate. Points are awarded for alignment with the average effective tax rate on a sliding scale until no points are awarded for deviations beyond 7 per cent below the target rate (FTM 2014a).

Since FTM was launched in February 2014, over 30 companies have been licensed to its solely UK standard and none to its UK-based multinational standard (FTM 2016b). Of the companies licensed to its solely UK standard, one is a FTSE 100 company, the energy provider SSE (originally Scottish and Southern Energy), which 'is involved in the generation, transmission, distribution and supply of electricity, in the production, storage, distribution and supply of gas and in other energy services' (SSE 2016). Of the other companies licensed to use the FTM logo, the majority are co-operatives, including Midcounties Co-operative, the Phone Co-op, East of England Co-op, the Radstock Co-operative, Co-operatives UK and the Co-operative Group. It is unclear why so many co-operatives have signed up to FTM, but it may reflect the fact that the core principles of the co-operative movement include 'voluntary and open membership' and 'concern for community', both of which are compatible with FTM's focus on transparency and fairness. It may also reflect the background of FTM's UK founders, many of whom have strong connections to the UK co-operative movement.

Assessing Fair Tax Mark's Legitimacy

It is difficult to judge whether the number and type of companies signing up to become licensed to use the FTM's logo represent significant success or not. Given the organisation has been operational for only a few years, the fact that it has successfully reviewed and licensed around 30 businesses may be regarded as a success. Indeed FTM staff are pleased with progress to date and argue that the rate of uptake of the standard has been faster than when early consumer product standards were introduced in the 1980s. On the other hand, the number of FTM businesses represents only a tiny fraction of solely UK-based businesses, and the non-issuing of any UK-based MNCs' licences must be a source of concern, since it is MNCs that have been especially targeted by tax justice activists for defending and exploiting national loopholes to minimise tax liabilities. While it is premature to pass judgement on FTM's success, the lessons from our case studies are that it will need to further evolve – in the UK and beyond – if it is to move from a niche to a mainstream standard and have a significant impact either indirectly by influencing national regulation (by demonstrating the feasibility of more transparent reporting standards) or by influencing corporate tax compliance standards directly.

To assess the legitimacy of FTM's current arrangements, we can compare its standards development, stakeholder engagement and institutional arrangements to those adopted by FSC and FI and articulated in the ISEAL Alliance's Code of Good Practice. Notably, FTM has come under significant criticism from internal and external stakeholders for aspects of its standards development process. Key criticisms have been the in-house nature of the standards development process, the lack of a standards development plan, opacity with regard to consultation procedures and, perhaps especially, the use of very short timelines for stakeholder feedback. FTM's official account of its standards development processes is set out in each of its two standards, with the standard for UK-based MNCs stating:

> The Fair Tax Mark criteria are the result of extensive research and development. This has involved a broad range of stakeholders including civil society NGOs, business representatives and industry practitioners. Input has also come from our group of independent technical advisors drawn from academia and the professions.
>
> As part of this process, feedback on at least two drafts of this document was invited via open consultation and the responses incorporated into the final

> version. The first consultation of two weeks was in June 2014 with an additional week for the second draft in September of the same year. (FTM 2014d, p. 5)

This account is both vague and concerning. Missing elements in the account include (a) the date of the public notification of the intention to develop the standard and (b) the date of circulation of the standard's terms of reference and for stakeholder input on these. Concerning elements are that, while information is provided of the general date of circulation of the first draft of the standard and the timelines for stakeholder feedback on the draft, these are very short and do not conform to the ISEAL Codes requirements (a minimum of 60 days for initial consultation and 30 days for subsequent consultation rounds). Finally, although a report was subsequently prepared of stakeholder comments, it is not clear how these were addressed in the final standard document.

That FTM's standards development process has caused some stakeholder concern is evident from the comments made on the UK-based MNC standard (FTM 2014b). The first of the five submissions noted that 'I would firstly note that 2 weeks is not a long time for this, and I have not been able to take the time I would have wished to examine the issues in detail.' The second respondent drew attention to 'a blink-and-you'll-miss-it open consultation period', while the third stated that 'It would have been helpful to allow a longer period for consultation, particularly as it has taken a year to develop the criteria.' The fourth submission, from the Confederation of British Industry, noted that 'the formal consultation period was too short', and only the fifth and final responder did not comment on the shortness of the consultation period. The fact that there were only five respondents could be taken as an indication of the very short consultation times utilised.

Another key area where FTM has been criticised is with regard to stakeholder engagement. As noted in the previous paragraph, only five submissions were received on FTM's draft standard, reflecting the very short timeline provided and a lack of outreach to the broader community. The perception within the TJN and beyond is that the FTM is dominated by a single personality, who is deeply involved in all aspects of its development and operation to the detriment of wider stakeholder participation and consultation. Highlighting this concern, a member of FTM's technical advisory panel is reported as seeking 'to dispel the "myth" that the FTM was "an emanation of Richard [Murphy]"' and that while 'Murphy was "clearly a driver" behind the FTM . . . my experience of it isn't of being steamrollered by Richard' (Goodall 2014, p. 3). While this observation regarding Murphy's role may be the case, external perceptions matter, and many stakeholders appear to be suspicious of FTM's motives and actions.

Thus, in making comments on the UK-based MNC standard, and in her personal capacity and not as an employee of the Confederation of British Industry, Heather Self commented on the short consultation period provided that, 'Unfortunately, the impression given is that the Fair Tax Mark organisation does not want to engage constructively with the wider business community' (FTM 2014b, p. 5). The former editor of *Taxation*, the British tax magazine published by LexisNexis, Mike Truman, is reported as suggesting that FTM's founders 'might have to give up some control and allow other interested parties to get involved. . ..“I do think it's going to need to be owned by the community”' (quoted in Goodall 2014, p. 3).

The above comments suggest the need for FTM to engage with the broader internal and external stakeholder community regarding tax transparency and fairness, a perception confirmed by a consideration of the ISEAL Alliance's requirements regarding the same. According to ISEAL's Code of Best Practice, GSOs are expected among other things (a) to develop and/or update a list of stakeholders, (b) to ensure participation is available to all stakeholders, (c) to identify stakeholder groups that are not adequately represented and seek to secure their representation, and (d) to ensure a reasonable balance of stakeholders on the committee responsible for standards development. The information available on FTM's website and the comments of internal and external stakeholders all suggest significant improvements are required with regard to stakeholder engagement. Our case studies of FSC and FI support this requirement, as both have sought to engage meaningfully with a larger number of stakeholders as part of their broader legitimating strategies.

As currently structured, FTM is a co-operative under the UK's Co-operative and Community Benefit Societies Act 2014. Of its current board of seven members, two are closely associated with activist groups on taxation, via the Tax Research UK website, and four with ethical consumption more broadly, with the Ethical Consumer Research Association. Practically, the Association manages FTM's operation on a day-to-day basis under the guidance of the directors, who meet every two months (FTM 2014c). FTM has also established an eight-member technical advisory panel with expertise in areas such as accounting, finance, international development and law to 'help shape the development of the Fair Tax Criteria from a range of different expert perspectives' (FTM 2016c). While FTM develops the standard and conducts assessments to the standard, it also has provisions for licensing independent assessors, with one licensee listed on its website (FTM 2016d). Not only is its board narrowly constituted and somewhat unbalanced in terms of representation, but the organisation is functioning as both a standard-setting and an accrediting organisation, in non-conformity with ISO 65/17065 provisions for the separation of these functions. While FTM remains a small, niche-focused organisation certifying mainly small, domestically oriented UK businesses, this may not be a critical issue. However, as the cases of FSC and FI indicate, if FTM intends to scale up its activity to influence the tax practices of globalised MNCs, it will need to give further consideration to how it structures its governing body and to whether it would be better served by splitting the standards development and accreditation functions.

Beyond these structural and operational concerns, and from a non-state market-driven perspective, there may be merit in FTM engaging in a conforming strategy and reaching out to two currently disengaged audiences. Our analysis highlights how FTM has focused on using informing and converting strategies to convince the general public and domestic, mainly co-operative, businesses of the merits of its approach. This strategy ignores the intersection between two other potentially supportive audiences. First, there is a segment of the UK business community that is already compliant with FTM's system but as yet sees no reason to support FTM's scheme. One reason for its reticence is that there is a second audience, a segment of the accounting profession interested in promoting greater tax fairness, that has been excluded from participation. The first audience is unlikely to sign up to FTM unless encouraged to do so by the second audience; and the second audience is unlikely to be so motivated unless FTM engages in some conforming moves towards it. Thus, while a conforming strategy targeting *all* businesses and *all* accountants would result in a race-to-the-bottom compromise, an opening up of FTM's operation and processes to greater engagement, scrutiny and participation by a larger segment of sympathetic accounting professionals could assist in rapidly mainstreaming tax certification through the segment of currently compliant businesses. In the absence of such a conforming strategy, FTM will likely remain a niche certification initiative and, to that extent, not as effective as intended.

11.6 CONCLUSIONS

In this chapter, we have teased out some of the lessons to be learned from case studies of two long-established GSOs for the structure and operation of FTM. Noting that both FSC and FI have undergone a significant evolution in terms of standards development procedures, governance structure and institutional arrangements, and that there is now a substantial degree of knowledge available to those developing environmental and social sustainability standards as contained in ISEAL's Codes of Good Practice, we examined the degree to which the lessons learned had been applied by a new GSO operating in the financial services sector. The results of our analysis suggest that FTM is still a niche GSO and that it has not yet fully considered the strategic environment in which it is operating. It is thus at a crossroads not dissimilar to that confronting the FSC and FI in the previous decade. Both FSC and FI were initiated by activists, the former deeply concerned about tropical deforestation and the latter about the exploitation of peasant producers in developing countries. Both sought to develop certification systems that would reward those companies that are 'doing the right thing'. However, both also evolved over the years to address a range of interests not originally included in the organisations' governance bodies or standards development processes and in doing so expanded their reach beyond the niche markets originally targeted. While some perceive this expansion as coming at the cost of diluting an otherwise rigorous standard, others may legitimately claim that it was a rebalancing of a standard's rigour to take account of the legitimate interests of previously excluded actors. If FTM chooses to follow in FSC's and FI's footsteps, then it will undoubtedly need to undergo a significant further evolution in governance structure, institutional form and standards development procedures.

NOTES

1. In 2012, ISO 65 was revised and replaced with ISO 17065, Conformity assessment – Requirements for bodies certifying products, processes and services. FLOCERT was reaccredited to the ISO 17065 Standard in 2015.
2. 'Greenwashing' is used to refer to firms that market themselves as more environmentally friendly than they actually are. It should also be noted that IOAS, a major organic accreditation organisation originally established by IFOAM in 1997, remains a member of the ISEAL Alliance. Like Accreditation Services International, which is also a member of the ISEAL Alliance, IOAS provides 'accreditation and assessment services to certification bodies working in organic agriculture' and 'works as the sole provider of accreditation against IFOAM norms and is heavily engaged in working in collaboration with regulators of the organic trade on international and national levels' (ISEAL Alliance 2016b). Therefore IFOAM's departure should not be construed as a blanket rejection by the organic sector of the ISEAL Alliance approach to meta-standards.
3. Curiously, FTM does not use the term 'standard' to refer to what is clearly otherwise a standard. Instead, both the UK-only and UK-multinational standards are referenced in 'Criteria Notes'.

REFERENCES

Auld, G. (2014), *Constructing Private Governance: The Rise and Evolution of Forest, Coffee, and Fisheries Certification*, New Haven, CT: Yale University Press.

Bahra, P. (2009), 'Tea Workers Still Waiting to Reap Fairtrade Benefits', *Times* (UK), published electronically 2 January, available at https://www.thetimes.co.uk/

article/tea-workers-still-waiting-to-reap-fairtrade-benefits-5pstzp6xgz5 (accessed 10 June 2015).
Cashore, B., G. Auld and D. Newsom (2004), *Governing through Markets: Forest Certification and the Emergence of Non-State Authority*, New Haven, CT: Yale University Press.
Christians, A. (2013), 'Tax Activists and the Global Movement for Development through Transparency', in Y. Brauner and M. Stewart (eds), *Tax, Law and Development*, Cheltenham, UK and Northampton, MA, USA: Edward Elgar Publishing, pp. 288–315.
Fairtrade Australia New Zealand (2014), 'Fairtrade Delivering Change', available at https://fairtrade.com.au/news/fairtrade-delivering-change (accessed 18 June 2015).
FI (Fairtrade International) (2011a), 'Aims of Fairtrade Standards', available at http://www.fairtrade.net/aims-of-fairtrade-standards.html (accessed 18 June 2015).
FI (Fairtrade International) (2011b), 'Certifying Fairtrade', available at http://www.fairtrade.net/certifying-fairtrade.html (accessed 18 June 2015).
FI (Fairtrade International) (2014), *Strong Producers, Strong Future: Annual Report 2013–14*, available at http://www.fairtrade.net/fileadmin/user_upload/content/2009/resources/2013-14_AnnualReport_FairtradeIntl_web.pdf (accessed 18 June 2015).
FLOCERT (2015), 'About Us', available at http://www.flocert.net/about-us/ (accessed 18 June 2015).
FSC (Forest Stewardship Council) (2012), *FSC Dispute Resolution System*, Bonn: FSC International Centre, available at https://ic.fsc.org/en/stakeholders/dispute-resolution (accessed 10 January 2015).
FTM (Fair Tax Mark) (2014a), 'Sample Company Assessment Form', available at http://www.fairtaxmark.net/wp-content/uploads/2014/02/Final-Company-Report-Template1.pdf (accessed 13 January 2016).
FTM (Fair Tax Mark) (2014b), 'Responses to UK-Based Multinational Companies Criteria Consultation June/July 2014', available at http://www.fairtaxmark.net/wpcontent/uploads/2014/09/ Consultation-Responses.pdf (accessed 12 January 2016).
FTM (Fair Tax Mark) (2014c), 'Community Share Offer Document', available at http://www.fairtaxmark.net/wp-content/uploads/2014/04/Fair-Tax-Mark-Community-Share-Offer-28-April-2014.1.pdf (accessed 12 January 2016).
FTM (Fair Tax Mark) (2014d), 'Fair Tax: Fair Tax Mark Criteria Notes – UK-Based Multinationals 2014–2015', available at http://www.fairtaxmark.net/wp-content/uploads/2014/10/MNC-Criteria-Notes-2014-15.pdf (accessed 27 June 2018).
FTM (Fair Tax Mark) (2016a), 'Criteria', available at http://www.fairtaxmark.net/criteria/ (accessed 12 January 2016).
FTM (Fair Tax Mark) (2016b), 'Who's Got It', available at http://www.fairtaxmark.net/whos-got-it/ (accessed 12 January 2016).
FTM (Fair Tax Mark) (2016c), 'Advisors', available at http://www.fairtaxmark.net/who-we-are/advisors/ (accessed 12 January 2016).
FTM (Fair Tax Mark), (2016d), 'For Accountants', available at http://www.fairtaxmark.net/accountants/ (accessed 12 January 2016).
Gale, F.P. (1998), *The Tropical Timber Trade Regime*, Basingstoke: Palgrave Macmillan.

Gale, F. (2004), 'The Consultation Dilemma in Private Regulatory Regimes: Negotiating FSC Regional Standards in the United States and Canada', *Journal of Environmental Policy and Planning* **6** (1), 57–84.

Gale, F. and M. Haward (2011), *Global Commodity Governance: State Responses to Sustainable Forestry and Fisheries Certification*, Basingstoke: Palgrave Macmillan.

Gamper-Rabindran, S. and S. Finger (2013), 'Does Industry Self-Regulation Reduce Pollution? Responsible Care in the Chemical Industry', *Journal of Regulatory Economics* **43** (1), 1–30.

Goodall, A. (2014), 'Fair to Middling: Transparency Was a Key Issue at a Debate on the New Tax Standard', *Taxation*, published electronically 23 April, available at http://www.taxation.co.uk/taxation/Articles/2014/04/22/323501/fair-middling (accessed 11 January 2016).

Green, J. (2014), *Rethinking Private Authority: Agents and Entrepreneurs in Global Environmental Governance*, Princeton, NJ: Princeton University Press.

Heires, M. (2008), 'The International Organization for Standardization (ISO)', *New Political Economy* **13** (3), 357–367.

Held, D., A. McGrew, D. Goldblatt and J. Perraton (1999), *Global Transformations: Politics, Economics, Culture*, Stanford, CA: Stanford University Press.

ISEAL Alliance (2016a), 'About Us', available at http://www.isealalliance.org/about-us (accessed 9 January 2016).

ISEAL Alliance (2016b), 'IOAS', available at http://www.isealalliance.org/online-community/organisations/ioas (accessed 11 January 2016).

Jaffee, D. and P.H. Howard (2010), 'Corporate Cooptation of Organic and Fair Trade Standards', *Agriculture and Human Values* **27** (4), 387–399.

King, A. and M. Lennox (2000), 'Industry Self-Regulation without Sanctions: The Chemical Industry's Responsible Care Program', *Academy of Management Journal* **43** (4), 698–716.

Lanis, R., B. Govendir and R. McClure (2015), 'So Now We Know Which Companies Did Not Pay Tax: Time to Target Aggressive Avoidance', *The Conversation*, published electronically 18 December, available at https://theconversation.com/so-now-we-know-which-companies-did-not-pay-tax-time-to-target-aggressive-avoidance-52490 (accessed 11 January 2016).

Loconto, A. and E. Fouilleux (2014), 'Politics of Private Regulation: ISEAL and the Shaping of Transnational Sustainability Governance', *Regulation and Governance* **8** (2), 166–185.

Mutersbaugh, T. (2005), 'Just-in-Space: Certified Rural Products, Labour of Quality, and Regulatory Spaces', *Journal of Rural Studies* **21** (4), 389–402.

Pattberg, P. (2008), *Private Institutions and Global Governance: The New Politics of Environmental Sustainability*, Cheltenham, UK and Northampton, MA, USA: Edward Elgar Publishing.

Prakash, A. (2000), 'Responsible Care: An Assessment', *Business and Society* **39** (2), 183–209.

Renard, M.-C. (2005), 'Quality Certification, Regulation and Power in Fair Trade', *Journal of Rural Studies* **21** (4), 419–431.

Schouten, G. and P. Glasbergen (2011), 'Creating Legitimacy in Global Private Governance: The Case of the Roundtable on Sustainable Palm Oil', *Ecological Economics* **70** (11), 1891–1899.

SSE (2016) 'What We Do: Keeping the Lights On', available at http://sse.com/whatwedo/ (accessed 11 January 2016).

Suchman, M.C. (1995), 'Managing Legitimacy: Strategic and Institutional Approaches', *Academy of Management Review* **34** (3), 346–357.
Synnott, T. (2005), 'Some Notes on the Early Years of FSC', available at https://ic.fsc.org/download.notes-on-the-early-years-of-fsc.a-797.pdf (accessed 11 January 2016).
TJN (Tax Justice Network) (2016), 'Our Goals and Methods', available at http://www.taxjustice.net/about/who-we-are/goals/ (accessed 11 January 2016).
Tollefson, C., F. Gale and D. Haley (2008), *Setting the Standard: Governance, Certification and the Forest Stewardship Council*, Vancouver: University of British Columbia Press.
Tucker, A. (2006), 'Fair Enough?', *New Internationalist* **395**, 7.
TWS (The Wilderness Society) (2005), *Certifying the Incredible: The Australian Forestry Standard: Barely Legal and Not Sustainable*, November, Hobart: The Wilderness Society, available at https://cdn.wilderness.org.au/archive/pdf/Certifying_the_IncredibleFULLv3.pdf (accessed 31 January 2016).
UNEP (United Nations Environment Programme) (2013), 'Forests', in *Green Economy and Trade: Trends, Challenges and Opportunities*, Nairobi: United Nations Environment Programme, available at http://www.unep.org/greeneconomy/Portals/88/GETReport/pdf/chapitre_4_Forest.pdf (accessed 10 January 2016).
Wenban-Smith, M. (2007), '"Certified Once, Accepted Everywhere": Is the International Accreditation Forum (IAF) Part of the Solution or Part of the Problem?', Dovetail Partners Inc, available at http://www.dovetailinc.org/report_pdfs/2007/dovetailiaf0807wq.pdf (accessed 26 June 2018).

12. Whistleblowing and investigative journalism: reputational damage and the private governance of aggressive tax planning

Lachlan Johnson

12.1 INTRODUCTION

This volume has identified and analysed the growing political, regulatory and cultural challenges to aggressive tax avoidance strategies that multinational corporations (MNCs) have been forced to confront over past decades. These include increasingly sophisticated legal instruments to claw back offshored revenue, and a renewed political imperative to plug leaks in the corporate tax base in the wake of the Financial Crisis (FC). In addition to the civil society organisations and legal developments discussed in earlier chapters, whistleblowers and journalists are emerging as important actors in the international tax regime, subjecting the tax strategies of some of the world's most profitable companies to unprecedented public scrutiny. The revelation of aggressive tax practices by whistleblowers, leakers and investigative journalists can have a variety of impacts. It can intensify the zeal of regulators and authorities by providing them with otherwise unobtainable information. It can also tarnish the reputations of those companies that trade on their brand equity. Revelations that have followed acts of corporate whistleblowing or investigative journalism include some of the most explosive news stories of recent years; LuxLeaks, the Panama Papers and the Paradise Papers implicated a slew of corporate actors, business people, celebrities, sports stars and politicians in the systemic (and, in some cases, criminal) reduction of tax liabilities worth billions of US dollars to national governments the world over. In the wake of these events, whistleblowers and journalists are increasingly being recognised as important agents of transparency with clear potential to inflict reputational damage. Indeed, the outgoing chair of Australia's corporate regulator, the Australian Securities and Investments Commission, has stated that reputational damage following massive data leaks by whistleblowers was poised to overtake governments and regulators as 'the number one risk' for MNCs involved in tax avoidance or other corporate malfeasance (Medcraft 2017). Similarly, David Bradbury, the head of tax policy and statistics at the OECD, contends that the growing size and pace of corporate data leaks means that, 'if [MNCs] have sought to hide their affairs from tax authorities in the past, then they'll only be able to do that for so much longer before they get detected' (Bradbury 2017).

Despite their importance, however, the theoretical or conceptual place of leakers, journalists and whistleblowers in the international anti-avoidance regime is under-researched. As a result, while the impact of these actors and events on the political dynamics of corporate tax policy is undeniable, many important questions remain about what form that impact actually takes. Does greater public scrutiny of corporate tax planning lead to less tax evasion or avoidance? Have journalists and whistleblowers really been a catalyst for the 'tax justice' movement, or merely an accelerant? How does the transparency provided by whistleblowing and financial data leaking promote corporate social responsibility and limit tax avoidance? Most importantly, where change in the culture of aggressive tax avoidance does occur, is it the result of public pressure that follows revelation or transparency, or of increased regulatory and compliance pressure from reactive governments?

This chapter addresses these questions by describing some of the ways in which whistleblowing and investigative journalism have drawn attention to, and helped to counter, aggressive tax planning strategies. It identifies three different models for understanding the complex processes by which public scrutiny can skew the calculus of corporate tax avoidance or evasion. The first of these three models of whistleblowing's influence on tax avoidance is 'regulation by revelation', whereby transparency and public pressure directly impact the cost–benefit calculus of tax avoidance and evasion – in other words, a form of private governance. The second model is the ability of whistleblowers and journalists to enhance an issue's political salience, thereby forcing politicians and governments to address it. The role of issue salience is crucial in determining not only the rigour of government compliance measures, but also the bargaining power of corporate actors that wish to reduce the public profile of their activities or influence the course of policy making. The third model is the regulatory effects of whistleblower protection and incentivisation in normalising or institutionalising the process of whistleblower revelation. These frameworks are then applied to three recent case studies from the corporate tax arena, demonstrating their relevance to some recent high-profile journalistic or whistleblower revelations. This case study analysis promotes the theory that mandatory publication of key data from corporate tax filings, strong whistleblower protections, and information exchange between jurisdictions should increase the impact of journalism and civil society activism on curtailing tax avoidance and evasion. While the importance of whistleblowers and journalists is clear, existing theories do not fully capture the complex processes at play. This chapter therefore discusses the increasingly significant role these actors play in the complex and diverse activist networks which exploit both public and private channels of authority to achieve political change.

It is assumed here, following Gallemore et al. (2014, p. 1104), that tax planners are rational actors (this volume, Chapter 6). When developing a firm's tax strategy, it is reasonable to assume that those responsible weigh up all the options, assessing the financial or reputational risks, costs and benefits of each in turn. Aggressive strategies yield significant tax advantages for companies – the average effective tax rate paid by US businesses has fallen by 10 per cent over the last decade, and two-thirds of this decline can be attributed to profit shifting alone (Zucman 2014) – and the legal consequences are generally not prohibitive; on the contrary, as outlined in Chapter 2, many of the most egregious tax avoidance strategies are particularly galling owing to their apparent legality. The nature of most tax avoidance strategies, given the legal grey area in which they operate, is that the legality of a firm's tax position can only be determined by authoritative bodies after the fact; there is no *ex ante* legal distinction between avoidance and evasion (Lee et al. 2015, p. 21; this volume, Chapter 6). Even the risk of suffering severe reputational damage seems relatively low, although evidence presented in this volume suggests it has increased in recent years. The evidence on whether reputational damage governs corporate tax strategies is complex and generally points to only a relatively minor impact: most accounting scholars argue that its effects are small, short-lived (adverse effects on a firm's share price following public scrutiny of aggressive tax practices typically last around one month), confined to a relatively small subset of industries, or even virtually non-existent (Hanlon and Heitzman 2010; Gallemore et al. 2014; Graham et al. 2014; this volume, Chapter 7). For instance, when Apple's preferential tax deal with Ireland was judged by the EU to be illegal in 2016, the Irish government challenged the ruling on the grounds that it would cause reputational damage not to Apple, but to *Ireland's* brand association with tax leniency (Farrell and McDonald 2016).

The crucial question, considering that corporate actors, especially those not heavily reliant on valuable consumer-based brand equity (Austin and Wilson 2017), can avoid large amounts of tax with relatively meagre consequences, is why many firms *do not* engage in aggressive tax minimisation strategies. This chapter aims to shed some light on this problem – often referred to as the 'under-sheltering puzzle' (see Gallemore et al. 2014) – by considering the impacts of whistleblowing and activist journalism upon public perceptions of the importance and morality of tax avoidance. By discussing how three models of private governance that have proven effective in other seemingly intractable policy domains may increasingly relate to the problem of MNC tax avoidance as well, this chapter aims to generate some insights into the regulation of aggressive tax planning.

12.2 REGULATION THROUGH REVELATION

A great deal of the power corporate actors wield in the conduct of their tax affairs comes from opacity and secrecy (Sikka 2010). MNCs enjoy a formidable ability not only to hide their tax arrangements from view (via complex transfer pricing arrangements, for example), but also to influence the regulatory regimes within which they operate. The costs of public sanction, regulatory crackdowns resulting from increased public scrutiny, or political responses to inflamed public sentiment mean that the effectiveness of MNC tax avoidance relies to some extent on the ability of corporate tax planners to conceal it. Evidence of MNC investment patterns in tax haven jurisdictions strongly supports this contention – corporate actors investing in tax havens do so not only for the low rates of tax they pay, but also for the opacity on offer (Braun and Weichenrieder 2015). Therefore, one way to interpret the impact of whistleblowing and investigative journalism on tax planning is to consider its effect on the likelihood of aggressive tax practices being exposed to public scrutiny. As the 'regulation through revelation' thesis, drawn from the environmental protection literature, proposes, sunlight may be the best disinfectant in the design of effective regulatory regimes.

The concept of regulation through revelation was propounded by James T. Hamilton to describe the impact of the US Toxic Release Inventory (TRI) on the transfer and disposal of toxic industrial chemicals in the United States (Hamilton 2005). Hamilton's history of the TRI, the first publicly accessible electronic database ever created by a US government agency, builds a compelling argument that transparency itself has been a powerful form of regulation of chemical transfers and disposal in manufacturing and heavy industry. In other words, subjecting industrial facilities above a threshold size to the scrutiny of routine public reporting has been more effective than increases in compliance pressures, emissions permit systems, or tax and subsidy programmes at reducing toxic chemical emissions. By way of example, Hamilton discusses the TRI's introduction in the state of Louisiana, where usage of the 650 different toxic chemicals reportable to the Environmental Protection Agency fell by 82 per cent between the first year of the TRI scheme (1987) and 2001. Its inception sparked an estimated US$5 billion in investment aimed at reducing toxic emissions during those years in Louisiana alone (Hamilton 2005, pp. 4–5).

The TRI presents an equally interesting study in policy transfer, with similar schemes being developed in Canada, Mexico, Norway, Wales, England, China, the Philippines, India and Australia following its successes in the US. Like the US, which saw national reductions in toxic chemical usage in industrial facilities of the order of 50 per cent, these countries experienced significant reductions in chemical pollution and emissions from manufacturing plants. In all of these jurisdictions, the success of mandatory reporting lay in the fact that these publicly accessible databases quickly became the primary barometer used by NGOs, government agencies, journalists, lawmakers and investors alike to evaluate an industrial manufacturer's environmental performance. Hamilton's (2005) conclusion that, for these reasons, increased transparency should be conceptualised as a regulatory tool alongside compliance and penalty measures presents an equally useful way to understand the impact of information revelation on tax avoidance. There is ample evidence to demonstrate that both government information reporting or exchange programmes and less official channels, like whistleblowing and investigative journalism, can function as regulation through revelation on corporate tax planning.

A very significant amount of the work of exposing evasive or opaque tax practices, particularly those strategies centred around offshoring profits or liabilities, has been carried out by journalists and NGOs. With help from leakers and whistleblowers, organisations such as the Tax Justice Network, Fair Tax Mark, Oxfam, Whistleblowers International, UK Uncut, the International Consortium of Investigative Journalists (ICIJ) and many others have been steadily increasing transparency in the international tax system. As Robert Dover writes, 'the major accelerants in making aggressive tax planning salient in the policy sphere have largely come through the series of leaks from whistleblowers in Luxembourg, Liechtenstein, and Panama' (Dover 2016b, p. 108). These leaks and investigations can serve to regulate tax avoidance by subjecting the activities of MNCs to a vastly increased level of public scrutiny.

One example of the negative impact of an MNC's implication in tax avoidance or evasion is the impact on the willingness of investors to buy stock in companies they perceive as having aggressive tax minimisation strategies. In a study investigating the likelihood of individual investors to buy stock in firms paying very low marginal tax rates,[1] Rego et al. (2017) found that firms engaged in avoidance are perceived as having a higher risk of detection or reputational damage, and are less favoured by investors as a result. Similarly, Graham et al. (2014) contend that tax planners' *perception* of the risk of reputational damage is a significant deterrent to aggressive tax avoidance even if there is scant evidence to indicate that such reputational damage will actually occur. They found, in a survey of 594 tax executives, that 69 per cent were deterred from adopting more aggressive tax planning strategies by the perceived risk of reputational damage. Furthermore, they point to the significance of reputation as a determinant of tax practices for different types of firms, showing that larger firms, publicly traded firms, and firms in the retail industry are more sensitive to the perceived risks associated with reputational damage (Graham et al. 2014, p. 993).

A good illustration of the reasons tax planners fear reputational damage is the case of Starbucks in the United Kingdom. As was mentioned in Chapters 5 and 7, in 2012 a Reuters special report revealed that Starbucks, despite a rapid expansion and growing market share in the UK, had paid just £8.6 million in corporate income tax over the preceding 14 years (Bergin 2012). The ensuing scandal saw protests at Starbucks outlets, public boycott campaigns, and heavy media coverage of the business's tax affairs. The café chain was even pilloried by British prime minister David Cameron at the World Economic Forum in Davos the following year, when he called on them to 'wake up and smell the coffee' (Elliott and Stewart 2013). The Starbucks case illustrates the important linkages between journalistic revelation, exposure and scrutiny, public pressure and political pressure. Importantly, even though it was never prosecuted for illegal evasion, Starbucks stated that it would forgo £20 million in legal deductions in an attempt to quell public disaffection. It is a valuable example of the reasons motivating firms with high consumer-based brand equity to be generally less likely to engage in tax avoidance that carries the risk of attracting negative publicity and public/political scrutiny like that faced by Starbucks (Austin and Wilson 2017, p. 68).

Starbucks' experience, although relatively sensational, should not be considered anomalous. On the contrary, there is strong evidence that, once knowledge of a company's aggressive tax practices becomes widespread and the practices are subjected to public condemnation, a significant proportion of consumers change their perceptions of that company. A survey of UK taxpayers in 2014 found that 84 per cent of respondents believed legal tax minimisation to be unethical. Moreover, at the time of the survey, 25 per cent were currently involved in boycotting a company that they saw as not paying a fair amount of tax, and 39 per cent of respondents indicated that they would boycott a company if they became aware of its involvement in aggressive tax planning (Christian Aid 2013). Even when the kind of reputational damage suffered by Starbucks might ultimately not be reflected in sales or its share prices, the perceived risk of being exposed to volatile changes in public attitudes can be enough to deter some firms from adopting more aggressive tax avoidance strategies. A developing public distaste for tax avoidance has not, however, had uniform effects. As the above polling data show, if interpreted another way, a large proportion of customers (almost two-thirds) are *not* willing to boycott firms implicated in tax avoidance. Indeed, some of the most notorious and frequently targeted offenders – such as Apple, Amazon and Google – show no signs of having suffered adverse reputational consequences following their implication in elaborate tax avoidance strategies.

Even despite this conflicting evidence, however, firms' fears of reputational damage and diminished investor confidence resulting from public implication in aggressive tax minimisation do follow a general trend in which increased transparency is associated with reduced tax avoidance. In US studies comparing various IRS mandatory tax disclosure regimes it has been shown that a firm's rate of compliance is strongly influenced by its perception of how informative that particular tax schedule is. Henry et al. (2016, p. 811), for example, show that tax disclosure regimes perceived to have less rigorous information provision requirements are associated with higher rates of tax avoidance, and those perceived to have more strenuous information requirements are associated with lower rates of avoidance. The regulation by revelation argument is a good fit for the governance of legal tax avoidance and minimisation strategies owing to the reluctance of MNCs to risk the adverse effects of reputational damage, media scandal and popular sanction. This same rationale underlies the continued calls of tax justice NGOs for information publication initiatives such as country-by-country reporting and registers of beneficial ownership (Murphy and Christensen 2012; Oxfam Australia 2016).

Campaigns for companies to report the location of their sales activity, employees, assets, and income taxes paid are rapidly gaining traction, and country-by-country reporting is being adopted in many jurisdictions, including Australia, Canada, the EU and Norway (Moss et al. 2016). Perhaps more importantly still, 64 countries have now signed on to the OECD's Multilateral Competent Authority Agreement on the Exchange of Country-by-Country Reports, which means that parties to the agreement will automatically share reporting information received through CbC reporting from MNCs with the tax authorities of all other jurisdictions in which that MNC operates, although, as has been noted previously, the OECD standard is intergovernmental and does not require the publication of CbCR data (OECD 2017). The Australian government has also taken the step of publishing income, taxable income and tax payable data for privately owned companies with incomes of $200 million or more (Liddy 2016).

12.3 ISSUE SALIENCE AND POLITICAL PRESSURE

The second conceptual approach to understanding the impact of whistle-blower revelations on tax avoidance is the argument that they spur political and regulatory momentum generated by increased issue salience. This approach is most useful in explaining legal tax minimisation rather than illegal evasion. As Robert Dover argues, it also lays a significant amount of blame at the feet of legislators and tax codes, as opposed to companies acting within the rules that may have an understandable incentive to minimise their liabilities using existing loopholes or weak provisions (Dover 2016a, p. 41). Thus, this approach hinges on the political potency of popular perceptions of what constitutes a fair or equitable tax burden for an MNC. For this reason, the impact of popular disaffection on tax policy has been criticised by those, like Allison Christians (see this volume, Chapter 10), who consider popular sentiment – a 'soft-law approach' – to be a dangerous influence on the drafting of tax provisions (Christians 2013, pp. 39–41).

Even though she believes that social sanction is not the best driver of tax policy, however, Christians concedes that it is often something of a political reality (Christians 2013, p. 39). High issue salience restricts the bargaining power of corporate actors because, even though they may have exercised significant influence through lobbying or campaign funding and donations in the past, the rising place of tax avoidance on the political agenda makes political actors more sensitive to the perception that they may be viewed as pandering to special interests. Culpepper refers to such issue arenas, in which corporate interests enjoy a high degree of influence away from the public spotlight, as 'quiet politics'. 'Organised managers', he argues, 'typically prevail in political conflicts over corporate control because those issues are of little immediate interest to most voters' (Culpepper 2011, p. 4). While this may have been true of corporation tax policy in the past, growing levels of awareness and concern about this issue, as well as conditions of sluggish wage growth and austerity following the Financial Crisis, are rapidly making MNC tax avoidance a hot button issue (this volume, Chapter 3). As Robert Dover argues,

> business interests are able to use their technical and structural advantages to shape legislative and regulatory reforms at times when an issue – such as corporate tax reform – has low issue salience. The converse is true when an issue is highly salient in public and political circles. Then the structural advantages can be minimised because legislators and international organisations are keen to guard against the charge that they are being unduly influenced by special/sectoral interests. (Dover 2016a, p. 42)

Where corporate actors may have had the upper hand prior to the FC, increased issue salience instead heightens the power of critics of aggressive tax planning, such as tax justice NGOs, whistleblowers and activist journalists.

This transition of corporate tax policy from a low to a high level of issue salience occurred following the Financial Crisis of 2007–08 (Dover 2016a). As documented in Chapter 3, this is because the FC increased public sensitivity to the 'unfairness' or 'injustice' of legal but 'unethical' offshoring of profits. Austerity measures, particularly in Europe, contributed to a heightened public awareness of the disparity between the contributions individuals and corporations were being asked to make to fiscal consolidation. As a result, the tangible feeling of a deep power imbalance between the abilities of ordinary people and MNCs to minimise their tax burden increased the political potency of tax avoidance, thus increasing the desire of policy makers to be seen to be addressing the problem. Furthermore, evidence from Australian public companies shows a significant positive correlation between the financial pressures associated with the FC and the likelihood that corporate actors would implement an aggressive tax minimisation strategy. As Richardson et al. (2015) show, the cost–benefit calculus of tax avoidance was skewed by the financial distress caused by investor risk shifting and the credit crunch in the wake of the US housing market collapse in 2007. Their analysis finds a strong correlation between financial stress and tax avoidance, magnified especially during the FC, and also observed that the relationship between board independence and financial distress is positively associated with aggressive tax minimisation (Richardson et al. 2015, pp. 112–113). The FC was the perfect storm for the issue salience of tax minimisation because, even as ordinary people were becoming more sensitive to its perceived unfairness and immorality, companies were engaging in tax avoidance more readily and more aggressively than ever before.

Journalistic and whistleblower revelations fitted into this dynamic in two ways. First, they fuelled the fire of public antipathy towards tax avoidance, and, second, they provided the evidence and information used by policy makers to either prosecute offenders or push for reforms. Examples of policy action that have been a result of the increasing issue salience of MNC tax avoidance include the OECD's Base Erosion and Profit Shifting (BEPS) Plan (2015), the European Commission's Anti-Tax Avoidance Package (2016), and a plethora of recent unilateral initiatives.

12.4 WHISTLEBLOWING AS GOVERNANCE

The third interpretation of the impact of whistleblowing on aggressive tax planning is evident in Porter and Ronit's framework for the normalisation and institutionalisation of whistleblowing itself acting as a form of governance. Porter and Ronit argue that a changing media landscape, evolving attitudes towards internal whistleblowing, technological data-sharing advances, and the growing expository power of private whistleblowing individuals compared with official agencies and governments are driving a cultural shift towards greater transparency. Rather than being viewed as either a 'heroic or a criminal act of an individual', they argue, whistleblowing should be understood as 'an increasingly well-established regulatory tool that is diffusing globally' (Porter and Ronit 2016, p. 4). This work follows a broader reconceptualisation of the role of whistleblowing both in internal corporate governance and in external regulation of business practices. Andrade argues that whistleblowers have formerly been subject to dichotomous attitudes and polarisation based on a central dilemma of conflicting loyalties, and thus either praised or scorned for exposing wrongdoing. Rather, a whistleblower should, according to Andrade, be viewed not as an anomalous representative of external interests, but as constituting 'the ethical boundary' of an organisation (Andrade 2015, p. 322).

Whistleblowing can be a crucially important element of an organisation's risk management strategy, as large corporate actors have an enormous incentive to manage allegations of wrongdoing 'in-house' rather than under the public spotlight. A large majority of whistleblowing reports occur internally rather than being passed on to the media or government agencies and, in most cases, are only directed externally after internal reporting is deemed to have failed (Porter and Ronit 2016, p. 5). Porter and Ronit (2016) outline the growing prominence of whistleblowing as a form of governance of aggressive tax planning in three dimensions.

First, it is characterised by the growing importance of private actors relative to institutional or official ones. A growing culture of popular antipathy towards tax avoidance coupled with corporate efforts to maintain a certain level of secrecy regarding their tax affairs has disproportionately empowered individuals acting from inside organisations. Disgruntled internal whistleblowers reacting against wrongdoing by their employer organisations, such as Hervé Falciani, Antoine Deltour and Heinrich Kieber, have been the source of some of the most incendiary financial data leaks of recent years. The second element is an increasing recognition of the benefits of encouraging or incentivising external whistleblowing. The IRS, for example, gives cash payments and rewards to private citizens who provide tip-offs about tax avoidance, and the European Commission loudly praised and lauded the whistleblowing efforts of Antoine Deltour even as he was being sentenced in Luxembourg. Thus, while the relationship between whistleblowers and governments is complex, and often typified by viciously competing interests, there is a growing acceptance of the value of whistleblowing, and in some cases it is becoming institutionalised and supported by governments. The protections available to external whistleblowers under the section 922 provisions of the Dodd–Frank Act are a strong example of this emerging trend. Porter and Ronit (2016)'s third element is the relationship between whistleblowing and the media. There is a clear and growing public appetite for stories about whistleblowers revealing tax avoidance and evasion by the world's wealthiest corporations and individuals. The ease with which whistleblowers can connect leaked or stolen data with well-resourced, transboundary digital media organisations (like the ICIJ) makes it quicker and easier for leakers to engage directly with a moralised international public sphere whose tax literacy is improving rapidly (Porter and Ronit 2016).

12.5 ILLUSTRATIVE CASE STUDIES

Whistleblowers and investigative journalists regularly bring information to light that official actors, for various reasons, fail to reveal. The practical importance of whistleblowing can be easily demonstrated in numerous cases where a whistleblower or a journalistic revelation has been instrumental to the recapturing of offshored revenues or to the detection of fraudulent accounting practices. This section will discuss the role of whistleblowers and investigative journalism in three such relevant case studies: Goldman Sachs's compromised settlement with HM Revenue and Customs (HMRC), Caterpillar's transfer pricing practices, and pharmaceuticals giant Shire's deal with the Luxembourg tax authorities. These cases share some important commonalities, which will be highlighted as an illustration of the increasingly prominent private governance roles played by whistleblowers and investigative journalists. They are also used to highlight the cyclical and interdependent nature, represented in Figure 12.1, of the relationship between public attitudes, regulatory appetite, corporate tax behaviour, and media interest in corporate tax practices.

The case studies discussed here demonstrate some of the ways in which whistleblowing and journalism can function as a private/non-official mode of governance of aggressive tax planning. The question remains, though,

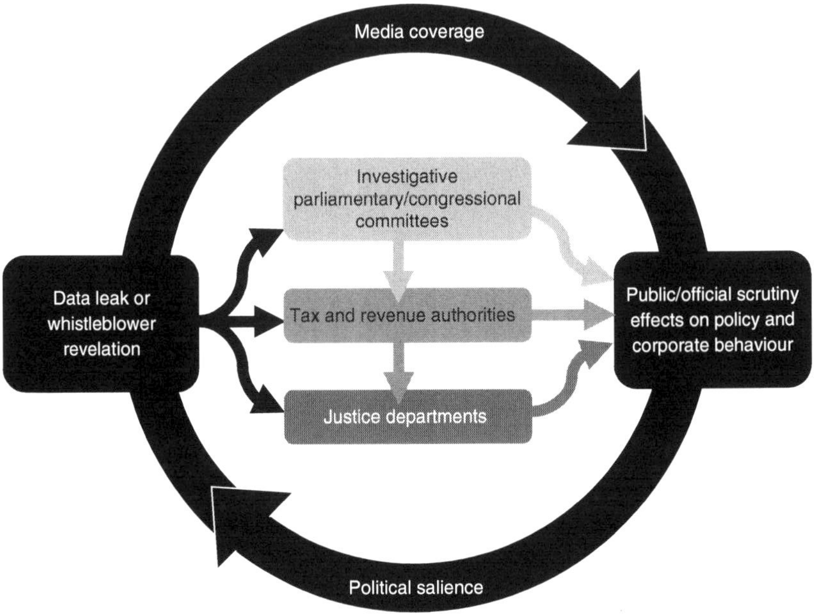

Figure 12.1 Issue salience/public attention cycle

how these studies should be linked in to the rational decision-making calculus of a tax planner. The answer is that the increasing incidence of whistleblowing in the tax avoidance space corresponds to a rapidly changing view of tax avoidance among the general population. Survey data show that the perceived moral severity of aggressive tax planning has increased enormously over the past three to five years (ActionAid 2013; Christian Aid 2013; Doherty 2015; Essential Research 2016; Shah 2016; Dawson 2017). This change towards the development of a moral or ethical dimension to the average person's perception of the problem, plus the advent of various measures either incentivising or protecting whistleblowers and the practice of whistleblowing, explains why the Dodd–Frank Office of the Whistleblower has been receiving an increasing number of tip-offs year on year and is gathering more revenue accordingly (US Securities and Exchange Commission 2016). Moreover, it is reflective of a trend whereby tax avoidance and deceptive accounting practices are quickly coming to be recognised with the same level of disdain and severity as various other kinds of white-collar crimes, frauds and false claims (Whistleblowers International 2017).

CASE STUDY NO. 1: PAC, HMRC AND GOLDMAN SACHS

The first case to be discussed here concerns the 2011 settlement between the UK arm of bank Goldman Sachs and HM Revenue and Customs. Goldman Sachs established a system whereby its employees were ostensibly 'seconded' from a subsidiary in the British Virgin Islands, allowing the company to avoid National Insurance contributions and obscuring the size of bonuses being paid to its bankers. This payment structure (along with similar systems used by other UK banks) was challenged by HMRC as an avoidance scheme in 2005, but Goldman Sachs refused to settle the outstanding payments, instead litigating the issue for a further five years. When the bank eventually settled, it was forgiven about £5 million to £8 million worth of interest that, according to HMRC guidelines, should have been collected (Syal and Mulholland 2011). Owing to provisions protecting the privacy of individual taxpayers, conflicting or hazy interpretations of administrative discretion and legal privilege within HMRC, and cosy relations between HMRC commissioners and finance executives, Parliament's exercise of any effective oversight of HMRC's decision was hamstrung. As former chair of the UK Public Accounts Committee (PAC) Margaret Hodge writes, 'we only learned about Goldman Sachs because of thorough and tough investigative journalism and the actions of a brave whistleblower' (Hodge 2016, p. 70).

The HMRC and Goldman Sachs case demonstrates some of the reasons why revelations about aggressive tax practices often come disproportionately from journalists, whistleblowers and civil society actors rather than through official channels. The first concerns issues of administrative discretion in non-ministerial departments, like HMRC, that are technically accountable to Parliament but that naturally require greater responsibility from high-level civil servants. In practice, this means that civil servants at HMRC must balance pragmatic considerations, such as the likelihood that they will succeed in litigation against any given party with the resources at their disposal, with ethical ones, such as their obligation not to treat any one taxpayer more leniently or more harshly than another (Freedman and Vella 2011, pp. 79–84). Where oversight is scant and resources are scarce, this balancing act can easily lead to perceptions of ethical compromise. In the HMRC example, proper process was compromised by the fact that the department's pool of expert tax commissioners was so small that the people who wrote the Goldman Sachs agreement were also responsible for signing off on its final approval. As the PAC's report concluded, 'there was no proper separation between the negotiation and approval of the settlement because one or both of the Commissioners signing off the settlement had also been involved in the negotiations' (UK Public Accounts Committee 2012).

The second problem is that the complexity of tax law creates opportunities for perverse influence and regulatory capture. A case Hodge cites in illustration of this point is the development of patent box tax relief, which was intended to support the commercialisation of patents and job creation from R&D in the UK. Patent box relief lowers the corporate tax rate on profits generated from patents incorporated in the UK. Companies thus calculate income that qualifies as a revenue stream flowing from a UK patent, and then calculate profits from this income using an HMRC formula and claim a corporate tax deduction on the eligible profits. Many such schemes are drafted with the help of expertise from the private sector, but for tax legislation this outside expertise is regularly drawn from companies whose core business activities involve minimising their clients' tax liabilities (this volume, Chapter 6). In the case of UK patent box relief, this took the form of an 18-month Treasury advisory role filled by a KPMG tax partner, who upon completing his secondment returned to KPMG to develop and market strategies of contrived licence agreement structuring that allowed their clients to claim dubious tax concessions under patent box provisions (Hodge 2016, pp. 50–53).

A similar story is evident in the Goldman Sachs case, during which former HMRC head David Hartnett personally engaged in meetings, negotiations and informal hospitality on several occasions (despite denying any relationship with Goldman Sachs) in the lead-up to the conclusion of HMRC's deal forgiving interest on their liabilities (Hodge 2016, pp. 63–65). The often uncomfortably close relationships between powerful business actors/accounting firms and governments (Sikka 2015, pp. 427–430), the paramount importance placed on individual taxpayers' privacy, and the difficult balancing of administrative discretion faced by civil servants all meant that information about HMRC's compromised settlement with Goldman Sachs could not have been revealed without whistleblowing and investigative journalism.

The role of whistleblowing in the Goldman Sachs/HMRC/PAC case highlights the complex dynamics at play in both private and public/official governance of tax avoidance. Whistleblowing and investigative journalism had the effect, in this case, of mobilising one public institution against another. Owing to asymmetries of information, competing incentives and opposing political imperatives, the information provided by whistleblowers and investigative journalists was used by a parliamentary committee to circumvent and reprimand a government department that came to be viewed as uncooperative, antagonistic and even vulnerable to regulatory capture (UK Public Accounts Committee 2012).

CASE STUDY NO. 2: CATERPILLAR

Many high-profile cases of the kinds of tax avoidance that are being discussed here are legally contentious because they involve dubious licensing arrangements for intellectual property – often for classes of products in which locating the jurisdiction of economic activity presents an added layer of complexity. For this reason, cases of tax avoidance that involve neither a finance corporation nor a tech giant can be especially illuminating, and Caterpillar's recent battle with the US tax and revenue authorities fits this bill well. This is because it provides a revealing example of legally dubious transfer pricing arrangements for a company where the economic activity itself relates to tangible products and occurs very clearly in one jurisdiction. Importantly, the industrial/construction heavy equipment manufacturer is also a darling of the American Midwest – a national icon and export giant that has kept 50 000 jobs in the country's embattled manufacturing heartland. Just one week before Caterpillar's Illinois headquarters were raided by federal agents seizing evidence and sequestering employees, President Donald Trump proudly declared, at a White House manufacturing summit, 'There's nothing like what you guys do. The Caterpillars are the best. . ..I love Caterpillar!' (Trump, quoted in White House Office of the Press Secretary 2017).

Caterpillar makes most of its profits from on-selling replacement parts for its vehicles rather than from their initial manufacture. It buys most of these parts from other manufacturers and stores them at its warehouses – mostly in Illinois. Until 1999, it conducted its parts business by selling them first to a Swiss subsidiary (though not actually shipping them via Switzerland), and from thence to the end consumer. However, Caterpillar's accountants at PwC advised that, while this strategy was incurring a tax liability in the US, it could facilitate the sale of parts from the manufacturers directly to its Swiss subsidiary and bypass its US headquarters, thus avoiding US tax on those transactions. Caterpillar continued to run its parts business through its factories in Illinois, but declared 85 per cent of the profits in its Swiss subsidiary. PwC even helped Caterpillar create an inventory system designed to defeat an audit, consisting of an arrangement whereby, if parts were shipped overseas, they were listed as owned by the Swiss operation despite the fact that both domestic and international orders remained indistinguishably commingled in the Illinois warehouse (Avi-Yonah and Xu 2016, p. 193).

Caterpillar's scheme was challenged in 2013 by the IRS, which concluded that it was employing an 'abusive' strategy wholly designed to avoid US taxes. In early 2014 the matter also became the subject of a US Senate Permanent Subcommittee on Investigations (PSI) probe. On 2 March 2017, the company's headquarters in Peoria was raided by agents of the IRS, the Federal Deposit Insurance Corporation and the Department of Commerce, who interviewed employees and confiscated computers, documents and encryption devices (Gruley et al. 2017, p. 44). As Avi-Yonah and Xu (2016) note, however, 'the disturbing fact is that [this] whole story would not have come to light but for a whistleblower, who alerted both PSI and the IRS' (Avi-Yonah and Xu 2016, pp. 193–194).

The whistleblower was Daniel Schlicksup, an accountant who had worked at Caterpillar for 16 years and had made repeated attempts to report his concerns about its tax strategy internally. As a result, he was chastised in performance reviews and eventually demoted. Schlicksup, thinking that his missives had been ignored, eventually sent 137 pages of Caterpillar and PwC documents to the IRS, showing how PwC, both as auditor and as consultant, had helped to obscure economic activity that was being undertaken in the US. The IRS used Schlicksup's documents to demand $2 billion in back taxes and penalties. These initial investigations culminated in the Senate Permanent Subcommittee on Investigations, to which Schlicksup gave evidence, concluding that Caterpillar had avoided more than $8 billion in taxes (Gruley et al. 2017, p. 43). The Subcommittee's final report on the matter describes a strategy in which Caterpillar 'replaced its leading Swiss affiliate with a new Swiss affiliate, CSARL, and then used a series of licensing transactions with CSARL to enable it to sell Caterpillar's third party manufactured replacement parts to its non-U.S. dealers and customers without showing the parts profits as U.S. income' (US Senate 2016, p. 4).

Interestingly, the US system has in recent years pursued tax avoidance and the tax avoidance industry with more rigour than the UK system has. Hearings of the UK Public Accounts Committee on tax avoidance and shady accounting schemes such as those devised by PwC for Accenture, Amazon, Aviva, Burberry, Citigroup,

Deutsche Bank, Disney, Dyson, Heinz, HSBC, IKEA, Koch, Pepsi, Procter & Gamble, Shire, Skype, Vodafone and many others have not been followed up with action by the Department of Justice, HMRC or the Treasury. In the US, however, Permanent Subcommittee on Investigations hearings have led to prosecutions, fines and even jail time for senior staff of 'big four' accounting firms. KPMG, for instance, was fined $456 million in 2005 for creating tax avoidance schemes that were later deemed illegal, and several of its senior tax professionals received prison sentences. Ernst & Young paid a $123 million fine in 2013 for instructing clients on how to shelter profit in tax havens, and a number of its staff were also jailed (Sikka 2015, p. 431). The US Securities and Exchange Commission Office of the Whistleblower's incentivisation and protection programmes have seen tip-offs increase (both in number and in the scale of avoidance reported) in every year of the Office's operation. The whistleblowers who report wrongdoing to the Office of the Whistleblower are allowed to receive 15–30 per cent of the proceeds recovered from any investigation to which their information has contributed significantly. Financial year 2015–16 saw the agency's pay-outs to whistleblowers increase to $57 million, which was higher than in all previous years combined. Financial year 2016–17 was set to break this record again (US Securities and Exchange Commission 2016, p. 1). Moreover, if Daniel Schlicksup's evidence leads to the recovery of the amount of tax that Caterpillar is alleged to have avoided, he could receive a pay-out of as much as $600 million, making him the most highly paid whistleblower in history (Gruley et al. 2017). The Caterpillar case is an excellent example of a situation in which a concerned but loyal employee, having exhausted all internal options, turned instead to working with the tax authorities to promote compliance.

CASE STUDY NO. 3: SHIRE PHARMACEUTICALS AND LUXLEAKS

Shire is a multinational pharmaceuticals corporation worth £24 billion. Shire is incorporated in Jersey and headquartered in Ireland, with large plants in Basingstoke in the UK and Massachusetts in the US. Most of its business is in North America – more than two-thirds of its revenue comes from sales in the US and Canada. Shire avoids paying large amounts of UK and US taxes using subsidiaries and holding corporations in Luxembourg that operate under special deals negotiated by PwC with the Luxembourg tax authorities. Through a system of contrived intra-group loans that nominally pass through these subsidiaries at inflated interest rates, Shire operations in higher-tax jurisdictions are able to write off interest payments to the holding company as deductions on their corporation tax filings. As a result, the Luxembourg entity has lent as much as $10 billion, at interest rates of up to 9 per cent, to other Shire group companies and booked profits of $1.87 billion over the last five years. These transactions have brought the overall average rate of tax Shire pays around the world to just 16.4 per cent (Bowers 2014). As a UK Parliamentary Accounts Committee hearing revealed, the

Luxembourg operation – ostensibly solely responsible for $10 billion worth of loans and having netted nearly $2 billion in profits for the company – employs only two people, at a cost to Shire of €135 000. These employees are also directors of dozens of other companies headquartered at the same premises in Luxembourg. As Margaret Hodge, the Committee chair, stated in the hearing, 'It is stretching our credulity [to suggest] that these two employees, who are also directors of umpteen other companies, are seriously the guys taking the decisions on loans totalling $10 billion' (UK Public Accounts Committee 2014).

Shire's aggressive tax strategies only came to the attention of the public (and the PAC) as a result of the 'LuxLeaks' scandal of November 2014. LuxLeaks was an ICIJ investigation, based on some 28 000 pages of leaked documents, divulging the details of 548 tax rulings between the Luxembourg tax authorities and around 340 companies. These rulings, granting favourable and lenient 'sweetheart' deals to a large number of high-profile corporates, were leaked to the ICIJ and published in full on its website, causing international outrage (Wayne et al. 2017). The main source of the leak was a PricewaterhouseCoopers employee named Antoine Deltour. Deltour used a secure messaging service to transfer the enormous cache of data to ICIJ reporters and was subsequently prosecuted in Luxembourg for theft and for violating Luxembourg's strict professional secrecy laws, receiving a 12-month suspended sentence in June 2016.

The ease with which such large amounts of data can be safely captured, stored, manipulated and transferred compared to even just four to five years ago means that leaks like LuxLeaks have become not only more straightforward and less expensive, but also vastly more damaging. Dover argues that increasingly simple, movable data storage technologies have the potential to radically alter the risk–reward calculus of tax avoidance, as the combination of technical capability and issue salience vastly raises the likelihood of aggressive tax practices being revealed in the public domain. Furthermore, the increasing accessibility of information to the public is rapidly translating into a political imperative to address the issue of corporate tax avoidance. The ICIJ's LuxLeaks investigation was, as Dover writes, 'the explicit trigger for the European Parliament's investigation and legislative initiative on corporate taxation' (Dover 2016b, p. 108). The growing political imperative of addressing corporate tax avoidance can be illustrated by the various government inquiries, taskforces and campaigns materialising across the Western world, including in Australia (Australian Tax Office 2017).

12.6 CONCLUSION

This chapter has argued that the role of whistleblowing and investigative journalism in the international anti-avoidance regime should be understood as a form of private governance. The three different regulatory theories presented here have been selected because of their documented impact in other complex policy problems in the areas of environmental regulation and corporate governance. This chapter has attempted to show the growing relevance of these regulatory mechanisms to corporate tax avoidance in three ways. First, the political salience and public profile of corporate tax avoidance as an issue are on the rise. Survey data, whistleblowing statistics and increasingly prolific and impactful investigative reporting all support the conclusion that perceptions of tax avoidance as a moral issue in the minds of ordinary voters is quickly developing. Second, as voters' tax literacy and awareness grow, the disdain for aggressive tax planning is translating into a burgeoning political imperative to be seen to be addressing the problem. Third, changing understandings of tax avoidance's moral dimension are contributing to the normalisation and institutionalisation of tax whistleblowing. Where tax avoidance has not, in past decades, been viewed as seriously as other kinds of white-collar crime or fraud, programmes of whistleblower incentivisation and protection have encouraged far greater transparency in the international tax system, establishing something of a feedback loop between public attitudes and whistleblower revelations. The gathering pace of whistleblowing in the tax arena has also been aided by technological advances, which now allow almost effortless collection, transfer, analysis and publication of the often-complex caches of information contained in financial data leaks.

Nevertheless, the evidence presented here does not point to whistleblowing and investigative journalism exerting a strong effect independently of government. These actors and events are undeniably exerting a private governance pressure on corporate tax avoidance practices, but they do so via varied mechanisms of influence over state responses. There are, essentially, three such identifiable mechanisms evident in the examples presented here:

1. Whistleblowing or investigative journalism can enable a willing government or tax authority to act. This effect is clear in the Caterpillar case, in which authorities with a documented appetite for prosecutions following whistleblower revelations were able to initiate proceedings following the release of vital documentation from a company insider that would otherwise have been near impossible to obtain.
2. Increased political pressure following a whistleblower or journalistic revelation can prompt a reluctant government or tax authority to act. This mechanism is visible in both UK Public Accounts Committee cases discussed here, wherein information from whistleblowers and investigative journalists effectively mobilised an activist government institution against a reluctant or uncooperative one, feeding a growing public appetite for rigorous government action in this policy space. Moreover, the revelations and subsequent reports produced by the PAC have led to reforms at the highest levels of HM Revenue and

Customs, including the appointment of more commissioners with deep tax and accounting expertise.

3. Evidence of the effectiveness of whistleblowing as a tool for regulation and information revelation can force government to institutionalise whistleblower protection and incentivisation, which acts as a regulatory governance framework. The American system is the best example of this mechanism, with tip-offs to the Securities and Exchange Commission leading to the recapturing of a larger quantum of avoided tax revenue every year as a result of its effectiveness.

While whistleblowing events and data leaks regularly generate media attention, political backlash and public sanction, some systems are ultimately better at recovering forgone revenue and punishing offenders than others. Convictions of accountants for tax avoidance offences and recovery of funds has been more successful in the US's system than the UK's (Sikka 2015), even despite the US's well-documented reluctance to contribute to international anti-avoidance programmes and efforts (Stiglitz 2013). Such differences in systems like those of the US and the UK provide a good illustration of a rational actor or principal–agent focused analysis of whistleblowing as a developing mode of private governance. This is because whistleblowing not only can demonstrate the exertion of differing sets of pressures on rational tax planners, but also underscores the various ways that transparency can bring the interests of tax planners, accounting professionals, shareholders and executives into conflict. Comparative analysis of whistleblowing in different tax systems, such as those of the US and the UK, may thus be a fruitful avenue for further research and analysis. Equally useful could be a comparative survey of the effects of regulation through revelation on the tax affairs of high-net-worth individuals versus corporate tax planners.

NOTE

1. Effective marginal tax rates are used by the authors as a proxy measure of avoidance, as they are the main source of publicly available information from a financial disclosure statement upon which an investor could make an assessment about whether a firm engages in aggressive tax avoidance.

REFERENCES

ActionAid (2013), *Community Attitudes towards Corporate Taxation and Tax Justice*, Polity Social Research Consulting, available at http://www.actionaid.org/sites/

files/actionaid/actionaid_tax_justice_report_final_public_release_14102013.pdf (accessed 15 July 2017).
Andrade, J.A. (2015), 'Reconceptualising Whistleblowing in a Complex World', *Journal of Business Ethics* **128**, 321–335, available at https://doi.org/10.1007/s10551-014-2105-z (accessed 4 August 2017).
Austin, C.R. and R.J. Wilson (2017), 'An Examination of Reputational Costs and Tax Avoidance: Evidence from Firms with Valuable Consumer Brands', *Journal of the American Taxation Association* **39** (1), 67–93.
Australian Tax Office (2017), 'Australian Tax Avoidance Taskforce', Parliament of Australia, available at https://www.ato.gov.au/general/Tax-avoidance-taskforce/ (accessed 6 August 2017).
Avi-Yonah, R.S. and H. Xu (2016), 'Evaluating BEPS: A Reconsideration of the Benefits Principle and Proposal for UN Oversight', *Harvard Business Law Review* **6** (2), 185–238.
Bergin, T. (2012), 'Special Report: How Starbucks Avoids UK Taxes', *Reuters*, published electronically 15 October, available at https://uk.reuters.com/article/uk-britain-starbucks-tax/special-report-how-starbucks-avoids-uk-taxes-idUKBRE89E0EW20121015 (accessed 28 August 2017).
Bowers, S. (2014), 'Luxembourg Tax Files: How a Tiny State Rubber-Stamped Tax Avoidance on an Industrial Scale', *Guardian UK*, published electronically 6 November, available at https://www.theguardian.com/business/2014/nov/05/-sp-luxembourg-tax-files-tax-avoidance-industrial-scale (accessed 20 July 2017).
Bradbury, D. (2017), 'Tax Avoiders Running Out of Time as Global Transparency Increases', Interview with Eleanor Hall, *The World Today*, ABC Radio National, broadcast 7 November, available at http://www.abc.net.au/radio/programs/worldtoday/tax-avoiders-running-out-of-time-global-transparency-increases/9125920 (accessed 5 August 2017).
Braun, J. and A. Weichenrieder (2015), *Does Exchange of Information between Tax Authorities Influence Multinationals' Use of Tax Havens?*, Discussion Paper No. 15-015, Mannheim: Centre for European Economic Research, available at http://ftp.zew.de/pub/zew-docs/dp/dp15015.pdf (accessed 17 July 2017).
Christian Aid (2013), 'Christian Aid Tax Avoidance Poll', ComRes Global, available at http://www.comresglobal.com/wp-content/themes/comres/poll/Christian_Aid_Tax_Avoidance_Feb_2013.pdf (accessed 12 October 2017).
Christians, A. (2013), 'Avoidance, Evasion, and Taxpayer Morality', *Washington University Journal of Law and Policy* **44**, 39–59.
Culpepper, P.D. (2011), *Quiet Politics and Business Power: Corporate Control in Europe and Japan*, New York: Cambridge University Press.
Dawson, E. with W. Smith (2017), *Per Capita Tax Survey 2017: Public Attitudes towards Taxation and Public Expenditure*, Per Capita: Fighting Inequality in Australia, available at https://percapita.org.au/wp-content/uploads/2017/06/2017-Tax-Survey_Final-1.pdf (accessed 4 August 2017).
Doherty, C. (2015), 'Federal Tax System Seen as in Need of Overhaul: Top Complaints – Wealthy Corporations "Don't Pay Fair Share"', Pew Research Center, available at http://www.people-press.org/2015/03/19/federal-tax-system-seen-in-need-of-overhaul/ (accessed 14 October 2017).
Dover, R. (2016a), 'Fixing Financial Plumbing: Tax, Leaks and Base Erosion and Profit Shifting in Europe', *Italian Journal of International Affairs* **51** (4), 40–50.

Dover, R. (2016b), 'Regulation by Revelation: The Opportunities and Challenges of Information Control in an Intelligence Era', *SAIS Review of International Affairs* **36** (2), 103–111.

Elliott, L. and H. Stewart (2013), 'David Cameron Makes Swipe at Starbucks as He Promises Focus on Tax', *Guardian Australia*, published electronically 25 January, available at https://www.theguardian.com/politics/2013/jan/24/david-cameron-starbucks-focus-tax (accessed 28 August 2017).

Essential Research (2016), *The Essential Report*, Australian Council of Trade Unions, available at http://www.actu.org.au/media/886516/essential-report_160412_actu.pdf (accessed 15 July 2017).

Farrell, S. and H. McDonald (2016), 'Apple Ordered to Pay €13bn after EU Rules Ireland Broke State Aid Laws', *Guardian UK*, published electronically 31 August, available at https://www.theguardian.com/business/2016/aug/30/apple-pay-back-taxes-eu-ruling-ireland-state-aid (accessed 12 October 2017).

Freedman, J. and J. Vella (2011), 'HMRC's Management of the UK Tax System: The Boundaries of Legitimate Discretion', in C. Evans, J. Freedman and R. Krever (eds), *The Delicate Balance: Tax, Discretion, and the Rule of Law*, Amsterdam: International Bureau of Fiscal Documentation, pp. 79–120.

Gallemore, J., E.L. Maydew and J.R. Thornock (2014), 'The Reputational Costs of Tax Avoidance', *Contemporary Accounting Research* **31** (4), 1103–1133.

Graham, J.R., M. Hanlon, T. Shevlin and N. Shroff (2014), 'Incentives for Tax Planning and Avoidance: Evidence from the Field', *Accounting Review* **89** (3), 991–1023.

Gruley, B., D. Voreacos, J. Deaux, M. Parker and A. Hoffman (2017), 'How Does Tax Avoidance Play in Peoria?', *Bloomberg Businessweek*, **4525** (2017), 42–47.

Hamilton, J.T. (2005), *Regulation through Revelation*, Cambridge: Cambridge University Press.

Hanlon, M. and S. Heitzman (2010), 'A Review of Tax Research', *Journal of Accounting and Economics* **50** (2–3), 127–178.

Henry, E., N. Massel and E. Towery (2016), 'Increased Tax Disclosures and Corporate Tax Avoidance', *National Tax Journal* **69** (4), 809–830.

Hodge, M. (2016), *Called to Account: How Corporate Bad Behaviour and Government Waste Combine to Cost Us Millions*, London: Little, Brown.

Lee, B.B., A. Dobiyanski and S. Minton (2015), 'Theories and Empirical Proxies for Corporate Tax Avoidance', *Journal of Applied Business and Economics* **17** (3), 21–34.

Liddy, M. (2016), 'Who Pays What? Big Private Companies' Tax Details Revealed', *Australian Broadcasting Corporation*, available at http://www.abc.net.au/news/2016-03-22/tax-transparency-private-companies-who-is-paying/7266184 (accessed 26 August 2017).

Medcraft, G. (2017), Interview with Fran Kelly, *Radio National Breakfast*, ABC Radio National, broadcast 8 November, available at http://radio.abc.net.au/programitem/pgE7Jgy33G?play=true (accessed 8 November 2017).

Moss, J., J. Ratna, G. O'Halloran and T. Murphy (2016), 'Tax Transparency: A New Era in Reporting?', Chartered Accountants Australia and New Zealand, PricewaterhouseCoopers, available at https://www.pwc.com.au/assurance/ifrs/assets/tax-transparency-a-new-era-in-reporting.pdf (accessed 4 August 2017).

Murphy, R. and J. Christensen (2012), *Tax Us if You Can*, Tax Justice Network, available at https://www.taxjustice.net/cms/upload/pdf/TUIYC_2012_FINAL.pdf (accessed 22 July 2017).

OECD (Organisation for Economic Co-operation and Development) (2017), *Signatories of the Multilateral Competent Authority Agreement on the Exchange of Country-by-Country Reports (CbC MCAA) and Signing Dates*, Paris: OECD Publishing, available at https://www.oecd.org/tax/beps/CbC-MCAA-Signatories.pdf (accessed 20 July 2017).

Oxfam Australia (2016), *The Hidden Billions: How Tax Havens Impact Lives at Home and Abroad*, available at https://www.oxfam.org.au/wp-content/uploads/2016/06/OXF003-Tax-Havens-Report-FA2-WEB.pdf (accessed 12 October 2017).

Porter, T. and K. Ronit (2016), 'The Institutionalization of Whistleblowing in Global Regulation: The Case of Taxation', Paper presented to the International Political Science Association Congress, Poznan, available at http://paperroom.ipsa.org/papers/paper_50176.pdf (accessed 28 August 2017).

Rego, S.O., B.M. Williams and R.J. Wilson (2017), 'Who Invests in Corporate Tax Avoiders?', Kelly School of Business Research Paper No. 17–16, available at https://papers.ssrn.com/sol3/papers.cfm?abstract_id=2919004 (accessed 21 October 2017).

Richardson, G., R. Lanis and G. Taylor (2015), 'Financial Distress, Outside Directors and Corporate Tax Aggressiveness Spanning the Global Financial Crisis: An Empirical Analysis', *Journal of Banking and Finance* **52**, 112–129.

Shah, P. (2016), *Exploring Public Attitudes to Tax Avoidance in 2015*, Research Report No. 401, HM Revenue and Customs, available at https://www.gov.uk/government/publications/exploring-public-attitudes-to-tax-avoidance-in-2015 (accessed 21 July 2017).

Sikka, P. (2010), 'Smoke and Mirrors: Corporate Social Responsibility and Tax Avoidance', *Accounting Forum* **34** (3–4), 153–168.

Sikka, P. (2015), 'No Accounting for Tax Avoidance', *Political Quarterly* **86** (3), 427–433.

Stiglitz, J. (2013), 'Globalisation Isn't Just about Profits, It's about Taxes Too', *Guardian Australia*, published electronically 28 May, available at https://www.theguardian.com/commentisfree/2013/may/27/globalisation-is-about-taxes-too (accessed 22 July 2017).

Syal, R. and H. Mulholland (2011), 'HMRC Hid "Sweetheart" Tax Deals for Big Business, MPs Say', *Guardian UK*, published electronically 20 December, available at https://www.theguardian.com/politics/2011/dec/20/inland-revenue-sweetheart-tax-deals (accessed 22 July 2017).

UK Public Accounts Committee (2012), 'HM Revenue & Customs 2010–11 Accounts: Public Accounts Committee', available at https://www.publications.parliament.uk/pa/cm201012/cmselect/cmpubacc/1531/153107.htm (accessed 20 July 2017).

UK Public Accounts Committee (2014), 'Meeting of the Public Accounts Committee: Hearing on Tax Avoidance, 8 November 2014', available at http://www.parliamentlive.tv/Event/Index/121850ef-001a-44af-9037-582f616ede41 (accessed 26 August 2017).

US Securities and Exchange Commission (2016), *2016 Annual Report to Congress on the Dodd–Frank Whistleblower Program*, Washington, DC: United States Securities and Exchange Commission, available at https://www.sec.gov/files/owb-annual-report-2016.pdf (accessed 20 July 2017).

US Senate (2016), *Majority Staff Report: Caterpillar's Offshore Tax Strategy*, Washington, DC: Permanent Subcommittee on Investigations, Committee on Homeland Security and Governmental Affairs, available at https://www.hsgac.senate.gov/download/report-caterpillars-offshore-tax-strategy-april-1-2014 (accessed 12 October 2017).

Wayne, L., K. Carr, M.G. Walker, M. Cabra and M. Hudson (2017), 'Leaked Documents Expose Global Companies' Secret Tax Deals in Luxembourg', International Consortium of Investigative Journalists, available at https://www.icij.org/project/luxembourg-leaks/leaked-documents-expose-global-companies-secret-tax-deals-luxembourg (accessed 16 October 2017).

Whistleblowers International (2017), 'The History of Whistleblowing', available at https://www.whistleblowersinternational.com/what-is-whistleblowing/history/ (accessed 21 July 2017).

White House Office of the Press Secretary (2017), 'Remarks by President Trump in Meeting with Manufacturing CEOs', Press release, 23 February, available at https://www.whitehouse.gov/the-press-office/2017/02/23/remarks-president-trump-meeting-manufacturing-ceos (accessed 14 October 2017).

Zucman, G. (2014), 'Taxing across Borders: Tracking Personal Wealth and Corporate Profits', *Journal of Economic Perspectives* **28** (4), 121–148.

Conclusion: business, civil society and the 'new' politics of corporate tax justice: paying a fair share?

Richard Eccleston and Ainsley Elbra

Economic liberalisation and the rise of MNCs in recent decades have been a double-edged sword. With the exception of the 2008 Financial Crisis and its aftermath, the rise of global capitalism has been a key driver of economic growth and technological innovation, but at the same time has undermined state sovereignty and exacerbated inequality (Mikler 2018). Nowhere has this dualism been more apparent than in the realm of corporate taxation, which has become a prime example of what Martin Wolf (2012) describes as a 'contemporary tragedy of the global commons'. The 'tragedy' is such that MNC tax avoidance is now estimated to deny governments over a quarter of a trillion US dollars per year, and after years of ignoring the issue governments and firms are being forced to act (Clausing 2015; OECD 2015).

As scholars with a strong interest in the political economy of taxation, and global governance more generally, we have been keen observers of the international campaign to address corporate tax avoidance over the past decade. This campaign, we believe, raises a number of significant questions concerning both the outlook for corporate tax policy and the theoretical debates relating to the future of global economic governance. This volume has addressed a number of questions concerning the future of corporate taxation – and the actors and ideas shaping its likely trajectory. The study has considered whether growing political and public scrutiny of MNCs will influence corporate tax behaviour, whether tax justice campaigns orchestrated by NGOs will have a significant and sustainable impact on tax compliance and whether they are an alternative or a complement to more formal regulation. At a broader level we consider what these developments say about the potential for new forms of tax governance in the twenty-first century. In this Conclusion these key themes and findings will be summarised, and assessments made of their likely implications for corporate tax justice and the future of global economic governance.

Given the growing complexity of the international tax regime, many of the threads of the corporate tax story are intertwined. In order to make sense of these developments, we begin by summarising the key contours of the 'new' politics of international taxation, and then provide an overview of the ongoing and critically important normative arguments about what constitutes a 'fair' level of taxation. The second aim of this Conclusion is to describe the emerging policy and governance response to the challenge of corporate tax avoidance before attempting to conceptualise this increasingly complex and dynamic issue arena.

This study is very much a preliminary academic foray into the political economy of post-Crisis corporate taxation, and, while finding that the corporate tax debate has become more contested and politicised over the past decade, we also acknowledge that it is too soon to predict the longer-term implications of these developments with any certainty. While awareness of the extent of corporate tax avoidance among governments and citizens is high, and regulators and firms alike are under unprecedented pressure to change their ways, formidable barriers to reform remain. Reflecting these themes, the volume concludes with a brief assessment of the outlook for corporate taxation and tax justice as well as the wider implications of the study for global governance and democratic accountability in the twenty-first century.

THE RISE OF THE TAX JUSTICE MOVEMENT AND THE NEW POLITICS OF INTERNATIONAL TAXATION

In the early 1960s, Bernard Cohen (1963) argued that political outcomes were not only determined by the actors with greatest capacity to win public debates and the hearts and minds of voters. Rather, real political power and influence came from being able to shape the political agenda and manage the specific issues being debated and scrutinised by political parties, interest groups and the mass public. Studies such as Cohen's gave rise to a broad literature on agenda control and 'non-decision making', which has highlighted the importance of raising an issue's profile in order to effect change (Bachrach and Baratz 1970). The corollary, of course, is that interests benefiting from the policy status quo often embark on a conscious strategy to keep an issue off the political agenda and away from serious scrutiny. There is now an extensive literature on the importance of agenda control and transparency in the field of business regulation, highlighting how corporate interests tend to benefit during times of 'quiet politics', during which regulatory decisions and frameworks are not subjected to close public scrutiny (Culpepper 2011).

Part I of this volume described the rise of corporate tax issues up the international policy agenda in the aftermath of the Financial Crisis. This volume outlined how international tax policy transitioned from a 'quiet' policy arena, dominated by technical experts and intergovernmental organisations such as the OECD, to an issue subject to unprecedented grassroots activism, international media campaigns and the deliberations of world leaders, a process described in detail in Chapter 3. The fact that media coverage of corporate avoidance increased fivefold between 2007 and 2012, during which time it went from being the sleeping giant of global governance to dominating discussion at the G20 leaders' forum in 2013, was no accident. Nor was it an inevitable consequence of the Financial Crisis and its aftermath. Rather, the 'new' politics of corporate tax justice was shaped by the agenda-setting and framing strategies employed by tax justice NGOs since the early 2000s. Chapters 3 and 4 highlighted how a network of activists managed to use the Financial Crisis as a window of opportunity to promote corporate tax reform. Groups such as Occupy and UK Uncut distilled broad-based opposition to corporate capitalism into focused social movements, which in turn prompted a more specific debate on corporate tax avoidance. In Chapter 4, Seabrooke and Wigan draw on their detailed knowledge of the tax justice movement to explain how a small group of activists with sufficient technical expertise can create networks and alliances with mainstream NGOs, media outlets and sympathetic politicians and academics capable of influencing the international policy agenda. The likes of Tax Justice Network and affiliated groups have played a significant role in highlighting the extent of corporate tax avoidance, but they also benefit from complementary developments such as increased tax transparency and disclosure courtesy of a combination of new regulatory initiatives and high-profile data leaks from whistleblowers (this volume, Chapter 12).

Unprecedented public awareness of the scope of corporate tax avoidance has forced world leaders and established intergovernmental organisations, such as the OECD, to act by making various commitments to ensure that MNCs pay their fair share of tax. However, the history of international tax governance (this volume, Chapters 1 and 2) highlights the need for caution, as platitudes and earnest commitments to implement reforms often fail to translate into effective action. This is especially the case when reform requires international agreement, and runs counter to the financial interests of the world's most powerful firms (Walter 2008; Eccleston 2012). Getting the issue of corporate tax avoidance on to the international political agenda is an important step towards meaningful reform, but significant hurdles remain. Chief among these is the difficulty of reaching a degree of consensus as to what constitutes a 'fair share' of taxation, and finding governance strategies that are likely to ensure more MNCs pay more tax, with proceeds distributed appropriately among the jurisdictions in which global firms operate. These normative and moral questions continue to loom large over the corporate tax avoidance debate.

THE BATTLE OF IDEAS: WHAT'S THE PROBLEM AND WHO'S TO BLAME?

It is one thing to highlight the growing problem of corporate tax avoidance, but, in order to achieve meaningful political change and influence corporate behaviour, the ongoing battle of ideas about what constitutes a 'fair share' of corporate taxation and whether firms have any moral obligation to stop using all legal means to minimise tax must be resolved.

There is growing recognition that effective global governance is dependent on compelling moral claims. Indeed, this volume reveals that the ongoing contestation of norms about what constitutes an appropriate corporate tax strategy is a major barrier to reform. In relation to the critical question of what constitutes a fair corporate tax burden, the study found that many corporations and their influential advisers continue to argue that their only responsibility is to meet their legal – rather than social – obligations to pay taxes and that it is the responsibility of governments to develop simpler, fairer corporate tax regimes (this volume, Chapters 6, 7 and 9). Thus, it is clear that effective and sustainable measures to address corporate tax avoidance will depend upon establishing a widely accepted ethical and moral foundation for what constitutes a 'fair' tax regime – a framework which in turn can inform the development of practical and effective reform programmes. The establishment of agreed-upon norms regarding 'tax fairness' will thus enhance the effectiveness of civil society campaigns targeting both governments and firms, while simultaneously shaping and legitimising more ambitious reform initiatives.

While the normative battle concerning corporate tax justice is far from resolved there is an emerging consensus, driven largely by NGOs and activists, concerning both the high-level principles which should inform corporate tax policy and how these might be applied to the international reform agenda. Chapter 2 provided a stylised sketch of the broad technical literature on corporate tax avoidance, highlighting how the central element of most aggressive tax planning strategies is to shift profits to low- or no-tax jurisdictions while booking tax-deductible costs (including debt) in high-tax countries. This base erosion and profit shifting (or BEPS, to use the language of the OECD) is made possible by the ability of MNCs to establish vast networks of related companies around the world (in some cases numbering in their hundreds), which are all taxed separately under the 'independent entity' principle established in the 1930s. This framework has allowed MNCs to decouple the reporting of profits for tax purposes from where real economic activity occurs and profits are created. While the details are technical, the central principle which defines a 'fair' taxation system is the idea that corporate profits must be recorded in the jurisdiction where they were earned, and that that country's sovereign right to tax those profits as it sees fit should be protected. Such principles have been affirmed by moral philosophers with expertise in corporate taxation such as Peter Dietsch (2015; see also this volume, Chapter 2), and were neatly captured in the G20 leaders' communiqué stating that MNC profits 'should be taxed where economic activities deriving the profits are performed and where value is created' (G20 2014, p. 3).

A chorus of tax justice campaigners, academics and independent analysts are converging on the argument that a form of 'unitary taxation', in which MNCs are treated as one large company for taxation purposes and then profits are taxed in the jurisdiction where they are created, should become the cornerstone of a fair tax system. Nevertheless, embarking on a paradigm shift from the current system of arm's-length transfer pricing to a unitary tax system is fiercely resisted by most firms, tax professionals and many national governments. To use the language of Finnemore and Sikkink (1998), we are yet to reach the tipping point of the 'norm lifecycle' where an emerging standard of what constitutes a fair tax system is accepted widely enough that it shapes societal views about appropriate corporate tax policy and the levels of taxation major MNCs should pay.

The contestation and debate about what constitutes a 'fair' level of taxation have a number of implications for tax politics and policy. In terms of legitimacy and moral claims, the fact that firms such as Apple, which engage in aggressive tax avoidance, can credibly say they pay all the tax they are legally obliged to pay allows them to successfully deflect claims that they are avoiding tax, while simultaneously placing the onus on governments to reform corporate tax laws to make them fairer. The significance of these discursive strategies was analysed in Chapter 6, which argued that MNCs and their advisers exploit the technical complexity of international taxation to create a veneer of legitimacy for their strategies and thus to counter claims that they have an ethical or moral obligation to pay more tax. This strategy may be successful in the short term, but in Chapter 7 Mikler and Elbra argue that it may have the unintended consequence of legitimising the state's sovereign right to tax MNCs if and when more robust and effective legislation is introduced.

Resolving the 'battle of ideas' concerning corporate taxation will have a number of consequences. If it becomes widely accepted that firms should report where profits are made and where taxes are paid, then this will enable NGOs to exert moral pressure on firms which don't conform, thereby increasing the efficacy of the voluntary and private governance initiatives described in this volume.

Exerting direct pressure on MNCs to change their tax strategies is one way to create a fairer tax system, but a central finding of this volume is that a range of actors, public and private, shape the governance of the complex and evolving international tax regime. Indeed, greater normative and moral clarity about what constitutes a fair taxation system will increase the pressure on both intergovernmental organisations and national governments to embrace more ambitious reform. For these reasons, it will be essential to consolidate the ethical foundations of a fair corporate tax system if the wider goal of addressing MNC tax avoidance is to be realised.

WHAT'S THE SOLUTION? A NEW MODEL OF CORPORATE TAXATION FOR THE TWENTY-FIRST CENTURY

Support for the idea that corporate taxes must be paid where economic value is created is building. Moreover, this principle represents the cornerstone of a fair and sustainable corporate tax regime. However, the question of the best regulatory framework for upholding this principle remains the subject of ongoing debate.

Conceptually, recent developments in international tax governance represent an important example of the growing fragmentation and complexity of global economic governance (Coen and Pegram 2018). The structures and institutions of the post-war economic order, such as the interests of great powers like the United States and the enduring influence of intergovernmental organisations such as the OECD, remain, but this volume has also demonstrated that the politics of international taxation is being shaped by a widening constellation of actors using varied strategies across a number of political arenas.

We have described the actors that have played a key role in highlighting the extent and implications of corporate tax avoidance, as well as the rise of alternative 'norms' concerning what constitutes an appropriate corporate tax strategy. Inevitably, these developments have had significant implications for policy development and the translation of growing popular concern about corporate tax avoidance into concrete policy proposals. Here too NGOs have played a significant role. Whereas international taxation was formerly dominated by national tax authorities and a handful of intergovernmental organisations developing policies and standards informed by the advice of tax professionals (this volume, Chapter 1), the Financial Crisis has made the international tax policy arena significantly more open and contested. Increasingly, activist academics and NGOs are developing alternative models for allocating the corporate tax base between jurisdictions, while insisting on greater levels of transparency. Having developed new reform agendas – such as country-by-country reporting and automatic information exchange – tax justice groups have promoted transparency by establishing private standards such as the EITI and Fair Tax Mark, while at the same time advocating that such principles be embodied in national law and international agreements.

The intergovernmental organisations, such as the OECD, which have traditionally dominated the international tax arena have also been forced to respond to this changing political context. In the face of growing pressure from the G20 and member countries, and advocacy from emerging NGOs such as Tax Justice Network, the OECD has been forced to confront arguments that its existing standards, such as the BEPS framework, are weak and ineffective. What is clear is that intergovernmental organisations can adopt only incremental reforms, wherein the rate of policy change is largely determined by the interests of powerful member states. In contrast, activist groups by their nature agitate for more radical, paradigmatic change, such as the adoption of a system of unitary taxation with formula apportionment. In contrast, the OECD strategy eschews root-and-branch reform of the existing transfer pricing regime, preferring instead a very tentative transition to country-by-country reporting, with data to be retained by national tax authorities rather than being made publicly available. While the OECD may be hamstrung by the interests of key member states such as the US, the EU is perhaps the most likely intergovernmental organisation to demand that MNCs outside the mining and forestry sector engage in country-by-country reporting. Under the European Commission's 2016 Directive on Corporate Tax Transparency, MNCs with a presence in the EU and a global turnover of more than €750 000 000 would have to produce comprehensive country-by-country reporting accounts. The prospects of the Directive being implemented improved in January 2018, when in Germany Angela Merkel's Christian Democratic Union and the Social Democratic Party agreed that addressing tax avoidance by large corporations would be a key element of their coalition negotiations.

The policy debate about the taxation of MNCs is thus at a critical juncture. There is unprecedented awareness of the scale of corporate tax avoidance, and significant pressure on political leaders to act. Moreover, there is growing consensus that the foundational principles that shaped the international tax system in the past must be recast. Whether this paradigm shift can be realised, either through the incremental adoption of the regime via the OECD's BEPS framework and associated measures or through the adoption of more fundamental reforms in the EU or elsewhere remains to be seen. It may be too early to predict the exact form of the international tax system in 10 or 20 years' time, but we can draw some conclusions about the implications of the developments documented in this volume for theories of global governance and policy change and identify the broad forces which are likely to shape the future trajectory of international tax reform.

CONCEPTUALISING THE 'NEW' TAX POLICY PROCESS: IMPLICATIONS FOR THEORY

The transformation of the international tax arena from being dominated by major states and intergovernmental organisations to a much more complex and dynamic constellation of actors and issues is but one example of wider trends in global governance. In a 2018 survey of these developments, David Coen and Tom Pegram identify three generations of global governance which are also evident in the international tax arena.

The first generation had its origins in liberal institutionalism and regime theory in the 1970s and 1980s, and was defined by the recognition that international and transnational governance was not shaped by interstate relations and associated intergovernmental organisations alone. Rather than relying on abstract theories of state action, in the words of Weiss and Wilkinson (2015, p. 405, quoted in Coen and Pegram 2018) this scholarship 'asked questions about how the world is governed and ordered at all levels and in every historical period'. This first-generation research revealed the growing power of non-state actors, including both MNCs (Mikler 2018) and countervailing forces such as new social movements which, through the use of technology and other innovative means, have been able to mobilise and exert political influence in ways that transcend the traditional state institutions and boundaries of national politics.

Reflecting the growing proliferation of new forms of governance emerging in response to a wide range of transboundary challenges, second-generation research focused on documenting these innovative responses at the level of specific policy arenas and problems. While the best of this research recognised that innovations in global governance were shaped by the broad structural context of geo-political and economic relations, it also documented growing complexity and diversity in specific issue arenas as well as the connections between them. This scholarship played a key role in framing the present study, with its focus on the growth of private or voluntary governance and the way in which tax justice NGOs have emulated the successful strategies of environmental campaigners. The goal here was to understand the consequences of complexity and fragmentation, and its relationship with systemic, macro-level change (Zürn 2018).

The emerging third generation of global governance scholarship seeks to synthesise the detailed empirical research of recent years to build a more coherent picture of which governance initiatives have been effective, and why. This is a critically important question given the widely held view that the post-war liberal order is in decline, and that we need new frameworks and strategies to address the growing number of governance challenges associated with economic, social and environmental interdependence. In the words of Coen and Pegram (2018, p. 112), 'the most pressing question in global governance is: what works and why?', a concern which closely aligns with the key political question posed in the Introduction to this volume: can MNCs, as increasingly powerful actors in the twenty-first century, be subject to democratic accountability? The answers to these fundamental questions may be unclear, but Coen and Pegram (2018) make the compelling case that global governance scholarship must draw on the tools of policy analysis and implementation theory so as to better understand 'what works and why' in global governance.

This study has responded to Coen and Pegram's (2018) call by applying tools and insights from policy analysis to conceptualise and evaluate recent developments in the international tax arena. Porter and Ronit (this volume, Chapter 8), for example, propose a more sophisticated model of the policy cycle, highlighting the range of roles that state, business and civil society actors have played at various stages of the policy process – a framework which is consistent with the findings of other contributions to this volume. Two broad conclusions can be drawn from this analysis. The first is that the established distinction between public and private governance is misleading. This study shows that global governance increasingly relies on combinations of public and private authority, and that the relative influence of different actors varies across policy arenas, institutional settings and stages of the policy cycle. The impact of new private standards such as EITI and Fair Tax Mark (this volume, Chapters 9, 10 and 11) on the international tax arena is a good example, because, while evidence of these new standards having a direct impact on corporate tax practice is limited, it is also clear that they influence 'formal' policy development by promoting new standards and models of reporting. Similarly, civil society organisations and 'first-mover' firms have a key role to play in the implementation and compliance stages of international tax reform. Porter and Ronit (this volume, Chapter 8) may have presented a stylised account of contemporary global governance, but it serves as an important heuristic for conceptualising the complexity of international policy making.

Conceptual frameworks provide important tools for analysing the international tax policy process, but they provide little guidance for the future trajectory of reform and the prospects for developing and implementing a more just and equitable corporate tax system. Ultimately, the outcome of political conflicts in which the interests of large corporations are pitted against those of national governments and many of their citizens is determined by power politics in all of its dimensions. It is to the changing distribution of power in the international tax arena and its likely implications that we now turn.

THE FUTURE: THE CHALLENGE OF CORPORATE TAX JUSTICE

Corporate leaders persist with defiant claims that the companies they lead have done nothing wrong in relation to their tax affairs, yet it is clear that the world has changed. Voters and the governments they elect are aware of the aggressive tax practices of many of the world's most powerful corporations, and of the impact of tax avoidance on government budgets and communities alike. What is also clear is that there are significant barriers to translating growing concern about corporate tax avoidance into effective and sustainable action. Corporate tax avoidance is a transnational problem, requiring an international solution devised and implemented in the face of formidable corporate lobbying and amid real potential for distributional conflicts among states. Even if there is an international commitment to elements of reform as exemplified by the OECD BEPS initiative, the effectiveness of such measures can always be undermined by partial implementation, weak enforcement, and the enduring incentives for tax professionals to develop and market new avoidance strategies. The barriers to reform are formidable, but the recent history of international tax reform suggests that meaningful change is possible under the right conditions (Eccleston 2012).

The first and most important precondition for successful and sustainable reform is transparency. Citizens and governments alike have the right to know how much tax large firms pay and where they pay it, because these data allow academics, tax authorities and NGOs to assess individual companies' tax practices and hold them to account. This study, and others like it, clearly demonstrates that in the absence of transparency and scrutiny firms can engage in aggressive avoidance with little or no repercussions. The corollary is that publicly available tax and financial data allow NGOs, often working with media outlets, to monitor the extent of the problem and highlight egregious breaches by specific firms. As we have noted, the resulting public awareness sustains political pressure for effective reform and provides incentives for individual companies to change their ways. Once consumers and investors can credibly distinguish companies that embrace ethical tax practices from those that don't then private certification schemes can take root while also increasing the pressure on government to implement and enforce regulation. While many corporations argue that they shouldn't have to disclose detailed tax and financial data on an entity basis, and successfully lobbied the OECD not to insist on public disclosure, the tide is starting to turn. As was noted in Chapter 9, many resource firms are disclosing this information on a voluntary basis, while many national tax authorities, such as the Australian Taxation Office, are now publishing tax data on MNCs. As noted above, the threshold development in the push for greater tax transparency is the EU's corporate tax transparency initiative, which when fully implemented will put pressure on other organisations, such as the OECD, to follow suit.

Improved tax transparency may be the foundation for international tax reform, but we have also argued that the politics of meaningful and sustained policy change depends not only on defining the policy problem at hand but on building a clear and credible consensus about the key features of a 'fair' tax system. There is an emerging consensus that MNCs should be taxed where economic activity occurs and profits are created, but there remains a good deal of debate about the best policy framework for achieving this norm and the relative merits of a reformed regime based on arm's-length transfer pricing relative to a full unitary tax model with taxable profits allocated by formula apportionment. What is clear is that the debate about the normative objectives of international tax reform and the associated policy implications must be resolved before meaningful reform can be achieved. This is especially important given the technical nature of corporate taxation and the fact that emerging norms concerning tax fairness run counter to core tenets of corporate capitalism.

Transparency and the establishment of a consensus about the key elements of a fair tax regime are both preconditions for substantive reform, but, in a complex system such as the international tax regime, fundamental reform often requires a specific catalyst which can trigger a tipping point and precipitate wider policy change. Individual political leaders and policy entrepreneurs who link policy solutions to established problems are important facilitators of change. The leaders of the Tax Justice Network and Pascal Saint-Amans, director of the OECD Centre for Tax Policy and Administration, have likewise been important agents for change within their respective domains. Yet the real challenge for reformers is getting major firms, governments and intergovernmental organisations to adopt new standards such as country-by-country reporting, because, once a critical mass of first movers have established institutional footholds and embraced change, others will follow. Our preliminary research on how MNCs are responding to the new politics of corporate tax justice suggests that some major corporates are giving serious consideration to adopting simpler tax structures and more transparent practices, but remain concerned that they would be at a competitive disadvantage if they pre-empt formal regulatory change or the adoption of new standards. This finding highlights the need for governments and intergovernmental organisations to formally commit to and implement new frameworks for taxing international business, such as standards for country-by-country reporting, and then over time a system of unitary taxation with formula apportionment.

The bottom line is that, while engaged citizens, NGOs, private governance regimes and corporations all have important roles to play in creating and sustaining a fairer tax regime, long-term change is dependent on key states and intergovernmental organisations adopting and implementing meaningful reform. At the political level, it appears that neither the United States nor the UK will provide political leadership on these issues in the near term, but, as noted above, there is a serious commitment within the EU to implement robust measures to address corporate tax avoidance. Whether these reforms will be fully implemented and institutionalised in the face of powerful countervailing forces remains to be seen. On a more optimistic note, this volume has demonstrated that committed citizens and civil society organisations can mobilise to highlight poor corporate behaviour and successfully advocate for change. It is also clear that it will be essential to sustain this democratic activism if citizens are to hold MNCs to account and ensure that they make a fair contribution to funding the public goods and social infrastructure on which we all depend.

REFERENCES

Bachrach, P. and M. Baratz (1970), *Power and Poverty: Theory and Practice*, Oxford: Oxford University Press.

Clausing, K.A. (2015), 'Beyond Territorial and Worldwide Systems of International Taxation', available online at http://dx.doi.org/10.2139/ssrn.2567952 (accessed 19 January 2017).

Coen, D. and T. Pegram (2018), 'Towards a Third Generation of Global Governance Scholarship', *Global Policy* **9** (1), 107–113, doi:10.1111/1758-5899.12527.

Cohen, B.C. (1963), *The Press and Foreign Policy*, Princeton, NJ: Princeton University Press.

Culpepper, P.D. (2011), *Quiet Politics and Business Power: Corporate Control in Europe and Japan*, New York: Cambridge University Press.

Dietsch, P. (2015), *Catching Capital*, Oxford: Oxford University Press.

Eccleston, R. (2012), *The Dynamics of Global Economic Governance*, Cheltenham, UK and Northampton, MA, USA: Edward Elgar Publishing.

Finnemore, M. and K. Sikkink (1998), 'International Norm Dynamics and Political Change', *International Organisation* **52** (4), 887–917.
G20 (2014), 'G20 Leaders' Communiqué, Brisbane Summit, 15–16 November 2014', Press release, available at http://www.consilium.europa.eu/uedocs/cms_Data/docs/pressdata/en/ec/145770.pdf (accessed 19 January 2017).
Mikler, J. (2018), *The Political Power of Global Corporations*, Cambridge: Polity Press.
OECD (2015), 'OECD Base Erosion and Profit Shifting Project', available online at http://www.oecd-ilibrary.org/taxation/oecd-g20-base-erosion-and-profit-shifting-project_23132612 (accessed 18 January 2017).
Walter, A. (2008), *Governing Finance: East Asia's Adoption of International Standards*, Ithaca, NY: Cornell University Press.
Weiss, T.G. and R. Wilkinson (2015), 'Change and Continuity in Global Governance', *Ethics and International Affairs* **29** (4), 397–406.
Wolf, M. (2012), 'The World's Hunger for Public Goods', *Financial Times*, published electronically 25 January, available at https://www.ft.com/content/517e31c8-45bd-11e1-93f1-00144feabdc0 (accessed 1 January 2017).
Zürn, M. (2018), *A Theory of Global Governance: Authority, Legitimation and Contestation*, Oxford: Oxford University Press.

Index